Transactions of the Royal Historical Society

SIXTH SERIES

XXII

CAMBRIDGE
UNIVERSITY PRESS

Published by the Press Syndicate of the University of Cambridge
The Edinburgh Building, Cambridge CB2 8RU, United Kingdom
32 Avenue of the Americas, New York, NY 10013-2473, USA
477 Williamstown Road, Port Melbourne, VIC 3207, Australia
C/Orense, 4, Planta 13, 28020 Madrid, Spain
Lower Ground Floor, Nautica Building, The Water Club,
Beach Road, Granger Bay, 8005 Cape Town, South Africa

First published 2012

A catalogue record for this book is available from the British Library

ISBN 9781107038967 hardback

SUBSCRIPTIONS. The serial publications of the Royal Historical Society, *Royal Historical Society Transactions* (ISSN 0080–4401) and Camden Fifth Series (ISSN 0960–1163) volumes, may be purchased together on annual subscription. The 2012 subscription price, which includes print and electronic access (but not VAT), is £130 (US $ 218 in the USA, Canada, and Mexico) and includes Camden Fifth Series, volumes 41 and 42 (published in September and November) and Transactions Sixth Series, volume 22 (published in December). Japanese prices are available from Kinokuniya Company Ltd, P.O. Box 55, Chitose, Tokyo 156, Japan. EU subscribers (outside the UK) who are not registered for VAT should add VAT at their country's rate. VAT registered subscribers should provide their VAT registration number. Prices include delivery by air.

Subscription orders, which must be accompanied by payment, may be sent to a bookseller, subscription agent, or direct to the publisher: Cambridge University Press, The Edinburgh Building, Shaftesbury Road, Cambridge CB2 8RU, UK; or in the USA, Canada, and Mexico: Cambridge University Press, Journals Fulfillment Department, 100 Brook Hill Drive, West Nyack, New York, 10994–2133, USA.

SINGLE VOLUMES AND BACK VOLUMES. A list of Royal Historical Society volumes available from Cambridge University Press may be obtained from the Humanities Marketing Department at the address above.

Printed in the UK by MPG Books Ltd

CONTENTS

Transactions of the RHS 22 (2012), p. 1 © Royal Historical Society 2012
doi:10.1017/S0080440112000035

EDITORIAL NOTE

We are continuing our policy of including some of the papers held at our regional symposia. Four contributions, by Alex Metcalfe, Andrew Jotischky, Naomi Tadmor and Michael Beckerman, come from the symposium 'Edges of Europe: Frontiers in Context' organised at the University of Lancaster on 16–17 June 2011. The article by Michael Beckerman and his collaborators represents a new departure for us, as the lecture was accompanied by a series of audio recordings which are available on the Cambridge University website (http://journals.cambridge.org/rht). It is generically rather different from the material we normally publish, but we think it is an exciting piece.

Transactions of the RHS 22 (2012), pp. 3–35 © Royal Historical Society 2012
doi:10.1017/S0080440112000047

TRANSACTIONS OF THE

ROYAL HISTORICAL SOCIETY

PRESIDENTIAL ADDRESS

By Colin Jones

FRENCH CROSSINGS: III. THE SMILE OF THE TIGER

READ 25 NOVEMBER 2011

ABSTRACT. This paper continues the theme of 'French Crossings' explored in other Presidential Addresses by focusing on the border zone between the human and the animal. The focus is on the allegedly tiger-like character attributed to Maximilien Robespierre, particularly after his fall from power and his execution in 1794. This theme is explored in terms of Thermidorian propaganda, French Revolutionary historiography and the ancient discipline of physiognomy, which was reactivated by Johann-Caspar Lavater in the late eighteenth century and was still influential through much of the nineteenth. Robespierre's animal rather than human status was also held to emerge in his inability to smile or laugh, a significant point also in that the meaning of the smile was changing in the same period.

On 6 February 1834, an old woman died on the Rue des Fontaines in Paris. Her full name was Marie-Marguerite-Charlotte Robespierre. Charlotte (1760–1834) was the younger sister of Maximilien and Augustin Robespierre. Some forty years earlier, on 28 July 1794, following the *coup d'état* of the previous day, 27 July 1794 (9 Thermidor Year II in the Revolutionary Calendar), Charlotte's two brothers, Maximilien and Augustin, had perished together on the guillotine. The *coup d'état* of 9 Thermidor led to the overthrow of the Committee of Public Safety on which Maximilien had been a leading light, and which had directed the Terror. Celebrations would be instantaneous, launching a tidal wave of attacks in print. *Le triomphe des Parisiens* and the *Portraits exécrables du traitre Robespierre et ses complices*, complete with images of the severed heads of Maximilien and his brother and their alleged accomplices from the Committee of Public Safety, Saint-Just and Couthon, are characteristic examples (Figures 1 and 2).[1] Much blame would focus – and has continued to focus in history-writing down to the present day – on Maximilien's role within the Committee of Public Safety, which had implemented violently repressive policies as a way of winning the war within France and without, and of instituting, so it was held, a 'republic of virtue'.[2]

In memoirs published posthumously in 1835, Charlotte Robespierre sought to rehabilitate her brothers from the calumnies which had buzzed like flies about their heads, ever since those heads had fallen into the guillotine basket over forty years earlier. She had taken to the grave a profound irritation in particular at the ways that Maximilien's physical appearance was generally described.

> Brother Augustin [she stated] was big, well made and had a face full of nobility and beauty. Maximilien did not share these features to the same extent. He was of average height and of delicate complexion. His face exuded sweetness and goodness, but was not as regular nor as fine as his brother's. He was nearly always smiling.[3]

Warming to her theme of a sweet, good, 'nearly always smiling' Maximilien Robespierre, she went on to excoriate the way that her brother had been portrayed since his death. One particular portrait, that had accompanied apocryphal memoirs published in 1830, drew her particular scorn. It was, she stated, 'an ignoble caricature' (Figure 3). 'His physiognomy is there disfigured, just as as his cowardly enemies have disfigured his character.' In fact, '[Maximilien's] physiognomy exuded sweetness and he had an expression of goodness which struck everyone who saw him.'[4] We can just about glimpse the faintest of smiles playing

---

[1] *Le triomphe des Parisiens dans les Journées des 9 et 10 Thermidor* (n.p., n.d.) and *Portraits exécrables du traître Robespierre et ses complices* (n.p., n.d.). Much of this post-Thermidor literature, cited below, does not signal either a place or date of publication. Unless otherwise indicated, one can assume that the pamphlets were published in Paris in late 1794. I have drawn extensively on the famous Croker collection at the British Library (BL), the largest collection of French Revolution publications outside the Bibliothèque Nationale de France. I have given the BL call-marks in the relevant cases, to assist in location of these ephemeral and not easily locatable pieces.

[2] An excellent entrée into the life and ideas of Robespierre, his role within the Committee of Public Safety and the circumstances of his death, is provided by two stimulating recent biographies: Ruth Scurr, *Fatal Purity: Robespierre and the French Revolution* (New York, 2006), and Peter McPhee, *Robespierre: A Revolutionary Life* (New Haven and London, 2012). Their bibliographies give a sense of the huge volume and wide range of reactions Robespierre has always evoked. We also now have the first biography of Maximilen's younger brother, Augustin: Sergio Luzzatto, *Bonbon Robespierre: Il Terrore dal volto umano* (Turin, 2009). The literature on the Terror is similarly immense. Helpful perspectives are provided by David Andress, *The Terror: Civil War in the French Revolution* (New York, 2005).

[3] *Mémoires de Charlotte Robespierre sur ses deux frères*, 2nd edn (Paris, 1835), 68. Throughout, all translations from the French are my own.

[4] *Ibid.*, 38, 159–60. The volume she attacked was *Mémoires authentiques de Maximilien Robespierre, ornés de son portrait tiré de ses mémoires* (Paris, 1830). The work is thought to be the work of Charles Reybaud.

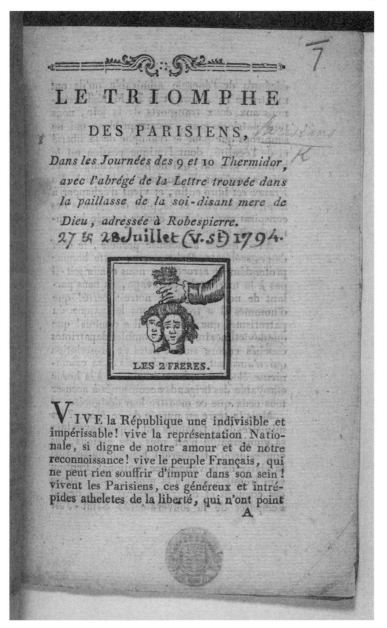

Figure 1 *Le triomphe des Parisiens* (Paris, 1794). © British Library Board: FR 598.

Figure 2 *Portraits exécrables du traitre Robespierre et ses complices.* © British Library Board: F856.

Figure 3 Portrait of Robespierre, from *Mémoires authentiques de Maximilien Robespierre, ornés de son portrait tiré de ses mémoires* (Paris, 1830). © British Library Board: 010661.c.28.

lightly around the lips of a number of the portraits of the future arch-terrorist, such as Adelaide Labille-Guiard's famous 1791 painting of him in his costume as deputy in the National Assembly.[5] Yet, loyal Charlotte's sisterly memory has cut little historiographical ice, and historians ever since have scoffed at the thought of sweet, smiley Robespierre.

Charlotte was attacking the attempt to read the alleged wickedness of Robespierre in his face. Physiognomical portraiture – the detection of character through bodily, and especially through facial, depiction – could be done in words as well as by pencil or paintbrush. An early, influential textual example of the genre, written just weeks after Robespierre's death, was the 'Portrait of Robespierre' by Antoine Merlin de Thionville, a deputy who had sat alongside him in the National Convention:

> People who like to find relationships between faces and moral qualities, between human faces and those of animals, have noted that just as Danton had the head of a mastiff, Marat that of an eagle, Mirabeau that of a lion, Robespierre had the face of a cat. But the face altered its physiognomy; at first it was the anxious but fairly soft look of a domestic cat; then the wild look of a feral cat; and then the ferocious look of a tiger.[6]

We may be surprised to think of a Robespierre who smiled. And by drawing on the conventions of physiognomy in this Revolutionary bestiary so as to make a tiger of him, Merlin de Thionville was of course adding to our doubts. For tigers do many things; smiling is not conventionally held to be among them. The smile of a tiger is a simple impossibility.

In my Presidential Addresses, under the general heading of 'French Crossings', I have taken the idea of crossing very broadly, ranging from the crossing of territorial boundaries, to the crossing of disciplinary frontiers, through to the meaning of crossing in the lives of my subjects. In 2009, I used the differential, Anglo-French reception of Charles Dickens's *A Tale of Two Cities*, and his own personal Channel-hoppings, to explore issues of personal and national identity under a transnational prism.[7] Last year, the book of comic drawings of the obscure French court embroiderer, Charles-Germain de Saint-Aubin, allowed me to examine the crossing of social boundaries and the role of laughter in sometimes transcending, sometimes reinforcing, class frontiers.[8] In the present paper, while incidentally passing back and forth over the disciplinary boundaries separating visual from textual studies, and the history of art and the history of science, I will be examining the crossing of another type of boundary, namely, the frontier between humans and animals.

---

[5] Adelaide Labille-Guiard, *Maximilien Robespierre en habit de député du Tiers Etat*. There is a good if outdated account of Robespierre's pictorial representations in Hippolyte Buffenoir, *Les portraits de Robespierre* (Paris, 1910).

[6] Merlin de Thionville, *Portrait de Robespierre*, 1 (BL, F852(1)).

[7] Colin Jones, 'Tales of Two Cities', *Transactions of the Royal Historical Society*, 20 (2010), 1–26.

[8] Colin Jones, 'Laughing over Boundaries', *ibid.*, 21 (2011), 1–38.

Yet, is the term 'frontier' justified in regard to human–animal relations? In recent years, a number of continental philosophers – Giorgio Agamben, Emmanuel Levinas, Gilles Deleuze, Jacques Derrida and others – have explored the human–animal relationship in an avowedly 'post-humanist' spirit that posits as its foundation porosity rather than rupture.[9] Oddly, early modern French society in some ways prefigured this. While people certainly viewed with horror monstrous beings that incorporated within their bodies human and animal components, suggesting a sense of incommensurability, yet at a more everyday level they were also well habituated to less extreme and prejudicial ideas involving the crossing of the human–animal frontier.[10] One of these was physiognomy, a discipline which historians have too often lost from view, and on which Merlin was drawing in composing his Revolutionary bestiary. Flourishing particularly between *c.* 1500 and *c.* 1850, physiognomical writing and analysis provided a space in which individuals could explore what united humans and animals and what differentiated them. It thus offers an appropriate lens through which to explore changing views of the human–animal relationship. Significantly, moreover, although we may (foolishly) imagine that smiling lies beyond historical analysis[11] and (misguidedly?) surmise that it is quintessentially human (and therefore presumably non-animal), the smile was a source of much physiognomical reflection. The putative smile on the face of an alleged tiger will thus allow us to reflect on the human–animal relationship while also considering the pressing political, ideological and historiographical issues in play concerning the French Revolutionary Terror in which physiognomy came to be caught up.

Considering how widespread and influential physiognomy has been as a form of knowledge which had currency for an exceptionally long period

[9] Key texts include Giorgio Agamben, *The Open: Man and Animal* (Stanford, 1998); Gilles Deleuze and Félix Guattari, *A Thousand Plateaus. Capitalism and Schizophrenia* (Minneapolis, 1990); Jacques Derrida, 'The Animal that Therefore I Am (More to Follow)', *Critical Enquiry*, 28 (2002), 369–418; Emmanuel Levinas, 'The Name of a Dog, or Natural Rights', in *Difficult Freedom: Essays on Judaism* (1990), 151–3. A good anthology of this literature is Peter Atterton and Matthew Calarco, eds., *Animal Philosophy. Essential Readings in Continental Thought* (2004). Joanna Bourke, in *What It Means To Be Human. Reflections from 1791 to the Present* (2011), seeks to historicise these approaches. See also Martin Kemp, *The Human Animal in Western Art and Science* (Chicago, 2007).

[10] Arnold Davidson, 'The Horror of Monsters', in *The Boundaries of Humanity. Humans, Animals and Machines*, ed. James J. Sheehan and Morton Sosna (Berkeley, 1991). Cf. Keith Thomas, *Man and the Natural World: Changing Attitudes in England, 1500–1800* (Oxford, 1983); Erica Fudge, *Perceiving Animals: Humans and Beasts in Early Modern English Culture* (New York, 1999); Katherine Park and Lorraine Daston, *Wonders and the Order of Nature 1150–1750* (New York, 1998); and Jean-Jacques Courtine, 'Le corps inhumain', in *Histoire du corps*, I: *De la Renaissance aux Lumières*, ed. *idem*, Alain Corbin and Georges Vigarello (Paris, 2005), 373–86.

[11] See however Angus Trumble, *A Brief History of the Smile* (New York, 2004).

across an impressively wide range of cultures, it remains surprisingly under-studied.[12] The discipline has a venerable pedigree in western and Arabic cultures, as well as long-established traditions in India, China, Japan and elsewhere. The earliest existing physiognomic dicta are to be found on Mesopotamian clay tablets carved over 3,000 years ago. They propound things such as: 'If a man has curly hair on his shoulders, women will fall in love with him', or 'If a man with a contorted face has a prominent right eye, far from home dogs will eat him.'[13] Physiognomy always had an air of pseudo-empirical non-falsifiability, that is evident in the shards of the discipline which remain in our own culture (such as the idea of individuals with red hair having fiery tempers). The basic notion behind physiognomy is that one can grasp an individual's character, identity and even destiny by close informed scrutiny of their outward physical appearance, especially their face. Developed in Antiquity, physiognomy was taught in medieval universities; it gained in intellectual cogency during the Renaissance; it was found in manuscript and printed sources in just about every European language in the early modern period from Icelandic to Welsh; and it was published in every imaginable print format from learned in-folios through to cheap almanachs and broadsheets.

One reason for physiognomy's astonishing longevity and cultural reach has been its capacity for adapting its precepts to harmonise with current ways of understanding the world. Like Galenic medical theory which for much of the early modern period still provided the standard way of thinking, about states of bodily health, for example, physiognomy was grounded in a cosmology expressing itself in correspondences between substances and qualities both within and between the supra- and sub-lunar worlds. This encompassed correspondence between humans and animals. A hoary physiognomic truism had it that one of the ways that character could be read was through detecting human resemblances with animals.

---

[12] The subject of physiognomy within the west European tradition has come increasingly into focus in recent decades, but still represents a poorly covered field. Much recent work has focused on the later phases of the movement, dating from the work of Lavater in the late eighteenth century (see below, n. 26). For the medieval and early modern period, particularly useful are Martin Porter, *Windows of the Soul. The Art of Physiognomy in European Culture, 1470–1780* (Oxford, 2005), and Jean-Jacques Courtine and Claudine Haroche, *Histoire du visage: exprimer et taire ses émotions, XVIe–début XIXe siècle* (Paris, 1988). See too Paolo Getrevi, *Le scritture des volto. Fisiognomica e modelli culturali dal Medioevo ad oggi* (Milan, 1991); Lucia Rodler, *I silenzi mimici del volto* (Pisa, 1991); Nadeije Laneyrie-Dagen, *L'invention du corps: la représentation de l'homme du Moyen Âge à la fin du XIXe siècle* (Paris, 1997); Ian Maclean, 'The Logic of Physiognomy in the Late Reanaissance', *Early Science and Medicine*, 16 (2011), 275–95; Jean-Jacques Courtine, 'Le miroir de l'âme', in *Histoire du corps*, ed. Courtine, Corbin and Vigarello. See too Martial Guédron, *L'art de la grimace: cinq siècles d'excès de visage* (Paris, 2011), 303–9.
[13] Porter, *Windows of the Soul*, 48.

Figure 4 Giambattista Della Porta, 'Lion Man', from idem, *De humana physiognomonia* (Turin, 1586). © Wellcome Library, London.

A key physiognomic syllogism went along the lines: a man looks like a lion; a lion is brave and masterful; the leonine man must therefore partake of the same qualities and be brave and masterful. Based on prestigious texts ranging from Antiquity through to the Renaissance and beyond, this strain of physiognomic analysis was given systematic visual illustration in Giambattista Della Porta's *De humana physiognomonia* (1586), a work highly influential among artists as well as physiognomists[14] (Figure 4).

Physiognomy caters to an essential, everyday social concern: namely, what sort of person stands in front of me? The discipline purports to offer help in answering this question. Its practitioners realised that it requires a degree of subtlety and sophistication, not least because some individuals do not want their characters to be read. If one of physiognomy's stock aphorisms was 'in facie legitur homo' ('the character of man is in his face'), another was 'fronti nulla fides' ('there's no trusting faces'). The apparent contradiction highlighted the point that it needed a trained physiognomic eye to see through pretences about their true nature with which individuals often obscured the underlying features of their face.

---

[14] Giambattista Della Porta, *De humana physiognomonia* (Turin, 1586). The work appeared in French as *La physionomie humaine* (Rouen, 1655). Cf. Tommaso Casini, *Ritratti parlanti. Collezione e biografie illustrate nei secoli XVI e XVII* (Florence, 2004).

Contradicting Shakespeare's Lady Macbeth, physiognomy was precisely that art which promised 'to find the mind's construction in the face'.[15]

During the eighteenth century, popular almanachs still blithely circulated physiognomic notions such as that a man born in November will have 'a white face with red spots, a big head, hard bones, and will be quite fleshy and big, with a cold complexion, plus ... fine delicate teeth' (and so on).[16] But by then, such views were no longer viewed as having scientific validity within elite circles, due to the decline of the Renaissance cosmology of correspondences in the Scientific Revolution and the Enlightenment that also, incidentally, undermined Galenic medical thought.[17]

Yet, physiognomy's end was far from nigh. Two major transformations ensured its passage as a powerful cultural force well into the nineteenth century. First, there was a fundamental reformulation of the analysis of facial expression. In the late seventeenth century, Louis XIV's premier painter, Charles Le Brun, attacked the theory of resemblances and cosmological analogies on which Della Porta's work had been based, and shifted physiognomic analysis towards the study of facial expression.[18] Indeed, his followers often claimed he had renounced physiognomy for what became known as pathognomy, the study of the facial expression of feelings.[19] Le Brun grounded his studies in contemporary science in fact, notably the physiology of René Descartes, who held that the human soul resided in the pineal gland located in the brain behind the bridge of the nose.[20] Le Brun developed a whole theory around the assumption that disturbance of the passions of the soul catalysed movement on the face from this originary spot, so that disturbances rippled from the eyebrows outwards (Figure 5). Mild passion might cause a slight disturbance in this area; extreme passion caused major distortions across the face. Le Brun's

---

[15] Shakespeare, *Macbeth*, I, iv, 12. Interestingly, Lady Macbeth also evokes the alternative version: 'Your face, my thane, is as a book where men / May read strange messages' (*ibid.*, I, v, 53–4).

[16] For this almanach-style literature, see Liese Andries, *La bibliothèque bleue au XVIIIe siècle: une tradition éditoriale* (Oxford, 1989), and D. Roche, 'Le rire bleu: comique et transgression dans la littérature de colportage', in 'Le Rire', special issue, *XVIIIe siècle*, 32 (2000), 19–32.

[17] See the general overview, stressing Galenism's attenuated survival, in Mary Lindemann, *Medicine and Society in Early Modern Europe* (Cambridge, 1999), and Peter Elmer, *The Healing Arts. Health, Disease and Society in Europe, 1500–1800* (Manchester, 2004).

[18] Charles Le Brun, *Conférence sur l'expression générale et particulière* (Paris, 1668). On this work, see esp. Jennifer Montagu, *The Expression of the Passions. The Origin and Influence of Charles Le Brun's 'Conférence sur l'expression générale et particulière'* (New Haven and London, 1994). Cf. too Thomas Kirchner, *L'expression des passions. Ausdruck als Darstellungsproblem in der französischen Kunst und Kunsttheorie des 17. und 18. Jahrhunderts* (Mainz, 1991).

[19] See the discussion on the distinction in Melissa Percival, *The Appearance of Character. Physiognomy and Facial Expression in Eighteenth-Century France* (Leeds, 1999), 30–2, 36–7 and *passim*.

[20] Montagu, *Expression of the Passions*, esp. 17 and Appendix III, 'The Sources', 156–61.

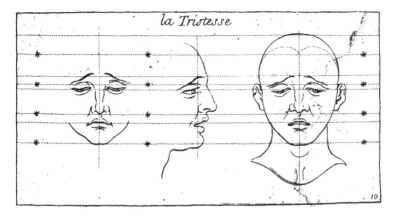

la Tristesse

Figure 5 Charles le Brun, 'Tristesse', after idem, Le Brun, *Conférence sur l'expression générale et particulière* (Paris, 1668) (1720). © Wellcome Library, London.

theological and physiological surmising became increasingly *dépassé* in the eighteenth century. But his book of drawings – with their almost geometrical facial calibrations of feeling – continued to be influential, going through numerous reeditions. Indeed, it became the way that people in the Enlightenment learned to draw: William Hogarth noted around mid-century, 'It is the common drawing book ... for the use of learners.'[21] If one wants a single example of the continuing strength of Le Brun's influence, one has only to compare his representation of despair (Figure 6) with the facial contortion (a century later) shown on the guillotined head of Saint-Just ('S.J.'), Robespierre's fellow Terrorist, in the Thermidorian pamphlet cited earlier.[22]

Descartes was held to have made an intervention in a very long-running polemic, by essentially cutting humanity off from the animal world. The human *cogito* emphatically and indeed definitionally did not extend into the animal realm. The Cartesian contention that the human soul was located in the pineal gland was based on the, in fact anatomically ungrounded, finding that only humans possess such a gland.[23] For his part, however, Charles Le Brun continued to be fascinated by analogies between animals and humans – as is attested by a collection of his drawings

[21] Cited in Montagu, *Expression of the Passions*, 85. Hogarth's regret reflected a general criticism of Le Brun for its overly mechanical view of expression, even while its influence continued to be strong. Cf. *ibid.*, 85, for the decline of Cartesian physiology.

[22] Cf. above, Figure 2. The Le Brun illustration drawing is from an eighteenth-century drawing primer.

[23] Subsequent commentators did not always appreciate the fact.

Figure 6 'Désespoir', after Charles Le Brun, *Conférence sur l'expression génerale et particulière* (Paris, 1668) (1770). © Wellcome Library, London.

on the subject that reprised and updated Della Porta. Significantly, however, these were only publicly known in France from 1797, just after Robespierre's fall.[24]

---

[24] Exhibited in the Paris Salon in 1797 where they caused a sensation, the images were first published in 1806. Montagu, *Expression of the Passions*, 193 n. 59. The lecture on physiognomy that Le Brun had given has been lost, though there were accounts of it in circulation.

The second incursion and force for renewal within the world of physiognomy also overtly downplayed overlaps between the human and the animal and assumed a radical, Cartesian incommensurability between the two. This was the oeuvre of the German pastor-physiognomist, Johann-Caspar Lavater.[25] From the 1770s down to his death in 1801, Lavater sought to re-cast Renaissance physiognomy from top to bottom. He claimed to throw out all earlier physiognomical writings except Aristotle and to start from scratch through close observation of his fellow-men. His *Essays on Physiognomy* – a European best-seller published in numerous editions, translations and vulgarisations, that established him as one of the celebrities of his age – put humans at the centre of the physiognomic vision.[26] Only humans had a face and that face was a version (albeit a degenerate version) of the face of God, who had made man in His own image.[27] Whereas Le Brun had increasingly shifted attention to facial mobility, Lavater placed more emphasis on the solid and unchanging parts of the human head as a guide to character. Despite its strongly religious inspiration, Lavaterian physiognomy also aspired to scientific status, specifically rejecting the traditional physiognomic lore about 'leonine' character, for example, in favour of mathematical and geometrical approaches. Lavater worked hard to develop ways of measuring and quantifying human heads, deploying, for example, the silhouette, craniometry and consideration of the so-called facial angle.[28] Just as Renaissance physiognomy had benefited from contemporary sciences, which underpinned their practices (Galenic physic and Aristotelian cosmology in particular), so Lavater

---

[25] Lavater's works started to appear in German in the early 1770s: see esp. his *Physiognomische Fragmente* (4 vols., Leipzig, 1775–8). Later editions were added to progressively. The first French edition of his work was *Essai sur la physiognomonie destiné à faire connaître l'homme et à le faire aimer* (4 vols., The Hague, 1781–1803). What became the standard work was published by Louis-Jacques Moreau de la Sarthe after Lavater's death as *L'art de connaître les hommes par la physiognomonie* (10 vols., Paris, 1806).

[26] Lavater's work in English and French has tended to become better known in recent years through works focused on the impact of his writings on nineteenth-century culture. See esp. in this vein *Physiognomy in Profile: Lavater's Impact on European Culture*, ed. Melissa Percival and Graeme Tytler (Newark, DE.), 2005; Sibylle Erle, *Blake, Lavater, and Physiognomy* (2010); Lucy Hartley, *Physiognomy and the Meaning of Expression in Nineteenth-Century Culture* (Cambridge, 2001); and Sharrona Pearl, *About Faces. Physiognomy in Nineteenth-Century Britain* (2010). See also Guédron, *L'art de la grimace*.

[27] Cf. Kemp, *The Human Animal*, 69–72.

[28] The 'facial angle' measuring the facial profile was particularly associated with Pierre Camper, and developed into a proto-racial science: *Dissertation sur les variétés naturelles qui ont pour object l'histoire naturelle, la physiologie et l'anatomie comparée* (Paris, 1791). Cf. David Bindman, *Ape to Apollo. Aesthetics and the Idea of Race in the Eighteenth Century* (Ithaca, NY, 2002). On other forms of pseudo-scientific measurement, see Barbara Maria Stafford, *Body Criticism. Imaging the Unseen in Enlightenment Art and Medicine* (Cambridge, MA, 1993), esp. 84–129; and Marc Renneville, *Le Langage des crânes: une histoire de la phrénologie* (Paris, 2000).

hitched physiognomy's wagon to the rise of quantitative and comparative methodologies in the social and medical sciences.[29]

Following on from the break-up of the medieval and Renaissance cosmology in which physiognomy had been formerly grounded, the effect of Le Brun and Lavater was to keep it in play as an intellectual discipline – and indeed to give it a strong impulsion. Moreover, even though both men stressed radical discontinuity and incommensurability between humans and animals, in fact both also showed themselves very open to the traditional physiognomical interest in human–animal resemblance. Lavaterian physiognomy was a very broad church that tended to have something for (and from) everyone. Lavater's disciples, for example, were soon blithely intermixing their master's work with that of Della Porta and Le Brun and with emergent disciplines such as phrenology.[30] There was thus nothing surprising or out of line with Merlin de Thionville in 1794 invoking physiognomy in making his Robespierre/tiger comparison. Notwithstanding Le Brun and Lavater, some men at least could still be beasts. Indeed, the Terror had revealed the bestial in humankind, just as it had revealed, as we shall see, the tiger in Robespierre.

What was it about tigers that made it possible for these poor creatures to be assimilated to Robespierre? Tigers were not well known in medieval Europe, and they made few appearances in medieval bestiaries or heraldic sources.[31] Neither did Renaissance physiognomical writings find a place for them – although both Della Porta and Le Brun made comparisons with the cat.[32] When the tiger did hove into view, its outstanding characteristic and its biggest liability was its stripeyness. Striped pelts, cloth and decor were generally viewed as denoting ignomiy and treachery in the Middle Ages and Renaissance.[33] This perspective may have influenced the great Enlightenment naturalist, Buffon. In his multi-volumed and hugely influential *Histoire naturelle* (1749–67), Buffon ranked the tiger, among carnivores, as a poor second to the lion, with which its character formed a

[29] Theodore M. Porter, *The Rise of Statistical Thinking, 1820–1900* (Princeton, 1986), and the classic Michel Foucault, *The Birth of the Clinic. An Archaeology of Medical Perception* (1973).

[30] See below, p. 25. This is evident in even early post-Lavaterian texts such J. M. Le Plane, *Physiologie ou l'art de connaître les hommes par leur physiognomie* (Meudon,1797), which draws as much on Le Brun as Lavater. The same is true of the illustrated text, *Etrennes physiognomiques, ou le Lavater historique des femmes célèbres* (Paris, 1810). For the incorporation of phrenology, see Isidore Bourdon, *La physionomie et la phrénologie* (Paris, 1842).

[31] Michel Pastoureau, *Bestiaires du Moyen Âge* (Paris, 2011), 77–9; *idem, L'art héraldique au Moyen Âge* (Paris 2009); and *idem, The Devil's Cloth. A History of Stripes and Striped Fabric* (New York, 1991). The status of a 'bad lion' assumed by the tiger in the eighteenth century was assumed in the Middle Ages by the spotted leopard; and tigers were sometimes shown with spots.

[32] Della Porta, *De humana physiognomonia*, 96.

[33] Pastoureau, *The Devil's Cloth*.

stark contrast. 'To pride, bravery and strength, the lion conjoins nobility, clemency and magnanimity; while the tiger is low and ferocious, and cruel without justice, that is to say, without need.'[34] He went on, using language which as we shall see echoes rather accurately polemical writings against Robespierre, to note how the tiger – almost like a 'bad lion' – 'though satisfied with flesh, seems always thirsty for blood'. Viciously cruel, seemingly for the sake of it, 'he desolates the country he inhabits, … he kills and devastates herds of domestic animals and he slaughters all wild beasts [he encounters]'.[35]

Buffon was not out of line with his contemporaries. The tiger's penchant for wilfully cruel destructiveness had been highlighted by Voltaire – who had made tigrishness a national characteristic. His French compatriots were, he complained, 'a nation divided into two species, one of idle monkeys who mock at everything, and one of tigers who tear'.[36] Over the course of the eighteenth century, the adjectives that qualified the tiger most frequently in French literary works were words like 'bloodied', 'inhuman', 'fierce', 'pitiless', 'wild', 'wicked' and 'treacherous'.[37] Symptomatically, one of eighteenth-century literature's greatest villains – Lovelace in Richardson's *Clarissa*, which was almost as much of a best-seller in France as in England – had a heart 'as hard as a tiger' and was 'cruel as a tiger'.[38]

It is also worth mentioning in passing that Buffon and his contemporaries were hardly more warm-hearted towards the cat. The sweet, loveable domestic pussy-cat would be a bourgeois creation of the *fin de siècle* around the late nineteenth century.[39] For Buffon, cats were characterised by 'innate malice, natural perverseness and a taste for evil'; 'they only appear to be affectionate'.[40] The great naturalist still saw cats in terms that made their massacre comprehensible and possibly

[34] Georges-Louis Leclerc, comte de Buffon, *Histoire naturelle, générale et particulière* (15 vols., Paris, 1749–67), IX (1761), 129.

[35] *Ibid.*, 130.

[36] Letter to Madame du Deffand in 1766: Voltaire, *Correspondance*, ed. T. Bestermann (107 vols., Geneva, 1953–77), LXIII, 116. This characterisation was to be picked up in 1803 by the English satirist James Gillray, who in his print, 'The Arms of France', portrayed the French Revolutionary Republic as ceremonially represented by the two animals, one a monkey under the motto of atheism, the other, under that of desolation, a tiger. British Museum, Prints and Drawings. 1868,0808.7189.

[37] I am drawing here on the canonical works of French literature available through Frantext (ARTFL in the USA): www.frantext.fr/.

[38] I am quoting from the French version of *Clarissa*, trans. by the abbé Prévost: *Lettres anglaises ou Histoire de Miss Clarisse Harlow* (Dresden edn, 1752), III, 303, 467. Interestingly, Richardson did not use the word tiger, but 'savage' and 'panther'.

[39] Kathleen Kete, *The Beast in the Boudoir: Pet-Keeping in Nineteenth-Century Paris* (Berkeley, 1994), esp. 117–19.

[40] Buffon, *Histoire naturelle*, VI (1756), 3–4.

even desirable.[41] His views were shared by Lavater. The sight of a tiger at its prey recalled 'Satan triumphing at the fall of a saint', and cats were, Lavater went on, 'tigers in miniature'. Even crueller with birds and mice than tigers with lambs, cats took pleasure in the sufferings of their victims.[42] Calling Robespierre a cat was clearly just as bad as calling him a tiger.

The zoomorphic was probably the most widely used of four registers in which Thermidorian polemicists attacked Robespierre. First, in terms of the historical record, he was 'a modern Cataline' (evoking the conspirator against the Roman *res publica*), 'Nero' and on occasion even 'Cromwell'.[43] Secondly, in terms of political ideas and institutions, Robespierre was a tyrant and a dictator – and even a would-be king.[44] Thirdly, he was a monstrous being: a vampire, a 'political chameleon', a sphinx and so on.[45] Monstrosity was a staple theme in French Revolutionary print culture – as Louis XVI and Marie-Antoinette already knew, to their cost; monster Robespierre was thus only the latest in an evolving series.[46] Fourthly, there was the zoomorphic depiction of Robespierre as a wild animal – sometimes a wolf, sometimes a reptile, but most frequently, most powerfully and most influentially, a tiger. A German print of 1794 or 1795, 'Greuelscenen der Jacobiner', portrayed Robespierre alongside prowling tigers. 'The tiger Robespierre' (a frequent formulation) had presided over

---

[41] Robert Darnton, *The Great Cat Massacre and Other Essays in French Cultural History* (1984).

[42] Lavater, *L'art de connaître*, IX, 33–4.

[43] For Cataline, see e.g. Michel-Julien Mathiey, *Réflexions sur les événements du 9 au 10 thermidor* (Nemours, Year II (1794); BL, F853(15)). For Nero, cf. (Félix), *La dictature renversée, la royauté abolie, et le fanatisme détruit; ou Robespierre et sa clique traités comme ils le méritent. Dédié aux Jacobins* (BL, F581(4)); and *Nouveaux dialogues des morts* (BL, F852 (10)). And for Cromwell, cf. *Nouvelles observations sur le caractère la politique et la conduite de Robespierre le dernier tyran . . . Par le Sans-Culotte Lesenscommun*, 5 (BL, F852(3)).

[44] This literature highlighting the allegedly monarchical ambitions of Robespierre is analysed in Bronislaw Baczko, *Ending the Terror: The French Revolution after Robespierre* (Cambridge, 1994). Cf. the same author's '"Comment est fait un tyran": Thermidor et la légende noire de Thermidor', in the excellent collection, *Images de Robespierre. Actes du colloque international de Naples (1993)*, ed. Jean Ehrard (Naples, 1996), 25–54.

[45] As vampire, cf. (Dejean), *Sur la chute de Robespierre et complices* (BL, F854(13)), 3. As chameleon, cf. (Franconville), *Discours prononcé le 25 Thermidor à l'Assemblée générale de la Section de la Fraternité sur la conjuration de Robespierre et de ses complices*, 2 (BL, FR581(4)). More generally on this kind of language, see Jean-Louis Jam, 'Images de Robespierre dans les chansons et les hymnes de la Révolution', in *Images de Robespierre*, ed. Ehrard, 299–321. And for its continuation into the nineteenth century, see, in the same volume, Antoinette Ehrard, 'Un sphynx moderne? De quelques images de Robespierre au XIXe siècle', 263–97; and Marie-Hélène Huet, *Mourning Glory: The Will of the French Revolution* (Philadelphia, 1997), esp. ch. 7.

[46] Antoine de Baecque, *The Body Politic: Corporeal Metaphor in Revolutionary France 1770–1800* (Stanford, 1997); *French Caricature and the French Revolution, 1789–99*, ed. James Cuno (Los Angeles, 1989); and *Monstrous Bodies: Political Monstrosities in Early Modern Europe*, ed. Laura Knoppens and Joan Landes (Ithaca, NY, 2004), esp. 158.

a political system that was in essence, as another pictural attack put it, a 'cadavero-faminocratic government' and a 'tigrocracy'.[47]

Two tigrish characteristics were particularly helpful to the perpetuation of Robespierre's zoomorphic identity. First, the tiger's immoderate taste for blood-curdling killing had evidently made Robespierre an excellent target for the comparison at a time where the fantasies ran that in directing the Terror he aimed to depopulate France through hecatombs of guillotinings.[48] All 'Robespierrists' (the word was a Thermidorian neologism) were so many 'blood-drinkers' ('buveurs de sang'), and their chief had a quasi-vampiric, bulimic appetite for the liquid.[49] Second, was the fact that this tiger had a tail. 'You can cut off my head, but I am leaving you my tail', Robespierre had apocryphally said as he mounted the scaffold (though as we shall see he was in no fit state to utter any last words).[50] *La queue de Robespierre* – 'Robespierre's tail' – was the term given to his supporters, men who either had been his willing collaborators before Thermidor or who were still seeking to implement his policies. For the pamphleteers, such men were tigers 'avid for carnage', tigers 'who seek to bring down the human species'.[51] In the event, the tiger's tail would soon be crushed, but not before the pamphlets had consolidated Robespierre's reputation as a voracious tiger, and established an enduring 'black legend' of his 'tigocracy'.[52]

Robespierre was thus in good (or rather, bad) tiger-cattish company – and has remained there for the duration. The power of the metaphor was supported by the physiognomic tradition which, as we have suggested, continued to endorse the human–animal connection. The English author John Adolphus, writing in 1799, noted how the ferocity of Robespierre's gaze led 'an accurate observer to compare his general aspect to that of the cat-tyger'.[53] Two decades later, in 1821, the marquis de Ferrières echoed Merlin de Thionville when he wrote that Robespierre's 'face had

---

[47] Bibliothèque Nationale de France, Cabinet des Estampes, Collection Hennin, 11845; 'Miroir du passé pour sauvegarder l'avenir / Tableau parlant du Gouvernement cadavero-faminocratique de 93, sous la Tigocratie de Robespierre et Compagnie', British Museum, Prints and Drawings, 1925,0701.60.

[48] See the well-known print, 'Robespierre guillotinant le bourreau après avoir guillotiné tous les Français'. Reproduced in Huet, *Mourning Glory*, 173.

[49] Ehrrard, 'Un sphynx moderne', 264.

[50] Cited in Baczko, '"Comment est fait un tyran"', 46 (Fethemesi), *La queue de Robespierre ou les dangers de la liberté de la presse* (BL, F356(6)). See below, pp. 34–5.

[51] There is an excellent collection of these numerous pamphlets at BL, F354–5 and 356–7. The phrases cited are taken from *Les crimes des terroristes* (Year III (1795), BL, F355(25)); and [Saintomer], *Jugement du peuple souverain, qui condamne à mort la Queue infernale de robespierre* (BL, FR375(2)).

[52] The 'black legend' phrase is Baczko's ('"Comment est fait un tyran"').

[53] John Adolphus, *Biographical Memoirs of the French Revolution* (2 vols., 1799), II, 43.

something of the cat and the tiger in it'.[54] Physiognomic handbooks confirmed the association. Isidore Bourdon's 1842 text on physiognomy and phrenology, for example, noted how 'the physiognomy of Robespierre resembled that of a tiger', as was evidenced by his 'sanguinary instinct'.[55] The tiger analogy was soon enshrined within French Revolutionary historiography. Michelet, for example, recalled a conversation with Merlin de Thionville, in which Merlin had exclaimed 'Ah! If only you had seen his green eyes, you would have condemned him as I did.' Green eyes, the eyes of a cat. The eyes of a cat that would become, as Merlin had stated categorically, a tiger. On another occasion, Michelet evoked Robespierre on the festival of the Supreme Being, the ill-starred revolutionary cult which he had created, as 'radiant', but with a 'disturbing' smile: 'Passion visibly has imbibed his blood and dried his bones, leaving only nervous life, like a drowned cat brought back to life by Galvanism' (i.e. by electric shock). Robespierre became, moreover, Michelet held, more and more cat-like as time went on.[56]

The tiger–cat comparison was deployed by historians across the political divide. For the liberal politician and historian Alphonse de Lamartine, 'the bony outline of [Robespierre's] face involuntarily made one think of a beardless tiger'.[57] Later in the century, the rabid reactionary, Hippolyte Taine, paraphrased Merlin de Thionville: Robespierre had 'a cat's physiognomy, which was at first that of a worried but fairly gentle house-cat [but] became the ferocious expression of a tiger-cat'.[58] At the other end of the political spectrum, his near-contemporary, the great socialist politician and historian, Jean Jaurès, noted the 'feline' character of a statesman 'who walked at the margins of his responsibilities like a cat on a roof's edge'.[59]

This sequence of quotations certainly does not exhaust the presence in French Revolutionary historiography of Robespierre the cat–tiger. It became a familiar trope, as it remains. In her compelling recent biography, *Fatal Purity*, for example, Ruth Scurr quotes Merlin de Thionville before noting Robespierre's 'feline' character that she claims, moreover, to be

---

[54] Cited in Huet, *Mourning Glory*, 152. Many other citations about Robespierre are contained in the anthology by Louis Jacob, *Robespierre vu par ses contemporains* (Paris, 1938). In terms of the argument here, it is noticable that virtually all the 'contemporary' verdicts were given after 9 Thermidor.

[55] Bourdon, *La physionomonie et la phrénologie*, 328–9.

[56] Jules Michelet, *Histoire de la Révolution française*, ed. Gérard Walter (2 vols., Paris, 1952), II, 61, 870. Cf. Jean Ehrard, 'Entre Marx et Plutarque: le Robespierre de Jaurès', in *Images de Robespierre*, ed. Ehrard, 139–61, at 144.

[57] Cited in Antoine Court, 'Lamartine et Robespierre', in *Images de Robespierre*, ed. Ehrard, 93.

[58] Cited in Huet, *Mourning Glory*, 154.

[59] Ehrard, 'Entre Marx et Plutarque', 144.

able to detect in his portrait.[60] Merely considering such a view is a latter-day homage, I believe, to the success of the Thermidorian campaign of vilification. For I have simply been unable locate any individual who made even the slightest reference to Robespierre in terms of cats or tigers before his death. People may have remembered or imagined Robespierre as a tiger–cat after his death; there is no contemporaneous evidence I have found that anyone experienced him directly as such during his lifetime.[61] John Carr, an English visitor to Paris in 1802, was perceptive enough to spot what was going on. Coming across a 'handsome' bust of Robespierre made before his death, Carr noted: 'History, enraged at the review of the insatiable crimes of Robespierre, has already bestowed upon him a fanciful physiognomy, which she has compounded of features which correspond with the ferocity of his soul, rather than with his real countenance.'[62] The feline–tigrish spectre that has haunted even the most respectable of historical scholarship ever since is an *ex post facto* creation. Robespierre the ferocious cat–tiger owes everything, in sum, to the force of Thermidorian ideology and the ambient ethos of physiognomical theory.

In his lifetime, in fact, what physical description of Robespierre there was downplayed the physiognomic idiom. Far from standing out as physically wild, fierce or farouche, Robespierre passed in the crowd. 'His somewhat sulky physiognomy had nothing exceptional about it', even one Thermidorian polemicist recorded. 'His physiognomy and his gaze were expressionless', admitted another.[63] Robespierre was normally represented, moreover, as punctiliously correct in his dress and demeanour. He studiously eschewed the baggy plebeian trousers of the sans-culottes for a primped, polite and puffed-up appearance. He also tended towards an earnest, po-faced seriousness that won him the sobriquet 'the Incorruptible'. But this also led to him being viewed at times as yawn-inducing, even laughable.[64] The 'delicate complexion' that sister Charlotte evoked matched the pallor that was probably the most frequently remarked on aspect of his facial appearance among contemporaries prior to his death in 1794. Ground in the Thermidorian

---

[60] Scurr, *Fatal Purity*, 11.

[61] It would be interesting to see whether the image crops up in Counter-Revolutionary journalism, for example. That field is, however, very little studied. In terms of images, note their paucity, as remarked by Ehrard, 'Un sphynx moderne'. As noted above, it was almost as though Robespierre was completely physically unremarkable before 9 Thermidor.

[62] John Carr, *A Stranger in France, or A Trip from Devonshire to Paris*, 2nd edn (Paris, 1807), 316.

[63] Jean-Joseph Dussault, *Fragment pour servir à l'histoire de la Convention nationale depuis le 10 thermidor jusqu'à la dénonciation de Lecointre, inclusivement* (Paris, (1794)); *Histoire de la conjuration de Maximilien Robespierre* ((Lausanne, 1795)), 57.

[64] Cf. Pierre Rétat, 'Note sur la présence de Robespierre dans les journaux de 1789', in *Images de Robespierre*, ed. Ehrard.

mill, this pallor would be viewed as a symptom of Robespierre's bulimic, vampiric appetite for blood.[65]

Thermidorian propagandists occasionally acknowledged Robespierre's suaveness of appearance. But they merely held that it was a deliberate smokescreen that he had thrown up to hide his true, ferociously mendacious character. *Fronti nulla fides*, after all. The claims of physiognomy were, moreover, neatly congruent with the concern for transparency that was a fundamental feature of Revolutionary political culture. Robespierre and his followers were obsessed, for example, by 'red caps worn by intriguers', and with plots against the Republic, grounded in a similar concern with the apparent ubiquity of dissimulation.[66] This could bring Robespierre himself close to a highly physiognomic stance: he attacked the ultra-Revolutionary Joseph Fouché, for example, saying that 'his face was the expression of crime'.[67] It required a connoisseurial eye to penetrate physiognomic dissembling and to see through the political pretences of an opponent of the Revolutionary cause.

Following Robespierre's fall, there were some who held that the physiognomic gaze had come into its own even more, and was serving the cause of democratic accountability. Writing in the weeks after 9 Thermidor, the journalist Jean-Joseph Dussault opined that the art of physiognomy had in fact progressed since 1789. 'Tricked by so many traitors, the people has felt the need to look outside of speeches and even of actions in order to locate the true thinking of their representatives.' He continued, in a way that showed that Thermidorian propaganda was doing its job:

> History's paint-brush offers not a single case, from Cataline through to Robespierre, of a single great conspirator who has concocted the loss of liberty within a republic, and who has a flowery countenance or an agreeable look . . . [Physiognomy] . . ., this dialect of nature that is so difficult to translate, is becoming a common and familiar language for a free people, prone to being betrayed.[68]

If physiognomy had hitherto failed to perform its democratic task in the case of Robespierre – for it had missed the tiger lurking underneath, in pussy-cat clothing – this was partly due to his dastardly dissimulation and partly to a rather personal characteristic that was increasingly evoked. Robespierre, it was noted, 'often clenched his fists, as in a nervous

---

[65] Robespierre's acknowledged pallor seems to have darkened into 'lividity' from 1792, which was ascribed to an excess of bile. Cf. Robespierre's former ally Jérôme Pétion, writing in that year (Jacob, *Robespierre vu par ses contemporains*, 217); and post-Thermidor, see, e.g., Moreau de la Sarthe, *Portrait de Robespierre*, 2.

[66] The 'red caps' quote is Saint-Just's: B. J. B. Buchez and P. C. Roux, *Histoire parlementaire de la Révolution française* (40 vols., Paris, 1833–8), XXXV, 434.

[67] *Mémoires de Barras*, ed. Georges Duruy (4 vols., Paris, 1895–6), I, 179.

[68] Dussault, *Fragment*, 28–9.

contraction, and the same movement was evident in his shoulders and his neck, that he agitated convulsively to left and right . . . [to which could be added] a frequent blinking [of the eyes] that seemed linked to the aforementioned convulsive agitation'.[69] Fréron, one of the architects of Robespierre's downfall on 9 Thermidor, had known him when they were both schoolboys at the Collège Louis-le-Grand. 'His mobile face', Fréron recalled, 'had [already] contracted those convulsive grimaces for which he was known.'[70] One contemporary later stated that it was 'a continual and embarrassing blinking of the eyes' that marked Robespierre out, while another noted 'a contraction in the mouth'.[71] Charles Nodier in the Restoration amplified this even more luridly, evoking 'the nervous trembling that shook his palpitating limbs, through to the habitual tic that tormented the muscles of his face which spontaneously gave them the expression of laughter or of pain, through to the twitching of his fingers on the speaker's lectern, as if he were playing the spinet'.[72] This quotation recalls Michelet's likening of his smile to the galvanic twitch of a vivisected cat, evoked earlier.[73]

In our own day, medical researchers tend to see facial tics either as expressions of Tourette's syndrome or else as the symptoms of an underlying neurological disorder. Indeed, the facial tic is a godsend to modern authors wishing to attempt a psychoanalytical sketch of Robespierre. Over the eighteenth century, however, the term 'tic' had come to denote any invariably ridiculous little habit that individuals adopted involuntarily – tugging at a wig, stroking one's nose, scratching one's arse (the latter example is from Diderot).[74] Yet, interestingly, and revealingly in this study of animal–human crossings, the first and continuing usage of the term relates to veterinary medicine. A tic had originated as 'a kind of illness that horses get which makes them from time to time have a kind of convulsive movement of the head, and they take hold of their manger with their teeth and gnaw it'.[75] To his contemporaries at least, Robespierre the tiger evidently had an equine air. Strangely, this emerged in the final stages of his life, as he was being transported to

---

[69] (Duperron), *Vie secrette politique et curieuse de Maximilien Robespierre* (Paris, Year II (= 1794)), 23.

[70] Fréron, cited in Jacob, *Robespierre vu par ses contemporains*, 41.

[71] Etienne Dumont and Barère, both cited in Jacob, *Robespierre vu par ses contemporains*, 88, 201.

[72] Cited in Jeannine Guichardet, 'L'image de Robespierre dans quelques dictionnaires du XIXe siècle', in *Images de Robespierre*, ed. Ehrard, 86.

[73] See above, pp. 20–1.

[74] Again, Frantext is of great help in tracking usage. Cf. Denis Diderot, *Les bijoux indiscrets*, ed. Jacques Rustin (Paris, 1981), 88.

[75] *Dictionnaire de l'Académie française*, 1st edn (1694), art. 'tic'. The veterinary meaning of the term remains primary in the major French dictionaries through to the present.

the Committee of Public Safety during the night of 9–10 Thermidor. Silenced by his pistol shot to his jaw and in great physical distress, 'he sought repeatedly to bite those carrying his stretcher on several occasions' – much like a tiger in his cage or a horse convulsively biting his manger.[76]

At the turn of the century, medical researchers were in fact becoming increasingly interested in the tic. There was a debate over whether the involuntary tic could be differentiated from horse sickness on one hand and on the other from facial neuralgia presenting symptoms of facial contraction. The issue was discussed in a number of medical works, notably Guillaume-Antoine Soulagne's thesis, *Essai sur le tic* in 1804, which described the kind of facial distortions involved.[77] While eyebrows furrow and eyelids draw close, the corner of the mouth is drawn back towards the ear, with the jaw remaining immobile producing the appearances of sardonic laughter. Writing several years later, another medical researcher, Jean-Auguste Hérail, compared the tic to the involuntary laughter, often described since Antiquity as canine or sardonic laughter, whose characteristic was the raising of the upper lip to reveal the dog teeth.[78] The Robespierre legend was thus formed at a time when medical men were writing of the facial tic as something that looked like involuntary, sardonic laughter.[79]

If Robespierre seemed unable to manage the sunny, smiling beam of humanity later to be praised by his sister as his everyday expression, it was because his facial tic was allegedly so extreme that it made his face difficult for even a trained physiognomic gaze to read and comprehend. His attempt at a smile was a kind of bestial and cunning jamming device that prevented the physiognomic gaze from performing its work of detection: 'The smile of confidence never rested on his lips', noted the English critic John Adophus, 'but they were nearly always contracted by the sour grin of envy aiming to appear disdain.'[80] It was also, as we have suggested, a further crossing, simultaneously equine and canine, into the world of animality in which Robespierre's reputation wallowed, post-Thermidor.

---

[76] (Duperron), *Vie secrète*, 29.

[77] Guillaume-Antoine Soulagne, *Essai sur le tic en général et en particulier sur le tic douleureux de la pommette* (Montpellier, Year XII (1804)).

[78] Jean-Auguste Hérail, *Essai sur le tic douleureux de la face* (Montpellier, 1818). This is a useful text for tracing research on the phenomenon across the Enlightenment. See too Chantal Marazia, '"Un piccolo flagello dell'umanità": note sul termine "tic"', *Medicina nei secoli. Arte et scienza*, 21 (2009), 1005–15. My thanks to Chantal Marazia for help on this point.

[79] For sardonic laughter over the eighteenth century, cf. Jones, 'Laughing over boundaries, 9.

[80] Adolphus, *Biographical Memoirs*, II, 443.

In his novel *Quatre-vingt treize*, published in 1874, Victor Hugo imagined a tavern scene in which Robespierre discussed the destiny of the Revolution with Marat and Danton. The exquisitely well-dressed Robespierre presents a picture of characterless dedication to work – he has a pile of papers before him. Marat has a cup of coffee on the go and Danton is drinking from a bottle of wine. Robespierre is also distinguished by having 'a nervous tic on his cheek which', Hugo noted, 'prevented him from smiling'.[81] The tic topos, that earlier critics had utilised to indicate the involuntary unnaturalness and artificiality of Robespierre's attempts at a smile, is here expanded so as to encompass a physiological incapacity to smile. We may place this plot device in the context of the incredulity of Victor Hugo's contemporaries (and subsequent historians) when confonted with the Robespierre's sister's claim that her brother had had a sweet and smiley disposition. It is also helpful to set it in the physiognomic tradition I have been discussing.

Master-physiognomist Johann-Caspar Lavater waxed famously lyrical about the human smile and laughter. Laughter is, he maintained, 'the touchstone of good judgement, of qualities of the heart and of the energy of the Creator ... With an agreeable laugh one can never be wicked.'[82] We note in passing that the smile and laugh – that Lavater often conflates – are historically and etymologically interrelated, the smile seeming to emerge as a kind of sub-laugh (the literal translation of the French verb noun and verb, *sourire* ('smile', 'to smile') or *sous-rire*). Although Lavater noted there was much theological debate over the question of whether Jesus had ever laughed, he thought it unimaginable that he had never smiled: 'for if Christ had never smiled, he would not have been a man'.[83] This neat formulation nodded towards Lavater's overriding notion of the human face created in God's image, but also evoked the long-established physiognomical precept that benign laughter was what set humankind apart from beasts. Aristotle was alleged to have claimed that the faculty of laughter was quintessentially and exclusively human, a notion that Rabelais had updated as 'laughter is of man alone'. Robespierre's inability to smile properly – partly due to his tigrish physiognomical disposition, partly because of his animal-like facial tic – was thus a symptom of his base inhumanity.[84] If man was an *animal risibile* – a creature capable of laughter – Robespierre certainly was not. 'No-one', recalled his school-friend Fréron, 'remembers having seen him laugh even once.'[85]

---

[81] Victor Hugo, *Quatre-vingt-treize* (1874), in his *Oeuvres complètes. Romans. III* (Paris, 1985), 871–2.

[82] Lavater, *L'art de connaître*, V, 139.

[83] *Ibid.*

[84] Cf. Jones, 'Laughing over boundaries', 8.

[85] Jacob, *Robespierre vu par ses contemporains*, 41.

The publication in 1872 of Charles Darwin's study, *The Expression of the Emotions in Man and Animals* is often viewed as the moment when physiognomy's long-maintained scientific pretensions finally hit the buffers. Darwin had nearly fallen foul of popular physiognomical analysis personally – the captain of the *Beagle* almost refused to allow him on board in 1831 because the shape of his nose revealed a lack of energy and resolution according to Lavaterian textbooks. Darwin's subsequent study of physiognomical writings led him towards formal disdain for them, and he dismissed them out of hand as 'surprising nonsense' at the very outset of his *Expression of the Emotions.*[86]

Paradoxically, however, Darwin's account of facial expression in fact allowed a greater longevity and indeed a form of scientific legitimation for one of the key notions behind millennia of physiognomic lore, namely that there was a meaningful relationship between human and animal facial conformation and gestures. (Yet, the word physiognomy was studiously eschewed, and the practice henceforth most likely to be evoked by cartoonists and caricaturists.) Darwin's evolutionary account of the main ways in which the emotions were expressed blew away any putative division between humans and animals on the basis of expressive behaviour. Darwin was attracted by the notion that his pet dog was wont to grin at him – a sentiment many anthropomorphically minded pet-owners must have shared.[87] But he also highlighted a fuller overlap in the expression of the emotions among animals closest to humans in the evolutionary chain. Thus orangutans could chuckle and grin. Chimpanzees could laugh. The *Cynopithecus niger* might even flash a smile – as Darwin endeavoured to demonstrate with one of the most devastatingly unconvincing images ever to appear in a canonical scientific text (Figure 7).[88]

Despite such comic top-notes, Darwin's denial of a rupture between humans and animals in the expression of emotions such as smiling and laughing continues to be scientifically pertinent to our own day.[89] The term physiognomy might have fallen into terminal discredit but the intellectual concerns it expressed remain embedded in the Darwinian science that still offers the framework in which evolutionary biologists and psychologists work. These view laughing and smiling as innate and universal attributes, noting, for example, that human babies can be found producing something approximating to a smile when they are less than

---

[86] Perle, *About Faces*, 47. Charles Darwin, *The Expression of the Emotions in Man and Animals* (1872), ed. Paul Ekman (1998), 7, 11.

[87] Darwin, *Expression of the Emotions*, 120–1.

[88] *Ibid.*, 132–4. The image is on 135.

[89] It is also the basis on which 'post-human' philosophy operates: see above, n. 9.

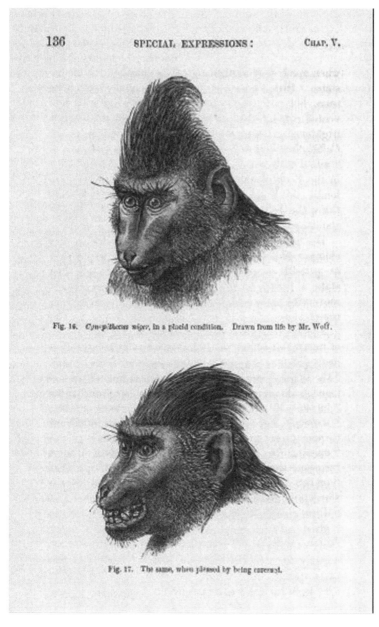

136　　　　　　SPECIAL EXPRESSIONS:　　　Chap. V.

Fig. 16. *Cynopithecus niger*, in a placid condition. Drawn from life by Mr. Wolf.

Fig. 17. The same, when pleased by being caressed.

Figure 7 *Cynopithecus niger*, from Charles Darwin, *The Expression of the Emotions in Man and Animals* (1872). © Wellcome Library, London.

three hours out of the womb.[90] Smiling is observed after three to four weeks, and laughter follows shortly afterwards. By three to four months, laughter is more developed, and 'social smiles' are evident as are the reservation of smiles for carers.[91] Evolutionary biologists also note that laughter and smiling are morphologically identical – that the basic facial changes associated with each gesture are essentially interchangeable.[92] Furthermore, they stretch this human universalism into the world of the great apes. But they divide over whether the human smile links to the benign play face of these mammals – as Darwin surmised – or else to gestures which communicate threat and aggression.

The smile (as we have seen with laughter)[93] thus comes fraught with complex meanings that allows it to cross boundaries – emotional boundaries – between love and hate, attraction and repulsion. It is a point of which Lavater was more than aware: he commented on the variability of the smile, contrasting 'the sweet smile' that 'adds to the eyes and mouth a grace and wit that an observer easily remarks' with, at the far extreme, the unpleasant 'sardonic laughter which degenerates into facial contortions'.[94] Beyond this broad generalisation, the universalist idiom of evolutionary psychology's take on the laugh and the smile might seem to proof it against merely historical analysis. Evolutionary time is so drawn out – the smile, it is seriously suggested, goes back ten million years – that it makes even the Braudelian framework of the *longue durée* seem the merest nano-second. Yet, the apparently timeless universalism of the evolutionary scientists still leaves some room for historians working with historical time-frames and deploying the methods of social and cultural construction. The scientist Paul Ekman has accumulated, for example, a list of some 180 different types of smile – which suggests that the gesture covers a particularly wide range of social situations and contexts, and that the smile's morphology and semantics of the smile are more various than the Darwinian approach appears at first blush to allow.[95]

That smiles are socially and culturally constructed within definable historical periods is evident when we consider their historical development over the course of the eighteenth century. For something akin to a 'French Smile Revolution' was under way, even within the lifetime of Maximilien

[90] M. K. Rothbart, 'Emotional Development: Changes in Reactivity and Self-Regulation', in *The Nature of Emotion. Fundamental Questions*, ed. P. Ekman and R. J. Davidson (Oxford, 1994).

[91] See esp. P. Ekman, *Emotion in the Human Face*, 2nd edn (Cambridge, 1982), 154.

[92] V. Bruce, *Recognising Faces* (1988), 43.

[93] Jones, 'Laughing over Boundaries'.

[94] Lavater, *L'art de connaître*, VI, 101–2.

[95] Ekman and Friesen (1978), cited in Bruce, *Recognising Faces*, 43.

Robespierre.[96] This emerges clearly, for example, in works of literature. It is striking to note the relative infrequency of the term *sourire* in late seventeenth- and early eighteenth-century texts. Any smiles around are invariably 'forced, 'arrogant', 'disdainful' and 'ironic' and notably, in light of the neurological discussion about Robespierre's convulsive grin, 'sardonic'.[97] They denote a gesture seemingly preferred by aristocrats and others in the social elite for condescending towards or being contemptuous of their social inferiors, or else they are a rictus aimed at hiding true feelings. This usage linked to the court culture that the absolute kings of France had established, wherein facial impassivity was the template for kings and courtiers alike.[98] According to La Bruyère, 'A man who knows the court is master of his gestures, his eyes and his face; … he smiles to his enemies, controls his temper, disguises his passions, belies his heart, speaks and acts against his real feelings.'[99] Any smiling or laughing in this context could only be top-down – *de haut en bas* – unspontaneous, disdainful, ironic, removed from authentic feelings and very much that sardonic smile 'degenerating into facial contortions' discussed by Lavater.[100]

The 1740s and 1750s, however, witnessed a dramatic step change in regard to usage of the term, *sourire*. First, there was a doubling, then a tripling in the frequency with which the word was used in works of literature.[101] Second, there was a detectable shift in the way in which the meaning of the smile was understood. What seems to have kick-started literary sensitivity to a new kind of smile was the translation into French at mid-century of Samuel Richardson's *Pamela* and *Clarissa*, foundational works of English sensibility.[102] This trend was subsequently taken forward and popularised by the influential novels of Jean-Jacques Rousseau notably *Julie, ou la Nouvelle Héloise* (1761) and *Émile* (1762) and the numerous literary works influenced by them. In this new literature of sensibility, smiles were 'enchanting', 'sweet', 'agreeable', 'friendly' and 'virtuous'. These smiles of sensibility were very much Lavater's 'sweet smiles'. They also notably transgressed codes of contrained good manners

---

[96] For fuller details on this section see my forthcoming book, *The French Smile Revolution: Identity and Dentistry in Eighteenth-Century Paris*.

[97] These conclusions are based on an analysis of the relevant entries in the Frantext/ARTFL database (see above, n. 37).

[98] Cf. Colin Jones, 'The King's Two Teeth', *History Workshop Journal*, 65 (2008), 79–95.

[99] Jean de La Bruyère, *Les caractères de Théophraste*, 10th edn (Paris, 1699), 238.

[100] See above, p. 27.

[101] Again, these conclusions are based on analysis of Frantext/ARTFL.

[102] *Pamela* (1740) was translated into French in 1745; and the abbé Prévost translated *Clarissa* (1748) as *Lettres anglaises ou Histoire de Miss Clarisse Harlowe* in 1751. Prévost was also responsible for the translation of Richardson's sequel, *Sir Charles Grandison* (1753), which appeared as *Nouvelles lettres anglaises ou Histoire du chevalier Grandisson* in 1755.

codified since the Renaissance by permitting the opening of lips to reveal white teeth – a gesture (to which I will return) that was now adjudged more sociable, more natural and in a way more moral.[103] The smile was not – as in the crushingly monotonous court culture still being performed out at Versailles – an insincere, artificial and tight-lipped grimace aimed at hiding true feelings or acting out repressed aggression. Rather, it offered a transparent pathway into the soul, a gesture that was shared on terms of equality, not hierarchy, between two evenly matched individuals. The ironical and sardonic superior smile did not of course disappear from the novel. Every plot had its villain, after all, every Clarissa its tiger-like Lovelace to encounter. Yet, it now seemed that the smile could be read for character, and that one could know what a person was like by their smile.

One might be tempted to dismiss all this as merely something that took place only in fiction – were it not the case that the literature of sensibility had an enormous impact on social attitudes and behaviour. A broad swathe of the upper reaches of society in both England and France sought not merely to read about Clarissa and Julie and their ilk – but to be like them.[104] The emulative behaviour certainly extended, incidentally, to smiling so as to reveal clean white teeth. A mouth-opening gesture in the past that had been hugely criticised in conduct books as plebeian, crude and impolite was now legitimated as emblematic of a new humane politeness and moral transparency. A new facial regime, a new regime of faciality, and what we can recognise as the new, modern smile was in gestation.[105]

Proof that the smile of sensibility was not just confined within the literary domain, but was strongly influencing behaviour in the public sphere is the fact that new technologies of mouth care were emergent precisely in this period, with Paris in the vanguard.[106] The tooth-puller of old now had a rival to contend with: the dentist. It is not an accident

---

[103] For sensibility, two helpful introductory works are Janet Todd, *Sensibility: An Introduction* (1986), and John Mullan, *Sentiment and Sociability: The Language of Feeling in the Eighteenth Century* (Oxford, 1988). Also focused on England is G. J. Barker-Benfield, *The Culture of Sensibility: Sex and Society in Eighteenth-Century Britain* (Chicago, 1992) – though cf. G. S. Rousseau, 'Sensibility Reconsidered', *Medical History*, 39 (1995), 375–7. For France, see esp. Anne C. Vila, *Enlightenment and Pathology: Sensibility in the Literature and Medicine of Eighteenth-Century France* (Baltimore, 1998), and Jessica Riskin, *Science in the Age of Sensibility. The Sentimental Empiricists of the French Enlightenment* (Chicago, 2002). On civility and the policing of orifices, see the classic Norbert Elias, *The Civilizing Process*, I: *The History of Manners* (New York, 1978).

[104] Robert Darnton, 'Readers Respond to Rousseau: The Fabrication of Romantic Sensitivity', in his *The Great Cat Massacre*, 215–56.

[105] As I seek to show in *The French Smile Revolution*, this process of the invention of the modern smile was not smoothly unproblematic, and was set back by the Revolutionary decade.

[106] Cf. Colin Jones, 'Pulling Teeth in Eighteenth-Century Paris', *Past and Present*, 166 (2000), 100–45.

Figure 8 Toothbrush of Napoleon Bonaparte. © Wellcome Library, London.

that the word dentist ('dentiste') dates from this period, for a vocational sub-grouping of practitioners emerged, using surgical know-how to create preventive dentistry. The public toothpuller had been something of a one-trick pony. The new dentist achieved new standards of care, developing an armamentarium of operative tools, passing far beyond mere tooth-extraction – the very last thing a good dentist should be doing – to tooth-filling, cleaning, whitening, straightening, transplanting and replacing. On the eve of the Revolution, the Parisian surgeon Nicolas Dubois de Chémant announced his invention of porcelain false teeth, thus allowing the white-toothed smile to become available even to the terminally toothless.[107] The regular cleaning of teeth had long been advocated. But now for the first time in human history, this was to be done not simply with a cloth and a toothpick, but with dental powder or paste and with a toothbrush, a shamefully unheralded innovation of this very period. (Napoleon's personal toothbrush may be viewed in the Wellcome Collection, London) (Figure 8).[108] Lavater characteristically set the seal of approval on the white-toothed smile: 'clean, white and well-arranged teeth [he held] . . . [show] a sweet and polished mind and a good and honest heart'. It was not the case, he maintained, that people with bad

[107] Colin Jones, 'English Teeth and French Dentists in the Long Eighteenth Century', in *Medicine, Madness and Social History: Essays in Honour of Roy Porter*, ed. Roberta Bivins and John V. Pickstone (Manchester, 2007), 73–89. English and American dentistry lagged far behind the French.
[108] Wellcome Collection, London.

teeth could not in some cases be estimable in their way. But, generally speaking, bad teeth revealed 'either sickness or else some melange of moral imperfection'.[109]

Where, then, in the 'French Smile Revolution' can we place the political revolutionary, Maximilien Robespierre? In the first part of this paper, I suggested that the tiger–cat reputation that Robespierre acquired on his death is more useful for comprehending an aspect of the nineteenth century's political imaginary, and the subterranean role that physiognomic portraiture has played in shaping subsequent historiography, than in allowing us to understand what Robespierre was really like or really all about. Robespierre inhabited the world of sensibility that was creating the French Smile Revolution. Had he died in 1789, moreover, recollections of him would not, we can wager, be dwelling on his tigrish disposition, but on his exemplary sensibility. The small-time country-town lawyer from provincial Arras had worked hard, built up his practice, specialised in pro bono litigation for the disadvantaged, liked country walks and picnics, dabbled in science, penned soppy verses (for example, an ode on the arts of nose-blowing and uses of the handkerchief) and written sentimental love-letters in the style of Jean-Jacques Rousseau. Put like this, he sounds the sort of character who, as his sister Charlotte would aver, would indeed be 'nearly always smiling'.[110]

Did he have white teeth, however? The evidence is that at least he tried to. In his memoirs, his fellow-deputy Barras recounted how he and fellow-deputy Fréron had visited Robespierre at his lodgings shortly before 9 Thermidor in an attempt to get him to reach a political compromise. They found him how? Cleaning his teeth (a point unnoticed by historians hitherto).[111] Barras noted that as Robespierre cleaned his teeth, he insouciantly spat out mouth-rinsing water at the feet of his fellow-deputies. The gesture conveyed, in Barras's account, a lack of civility on Robespierre's part and an overload of contempt for individuals he regarded as his inferiors rather than his fraternal equals. (Clearly, the man had never read his Norbert Elias.) But there is also a hint of the public display of private functions that had characterised the Bourbon court: Robespierre was thus displaying manners that were both reprehensibly Bourbon and irredeemably bestial. Even while noting Barras's spin on the incident, the anecdote reveals that Robespierre did, until the end of his days, maintain the new forms of dental hygiene. He was dentally equipped

[109] Lavater, *L'art de connaître*, II, 244–5.
[110] See above, p. 4. Peter McPhee's biography of Robespierre is particularly insistent on this aspect of Robespierre's character.
[111] *Mémoires de Barras*, ed. Duruy, I, 149.

as a regular man of feeling. (And indeed, flippantly, one might think: 'the Incorruptible' – what a wonderful brand-name for a tooth-paste.[112])

I began this paper with Charlotte Robespierre's memory of her brother's smiling physiognomy, and have gone on to set this personal recollection contrastively against not only the 'black legend' which sprang up as soon as Robespierre was executed but also the historiographical polemics that have circled around this contentious figure ever since. What has been striking is the extent to which debates among historians and biographers have been influenced (even to the present day) by the strongly physiognomical hatchet-job performed on his character after his death, notably the *ex post facto* invention of his tigrish proclivities. This may partly be explained by physiognomy's perennial wish to penetrate beneath facial and bodily appearance to the 'reality' of sub-jacent character, which evidently strikes a chord in our own era of emergent facial recognition technologies.[113] But the insistence on Robespierre's tiger-like characteristics seems to owe less to physiognomy's claims to explain than to its power to depreciate and diminish. By pushing Robespierre across the human–animal frontier, by making a tiger of him, in other words, we make it impossible to take his humanity seriously – let alone the possibility that he might, as his sister claimed, have managed a smile (at a time moreover when that gesture was being viewed as the key indicator to character). It is all too easy, I would contend, to 'understand' the Terror if we consider that its artisans were so many beasts and monsters. What is much more of a challenge is to understand how the Terror could have been created by men of feeling and good will. Robespierre was – of course – no angel. But we can only hope to manage some sort of dispassionate historical judgement on such a complex figure if we deal firmly with the physiognomic language which has accompanied his reputation. If we do not, we risk being only the ventriloquist dummies of Thermidorian propagandists.

Readers may have felt that in the course of my argument, the smile of Robespierre has been waxing and waning before their eyes rather like the grin of a Cheshire cat. I would like to end with one final image of Robespierre's face and capacity to smile that was to prove extremely influential over the next century. It set the seal on his alleged bestiality,

---

[112] The dental entrepreneur Dubois de Chémant marketed his patent porcelain white dentures under the heading of 'incorruptible teeth of mineral paste'. See Jones, 'French Dentists and English Teeth', 76–9. Barras's implication of monarchical tendencies fitted in with the attack on Robespierre's character on and after 9 Thermidor: see Bazcko, *Ending the Terror*, esp. ch. 1.

[113] See the interesting links between the two technologies in *La Fabrique du visage. De la physiognomonie antique à la première greffe*, ed. François Delaporte, Emmanuel Fournier and Bernard Devauchaell (Turnhout, 2010).

and did so in style and in a way that has proved difficult to efface from the memory. That image derives from his execution.

Arrested in the National Convention on 9 Thermidor, Robespierre escaped custody and sought to lead a counter-coup against the assembly. Later that night, faced with its failure, he sought to blow his brains out with a pistol.[114] He missed. Or at least he missed his brains. He blew a huge hole in his lower jaw, part detaching it from his face. His captors that night bandaged up his face, subjecting him to taunting to which he was powerless to reply. Rushed through the Revolutionary Tribunal next morning, he was conveyed in a tumbril through the streets of Paris. The socialist historian Jean Jaurès recorded that women were dancing wildly in celebration outside his lodgings on the Rue Saint-Honoré as the tumbril passed. Robespierre smiled sadly at the sight, Jaurès tells us (though on what evidence it is not clear, and quite what this smile might have actually have looked like we can only shudder to think).[115]

What happened when the tumbril reached the guillotine is better attested. I will follow Michelet's account. As Robespierre climbed the steps of the scaffold:

> One of the guillotine crew brutally snatched away the bandage that held his poor broken jaw together. He let out a howl . . . He could for an instant be seen pale, hideous, his mouth wide open and his teeth falling to the ground . . . there was a heavy thud.[116]

End of story. Or maybe – maybe equally correctly – the start of one. For this macabre episode would be much recounted and gleefully elaborated upon in histories of the Revolution throughout the nineteenth century (twentieth-century historians tend to be more circumspect with the detail, or more squeamish). The animal shriek had irrevocably wiped the smile off Robespierre's face, and established his subhuman bestiality at a stroke. The tiger had lost its white and well-kept teeth even before its head had hit the bottom of the basket. For many of those throughout the nineteenth century who contemplated the French Revolution, this was a fitting end for a tyrannical and bestial monster, pointing a moral, adorning a tale and exemplifying a physiognominal precept. The thought of Robespierre's 'nearly always smiling' face would now seem a chimerical fantasy that it would prove impossible, save for sister Charlotte and her ilk, even to imagine. What lingered in the mind was not the well-groomed smile of sensibility, but rather the gaping, gothic black hole where once a smile

---

[114] See the accounts of the day in Scull's and McPhee's biographies.

[115] Jean Jaurès, *Histoire socialiste de la Révolution française*, ed. Albert Soboul (7 vols., Paris, 1968–73), VI, 515.

[116] Michelet, *Histoire de la Révolution française*, II, 989. See Baczko, '"Comment est fait un tyran"', 25–6, for another version of the final events.

had been. By reducing Robespierre to a kind of degree zero of humanity, suffused by a sheer animality that was proclaimed by that final, bestial howl, the nineteenth century would live with a monstrous, ideologically hyper-charged and nightmare vision of what revolutions were all about. The bestialisation of Robespierre was equated with the bestiality of all revolutions and all revolutionaries.

Transactions of the RHS 22 (2012), pp. 37–55 © Royal Historical Society 2012
doi:10.1017/S0080440112000059

ORIENTATION IN THREE SPHERES: MEDIEVAL MEDITERRANEAN BOUNDARY CLAUSES IN LATIN, GREEK AND ARABIC*

By Alex Metcalfe

READ AT THE UNIVERSITY OF LANCASTER

ABSTRACT. This paper investigates the development of land registry traditions in the medieval Mediterranean by examining a distinctive aspect of Latin, Greek and Arabic formularies used in boundary clauses. The paper makes particular reference to Islamic and Norman Sicily. The argument begins by recalling that the archetypal way of defining limits according to Classical Roman land surveyors was to begin *ab oriente*. Many practices from Antiquity were discontinued in the Latin West, but the idea of starting with or from the East endured in many cases where boundaries were assigned cardinal directions. In the Byzantine Empire, the 'Roman' model was prescribed and emulated by Greek surveyors and scribes too. But in the Arab-Muslim Mediterranean, lands were defined with the southern limit first. This contrast forms the basis of a typology that can be tested against charter evidence in frontier zones – for example, in twelfth-century Sicily, which had been under Byzantine, Muslim and Norman rulers. It concludes that, under the Normans, private documents drawn up in Arabic began mainly with the southern limit following the 'Islamic' model. However, Arabic descriptions of crown lands started mainly in the 'Romano-Byzantine' way. These findings offer a higher resolution view of early Norman governance and suggest that such boundary definitions of the royal chancery could not have been based on older ones written in the Islamic period.

Introduction

When landed property was defined in the medieval Mediterranean, many boundary clauses were described in ways which still loosely resembled model compositions of *limites* drawn up in Classical Roman texts, even if direct knowledge of that surveying and notarial ancestry was exceptional

* I would like to thank the Arts and Humanities Research Council for their funding of 'The Norman Edge: Identity and State Formation on the Frontiers of Europe' project of which the author was a co-investigator (2008–11); the British Academy for their award of a Mid-Career Fellowship (2011–12); Wolfson College, the Oriental Institute and the Khalili Research Centre at the University of Oxford for hosting me as a Visiting Scholar and Research Associate (2010–12). I am also grateful to Chris Wickham and Jon Jarrett for their comments on a draft version of this paper. This is an adapted version of a paper read to the Society.

– and, more usually, non-existent. In itself, this observation is of no great consequence since it is well known that the art of land surveying in the Middle Ages had radically changed from that of Antiquity when professional *agrimensores*, experts in geometry and trigonometry, fastidiously noted every type of land, limit, local idiosyncrasy and cause of dispute.[1] The methodical precision of the *ars gromatica* rarely troubled the medieval notary. No longer was it standard practice to illustrate a work with sketches; to explain precedents, customs and jargon of land tenure, or, indeed, to link land survey, settlement and viability with cartography, cosmology or wider regional subdivision.[2]

It is equally obvious to note how political, legal and socio-economic relationships between landholder and the land were fundamentally different to those of later lordships in the Latin West, Byzantine East or, indeed, between a Mediterranean Muslim ruler and his salaried troops and officials. The colonising policy of the Roman Empire with its orderly resettlement of army veterans in the first centuries BC and AD were processes inconceivable to any medieval ruler, and the quintessential techniques of Roman surveying, a function of such imperial mandates, all but lapsed in the medieval Latin West and Balkans.[3] Instead, there was a far more haphazard approach to land definition with little effort made to measure boundary lengths and hardly ever any attempt to calculate the surface area of an estate.

However, not all ancient practice was discontinued. In the south of the Italian Peninsula for example, during and after the Norman period when document survival for the region improves significantly, echoes of Roman land surveying techniques are detectable in charters and cartularies. The notion that plots of land should be ideally conceived as quadrilateral had endured, and boundary markers were still of avail, albeit irregularly set, sized and devoid of any pagan aura.

---

[1] The gromatic texts have been compiled into a new critical edition by Brian Campbell, *The Writings of the Roman Land Surveyors. Introduction, Text, Translation and Commentary* (2000). On the *constitutio limitum*, see Hyginus in *ibid.*, 134–63. Among secondary sources, see O. A. W. Dilke, *The Roman Land Surveyors: An Introduction to the Agrimensores* (Newton Abbot, 1971); M. Clavel-Lévéque, *Cadastres et espace rural. Approches et réalités antiques. Table ronde de Besançon, mai 1980* (Paris, 1983); G. Chouquer, M. Clavel-Lévéque, F. Favry and J.-P. Vallat, *Structures agraires en Italie centro-méridionale. Cadastres et paysages ruraux* (Rome, 1987); C. Nicolet, *L'inventaire du monde. Géographie et politique aux origines de L'Empire romain* (Paris, 1988).

[2] For atypical medieval interest in Roman surveying texts, see Lucio Toneatto, 'Note sulla tradizione del *Corpus agrimensorum romanorum*, I. Contenuti e struttura dell'Ars gromatica di Gisemundus (IX sec.)', *Mélanges de l'École française de Rome: Moyen-Âge*, 94 (Rome, 1982), I, 191–313.

[3] One of the last references to the term 'agrimensor' dates to 597 when Gregory the Great dispatched a surveyor from Rome to resolve a dispute on church lands in Sicily where there was presumably no one suitable. *Monumenta Germaniae Historica, Epist. I.1, Gregorii I Registri Lib. I–IV*, ed. P. Ewald (Berlin, 1887), 484–5, Letter VII.36.

But the most striking links to the past were in the orientation of estates. In particular, the order in which boundaries were recorded when their limits were assigned cardinal points. In these descriptions, confines predominantly began *ab oriente* running laterally from a point at the top of the eastern limit. This system derived directly from the ancient Roman custom of land division. On this, its most basic precept, the early gromatic writer Julius Frontinus reflected how 'our ancestors . . . first drew out two *limites*, one stretching from east to west, which they called the *decumanus*, the other from south to north which they called the *kardo*'.[4]

Boundary clauses in pre- and early Norman Italy

Across the south Italian mainland, the period from late Antiquity to the early eleventh century is marked by a relative lack of charter materials. In part, this is due to questions of document production, but it is also due to document loss, which in many regions, such as Byzantine and Islamic Sicily, is extreme. From the twelfth century, a relative proliferation of charter material resulted from increasingly sophisticated forms of civil governance and complementary roles played by trained, literate functionaries.[5] Ironically, this period of nascent bureaucracy, which inflated the importance of documents as instruments of command, control and legitimacy, coincided with the rise of those most illegitimate and illiterate of newcomers – the Normans – who carved out new demesnes from which parcels of land could be granted. Norman patronage of ecclesiastical lordships generated new, and renovated old, institutional frameworks for the conservation of charter and cartulary materials, thus providing both means and motives for increased document production and conservation. Territorial consolidation and record-keeping further promoted the status of trained notaries, while also reinforcing the association between religious houses and the comital (later royal) administration on the one hand, and the scribal classes on the other. Indeed, it was through their agency that the outcomes of boundary inquests were expressed in the idiom of diplomatic and legal formularies, not the language of the landholders or that of the local *boni homines*, *kaloi anthrōpoi* or *shaykh*s. So in spite of reliance on oral testimony of the

---

[4] Julius Frontinus, *De agri mensura*, in Campbell, *Writings of the Roman Land Surveyors*, 10.

[5] For issues of document production, survival, as well as notarial status and traditions across medieval south Italy, see the following important collections: *Civiltà del Mezzogiorno d'Italia. Libro scrittura documento in età normanno–sveva. Atti del convegno dell'associazione italiana dei paleografi e diplomatisti (Napoli–Badia di Cava dei Tirreni, 14–18 ottobre, 1991)*, ed. Filippo D'Oria (Salerno, 1994); *Per una storia del notariato meridionale*, ed. Mario Amelotti *et al.* (Rome, 1982); Francesco Magistrale, *Notariato e documentazione in terra di Bari: ricerche su forme, rogatari, credibilità dei documenti latini nei secoli IX–XI* (Bari, 1984).

above parties, written boundary clauses in Latin, Greek or Arabic seldom contained any element of spoken vernacular.

The demarcated, straight-line rigour of Classical Roman boundaries reduced the need to record the precise course of limits. But with the dereliction of this system, emphasis shifted to noting the physical attributes of land which lay on the limits themselves, fixing a location either by citing that of adjacent properties, with boundary sides designated by number ('the first part is from the land of so-and-so');[6] or in terms of limits with an upper and lower 'head' or *caput*, each appended with a flank (*latus*);[7] or by orientation ('from the east there is such-and-such').[8] Cartulary collections, such as those compiled by the Longobard scribes of Cava, tended towards relatively fine descriptions of physical relief and included data relating to land use. However, in many Latin charters, landed property was given *cum omnibus pertinentiis*, rarely specifying what those things were.[9] Such styles of composition in grants, endowments, conveyances, deeds of sale and purchase can be found in all areas where Latin notaries operated.

Shades of difference existed within these debased, Romanised schemes, as Jean-Marie Martin has shown in a cursory assessment of terms used in

[6] Illustrative examples thus: 'de secunda parte a medio limite terra qui venit in sorte Nicyfori. Tertia parte a medio limite terra Rodelgardi et Petri. Quarta parte a medio limite terra qui venit in sorte Nicyfori', *Codice diplomatico Barese (Le pergamene di S. Nicola di Bari: periodo greco, 939–1071)*, ed. F. Nitti di Vito (Bari, 1900), IV, 5–6 from the year 962. For three eleventh-century examples, see *Les chartres de Troia. Édition et étude critique des plus anciens documents conservés à l'Archivio Capitolare (1024–1266)*, ed. J.-M. Martin (Bari, 1976), 87–9 (88) from 1039; 94–5 from 1047; 111–14 (113) from 1083.

[7] As frequently found in the Lombard *Regnum* and later in Campania, for example in an Amalfitan deed of sale from 1080, 'et predictae casalis fuit divisum capud fixum de susu in iusu et termines de petra e de sabuci inter illam et illam portionem constituti sunt', *Codice diplomatico amalfitano*, ed. R. Filangieri di Candida (Naples, 1917), 121–2.

[8] As a typical example: 'primum ab oriente a medio pariete est terra Nicolai pape. Secundus a meridie extra parietem est via publica. Tertium ab occidente extra parietem est introitus et exitus Ursi f. Maionis. Quartus autem finis a septemtrione extra parietem est terra eiusdem Ursi', see *Le pergamene di S. Nicola di Bari: periodo normanno, 1075–1194)*, ed. F. Nitti di Vito (Bari, 1902) (*Cod. dipl. Barese*, V), 47 from 1098. For twelfth-century descriptions that are directly comparable, see 145 and 153. In September 1125, a donation of land and an olive grove in Massafra to the church of San Pietro dell'Isola Grande di Táranto gave the limits as 'ab orientis parte via antica; ab occidente via Patemisium descendens; a boreę parte casilia ecclesiaę Sancti Martini; ab austro clausura Sancti Angeli'. *Le pergamene dell'archivio arcivescovile di Taranto (1083–1258)*, ed. F. Magistrale (2 vols., Galatina, 1999), I, 16–18 (17). In a private deed of sale from Brindisi from 1187: 'ab oriente in occidentem pedes manuales decem et octo et dimidium ... ab oriente domus Basilii. Ab occidente domus Laurencii. A borea terra mea. Ab austro via publica et introitus et exitus eius', *Codice diplomatico Brindisino (492–1299)*, ed. A. De Leo and G. M. Monti (Trani, 1940), I, 43, lines 7–8 and 10–12.

[9] In a grant from Venosa, an unspecified parcel of lands was accepted to be 'ut apparet ex instrumento Grece exarato'. See *Die Abtei Venosa und das Mönchtum im normannisch-staufischen Süditalien*, ed. Hubert Houben (Tübingen, 1995), 327–8 (328). On such Greek *deperdita*, see Vera von Falkenhausen, 'L'atto notarile greco in epoca normanno-sveva', in *Civiltà del Mezzogiorno d'Italia*, 241–70.

notarial acts to depict the rural landscape of south Italy.[10] While stressing broad uniformity interrupted by local variation contingent on both scribe and terrain, Martin found the sharpest distinctions to be in pre-Norman Campania, between the scribes of the *curiales* in the duchy of Naples and the Longobard notaries of the principality of Salerno, particularly Cava. Although the former were generally more conservative and closer to the practices of late Antiquity than their Salernitan counterparts, both 'schools' harmonised during the first half of the tenth century and defined limits with cardinal points or with numbered sides around plots conceived as quadrilateral.

Land survey models of the eastern Roman Empire

Classical Roman land surveyors were never sure why they set out land boundaries *ab oriente*, but they associated it with pagan practices from a time immemorial.[11] Over the course of the next millennium, the concept of the east as the foremost of bearings was increasingly bound up in Christian thought with the orientation of churches, heaven and holy Jerusalem.[12] The east even gave rise to the popular eastern Christian name, Anatolius.[13] For Gervase of Tilbury, echoing Augustine of Hippo, the sequential arrangement of cardinal points in Greek revealed the primordial, quadripartite division of the earth.[14] Why else would the initial letters of ἀνατολή ('east'), δύσις ('west'), ἄρκτος ('north') and μεσημβρία ('south') spell out the name of A-d-a-m? Although this did not entirely resolve the problem, the long-held view of prioritising and

---

[10] Jean-Marie Martin, 'Perception et description du paysage rural dans les actes notariés sud-italiens (IXe–XIIe siècles)', in *Castrum 5. Archéologie des espaces agraires méditerranéens au Moyen Âge*, ed. A. Bazzana (Madrid, Rome and Murcie, 1999), 113–27. No similar survey has been conducted for insular Sicily.

[11] On eastward-facing aspects of land and sacred buildings, see Hyginus, 'Gromaticus', in Campbell, *Writings of the Roman Land Surveyors*, 137. For Roman belief in Etruscan precedents, see *ibid.*, xlv and 326.

[12] For a recent critique with particular emphasis on visual representation, see Alessandro Scafi, *Mapping Paradise: A History of Heaven on Earth* (Chicago, 2006).

[13] In part, emulating Saint Anatolius, bishop of Laodicea (d. 283). In twelfth-century south Italy it was attested as both a first name, Ἀνατόλιος and Ἀνατόλης, and as a cognomen as in Νικόλαος τοῦ Ἀνατολοῦ and Ἰωάννης Ἀνατολός, see *Syllabus graecarum membranorum*, ed. F. Trinchera (Naples, 1865), 185 and 332. Cf. also the modern Italian surname, Natoli, frequently found in the province of Messina, specifically on the Aeolian islands and to the north of the Nébrodi mountains in what was once the Val Démone of the Norman period. Girolamo Caracausi, *Dizionario onomastico della Sicilia* (2 vols., Palermo, 1993), II, 1101.

[14] Gervase of Tilbury, *Otia imperialia. Recreations for an Emperor*, ed. and trans. S. E. Banks and J. W. Binns (Oxford, 2002), I, 10, 64–5; Augustine of Hippo, *Homilies on the Gospel according to St. John, and his First Epistle*, trans. John Henry Parker (2 vols., Oxford 1848–9), I, Homily X.12, 162. The link between Adam and the Greek cardinal points appears to have derived from apocalyptic literature of the Hellenistic period; cf. the same idea repeated in *The Sibylline Oracles*, ed. H. N. Bate (1918), Book III, *Prologue*, 46, and in 2 Enoch 30, 13.

outlining the first land boundary from the east continued long after the fall of Rome, not least in the Eastern Empire where the Classical principles of surveying were more deeply ingrained than in the Latin West.

In medieval Greek, didactic treatises on land definitions (περιορισμοί) were as detailed as their Classical Latin predecessors, and continuities between these cognate traditions are easily recognisable: the use of specialist scribes and surveyors; the compilation of cadastral records; the classification of land types; the use of boundary markers, and ways to measure boundary lengths.[15] Origins of the art were often attributed, not incorrectly or without precedent, to pharaonic Egypt.[16] Nevertheless, in both theory and practice, there remained the same propensity to sequence cardinal directions and to begin a boundary clause with reference to the east. These were set out in archetypal models, such as this:

> First, write the boundaries in order like this; taking the east as a start they lead away to the west leaving the property of so-and-so on the right where there stands a tree, an olive, myrtle, pine or plane, or a river or stream. To here, there are fifteen rope-lengths. It turns back, rises to the south leaving the fields of so-and-so on the right, and they go straight on until some-such place in which there is a rocky mound and a bay tree that has a cross, letters or a certain mark, by which point it has taken 100 rope-lengths. It turns to the east, continues right along the road that is the one leading from a certain *castrum*, leaving the property of so-and-so on the right and the trees planted in a row there. On them is found a mark drawn on high, a cross made as a sign for all; and going straight on, it reaches a certain spot completing a measure of 200 rope-lengths. Next they go away eastward for a little and downhill to the bend of a certain river where the measure is found to be fifteen rope-lengths. It curves back to the south, goes straight on, leaves on the right someone's vineyard, and downhill to the boundary of so-and-so's field in which there is an ancient mound where it is necessary to renew the place-marker, show the truth and keep the neighbours' peace. There, the rope-lengths are found to be thirty-five. Then they head off again to the east leaning up against the boundary and the property of so-and-so where a large rock is planted; the measure to here is found to be twenty-five rope-lengths. To the north again, they go along the road of the village heading straight towards the seashore joining the boundary where the start began, and where there are again found to be fifteen rope-lengths.[17]

---

[15] See the collected texts in *Géométries du fisc byzantin*, ed. J. Lefort, R. Bondoux, J.-CL. Cheynet, J.-P. Grélois and V. Kravari, Réalités byzantines 4 (Paris, 1991). For landholding contexts, see Paul Lemerle, *The Agrarian History of Byzantium from the Origins to the Twelfth Century: Sources and Problems* (Galway, 1979); Nicolas Svoronos, 'Recherches sur le cadastre byzantin et la fiscalité aux XIe et XIIIe siècle: le cadastre de Thèbes', *Bulletin de Correspondence Hellenique*, 83 (1959), 1–164.

[16] Classical Greek historians and geographers often alleged that the earliest origins of land division were Egyptian. Herodotus 2.109; Diodorus Siculus 1.81.2; Strabo 17.787. For Byzantine views on these precedents, see *Géométries du fisc byzantin*, 48–9, §17 and 136–7, §205.

[17] Ἀπάρξου, γράφε καθεξῆς τὰ σύνορα τοιῶσδε· ἀρχὴν λαβὼν ἀνατολῆς ἄπεισιν ὡς πρὸς δύσιν καταλιμπάνων δεξιὰ τὰ δίκαια τοῦ δεῖνα, ἐν οἷς καὶ δένδρον ἵσταται, ἐλαί ἢ μυρσίνη ἢ ἔλατος ἢ πλάτονος, ἢ ποταμὸς ἢ ῥύαξ, ἄχρι δὲ τούτου εὕρηνται σχοινία δεκαπέντε. Κλίνει δ'αὖθις, ἀνέρχεται ὡς πρὸς τὴν μεσημβρίαν καταλιμπάνων δεξιὰ χωράφια τοῦ δεῖνα, καὶ κατ'εὐθεῖαν ἄπεισιν ἄχρι τοῦδε τοῦ τόπου, ἐν ᾧ λαυράτου ἵσταται λίθινον κεχωσμένον ἔχον σταυρὸν ἢ γράμματα ἢ γνώρισμα τοιόνδε, ἐν ᾧ καὶ

It should be reiterated that some scribes adhered to such prescribed ideals more closely than others, and many definitions did not even include references to boundary sides. Moreover, it is unfortunate that the bulk of surviving evidence in Greek comes from the fourteenth and fifteenth centuries, much relating to the Balkans, at times and in places where limits were not always plotted systematically.[18] Nonetheless, Greek boundary-clause models consistently followed the same principles as seen in the three examples below:

> Consider the directions when starting a survey, and write down the notable parts quite precisely, pointing out the start, end, and any change to the direction. Thus, a field of such-and-such a person starts from the east, runs to the west, turns to the south until it reaches a certain spot, back to the east to a particular known point, and turns back up to the north.[19]

> Much as you must also know the directions well: the east, the west, the north, and the south. For the east is always the top (κεφαλή) boundary.[20]

> Land surveying on the level comprises directions, observation points, lines and angles; it includes types, forms, figures, and principles. There are four directions – east, west, north, and south.[21]

In former Byzantine areas of southern Italy, including Latinised regions such as Apulia, the strong tendency to begin with reference to the east

---

τέλος εἴληφε τὰ ἑκατὸν σχοινία. Στρέφεται πρὸς ἀνατολάς, κρατεῖ τὸν δρόμον δρόμον, τὸν δρόμον τὸν ἐρχόμενον ἀπὸ τοῦ δεῖνα κάστρου, καταλιμπάνει δεξιὰ τὰ δίκαια τοῦ δεῖνα καὶ τοὺς κατ'ὅρδινον ἐκεῖ πεφυτευμένους δρύας, ἐν οἷς καὶ τύπος εὕρηται σχηματισθεὶς εἰς ὥραν ἄνωθεν τούτου δὲ σταυρὸς εἰς γνώρισμα τοῖς πᾶσι, καὶ κατ'εὐθεῖαν ἀπιὼν ἄχρι τοῦ δεῖνα τόπου ἀποτελεῖ ποσότητα διακοσίων σχοίνων. Εἶτ' ἀνατολικώτερον ἄπεισι πρὸς ὀλίγον, καὶ καταντᾷ εἰς ἀγκάλισμα τοῦ ποταμοῦ τοῦ δεῖνα, ἐν ᾧ καὶ μέτρον εὕρηται σχοινίων δεκαπέντε. Πρὸς ἄρκτον αὖθις ἀνακλᾷ, ἄπεισι κατ'εὐθεῖαν, καταλιμπάνει δεξιὰ ἀμπέλιον τοῦ δεῖνα, καὶ καταντᾷ εἰς σύνορα τοῦ δεῖνα χωραφίου, ἐν ᾧ χωματοβούνιον παμπάλαιον εὑρέθη, ὅπερ ἀνακαινίζειν δεῖ εἰς γνώρισμα τοῦ τόπου, εἰς ἀληθείας δήλωσιν, εἰς ἄμαχον γειτόνων, σχοῖνοι κἂν τούτῳ εὕρηνται τριάκοντα καὶ πέντε. Εἶτ' αὖθις πρὸς ἀνατολὰς ἄπεισιν ἀκουμβίζων εἰς σύνορον καὶ δίκαια τοῦ κτήματος τοῦ δεῖνα, ἐν ᾧ καὶ πέτρα εὕρηται μεγάλη ῥιζημαία, μέτρον δ'ἐν τούτοις εὕρηνται σχοινία εἰκοσιπέντε. Πρὸς ἄρκτον αὖθις ἄπεισι τὸν δρόμον τοῦ χωρίου τὸν κατερχόμενον εὐθὺ πρὸς τὴν ἀκτὴν θαλάσσης, καταλαμβάνει σύνορον ὅθεν ἀρχὴν εἰλήφει, ἐν ᾧ καὶ πάλιν εὕρηνται σχοινία δεκαπέντε. Taken from Τοῦ σοφωτάτου Ψελλοῦ γεωμετρία διὰ στίχων ('Land surveying in verses of the most learned Psellos'), in *Géométries du fisc Byzantin*, 191–3, §299. This anonymous work pre-dates 1204 and was optimistically attributed to the eleventh-century historian Michael Psellos.

[18] For example, the long *praktikon* of John Vatatzis from 1341 with its haphazard starting points. *Archives d'Athos: Actes d'Iviron IV*, ed. J. Lefort, N. Oikonomidès, D. Papachryssanthou and V. Kravari (Paris, 1995), 53–78.

[19] From Τοῦ σοφωτάτου Ψελλοῦ γεωμετρία διὰ στίχων ('Land surveying in verses of the most learned Psellos'), in *Géométries du fisc Byzantin*, 184–5, §287.

[20] From Ἀρχὴ τῆς γεωμετρίας ('Principle of land surveying'). Greek text in *Géométries du fisc Byzantin*, 48–9, §21.

[21] From Μέθοδος τῆς γεωμετρίας ('Method of land surveying'), in *Géométries du fisc Byzantin*, 38–9, §2. This is repeated almost verbatim in the treatise of Γεωργίου γεωμέτρου περὶ γεωδαισίας, 136–7, §207.

remained.[22] Further to the south, in Calabria, southern Basilicata and the Salento Peninsula (Terra d'Ótranto), where Byzantine notarial influence persisted and where Greek-speakers were more in evidence, the basic principle of conceiving land units as quadrilateral and of beginning their limits with reference to the east was also more standard than not.[23]

Arab-Muslim land surveying

The meagre pickings scattered in papyri, narrative texts and borrowings from Greek into Arabic which relate to landholding, settlement and tax-collection in the century after the Arab conquests of the Byzantine Near East show that much of the existing infrastructure, including local officials, their administrative memory, terminology and savoir faire was carried forward into the Islamic period, even if the dynamics of land grants, landholding and lordship in the Islamic world were to evolve in quite different ways.[24]

Under the Umayyads, the population census (*iḥṣā'*) and land survey (*masḥ* or *tā'dīl*) remained basic, if irregular, tools of post-conquest authority, control and organisation.[25] The first gauged revenues from the *jizya* or religious head-tax payable by non-Muslims; the second served to estimate and, if necessary, adjust the amount of income obtainable from the land. As a result, it was the names of landed properties, their taxable value and fiscal relationship with landholders and/or the treasury which tended to be documented in state registers, rather than the physical limits of the estates themselves.

Gathering and confirming essential data of this type in this way continued into later periods, exacerbating points of differentiation with non-Muslim regions where there was a more diverse range of record-keeping landlords for whom land use, rights, obligations and fiscal dues were inextricably linked to the act of describing boundaries for

---

[22] For example, a donation of various landed properties made to the church of Santa Maria Veteranis in Brindisi in the year 1107, *Codice diplomatico Brindisino*, I (492–1299), 20–3 (21, lines 17, 30, 42, 49; 22, lines 56, 61, 66 and 84).

[23] For early mainland examples from 981 and 1005, see *Syllabus Graecarum membranarum*, 6–7 and 13 respectively. Cf. *inter alia* the later βρέβιον ('inventory') of Reggio: ἔστιν δὲ ὁ συνορισμὸς πρὸς μὲν ἀνατολὰς τὸ σύνορον τῆς Ἁγίας Θεοτόκου τοῦ Ἀθανάτου, πρὸς δὲ δυσμὰς τό σύνορον Μαρίας μοναχῆς τῆς Ταβρομενίτις, ἐπὶ δὲ ἄρκτον εἰς τὸ ῥυάκιν τῆς αὐτῆς Ἁγίας Θεοτόκου τοῦ Ἀθανάτου. *Le Brébion de la métropole byzantine de Région (vers 1050)*, ed. André Guillou (Vatican City, 1974), 183, lines 18–21.

[24] See the important collection of essays in *Land Tenure and Social Transformation in the Middle East*, ed. Tarif Khalidi (Beirut, 1984); Kosei Morimoto, 'Land Tenure in Egypt during the Early Islamic Period', *Orient*, 11 (1975), 109–53; Michael G. Morony, 'Landholding in Seventh-Century Iraq: Late Sassanian and Early Islamic Patterns', in *The Islamic Middle East 700–1900*, ed. A. L. Udovitch (Princeton, 1981), 135–77.

[25] Wadād al-Qāḍī, 'Population Census and Land Surveys under the Umayyads (41–132/661–750)', *Der Islam*, 83 (2006), 341–416.

cartularies, inventories, concessions, sales and endowments. Instead, in the Islamic world, clearer lines of separation materialised between cultivation, productivity and state taxation strategies on the one hand, and the legally correct way of drawing up acts of alienation by trained Muslim jurists on the other. Thus, there is nothing in the treatises of Ibn Mammātī and al-Makhzūmī which explains how to make boundary definitions of landed estates, regardless of the wealth of other information relating to agronomy, agricultural surveys or tax assessment procedures.[26]

Document loss narrows our view of medieval chancery practice, but even so evidence of a Muslim fiscal administration routinely engaged in defining actual estate boundaries remains scarce. An exception, and also one of the earliest boundary clauses in Arabic, resulted from a land grant (qaṭīʿa) in Mosul made by the caliph al-Muʿtamid to make taxably productive a large, uncultivated plot on the city's outskirts by the Tigris river. Dating from 754, the limits were recorded by al-Azdī in his tenth-century regional history.[27] The chronicler had personally seen the original document (kitāb) and cited the boundaries verbatim. With a quadrilateral outline, point-to-point markers and assigning of cardinal directions to boundary sides, it bears tantalising, familial resemblances to European counterparts, distinguished only by an estimated area.[28] But beyond the superficial, there is nothing of substance to link it to any identifiable precedent.

While it is unusual to encounter detailed definitions made in Arabic by scribes of state offices or religious institutions, it is common to find descriptions of landed property in private deeds of sale. Moreover, after the first century AH, with increasingly refined articulation of Islamic thought by scholars and theorists, even the most mundane boundary delineations fell within legal, theological and cosmological frameworks constructed to define and regulate ideas of sacred geography.[29] By and from the 800s,

---

[26] Ibn Mammātī (d. 1209), Qawānīn wa-Dawāwīn, ed. A. S. Atiya (Cairo, 1943); Al-Makhzūmī (fl. 1169–85), Kitāb al-minhāj fī ʿilm kharāj Miṣr, ed. C. Cahen and Y. Ragib (Cairo, 1986). For particular reference to terminology arising from this, see Gladys Frantz-Murphy, The Agrarian Administration of Egypt from the Arabs to the Ottomans (Cairo, 1986).

[27] Al-Azdī, Taʾrīkh al-Mawṣil, ed. ʿAlī Ḥabība (Cairo, 1967), 171–2. The grant was made in Rabīʿ al-Thānī, 137 AH. See 158 for the terms of the concession. For a translation and discussion, see Hugh Kennedy, 'Elite Incomes in the Early Islamic State', in Studies in Late Antiquity and Early Islam 1. The Byzantine and Early Islamic Near East 6: Elites Old and New in the Byzantine and Early Islamic Near East, ed. John Haldon and Lawrence I. Conrad (Princeton, 2004), 13–28 (17–18).

[28] The area was reckoned as fifty-two jarīb. Only two boundaries (the south and the west) were mentioned by name, but the estate appears to have begun with the eastern boundary. Al-Azdī, Taʾrīkh al-Mawṣil, 172.

[29] In Muslim tradition, a mosque should ideally be entered with the right foot first, while exiting is done with the left foot first. Similarly, a toilet or place of cleansing (mirḥāḍ) should be entered by leading with the left foot and leaving, cleansed, with the right. Such

when boundary clauses are attested in greater numbers, an empirically observable point of difference emerges between the Muslim ordering of boundaries and the 'Romano-Byzantine' arrangement. In the Arab-Muslim world, pole position went to the southern limit (*al-ḥadd al-qiblī*), not the eastern one, as the first to be described.[30]

Why the south-first archetype became standard in Muslim land surveys is easier to guess than to ascertain with confidence but we need not be embroiled here in the debate about the *qibla* as the chosen direction of prayer for Muslims, since issues surrounding this were settled before Muslim legal tradition recognised *al-qiblī* ('the south') as pre-eminent among directions.[31] Less speculation is needed to explain the diffusion of the south-first model. For this, the efforts of Muslim jurists to reconcile legal theory and implementation, while ensuring that the parameters of orthodox practice were not exceeded, fostered a prodigious output in

conceptual links are reflected in Arabic etymology; the right hand and right-hand side (*yaman*) is fortunate (*yumn*). The Muslim orientation of the world, from the perspective of the central Arabian Peninsula, connects the right-hand side with the south, and the left (*al-shamāl*) with the north along a roughly north–south axis between Syria (*al-Shām*) and Yemen (*al-Yaman*). There are also associations between elevation (*ʿalyā*) and the heavenly sublime; and correspondingly negative links between the lower world (*al-dunyā*) and baseness (*danāya*). On sacred geography in Islam, see Annemarie Schimmel, *Deciphering the Signs of God: A Phenomenological Approach to Islam* (Albany, 1994), 47–87; Angelika Neuwirth, 'Spatial Relations', in *Encyclopaedia of the Quran*, ed. Jane Dammen McAuliffe (6 vols., Leiden, 2001–6), V, 104–8; Joseph Chelhod, *Les structures du sacré chez les arabes* (Paris, 1965; new edn, Paris, 1986), 35–65 and 209–45; James R. Lewis, 'Some Aspects of Sacred Space and Time in Islam', *Studies in Islam*, 19/3 (1982), 167–78; Clinton Bennett, 'Islam', in *Sacred Place*, ed. Jean Holm and John Bowker (London and New York, 1994), 88–114.

[30] In Egypt, Syria and al-Andalus, when *al-qiblī* appears in a quartet of cardinal points it is evident that it referred to the southern limit. The boundary diametrically opposite was often called *zahr al-qibla*, *dabūr al-qibla*, or *al-ḥadd al-dabūrī* (literally, 'the back of the *qibla*' i.e. 'north'). In Sicily, *dabūrī/an* was translated into Latin as *septemtrionaliter*, *a septemtrionali* or *versus septemtrionem*. However, in Classical Arabic the root *d-b-r* is associated with the rear or backside of something, of turning one's back or being 'of the west'. Indeed, *al-Dabūr* is the west wind attested in the *ḥadīth* (see *Saḥīḥ Bukhārī*, 4: 54.427), so called because it was thought to come from the back of the Kaʿba (see M. Forcada, *Rīh*, in *Encyclopaedia of Islam*, 2nd edn (11 vols. and Supplement, Leiden, 1960–2005) (henceforth *EF*), VIII, 526, and D. A. King, *al-Maṭlʿ*, in *EF*, VI, 839). The problem of twin meanings for *d-b-r* was raised, but not solved, by Adalgisa De Simone, 'Su alcune corrispondenze lessicali in diplomi arabo–latini della Sicilia medievale', in *Gli interscambi culturali e socio-economici fra l'Africa settentrionale e l'Europa mediterranea. Atti del congresso internazionale di Amalfi, 5–8 dicembre 1983*, ed. Luigi Serra (Naples, 1986), 469–84 (483–4).

[31] On the pre-Islamic precedents for the *qibla*; its directional switch during the lifetime of Muḥammad; the non-Meccan orientation of early mosques; the cosmological status acquired by the Kaʿba and the *qibla*'s scientific calculation, see Robert G. Hoyland, *Seeing Islam as Others Saw It: A Survey and Evaluation of Christian, Jewish and Zoroastrian Writing on Early Islam* (Princeton, 1997), 560–73; A. J. Wensinck and D. A. King, *Kibla*, in *EF*, V, 82–8. On later mathematical geography, see David A. King, *World-Maps for Finding the Direction and Distance to Mecca: Innovation and Tradition in Islamic Science* (Leiden, 1999); Petra Schmidl, *Volkstümliche Astronomie im islamischen Mittelalter* (2 vols., Leiden, 2007), both with full bibliographies.

ʿilm al-shurūṭ ('the study of contracts').[32] In tandem with other peripheral branches of the law, such as records of court minutes, verdicts and legal stratagems, they established and propagated formularies and paradigms as practical, professional aids for *qāḍī*s (judges), jurists, officials and scribes. By the end of the 800s, a unified notion of how a south-first 'Islamic' boundary definition should be written was as widely accepted as it was disseminated. On occasion, *shurūṭ* authors accompanied their boundary definition models with explanatory passages, such as this from al-Sarakhsī's eleventh-century *Kitāb al-Mabsūṭ*:

> The first boundary: from the direction of the south there is the house of so-and-so. The second boundary: to the east of the house is the house of so-and-so. And the third boundary: north there is the house of so-and-so. And the fourth boundary is western: the house of so-and-so. As the direction of the *qibla* is the most noble of directions (*'ashraf al-jihāt*), so its foremost part is the start.[33]

Thus, in an Egyptian papyrus relating a house sale in Alexandria from the year 820, the boundaries were given as south–north–west–east.[34] Other Arabic deeds of sale from the ninth- and tenth-century Egypt also begin with the southern boundary and proceed to cite the northern, eastern and western limits.[35] In a Syrian papyrus from the ninth century, we read that 'the first boundary: to the south there is the village [text missing], and the third boundary: there is, to the north the village of Burayj; and the fourth boundary: from the direction of the west'.[36] In sales of two estates outside Damascus in the year 922, the boundaries of both began *min al-qibla*, and

---

[32] W. B. Hallaq, 'Sharṭ', in *EI²*, IX, 358–9; Émile Tyan, *Le notariat et le régime de la preuve par écrit dans la pratique du droit musulman*, 2nd edn (Harissa, 1959), 1–99; al-Ṭaḥāwī (d. 933), *Kitāb al-shurūṭ al-saghīr*, ed. ʿA. M. al-Jubūrī (Baghdad, 1974); *Kitāb al-buyūʿ min al-shurūṭ al-kabīr*, ed. with introduction and notes by Jeanette A. Wakin, *The Functions of Documents in Islamic Law* (New York, 1972), 1–203.

[33] Al-Sarakhsī, *Kitāb al-Mabsūṭ fī l-Furūʿ* (30 vols., Cairo, 1906–13), XXX, 178, lines 2–4: *al-ḥadd al-awwal min qibla dār fulān wa-'l-ḥadd al-thānī fī sharq al-dār dār fulān wa-'l-ḥadd al-thālith dabr al-qibla dār fulān wa-'l-ḥadd al-rābiʿ al-gharbī dār fulān li-anna jihat al-qibla ashraf al-jihāt fa-'l-bidāya awwal min-hā*. The second boundary to be defined could vary between the north and the east, but since jurists were defining property for alienation and to correspond to an Islamic 'ideal' (and not to calculate surface area), there was less practical need to describe opposite sides consecutively in order to assist in working out their average lengths.

[34] *al-qiblī . . . al-baḥrī . . . al-gharbī . . . al-sharqī*. See Charles C. Torrey, 'An Arabic Papyrus Dated 205 AH', *Journal of the American Oriental Society*, 56 (1936), 288–92.

[35] For examples see Adolf Grohmann, *Arabic Papyri in the Egyptian Library* (6 vols., Cairo, 1934), I, 141ff. For illustrated examples, see Geoffrey Khan, *Bills, Letters and Deeds: Arabic Papyri of the 7th to 11th Centuries* (1993).

[36] *al-ḥadd al-awwal min al-qibla al-qarya* [MS text missing] *wa-'l-ḥadd al-thālith min qibal zahr al-qibla al-qarya Burayj, wa-'l-ḥadd al-rābiʿ min qibal al-maghrib*. i.e. S–[E]–N–W. See Nabia Abbott, 'Arabic Papyri of the Reign of Ǧaʿfar al-Mutawwakil ʿalā-llāh (AH 232–47/AD 847–61)', *Zeitschrift der Deutschen Morgenländischen Gesellschaft*, 92 (1938), 88–135 (110–13). As in al-Azdī's boundary definition, measures were given for lengths (reckoned in *jall*), but no calculations of area were included.

then ran east–north–west.[37] Moreover, the south-first model endured: in twenty deeds of sale, purchase and conveyance, mainly relating to houses in Cairo from the 1400s, all begin with the southern boundary, continuing north–east–west thereafter.[38]

Shurūṭ works, also known as *wathāʾiq* among the Mālikī jurists of the Iberian Peninsula and North Africa, may again provide a point of transmission, this time between Egypt–Syria and the south-central and western Mediterranean. The works of Ḥanafī *shurūṭ* scholars such as Ibn ʿAbdūn, *qāḍī* of Qayrawān in 888 AD under the Aghlabids, were widely consulted, influential – and now lost.[39] In any event, beginning with the south as 'the noblest of directions' was also the Andalusi practice as prescribed by the eleventh-century *shurūṭ* scholar Aḥmad al-Ṭulayṭulī ('from Toledo').[40] Deeds of sale from fifteenth-century Nasrid Granada show how the south-first model was a lasting one.[41] But such firmly rooted practices in Muslim al-Andalus were not pervasive to all parts of the Iberian Peninsula, as examples from the Catalonian cathedral of Sant Pere de Vic and others indicate, which tended to define properties with the east first.[42] Significant is an apparent switch between styles in pre- and post-*Reconquista* Toledo revealing how the south-first model

[37] Dominique Sourdel and Janine Sourdel-Thomine, 'Trois actes de vente Damascains du début du IVe/Xe siècle', *Journal of the Economic and Social History of the Orient*, 8 (1965), 164–84 (167 and 178).

[38] D. S. Richards, 'Documents from Sinai concerning Mainly Cairene Property', *Journal of the Economic and Social History of the Orient*, 28 (1985), 225–93.

[39] On the development of *shurūṭ* works under the Ḥanafī *madhhab*, see Wakin, *Documents in Islamic Law*, 10–29. For the situation in Ifrīqiya and Sicily, see William Granara, 'Islamic Education and the Transmission of Knowledge in Muslim Sicily', in *Law and Education in Medieval Islam*, ed. J. E. Lowry, D. J. Stewart and S. M. Toorawa (Gibb Memorial Trust, 2004), 150–73.

[40] For an archetypal, Andalusi, Arab–Muslim boundary definition running S–N–E–W (*al-qibla ... al-jawf ... al-sharq ... al-gharb*), see al-Ṭulayṭulī (d. 1067), *Al-Muqniʿ fī ʿilm al-shurūṭ*, ed. F. J. Aguirre Sábada (Madrid, 2004), 129.

[41] M. Dolores Rodríguez Gómez and Salud M. Domínguez Rojas, 'La compraventa de fincas urbanas en la Granada del siglo XV a través de dos documentos notariales árabes', *Anaquel de Estudios Árabes*, 19 (2008), 175–99 (195, doc #2, lines 4–5).

[42] For example: 'et afrontat ipsa vinea de parte orientis in strata qui pergit ubique, et de meridie in torrente, et de occiduo in vinea de nos donatores, et de circii similiter in vinea de nos donatores', in *Catalunya Carolíngia IV: els comtats d'Osona i de Manresa, Memòries de la Secció històrico-arqueològica LIII*, ed. Ramon Ordeig i Mata *et al.* (Barcelona, 1999), doc. no. 367. I am grateful to Jon Jarrett for alerting me to land-definition practices (and customary variations) in tenth-century Christian Catalonia, and also to Amalia Zomeño for her informal communication to me about boundary orientations in the corpus of 160 documents from Nasrid Granada, of which ninety-five were published with Spanish translations in *Documentos arábigos-granadinos*, ed. L. Seco de Lucena (Madrid, 1961). For a complete inventory, see A. Zomeño, 'Repertorio documental arábigo-granadino: LOS documentos árabes de la Biblioteca Universitaria de Granada', *Qurtuba. Estudios Andalusíes*, 6 (2001), 275–96.

was expressly linked to Muslim notarial practice before its fall in 1085. Thus, in an Arabic deed of sale dated to Ramaḍān 475 AH/AD 1083, the boundaries of a vineyard were given as south–north–east–west[43] However, the boundaries of 'Mozarab' Christian deeds of sale thereafter tended to begin with the east.[44]

The contrasting formulae from different administrative–religious traditions are sufficient to form the basis of a typology that can be tested against charter evidence from frontier zones in order to establish questions of continuity, disjuncture and the co-existence of land survey practices. At this point, we can return to the central Mediterranean and the contested island of Sicily which from 535 to 827 had been under the Byzantines, and then under Muslim rule until the fall of Palermo to the Normans in 1072.

Boundary delimitations in Norman Sicily[45]

In the 1090s, when the piecemeal Norman Conquest and pacification of Muslim Sicily was complete, two types of document emerged to confirm the details of granted lands and men: lists on which the local population was registered, and descriptions confirming the boundaries of conceded estates. In Greek, these were generally known as *plateiai*; in Arabic, they were called the *jarā'id al-rijāl* (literally 'lists of men'), and the *jarā'id al-ḥudūd* ('lists of boundaries'). Examples are known from comital and royal charters as well as from later cartulary collections. In the absence of any trained cadre of Latin scribes on the island, the Norman rulers' early use of Arabic and Greek, later combined in bilingual confirmations, is striking. Also of note is that Latin charters purport to date from this early period, but almost all are later copies, known forgeries or of dubious authenticity.[46]

---

[43] *Los Mozárabes de Toledo en los siglos XII y XIII*, ed. Angel González Palencia (3 vols., Madrid, 1926), I, 1 and 2–3. document no. 1 (475/1083): (*fī-'l-qibla . . . fī-'l-jawf . . . fī-'l-sharq . . . fī-'l-gharb*). For a brief commentary, see Francisco Pons Boigues, *Apuntes sobre las escrituras mozárabes Toledanas que se conservan en el archivo histórico nacional* (Madrid, 1897), 19–21.

[44] Of many similar examples, see documents no. 2 (Nov. 1092) and no. 3 (Apr. 1093), which open with the eastern boundary. *Los Mozárabes de Toledo*, 2–3.

[45] On Arabic deeds of sale and purchase in Sicily, see Antonio D'Emilia, 'Diplomi arabi siciliani di compravendita del secolo VI Egira e loro raffronto con documenti egiziani dei secoli III–V Egira', *Annali (Istituto Universitario Orientale di Napoli)*, 14 (1964), 83–109; Olivia Remie Constable, 'Cross-Cultural Contacts: Sales of Land between Christians and Muslims in 12th-Century Palermo', *Studia Islamica*, 85/1 (1997), 67–84; Henri Bresc, 'La propriété foncière des musulmans dans la Sicile du XIIe siècle: trois documents inédits', in *Giornata di studio: del nuovo sulla Sicilia musulmana (Roma, 3 maggio 1993)*, ed. Biancamaria Scarcia Amoretti (Rome, 1995), 69–97. Reprinted in *Una stagione in Sicilia* (2 vols., Palermo, 2010), I, no. 3.

[46] For an assessment of the problems of document counts, survival rates and forgeries, see Graham A. Loud, 'The chancery and charters of the kings of Sicily (1130–1212)', *English Historical Review*, 124 (2009), 779–810.

The *jarā'id* lists were to become the main written instruments of the Arab-Norman *Dīwān* or royal fiscal administration which managed estates and men of the royal demesnes in Sicily and Calabria.[47] Yet, the precise origins of the *jarā'id* are difficult to ascertain, not least because no charters have survived from either the Byzantine or Islamic periods. Even in the Norman period, there are no extant Arabic documents before the 1090s; nor were any apparently issued from 1112 until after the foundation of the kingdom in 1130.[48]

As for the 'lists of men', it is now accepted that they were based on pre-Norman precedents as it can be inferred that they had been compiled with reference to pre-existing Arabic records.[49] But the precedents for the land boundaries remain obscure – frustratingly so, because Norman Sicilian rulership is conspicuous for its borrowings from the Latin West, Byzantium and from the Islamic world, including the combined use of three languages in the royal palaces, and three diplomatic traditions in the royal chancery.

So, how original was the Norman land registry tradition in Sicily? Did it also have local Arabic roots from the Islamic period? Or had ways of defining limits been introduced with the Normans, perhaps from Latin Longobard or Byzantine Greek areas?

The orientation of boundaries in Sicilian Arabic charters

Of the earliest surviving, authentic, post-Norman Conquest land grants, those written in Greek are prominent, such as the description of the newly constructed *kastron* of Focerò in north-eastern Sicily, whose limits were composed in Greek from scratch in the mid-1090s on the order of Count Roger I himself.[50] The proceedings were overseen by twelve 'archons', almost all of whom had Greek names and some of whom can be identified with influential kin groups from around the area.[51] Recently, both this hilltop site and its extensive boundaries have been identified, and we now know that they began from the east, from a point at the

---

[47] For detailed analysis, see Jeremy Johns, *Arabic Administration in Norman Sicily: The Royal Dīwān* (Cambridge, 2002), 39–62, 91–169, for the *jarā'id al-rijāl*. For the *ḥudūd*, see 170–92.

[48] Johns, *Arabic Administration*, 78–80.

[49] For this argument, see *ibid.*, 42–62.

[50] For an unreliable edition of the petition (ἐπιστολή) of Carpetazza fol. 20 from the Archivio Capitolare at Patti, see *I diplomi greci ed arabi di Sicilia*, ed. Salvatore Cusa (Palermo, 1868–82; repr. Cologne and Vienna, 1982), 532–5 (henceforth Cusa, *I diplomi*).

[51] 'Those who defined the land of Focerò are: Giorgios, uncle of lord Eugenios the *amīr*; lord Melis the Frank of Troina; and the headman ('*arīf*) with those from Marsatina at Troina; Petros Philonitis from Catouna at Maniace; the notary Leon of Adrano; Basilis Tricharis of San Marco; Menglavitis of San Marco; Moules of Mavrachóma; the abbot of Galati; the *archistrategos* Michael; the notary, Leon Sakkas, and the notary, Philippos Kolokinthos.' Cusa, *I diplomi*, 533.

top of the eastern limit.[52] Indeed, of the earliest examples of boundary clauses in Sicilian Greek with specifically named boundary sides, the vast majority open with reference to the eastern boundary first.[53]

Arabic boundary descriptions made under the Norman rulers are in relatively short supply and are attested later. The earliest is a bilingual (Greek–Arabic) copy of a confirmation from 1133, in which the Arabic was based on the Greek.[54] The first monolingual boundary clause from the royal Arab-Norman *Dīwān* comes even later, in 1141.[55] Of all Arabic boundary clauses, the largest and most coherent corpus is found in a royal confirmation of lands granted to the church of Santa Maria Nuova at Monreale.[56] These were definitions of open villages and fertile farmlands in western Sicily – well-populated areas that had been overwhelmingly Muslim since the ninth century. The boundaries of four large provinces and some fifty of their internal estates were described in detail.[57]

When the data for Arabic boundary clauses is set out, there is a clear difference between private acts of alienation on the one hand and royal charters issued by the Norman *Dīwān* on the other. As can be seen in Tables 1 and 2, the private documents are mixed, but boundaries began mainly with the south – as if composed by Arab-Muslim scribes cognisant of the received 'Islamic' model.[58] However, confirmations of lands drawn up in Arabic and issued by the royal *Dīwān* opened mainly with the east in the 'Roman' Christian way.

---

[52] See Michele Fasolo, *Alla ricerca di Focerò* (Rome, 2008), for the careful identification of Focerò with the mountain peak and plateau of Fossa della Neve, and 66–7 for a reconstruction of the *kastron*'s limits circumscribing approximately 120km².

[53] See Cusa, *I diplomi*, 367–8 (from the year 1095: E–W), 509–10 (date 1097: E–), 549–50 (date 1102: E–S), 405–7 (date 1110: S–), 407–8 (date 1112: W–), 599–601 (date 1112: E–W–N–S), 413–14 (date 1122: E–); see also *Le pergamene greche esistenti nel grande archivio di Palermo*, ed. G. Spata (Palermo, 1862), 163–5 (date 1091), 173–5 (date 1092), 257–9 (date 1122); *Les actes grecs de Messina*, ed. André Guillou (Palermo, 1963), 60–1 (date 1123; E–W–).

[54] Cusa, *I diplomi*, 515–17. For an important discussion, see Albrecht Noth, 'I documenti arabi di Ruggero II', in Carlrichard Brühl, *Diplomi e cancelleria di Ruggero II* (Palermo, 1983), 190–1, and Johns, *Arabic Administration*, 94–9.

[55] Archivo Ducal de Medinacali, Toledo, 1104 (S796) *recto*. For further context of the Medinaceli documents in Sicily, see Johns, *Arabic Administration*, 58, 102–6 and 304–5.

[56] Cusa, *I diplomi*, 179–244. A new critical edition of the Arabic–Latin boundaries by Jeremy Johns and Alex Metcalfe is forthcoming.

[57] The provincial boundaries (Arabic: *iqlīm*, plural *aqālīm*; in Latin, *magnae divisae*) of Jāṭū (modern S. Giuseppe Iato), Qurullūn (Corleone), Baṭṭallārū (Battallaro) and Qalʿat al-Trazī (Calatrasi) covered over 1,200 km². They were conceived as amorphous or polygonal, not quadrilateral, and were not defined in terms of side or cardinal points. For attempts to trace the limits of Battallaro, see Maria Adelaide Vaggioli, 'Note di topografia nella Sicilia medievale: una rilettura della *jarīda* di Monreale (*divise Battallarii, divisa Fantasine*)', in *Quarte giornate internazionali di studi sull'area Elima, Erice, 1–4 dicembre 2000* (Pisa, 2003), 1247–324.

[58] Several appear to have Arab-Muslim vendors and (mainly Arab-)Christian purchasers. The exceptions to this are nos. 2, 9(?), 10, 11 and 12. See Table 1 (below).

Conclusions

In view of 250 years of Arab-Muslim rule in Sicily before the Normans, it is slightly surprising to find royal chancery scribes writing out boundaries in Arabic based on a Romano-Byzantine orientation model. There seem to me two plausible, but very different, explanations for this. The first is a conservative argument of long continuity: namely, that during the Islamic period, scribes drew on existing Byzantine records, superimposing new boundaries over old, but writing out subsequent descriptions in Arabic. Hence, the Arabic boundaries of Norman crown lands still started with the east.

This possibility, however, is a problematic one given the prevailing tendency for scribes everywhere else in the Islamic world to follow a south-first model in Arabic. Moreover, in Sicily, the protracted processes of conquest are likely to have dislocated old Byzantine boundaries – processes which continued with the division of imperial and ecclesiastical *latifundia*; colonisation and settlement from Ifrīqiya; the subdivision of property due to the literal application of Mālikī inheritance law which advocated splitting lands between heirs, and the 'green revolution' which can only have disrupted the rural landscape yet further. As such, there are many reasons to believe that Byzantine estates' boundaries could not have survived unadulterated throughout the Islamic period until the time of the Normans in the eleventh and twelfth centuries.

Moreover, the evidence for administrative records from Fatimid times prior to the Norman Conquest points primarily to the use of population censuses: recording the people on the land whose memory confirmed its limits, rather than defining the actual land boundaries themselves in writing. Indeed, this might explain the absence of any claim to lands in the Norman period on the pretext of some older documentation in Arabic. Otherwise for the Islamic period in Sicily, we can at best infer the existence of state records for landed property, perhaps with lists of provincial officials, landholders and presumably some estimate of land tax revenue. But there is too little evidence to go beyond this or to assume that they had compiled cadastral registers of detailed physical boundary descriptions.

An alternative explanation may offer a solution to this dilemma. Recent studies of the royal Norman *Dīwān* have shown the extent to which it was a confection of the Norman kingdom post-1130 under Roger II and his chief minister, George of Antioch.[59] It was also a late developer: after the period of 1112–30 when no documents in Arabic were apparently issued at all, the first boundary definition to be written using only Arabic is not attested before the 1140s. Moreover, when royal Norman charters

[59] Johns, *Arabic Administration*, 80–114.

in Arabic were reintroduced, they were characterised by the presence of non-Arabic loan terms, and occasional references to people and events of the 1100s.[60]

This scenario suggests a very different reason for the 'Romano-Byzantine' influence in Arab-Norman chancery documents; namely, that the Arabic boundary clauses were actually a modern product of Roger II's day when land inquests to verify property conceded to, or disputed by, newly privileged landholders were overseen by Christian officials familiar with the conventions of Byzantine land inquests. From time to time, the findings of these were written out by scribes of the newly created royal *Dīwān* in Arabic. On the face of it, their elegant external features had the style and hallmarks of Arab-Islamic chancery documents, but their content reveals a distinctly non-Muslim provenance. Such a scenario fits well with the known development of the Norman bureaucracy from the early days of territorial reorganisation in the post-conquest period of the 1090s when bilingual (Arabic–Greek) functionaries and officials rose to prominence as agents, authors and actors in the comital and royal entourage.[61] Was it these 'go-to' men, the Christian archons, amirs, strategots and scribes of the early Norman rulers, who had been responsible for initiating this change of course in post-Islamic Sicily?

This is a tentative conclusion by way of a suggestion. But even so, the royal charter evidence appears to indicate that the Arabic boundary documents of Norman Sicily had no diplomatic connection with the Arab-Muslim past.

[60] For contemporary references to the Norman period in Arabic boundary clauses, see Cusa, *I diplomi*, 515–16, for George of Antioch as the *strategot* or *ʿāmil* (district official) of Iato in 1114, 212 and 215 for lands and men of the *Dīwān*, 242 for lands of the Norman knight, Paganus de Gorgis. On loan words in chancery contexts, see Alex Metcalfe, *Muslims and Christians in Norman Sicily: Arabic Speakers and the End of Islam* (London and New York, 2003), 127–40. Of particular importance is the frequent use of noun reduplication in boundary clauses e.g. τὴν ὁδὸν ὁδόν; *per viam viam*; *al-ṭarīq al-ṭarīq* ('right along the road'), which was a distinctive trait of medieval Greek that was transmitted into Latin and Arabic as a loan term.

[61] Vera von Falkenhausen, 'The Greek Presence in Norman Sicily', in *The Society of Norman Italy*, ed. G. A. Loud and Alex Metcalfe (Leiden, 2002), 253–87; Hiroshi Takayama, *The Administration of the Norman Kingdom of Sicily* (Leiden, 1993), 25–56, and Johns, *Arabic Administration*, 63–90.

Table 1 *Private deeds of sale from Sicily with boundary definitions in Arabic*

		Boundary order
1	Deed of sale from 1112[a]	S–E–W–N
2	Deed of sale from 1116[b]	E–N–W–S
3	Deed of sale from 1130[c]	E–N–W–S
4	Deed of sale from 1137[d]	S–E–N–W
5	Deed of sale from 1161 overseen by the Muslim *qāḍī* of Palermo[e]	S–E–W–
6	Deed of sale from 1180[f]	S–E–W–N
7	Deed of sale from 1183[g]	S–W–E–N
8	Deed of sale from 1187[h]	E–S–W–N
9	Deed of sale from 1190[i]	S–N–E–W
10	Deed of sale from 1193[j]	E–S–W–N
11	Deed of sale from 1196 said to be have made according to *Sharīʿa* law[k]	S–W–N–E
12	Arab-Christian deed of sale (undated, but probably later 1100s)[l]	E–S–W–N

[a] *al-ḥadd al-qiblī ... al-sharqī ... al-ḥadd al-gharbī ... wa-'l-dabūr min-hi.* Cusa, *I diplomi*, 610–13 (611). [b] Known from a Latin transumpt of 1266, see Bresc, 'La propriété foncière', 93–6. [c] Latin transumpt of 1255, see Bresc, 'La propriété foncière', 96–9. Here, an estate in western Sicily – Raḥl Karrām – was named after the Muslim family who owned it (not simply held it), and was sold by them for 1,000 *tarì* to a Christian buyer. [d] *al-ḥadd al-qiblī ... al-ḥadd al-sharqī ... al-ḥadd al-dabūrī ... al-ḥadd al-gharbī.* Cusa, *I diplomi*, 61–7 (62). [e] *al-ḥadd al-qiblī ... wa-sharqī-hā ... wa-gharbī-hā.* Cusa, *I diplomi*, 101–6 (102). [f] *al-ḥadd al-qiblī ... al-ḥadd al-sharqī ... al-ḥadd al-gharbī ... al-ḥadd al-dabūrī.* Cusa, *I diplomi*, 39–43 (40). [g] *fa-ḥadd-hā al-qiblī ... al-gharbiyya ... wa-sharqī-hā ... wa-ẓahr al-qibla min-hā.* Cusa, *I diplomi*, 491–3 (491). [h] Latin transumpt of 1282, see Bresc, 'La propriété foncière', 99–101. [i] *min jiha qibliyya ... bi-dabūrī-hā ... wa-sharqī-hā ... wa-qiblī-hā* (sic) *... wa-gharbī-hā.* Cusa, *I diplomi*, 44–6 (44). [j] *al-ḥadd al-sharqī...al-ḥadd al-qiblī...al-ḥadd al-gharbī...wa-'l-ḥadd al-rābiʿ wa-huwa dabūr al-qibla.* Cusa, *I diplomi*, 496–8 (496–7). [k] *al-ḥadd al-qiblī ... al-ḥadd al-gharbī ... wa-dabūr al-qibla ... wa-'l-sharqī.* Cusa, *I diplomi*, 499–501 (499–500). [l] *al-ḥadd al-sharqī ... wa-'l-qiblī ... wa-'l-gharbī ... wa-'l-baḥrī.* Cusa, *I diplomi*, 505–6 (505).

Table 2 *Royal estates with cardinal-pointed boundary sides in Arabic*

Name of estate (*raḥl*)	Boundary order
Greek–Arabic grant from 1136[a]	E–S–W–N
Arabic boundaries of Raḥl Ibn Sahl from 1154[b]	E–W–S–
Greek–Arabic deed of purchase from 1161[c]	E–W–S–N
Maghnūja (estate of Monreale, 1182)	S–E–W–
al-Duqqī	E–S–W–
al-Maghāghī	E–W–
Sūminī	E–W–
Malbīṭ	E?
Qurūbnish	E–
al-Andalusīn	S–N–
Manzil Zarqūn	S–N–
Raḥl al-Būqāl	S–W–
Raḥl al-Ghalīẓ	E–W–
Raḥl al-Balāṭ	E–S–W–N
Raḥl al-Mudd	E–S–
Raḥl al-Sikkāk	E–S–W–
Dasīsa	E–W–S–
Manzil Zammūr	E–
Manzil Kirashatī	E–N–W–
Ghār Shuʿayb	E–W–N–
Raḥl Ibn Sahl	E–N–W–S
Jurf Bū Karīm	E–W–N–
Raḥl Bijānū	E–W–
Manzil ʿAbd al-Raḥmān	E–S–N–
al-Qumayṭ	E–S–W–N
Jaṭīna	E–S–W–N
al-Ghār	E–S–W–
al-Randa	E–N–W–
Raḥl al-Jawz	E–S–W–N
al-Aqbāṭ	E–S–W–N

[a] The original Arabic parts of the text are lost and survive only in later Latin and Italian translations of the Greek. Indeed, it is not even clear whether the boundaries were ever described in Arabic. Here, the boundary directions are taken from the Greek *periorismos*. See Cusa, *I diploma*, 115–16. [b] See Jeremy Johns and Alex Metcalfe, 'The mystery at Chúrchuro: conspiracy or incompetence in twelfth-century Sicily', *Bulletin of the School of Oriental and African Studies*, 62/1 (1999), 226–59, (esp. pp. 248–52). [c] *al-ḥadd al-sharqī . . . al-ḥadd al-gharbī . . . wa-'l-qiblī . . . wa-dabūr al-qibla*. Cusa, *I diplomi*, pp. 622–6 (pp. 624–5). The order of the boundaries in the Greek, which precedes the Arabic, is the same: τὸ ἀνατολικὸν, τὸ δυτικὸν, τὸ νοτιὸν, τὸ βόριον (ibid. p. 623).

Transactions of the RHS 22 (2012), pp. 57–74 © Royal Historical Society 2012
doi:10.1017/S0080440112000060

MONASTIC REFORM AND THE GEOGRAPHY OF CHRISTENDOM: EXPERIENCE, OBSERVATION AND INFLUENCE

By Andrew Jotischky

READ 17 JUNE 2011 AT THE UNIVERSITY OF LANCASTER

ABSTRACT. Monastic reform is generally understood as a textually driven process governed by a renewed interest in early monastic ideals and practices in the eleventh and twelfth centuries, and focusing on the discourses of reformers about the Egyptian 'desert fathers' as the originators of monasticism. Historians have suggested that tropes about the desert, solitude, etc., drawn from early texts found their way into mainstream accounts of monastic change in the period *c.* 1080–1150. This paper challenges this model by proposing that considerations of 'reform' must take into account parallel movements in Greek Orthodox monasticism and interactions of practice between the two monastic environments. Three case-studies of non-textually derived parallel practices are discussed, and the importance of the Holy Land as a source of inspiration for such practices is advanced in place of Egypt.

In 1151, Aelwin, a monk of Durham living in retreat on the island of Inner Farne off the coast of Northumbria, was surprised by the arrival of another Durham monk, Bartholomew. Aelwin's surprise was doubtless occasioned not only by the disturbance to his solitude but also by the startling appearance of the new arrival. Bartholomew was dressed in a long-sleeved tunic of animal skins and a separate hood or *cuculla*, over which he wore a black cloak (*pallium*). In this costume 'he showed to all who saw him', asserts his biographer, 'the figure of the ancient fathers'.[1] Bartholomew was, in fact, bringing the Egyptian desert to the North Sea. His clothing was the closest approximation he could manage to the garb of the monks of Egypt, as described in John Cassian's *Institutes*.[2]

---

[1] *Vita Bartholomaei Farnensis*, VIII–IX, Symeon of Durham, *Historia Ecclesiae Dunhemlensis. Appendix II*, ed. Thomas Arnold, Rolls Series (1882), I, 300–2. See also V. M. Tudor, 'Durham Priory and its Hermits in the Twelfth Century', in *Anglo-Norman Durham 1093–1193*, ed. David Rollason, Margaret Harvey and Michael Prestwich (Woodbridge, 1994), 67–78.

[2] John Cassian, *De institutis monachorum*, I, 3–9, ed. J.-C. Guy, Sources Chrétiennes 109 (Paris, 1965), 43–51, specified a 'cuculla', 'pallium' and linen tunic to be worn at all times together with 'subcinctoria', or shoulder straps. This clothing is also described in the earlier *Historia monachorum in Aegypto*, III, *Patrologia Latina*, ed. J.-P. Migne (215 vols., Paris, 1844–)

Bartholomew was signalling his adherence to a specific way of life – the monasticism of the 'golden age' of the desert fathers.

The keynote of the religious life of the late eleventh and early twelfth centuries has been characterised in two particular features: the range and variety of the types of life adopted and the foundation of new monastic houses, often in rejection of existing ones. The discourse of contemporary writers invites such assessments: there is talk in the sources of *renovatio*; monks are said to be engaged in processes characterised by words such as *recalescere* and *recuperari*.[3] One of the most obvious elements of this 'new monasticism' was the notion that it represented a return to an original form of the religious life. Thus, new foundations laid emphasis on the idea that they were not in fact starting anything new but simply polishing up a model that had become tarnished. The circumstances and types of reform enterprise were almost infinitely varied, but much of the language accompanying reform assumes that there is a model of 'proper' monastic life, and that this model, however resistant to definition, conforms to some historical prototype.[4] In his own small way, Bartholomew was taking a part in this discourse by signalling his search for authenticity in the religious life.

If there was an historical prototype – a moment at which monasticism was born – it follows that there must also have been some geographical specificity to this ur-monaticism. Another Benedictine, William of Saint-Thierry, described the early days of the Cistercian foundation of Clairvaux in the 1120s thus: 'Wherever I turned my eyes I was amazed to see as it were a new heaven and a new earth, and the well-worn path trodden by the monks of old, *our fathers out of Egypt*, bearing the footprints left by men of our own time.'[5] William sees a direct association between the monastic reform of his day and the emergence of monastic life in the Egyptian desert. The East – specifically, the Egyptian desert of Anthony, the first solitary monk, and Pachomius, the first to found monastic communities – was similarly identified by Orderic Vitalis as the wellspring of Cistercian reforming ideals. In his account of the founding of Citeaux in 1098, he makes the reforming prior Robert of Molesme try to persuade his monks that they needed to imitate the lives lived by their fathers in the Egyptian desert.[6] The Cistercians were willing to take on this parentage for themselves. Two generations or so after

(*PL*), XXI, col. 407. For standard Benedictine clothing, *La règle de Saint Benoit*, V–VI, ed. A. De Vogué and J. Neufville, Sources Chrétiennes 35 (2 vols., Paris, 1972), II, 618.

[3] Among many examples, Haimo of Hirsau, *Vita Willelmi Hirsaugiensis* XXI, *PL*, CL, col. 913; Giles Constable, *The Reformation of the Twelfth Century* (Cambridge, 1996), 144, 153–61.

[4] See the remark of Constable, *Reformation*, 125.

[5] William of Saint-Thierry, *Vita prima sancti Bernardi*, I, vii, 34, *PL*, CLXXXV, col. 247.

[6] *The Ecclesiastical History of Orderic Vitalis*, VIII, 26, ed. Marjorie Chibnall (6 vols., Oxford, 1969–80), IV, 312–14.

Orderic, the Cistercian Conrad of Eberbach's *Exordium Magnum* sought to give his Order an historical lineage reaching back to the Egyptian desert and beyond. According to his spiritual genealogy, the pioneers of monastic life in Egypt were themselves conscious heirs of the first Christians to live communally: the disciples of Christ in Jerusalem, as described in Acts. Monasticism – genuine monasticism – inescapably had its origins in the East, in the birthplace of Christianity.[7] There was nothing startlingly original about Conrad's formulation of the monastic heritage. The conviction that monasticism began with the Apostles and was transferred to Egypt, where it developed the forms that subsequently became recognisable as the reference point for 'correct' religious life, had been popularised in the West as early as the fifth century by John Cassian.[8] The idea of Egypt as the true heartland of monasticism owed its force to Cassian's own travels among the monks of Nitria and Skete, in the Nile Delta. Cassian's textual elaboration of this idea became canonical in the West through the adoption of his *Conferences* and *Institutes* by Benedict's Rule in the sixth century.[9] Alongside the Rule itself, the non-liturgical books most Benedictine monasteries could be relied on to own were probably those by Cassian, and the *Sayings of the Fathers*.[10]

Modern historians of monasticism have been rightly sceptical about how much meaning we should ascribe to the knowledge of such texts, and of the 'myth of Egypt', among monastic western reformers. As Orderic Vitalis pointed out in his commentary on Cistercian reform, northern France was not Egypt, and it was foolish to pretend that monks who wanted to live a purer monastic life could do so by pretending that they lived in a real desert rather than wooded valleys, and by cooking in olive oil instead of butter.[11] The appeal to Near Eastern origins was, in the words of one recent historian, 'the desert myth' – a 'literary ideology' constructed in search of the kind of respectability conferred by a sense of antiquity, rather than a genuine programme of reform.[12] Indeed, Orderic's account of the origins of Cîteaux can be read as a critique of such an ideology.

---

[7] Conrad of Eberbach, *Exordium Magnum Cisterciense*, Dist. I, 2–3, ed. B. Griesser, Corpus Christianorum Continuatio Medievalis (CCCM), 138 (Turnhout, 1994), 7–9.

[8] John Cassian, *Conférences XVIII–XXIV*, XVIII, 4–6, ed. E. Pichery, Sources Chrétiennes 64 (Paris, 1959), 13–18.

[9] *La règle*, LXXIII, 672.

[10] Taking England as an example, the *Vitas patrum* was certainly known at these monasteries by the early thirteenth century: Burton, Bury, Christ Church Canterbury, Flaxley, Glastonbury, Peterborough, Reading and Rochester. Cassian (either the *Institutes* or *Conferences* or both) was known at all the same houses, and also at Whitby and Rievaulx before the end of the twelfth century: list by Richard Sharpe at www.history.ox.ac.uk/sharpe/key.pdf.

[11] *Orderic Vitalis*, VIII, 26, 314–20.

[12] Benedicta Ward, 'The Desert Myth. Reflections on the Desert Ideal in Early Cistercian Monasticism', in *One Yet Two. Monastic Tradition East and West*, ed. M. Basil Pennington

If Robert of Molesme was in this account trying to persuade his monks to imitate the Egyptian desert fathers, the monks in response offered an alternative reading of monastic history, according to which the true essence of monasticism had passed from Egypt to Italy, with the writing of Benedict's Rule in the sixth century, and from Italy to France with the spread of the Rule westwards. Besides, Egypt was not invariably associated in monastic discourse with monastic precursors. Walter Daniel's *Life of Ailred of Rievaulx*, for example, uses Egypt to invoke the lives led by the secular clergy, in the story of the unstable clerk whose struggles with the Cistercian life cause such troubles to Ailred.[13] Authority had moved from East to West.

Moreover, consciousness of a lineage traceable back to Egypt did not necessarily incline monks such as Guibert to look favourably or respectfully at his contemporary eastern Christian brethren – in Egypt or elsewhere. Writing about the preaching of the first crusade in 1095, Guibert invoked the idea of a world beset by perversions of the Christian truth, in which the Frankish people have the sole responsibility of leading the defence of true religion. His configuration of Europe was the world outside the cloister, writ large. 'The East' was an amorphous region whence threats to Truth arose. In Guibert's eyes, it was no coincidence that Islam, the latest such threat, had arisen in the East. Climatic conditions made it inevitable that the East, once the birthplace of truth, should in his own times be the arena of confusion, doubt and error, because dry heat rendered peoples inconstant. Citing Isidore of Seville, Guibert pinpointed the overriding psychological characteristic of the East as *levitas* – 'lightness'. It was not only Turks and Arabs who were prey to such climatic forces, but also the Greeks: 'According to the purity of the air in which they are born, the Greeks have a lightness of body, and therefore keen talent.' But the Greeks of his day – the Byzantines – had abused this talent with 'Asiatic instability' to question the true faith with 'many useless commentaries'. In consequence, the faith of all peoples in the East was 'staggering and inconstant ... always derailing the rules of true belief'. Guibert's account of the first crusade is notable for the hostility he shows not only to the Turks and Islam but to the Greek Orthodox Christians whose delivery from oppression represented the *casus belli*. It was not surprising that they needed military intervention from the West: feeble and unwarlike, they were unable to defend either themselves or Jerusalem, the iconic centre of the world.[14]

(Kalamazoo, 1976), 183–99; Constable, *Reformation*, 136, and see also 131, where he doubts whether most twelfth-century monks knew much about the early Church.
[13] Walter Daniel, *Life of Ailred of Rievaulx*, XV, ed. F. M. Powicke (Edinburgh, 1950), 24.
[14] Guibert de Nogent, *Dei gesta per Francos*, II, ed. R. B. C. Huygens, CCCM, 127A (Turnhout, 1996), 89–90. See now LéanNi Chléirigh, 'The Impact of the First Crusade on

Guibert's prejudices against 'the East' explain why, in describing the phenomenon of monastic reform, he looks no further than French-speaking territories, implying that the 'swarms of new monks' were spontaneously generated from his own Gallic soil. But even if we dismiss the 'myth of the desert' as just that, there are other possibilities to be considered in thinking about the relationship between monastic reform and the East. Not least is the fact that reform of monastic communities was also going on throughout the Greek Orthodox world in the same period – the second half of the eleventh and first half of the twelfth centuries. As in the West, existing monasteries were restored and new ones founded by combinations of pious lay benefactors and energetic monastic entrepreneurs.[15] Among the ideals articulated as a reason for reform in the Orthodox world was one that would have been familiar to Guibert – the need to 'return' to a supposed lost 'original' form of religious life.[16] The reasons assumed for the loss of this original form may have differed in West and East, but the desired end result was often the same: cenobitic monasteries organised on coherent principles under strict observance of a given set of disciplinary codes.

How much of reforming Orthodox monastic practices was known to western monks in the eleventh century is unclear. The costume adopted by Bartholomew of Farne was more or less that still worn by Greek Orthodox monks in Egypt in his own day: a manuscript of John Climachos's *Heavenly Ladder* illuminated at Mt Sinai in the eleventh century shows Sinai monks wearing tunic, *cuculla* and *pallium* with scapular over the shoulders.[17] Bartholomew, however, is more likely to have obtained his knowledge of monastic dress textually than from actual observation.[18]

Monasticism that tends to be characterised as 'traditional' or pre-reforming had also looked to the East – but to a different east: Jerusalem. As Daniel Callahan and John France have shown, evidence for the place of Jerusalem in the western monastic imagination of the eleventh century is abundant.[19] The accounts of the Fatimid threat to Jerusalem in the

Western Opinion towards the Byzantine Empire', in *The Crusades and the Near East. Cultural Histories*, ed. Conor Kostick (2011), 164–8.

[15] John P. Thomas, *Private Religious Foundations in the Byzantine Empire* (Washington, DC, 1987), 186–213; Rosemary Morris, *Monks and Laymen in Byzantium* (Cambridge, 1995), 9–31.

[16] Compare the ideas expressed by John the Oxite in late eleventh-century Byzantium about monastic origins to those of Conrad of Eberbach a century or so later, 'Requisitoire du Patriarche Jean d'Antioche contre le charistikarioi', ed. P. Gautier, *Revue des Études Byzantines*, 33 (1975), 77–131.

[17] Princeton University Library Garrett MS 16, fo. 194r.

[18] Durham Cathedral MS B.IV.10 (Cassian's *Conferences*) and Durham Cathedral B.IV.11 (Cassian's *Institutes*).

[19] Daniel Callahan, 'Jerusalem in the Monastic Imaginations of the Early Eleventh Century', *Haskins Society Journal*, 6 (1994), 119–27; John France, 'The Destruction of Jerusalem and the First Crusade', *Journal of Ecclesiastical History*, 47 (1996), 1–17.

monastic chronicles of Ralph Glaber, Adhémar of Chabannes and Hugh of Flavigny show a long-standing attachment to the earthly Jerusalem as a place of pilgrimage, and therefore as the source of penitential absolution, in the Benedictine mentalité.[20] The affinity for Jerusalem found material form in various ways, among them the annual re-enactments of the Resurrection in purpose-built copies of the Holy Sepulchre at Easter in German, French and English monasteries from the tenth century onward.[21] It also took liturgical form. Prayers associated with the holy cross survive from Benedictine sources as far apart as England and the Iberian peninsula.[22] This attachment, moreover, did not necessarily reify the symbolic or spiritual at the expense of contemporary realities. Jerusalem was the source of salvation, but it was also the centre of a living church. Hugh of Flavigny, writing in the 1090s, records the participation in the Easter liturgy at Jerusalem by the Benedictine abbot Richard of Saint-Vanne on the 'Norman pilgrimage' of 1027.[23] It was a church, moreover, that stood in need of continuing support from the West. The returning pilgrim Odilo, son of the count of Rouerge, founded a monastery on his return from the Holy Land in 1053 dedicated to the Holy Sepulchre. The abbot appears to have been an honorary member *ex officio* of the clergy serving at the Church of the Holy Sepulchre, and an annual donation was to be paid for the incense burned at the tomb of Christ itself. [24]

Pilgrimage to Jerusalem in the eleventh century was a distinctively Benedictine practice, and nowhere was the practice more firmly established than in Normandy. Ralph, abbot of Mont Saint-Michel resigned his office in order to make a pilgrimage to the Holy Land in 1054, from which he may not have returned, since he died in 1055/6. Thierry de Mathinville, abbot of Saint-Evroult, did the same in 1057, dying in Cyprus on his return. Likewise Nicholas of Saint-Ouen in Rouen died in 1092 on his return from Jerusalem. William, later the first abbot of Saint-Etienne, Caen, made a pilgrimage to Jerusalem as archdeacon of Rouen before 1070.[25] Although eleventh-century Benedictine pilgrimage

---

[20] Adhémar, *Chronicon*, III, 47, ed. P. Bourgain, CCCM 129 (Turnhout, 1999), 166–7; *Rodulfi Glabri Historiarum Libri Quinti*, I, 21, III, 24, ed. J. France (Oxford, 1989), 37, 132–6; Hugh of Flavigny, *Chronicon*, II, 27, ed. G. Pertz, *Monumenta Germaniae Historica (MGH)* (SS), VIII (Hanover, 1848), 399.

[21] Colin Morris, *The Sepulchre of Christ and the Medieval West* (Oxford, 2005), 107–27.

[22] *Corpus Orationum*, ed. Edmond Eugène Moeller, Jean-Marie Clément and Bertrand C. T. Wallant, CCSL 160 A–L (13 vols., Turnhout, 1992–2003), I, 83–4.

[23] Hugh of Flavigny, *Chronicon*, II, 21–2, *MGH* (SS), VIII, 395–6.

[24] J. Bousquet, 'La foundation de Villeneuve d'Aveyron (1053) et l'expansion de l'abbaye de Moissac en Rouergue', *Annales du Midi*, 75 (1963), 517–42, with foundation document at 538–9. See also Andrew Jotischky, 'The Christians of Jerusalem, the Holy Sepulchre and the Origins of the First Crusade', *Crusades*, 7 (2008), 53–4.

[25] Veronique Gazeau, *Normannia Monastica* (2 vols., Caen, 2007), II: *Prosopographie des abbés bénédictins*, 208, 244–7, 254, 274.

to Jerusalem was certainly not exclusive to Norman monasticism,[26] it is especially striking to find enthusiasm for the Holy Land in a region where Benedictine monasticism was still relatively young. Saint-Etienne, Caen, was founded as late as 1070. Another Norman monastery that had connections to the Holy Land through pilgrimage and in supporting at least three first crusading families financially – Troarn – was founded in c. 1050.[27] Moreover, much of the new impetus for Norman Benedictinism continued to come from outside Normandy and northern France, just as the first steps had been taken by importing the Italian William of Volpiano, via Saint-Benigne, Dijon, to found Fécamp in 1001. Troarn's first abbot, Durand (1059–88), had been a monk of Fécamp before entering Holy Trinity Rouen, itself a foundation of c. 1030, whose first abbot was the German Isembert.[28] If the myth of Egypt was part of a new rhetoric of reform from the early twelfth century, an affinity to Jerusalem may be characterised as a feature of a previous, eleventh-century wave of monastic reform.

Monastic pilgrimages to Jerusalem engendered contacts with monasteries and monastic communities in the Holy Land. Yet, just as historians have seen through the rhetoric of antiquity, so they have tended to dismiss the possibility that any mutual influences might have been at work in the reform phenomenon in the Orthodox and Latin worlds. The proximity of Latin- and Greek-speaking monks in eleventh-century Calabria, Apulia and Sicily; the presence of Nilus of Rossano, the doyen of Orthodox Calabrian monks, at Monte Cassino in the late tenth century; the adoption of Orthodox saints' cults, including those of St George, St Nicholas of Myra and St Katherine of Alexandria, to western monasteries can be seen as contextual but not explanatory factors in the emergence of 'monastic reform' in the West.[29] The current consensus

---

[26] See for example, Meinwerk, bishop of Paderborn, who sent monks to Jerusalem to take the dimensions of the Holy Sepulchre to copy the building for his own new monastic foundation, *Vita Meinwerci episcopi*, CCXVII, ed. G. Pertz, *MGH* (SS), XI (Hanover, 1854), 158–9.

[27] Gazeau, *Normannia Monastica*, II, 374–6, for details of contracts with Adelaide and William de Bordouville, Richard de Troarn and William de Milly; *L'abbaye de Saint-Martin de Troarn*, ed. R. N. Sauvage, Mémoires de la Société des Antiquaires de Normandie, 4th series, 4 (Caen, 1911), 26, 222. For the Milly descendants in the Holy Land, see Malcolm Barber, 'The Career of Philip of Nablus in the Kingdom of Jerusalem', in *The Experience of Crusading*, II: *Defining the Crusader Kingdom*, ed. Peter Edbury and Jonathan Phillips (Cambridge, 2003), 60–75.

[28] Gazeau, *Normannia monastica*, II, 263–5.

[29] *Vita sancti Nili*, *PL*, CXX, cols. 124–32, for the impression made by St Nilus on the monks of Montecassino. See also Bernard Hamilton and P. A. McNulty, '*Orientale lumen et magistra Latinitas*: Greek Influence on Western Monasticism (900–1100)', in *Le millénaire du Mont Athos. Études et mélanges* (2 vols., Chevtogne, 1963), I, 181–216; Graham Loud, 'Montecassino and Byzantium in the Tenth and Eleventh Centuries', in *The Theotokos Evergetis and Eleventh-Century Monasticism*, ed. M. Mullett and A. Kirby (Belfast, 1994), 30–58; H. Bloch, 'Montecassino,

among monastic historians is that the reform movement in the West was self-generated. Similarities between ideals and practices found in both Orthodox and Latin monasticism are thus put down to the coincidence of reformers in both spheres reading and being influenced by the same 'classic' early monastic texts, especially Cassian, the corpus of Basilian and pseudo-Basilian regulatory texts and the 'literature of the desert' such as the *Sayings of the Fathers*.[30] This process entailed the emergence of new 'textual communities' with mindsets that enabled them to articulate their own positions in relation to past ideals: such communities identified themselves as 'reformers'; as undertaking *renovatio*. A corollary is that those who were not so identified were, by definition, 'unreformed', or enemies of 'reform'.[31] Western monastic discourses of the period from *c.* 1050 to 1200 were very largely informed by this agenda. It is hard to escape the conclusion that the historiography of monasticism has been no less driven by the same agenda, an agenda that sees religious life in this period according to a model of 'reform' versus 'tradition'. Such an agenda allows little place for reform to have come from anywhere but within, from reading texts, rather than from observation and shared experience; in fact, it allows no place for the geography of monasticism. In what follows, I offer a few examples that suggest greater complexity than the current model allows, and that might make us rethink the context of the 'myth of the desert'.

One of the underlying principles of reform in practice in the West, insisted upon in the rhetoric of just about all reforming foundations, was the performance of manual labour by the monks.[32] The first monks had done manual labour, therefore monks who did not perform such labour were not to be classed alongside the progenitors of the monastic profession. One of the earliest texts to mention manual labour in this

Byzantium and the West in the Early Middle Ages', in H. Bloch, *Montecassino in the Middle Ages* (Rome, 1968), 1–136; J. MacGregor, 'Negotiating Knightly Piety: The Cult of the Warrior Saints in the West ca. 1070–ca. 1200', *Church History*, 73 (2004), 317–45; Elizabeth Lapina, 'Demetrius of Thessaloniki, Patron Saint of Crusaders', *Viator*, 40 (2009), 93–112; Paul Oldfield, 'St Nicholas the Pilgrim and the City of Trani between Greeks and Normans c. 1090–1140', *Anglo-Norman Studies*, 30 (2008), 168–81; C. W. Jones, 'The Norman Cults of Saints Catherine and Nicholas', in *Hommages à André Boutemy*, ed. G. Cambier (Brussels, 1976), 216–31; Christine Walsh, *The Cult of Saint Katherine of Alexandria in Early Medieval Europe* (Aldershot, 2007).

[30] Thus Henrietta Leyser, *Hermits and the New Monasticism* (New York, 1992), 24–5; Marilyn Dunn, 'Eastern Influence on Western Monasticism in the Eleventh and Twelfth Centuries', *Byzantinische Forschungen*, 13 (1988), 245–59.

[31] See the discussions by Conrad Leyser, 'Custom, Truth and Gender in Eleventh-Century Reform', in *Gender and Christian Religion*, ed. R. N. Swanson, Studies in Church History, 34 (Woodbridge, 1998), 75–91; and Kathleen Cushing, *Reform and the Papacy in the Eleventh Century* (Manchester, 2005), 111–33.

[32] Constable, *Reformation*, 210–12.

context, however, is not a classic 'reform' text at all, but the chronicle of Monte Cassino, Benedict's original foundation in Campania. In the 990s, a group of monks left Monte Cassino for a pilgrimage to Jerusalem, then went on to the Greek monastery of Mt Sinai, and on to Mt Athos. On their return to Monte Cassino in 998, one of the monks, Liutius, founded a dependent cell where he devoted himself to a life of asceticism and, to the astonishment of both his contemporaries and to the Monte Cassino chronicler writing nearly a century later, to manual labour such as grinding the corn for the monks' food.[33] This episode appears to show – at least, in the mind of the chronicler who juxtaposes the story of the pilgrimage with the introduction of manual labour – the influence of a rather different monastic tradition – the laura monasticism of Mt Athos, founded earlier in the tenth century as a conscious revival of the practices of the early monks of the Holy Land.[34] In fact, this was not the first time such an influence had informed practice in a western monastery: in 933, John of Gorze had introduced manual labour at his new foundation after seeing Greek monks at work at Monte Gargano in Italy.[35]

Influences can be subtler than the appropriation of a custom or way of life. One of the earliest of the new monastic foundations in Normandy in the eleventh century was Holy Trinity, Rouen, founded in 1030. Within a few years of its foundation, the monastery had developed a cult dedicated to St Katherine of Alexandria, at that time a relatively obscure virgin martyr known largely in the Greek-speaking world.[36] By mid-century, Holy Trinity, Rouen, claimed to possess relics of the saint's finger bones, which oozed a clear oil that performed miracles of healing.[37] An anonymous account of the foundation of the monastery and of the acquisition of the relics was written by a Rouen monk at some point in the second half of the eleventh century. The account seeks to tie the founding of the monastery to the colourful Greek monk, Symeon, originally a native of Sicily who subsequently became a monk in the Holy Land and at Sinai, and who apparently brought the relics of the saint with him to Normandy after participating in the pilgrimage to Jerusalem led by Richard of Saint-Vannes and Richard II of Normandy.[38] In fact,

[33] *Chronica Monasterii Casinensis*, II, 12, 22, ed. H. Hoffman, *MGH* (SS), XXXIV (Hanover, 1980), 190, 206.

[34] '*Rule* of Athanasios the Athonite for the Lavra Monastery', XXIX–XXX, trans. George Dennis, in *Byzantine Monastic Foundation Documents*, ed. John Thomas and Angela Hero (5 vols., Washington, DC, 2000), I, 227.

[35] *Miracula Sancti Gorgonii*, XXVI, *MGH* (SS), IV (Hanover, 1841), 246.

[36] Walsh, *Cult of Saint Katherine*, 63–78.

[37] *Cartulaire de l'abbaye de la Sainte-Trinité de Rouen*, ed. A. Delville, in *Le cartulaire de l'abbaye de Saint-Bertin*, ed. M. Guérard (Paris, 1841), no. 97, 466–7.

[38] 'Sanctae Catherinae virginis et marytris translatio et miracula Rotomagenia saec. XI', ed. A. Poncelet *Analecta Bollandiana*, 22 (1903), 423–38.

Symeon cannot be shown to have had anything to do with the founding of Holy Trinity, and the whole account can be seen as part of a genre of institutional foundation-legends.[39] But the significance of the account lies not in whether Holy Trinity was or was not founded by a Greek monk, but the plausibility of such a claim to contemporaries. Perhaps the most interesting aspect of the foundation story is the insouciance with which a Benedictine monastic author of the second half of the eleventh century can narrate the circumstances of the foundation of his house by a Greek Orthodox monk. We assume that the chronicler was aware of the quite separate regulatory traditions operating in the Orthodox world, where the Rule of Benedict was, although known, not followed by Greek monks;[40] where, in fact, monastic founders adopted or composed their own Rules. There is nothing in the known history of Holy Trinity that suggests anything other than Benedictine observance; yet, according to the Rouen chronicler, Symeon not only founded the monastery according to his own customs, but put its running in charge of Greek companions he had brought with him from Sinai.[41] One might argue that the purpose of the text – promotion of the monastery's claims to powerful relics – trumped the need for anything like historical veracity or even plausibility. The fact remains that in the language and terms of reference of the text itself, for a Norman monastery to have been founded by a Greek monk was apparently uncontroversial – or, to put it another way, a Norman contemporary of Guibert of Nogent had no objection to being thought of as the product of a Greek Orthodox foundation.

Perhaps it was uncontroversial because to monks adherence to a particular set of regulations or to a doctrinally determined body of religious customs was a secondary consideration. During the siege of Antioch on the first crusade, the Frankish knight Peter Jordan of Châtillon, who had been wounded and thought he would not recover, wanted to end his life as a monk. He professed at the only monastery available in Antioch – the Greek Orthodox monastery of St Paul.[42] Neither the knight nor the Greek monks saw any difficulty about a Latin becoming a monk at an Orthodox monastery. Nor did this kind of interchange only apply to the dying. The Orthodox laura of St Sabas, in the Judaean desert south of Jerusalem, altered its *typikon* in the early years of the twelfth century in order to make liturgical provision for Franks who might become monks

[39] R. Fawtier, 'Les reliques rouennaises de Sainte Catherine d'Alexandrie', *Analecta Bolladiana*, 41 (1923), 365.

[40] Jerusalem, Greek Orthodox Patriarchate Taphou MS 35, an eleventh-century codex owned by the monastery of St Theodosius, south of Jerusalem, contains the *Dialogues* of Gregory the Great in Greek.

[41] 'Sanctae Catherinae', ed. Poncelet, 429.

[42] *Le cartulaire de Cormery*, ed. J. J. Bourassé (Tours, 1861), 104.

there.[43] There would be no point in making the change unless it reflected some kind of reality. There were precedents for this. Toward the end of the tenth century, a Latin bishop on pilgrimage in the East as a penance for the accidental murder of his nephew asked the advice of Patriarch Genasios, while in Constantinople, for a suitable place to settle as a hermit. Genasios discouraged him from this course, but recommended instead that he follow an eremitical life within a cenobitic community. The bishop asked where such a thing, of which he had never heard, might be done, and was sent to the monastery of St Mamas, where he would find 'another Arsenios the Great' in the person of the superior Symeon 'the New Theologian'. The bishop professed as a monk, taking the name Hierotheos.[44]

The conquest and settlement of the Holy Land and western Syria by Franks as a result of the crusade brought two overlapping monastic traditions, the Benedictine and the Greek Orthodox, into the same geographical space. Some of the results of this sharing of space have already been noted in the religious architecture of the Crusader States: for example, the extension of the Orthodox church at 'Abud to allow for Latin congregations, the double use of the shrine church of St John the Baptist at 'Ain Karim, and the monastery at al-Ba'ina, the confessional status of which remains uncertain.[45] I offer three examples of how the Holy Land functioned as what might be termed a laboratory of monastic 'invention' – in the original sense of the word, as a 'finding' of practices transmitted through observation and imitation.

The first concerns a link between demonic possession and certain types of manual labour. A fragmentary monastic text of the mid-twelfth century from the Crusader States, Gerard of Nazareth's *On the Way of Life of the Servants of God* gives a brief account of a solitary hermit called Ursus who lived on the Jebel Lakoum (Black Mountain) north-west of Antioch. Periodically tormented by demons in his solitude, he rid himself of the problem by entering a monastery and undertaking a particularly menial kind of labour – work in the kitchen and bakery.[46] The connection

---

[43] 'Die klösterregeln des hl. Sabbas', ed. E. Kurtz, *Byzantinische Zeitschrift*, 3 (1894), 167–70.

[44] *Un grand mystique byzantine: la Vie de Syméon le nouveau théologien*, ed. and trans. I. Hausherr, LII–LVII, Orientalia Christiana XII (Rome, 1928), 68–72.

[45] Ronnie Ellenblum, *Frankish Rural Settlement in the Kingdom of Jerusalem* (Cambridge, 1996), 128–36; Andrew Jotischky, 'The Frankish Encounter with the Greek Orthodox in the Crusader States', in *Tolerance and Intolerance. Social Conflict in the Age of the Crusades*, ed. Michael Gervers and James M. Powell (Syracuse, 2001), 102; *Les sains pelerinages*, V, 20, *Pelerinaiges*, XX, *Chemins et pelerinages*, A.IV, 17, in *Itinéraires à Jérusalem et descriptions de la Terre-Sainte rédigés en français au XIe, XIIe et XIII siècles*, ed. H. Michelant and G. Raynaud (2 vols., Geneva, 1879–80), II, 104, 102, 188; Denys Pringle, *The Churches of the Latin Kingdom of Jerusalem. A Corpus. Vol. I A–K* (Cambridge, 1993), 82–92.

[46] Benjamin Z. Kedar, 'Gerard of Nazareth, a Neglected Twelfth Century Writer in the Latin East', *Dumbarton Oaks Papers*, 37 (1983), 71–7, from Matthias Illyricus Flacius, *Historia*

between mental health and this specific kind of manual labour is striking. The only parallels known to me come from the Orthodox monastic tradition. A younger contemporary of Ursus was the Georgian monk Gabriel, who, although a monk of St Sabas, was living of his own volition as a stylite on a pillar in the desert near the monastery. What is known about Gabriel comes from a Greek instructional homily by the Cypriot monk Neophytos the Recluse, the purpose of which is to advise monks how to recognise and deal with demons and demonic possession. Gabriel, assailed by demons on his pillar, failed to recognise them for what they were, and after trying unsuccessfully under their influence to murder another solitary monk, he was taken in disgrace back to St Sabas. The superior of St Sabas expelled him to the cenobitic monastery of St Euthymius, also in the Judaean desert. Here, he was put to work collecting and carrying wood for the monastery's kitchen and bakery. Each load, says Neophytos, was like the cargo borne by a camel on its back: 'You could see this man every day bringing a load of wood on his shoulders hardly less than a camel's load . . . he was in subjection, slaving away zealously in the monastery.'[47] The purpose of this was clearly to rid Gabriel of the demons. There were established connections between monastic discipline, kitchen work and humility in the early Palestinian tradition, with which Neophytos was certainly familiar. According to Cyril of Scythopolis, John the Hesychast, wishing to hide his real identity as a bishop when he entered the *laura* of St Sabas, welcomed the job of kitchen servant. Similarly Cyriacus, when turned away from St Euthymius because of his youth, proved himself as a monk by chopping wood and carrying water for the kitchen.[48] In these cases, volunteering for low-status manual labour associated with the kitchen was a means of proving oneself in the *coenobium*. In the early Egyptian monastic tradition, a further connection tied manual labour concerned with kitchen and bakery to demonic possession. In Palladius's *Lausiac History*, a nun at Tabennisi pretends to be possessed by demons so that she can be assigned the most menial of kitchen work – serving the food and clearing plates afterwards. The nun is continually maltreated and mocked by the others for her apparent affliction and for her willingness to carry out humble work. An anchorite, told about the nun in a vision, visits the convent and tells the nuns that she whom they think is the lowest of them all is in fact their

Ecclesiastica, integram ecclesiae Christi ideam . . . secunda singulas centurias perspicuo ordine complectens (7 vols., Basel, 1562–74), XII, *Duodecima Centuria*, cols. 1603–10.

[47] *Narratio de monachi Palestinensis, in* 'Saints de Chypre', ed. H. Delehaye, *Analecta Bollandiana*, 26 (1907), 162–75.

[48] *Kyrillos von Skythopolis*, ed. E. Schwartz (Leipzig, 1939), 205–6, 225.

spiritual mother. As in Gabriel's story, a menial form of manual labour becomes a path to spiritual growth.[49]

It is easy enough to trace the influences on Neophytos in compiling his homily on Gabriel. More puzzling is the question of how Gerard of Nazareth, the earlier writer of the two, might have known about them. Knowledge of Greek was nugatory among western clerics such as Gerard, and none of the texts in which these practices occur was available in Latin. We are seeing, then, either the parallel development of the same traditions – manual labour as a disciplinary antidote to demonic possession, coupled with a particular relationship between solitary and communal monasticism – or evidence for interplay between Orthodox and Latin practices based not on textual influences but on observation and experience. A recent study of demonic visitation in twelfth-century western monasticism has concluded that although demons and the dangers of demonic affliction were common in monastic discourse, the treatment of the subject by most writers concentrated on the heroism of monks' resistance to demons, without showing much interest in the spiritual meaning of demonic assaults on monks.[50] Only among twelfth-century Cistercians, Tom Licence argues, can a more ambiguous and adventurous attitude to demonic visitation be discerned. The ability to see demons was explored by Cistercian writers, notably Herbert of Clairvaux and Caesarius of Heisterbach, as a spiritual gift and therefore as a mark of special visionary powers.[51] This does not quite correspond to Neophytos's use of Gabriel, who is set up by Neophytos as a cautionary example to be avoided rather than emulated. Nor do the Cistercian writers explore the possible meanings of demonic visitation in the same manner as Neophytos in his discussion of Gabriel. It is nevertheless striking to find an interest among the Cistercians in the spirituality of demonic visitation as it reflects on the experience and inner life of the monk in a way that is markedly different from the usual treatment of the theme in western hagiography.

Two further examples take us from the Holy Land to England. Ten years before his death in 1167, Aelred, abbot of Rievaulx, had a special building constructed for him at the monastery in which he could live because his infirmities no longer permitted him to move around or to exercise his office freely. The exact form of this building remains unclear, but it is described in Walter Daniel's *Life of Aelred* as a 'mausoleum', or free-standing tomb.[52] It was large enough to house up to thirty monks at

[49] Palladius, *The Lausiac History*, XXXIV, ed. Cuthbert Butler (Cambridge, 1898–1904), 98–100.
[50] Tom Licence, 'The Gift of Seeing Demons in Early Cistercian Spirituality', *Cistercian Studies Quarterly*, 39 (2004), 49–65.
[51] *Ibid.*, 62–4.
[52] Walter Daniel, *Life of Aelred of Rievaulx*, XXXI, 39–40.

a time, and it functioned as a separate cell in which he followed his own dispensation: its purpose was to free him from strict observance of the Rule on health grounds, without the need to be confined to the infirmary. The curious feature is the term used to describe it. There is no comparable usage known to me in medieval Latin of 'mausoleum' as a space for the living rather than the dead; nor is a strictly comparable monastic structure known from archaeological or literary evidence. One can see why it made particular sense in this instance, given that Aelred was considered to be near death, and the rich symbolism of inhabiting a mausoleum reinforced the image of the monk as dead to the world. But the construction of a building called a mausoleum but not actually functioning as such, in a monastic setting, is unusual, perhaps unique. There is a specific example that we can connect to Ailred's 'mausoleum'. Aelred's contemporary Godric of Finchale, the anchorite of Wearside, had according to his biographer Reginald of Durham been inspired by the example of solitary monks he had encountered in Jerusalem on pilgrimage. Now, hermits are known to have inhabited the rock tombs in the Kidron Valley, to the east of the city walls, in the twelfth century.[53] These tombs offered at the same time commodious accommodation near the holy city and the symbolism of being dead to the world. Aelred of Rievaulx's connections with the monks of Durham are well known, and the earliest manuscript of his *Life* comes from the Durham monastic library.[54] Moreover, Aelred is known to have sought out Godric himself in 1159, perhaps in the company of Godric's biographer, Reginald; certainly Reginald attests that it was at Aelred's prompting that he wrote the biography of Godric.[55] I suggest that the mausoleum he had built for him at Rievaulx came from the direct example of the tomb chambers at Jerusalem, through the mediation of Godric. More broadly speaking, Aelred's removal of himself as abbot from the community into a dwelling sited within the monastery but immune from the monastery's regulation is reminiscent of contemporary Orthodox rather than Benedictine practices – Neophytos's cave at the Enkleistra comes to mind.[56]

Another Godric, the anchorite of Throkenholt recently rescued from oblivion by Tom Licence, provides a further possible example of such a

[53] Andrew Jotischky, *The Perfection of Solitude. Hermits and Monks in the Crusader States* (University Park, PA, 1995), 69–71.

[54] Walter Daniel, *Life of Aelred of Rievaulx*, XXVIII–XXIX.

[55] Reginald of Durham, *De vita et miraculis S. Godrici heremitae de Finchale*, ed. J. Stevenson, Surtees Society (1847), 176–7.

[56] 'The Rule of Neophytos the Recluse', XIV–XV, ed. and trans. Nicholas Coureas, *The Foundation Rules of Medieval Cypriot Monasteries: Makhairas and Neophytos*, Cyprus Research Centre Texts and Studies in the History of Cyprus XLVI (Nicosia, 2003), 146–9.

link in monastic practices.[57] Godric retired to a purpose-built hermitage in East Anglia in the late eleventh century. Among the amenities of his hermitage was a chair with a curved back of shoulder height and with a separate neck-rest that he designed himself. This he used instead of a bed, so that he could stay up all night in vigils of prayer while still availing himself of some rest.[58] Godric's chair is worthy of note as an unusual detail of twelfth-century western ascetic practices. Where did the idea come from? It is possible, of course, that the idea as well as the design originated with Godric himself. Nevertheless, the practice of spending the night in a chair rather than lying down is also found among early Orthodox monks. It is first attested in Pachomius's *Rule*, as cited by Palladius, in a passage that requires monks to sleep on inclined benches or seats rather than in a fully supine position.[59] It seems to have been more common, however, in Palestine rather than Egypt or Syria, where mats on the floor became standard.[60] John Moschus reports that the monks of the laura of Ailiotes slept on chairs made of wicker (*sella viminea*).[61] But even if Godric had been educated, he is unlikely to have known Moschus or the Syrian texts. Although Pachomius's *Rule* was known in the West through the Latin translation by Jerome, tellingly, Jerome's version omits any mention of a chair, preferring the more common sleeping mat.[62] Contemporary Orthodox monastic practice preferred the use of mats or benches of wood or stone. At the monastery of St John on Patmos, for example, the only beds were of the collapsible variety, and used exclusively for sick monks.[63] The closest near-contemporary use of a chair for sleeping appears to be in the *Life of Lazaros of Mount Galesion*, a mid-eleventh-century text. Lazaros, who became a stylite in his own foundation at Mt Galesion in Asia Minor, had learned his ascetic practices as a monk of St Sabas in the last decade of the tenth and first decade of the eleventh century. According to his biographer, Lazaros used a specially designed chair rather than a bed so

---

[57] 'The *Life and Miracles* of Godric of Throkenholt', ed. Tom Licence, *Analecta Bollandiana*, 124 (2006), 15–43.

[58] 'ligneum sedile usque ad humeros in altitudine, in modum circuli rotundi, super quod die noctuque sedit', Licence, '*Life and Miracles*', 25–8. At other times he sat outside on a particular piece of turf for the same purpose, which after his death was kept and venerated by his patron.

[59] Pachomius, *Koinonia*, II. *Pachomian Chronicles and Rules*, trans. A. Veilleux (Kalamazoo, 1981), 126; also Palladius, *Historia Lausiaca*, XXXII, 3, ed. Butler, 88.

[60] For early Syrian practices, see A. Voobus, *History of Asceticism in the Syrian Orient*, Corpus Scriptorum Christianorum Orientalum 184, 197 (2 vols., Louvain, 1958–60), II, 264–5, where examples of standing and lying in contorted positions are given, but without reference to chairs.

[61] John Moschus, *Pratum Spirituale*, LXIII, *PL*, LXXIV, col. 148.

[62] Pachomius, *Regula*, LXXXVIII, *PL*, XXIII, col. 74.

[63] N. Oikonimides, 'The Contents of the Byzantine House from the Eleventh to the Fifteenth Centuries', *Dumbarton Oaks Papers*, 44 (1990), 205–14.

that he could never lie down at full stretch.[64] This practice Lazaros derived from the story that an angel had instructed Pachomius that monks should not lie down on their sides to sleep but doze while sitting up.[65] The word used to describe the preferred seat, *pezoulion*, has only one other known usage in Byzantine Greek: a Palestinian monastic text of the sixth century, the *Life of George of Choziba*.[66] All the evidence, therefore, points to the chair as a Palestinian Orthodox monastic practice, apparently still in use in the early eleventh century. Now, Godric certainly could not have known the *Life of Lazaros*, which did not achieve wide circulation even in the Byzantine world before a short summary version was composed in the fourteenth century.[67] It is quite possible that the custom arose independently in East and West, and that its adoption by Godric was coincidental. This might be a convincing argument for a custom so widespread or so obviously derivative from standard sources in common use in both Orthodox and Latin Christendom as to be picked up sooner or later without reference to corresponding usage by contemporaries. But the 'sleeping chair' is in fact a rather unusual detail, evidently known but not widespread in either East or West, and the likeliest explanation therefore is that it is a further example of a non-textual influence, picked up at some degree of remoteness – perhaps from something heard by a pilgrim or crusader returning from the East.

The fact that in none of these cases is there any textual attestation of influence should not deter us from seeing the transmission of ideas. Reluctance to attribute any aspects of reforming monasticism to knowledge of the contemporary monastic scene in the East is rooted in a methodology that reifies textual transmission as the main agent of praxis. Influences are generally established by historians' demonstrations through textual reference points that a given source of knowledge was available to a writer at a given time and could thus be transmitted through reading, internal absorption and composition. Reform monasticism thus takes the form of a 'communicative repertoire' through the composition and dissemination of texts from one monastic community to another. Reform texts generated by a fluid group of like-minded writers communicated ideologies through rhetorical conventions. Monasticism, however, provides a field of enquiry in which textual study offers only partial understanding of praxis. The regular life was based on

---

[64] *The Life of Lazaros of Mt Galesion*, XVIII, XXXV, ed. and trans. Richard P. Greenfield (Washington, DC, 2000), 99, 122. Lazaros, as superior at Mt Galesion, refused to permit beds even for sick monks, CLXII, 253–4.

[65] *Ibid.*, CLII, 253–4.

[66] A. N. Athanassakis and T. Vivian, 'Unattested Greek Words in the *Life of St George of Choziba* and the *Miracles of the Most Holy Mother of God of Choziba*', *Journal of Theological Studies*, 45 (1994), 625.

[67] *The Life of Lazaros*, 1.

imitation and repetition: the continual practice of 'regulation of cycles of repetition'.[68] This is, indeed, implicitly recognised in some twelfth-century western monastic discourses. As Caroline Bynum remarked, Cistercian spirituality provided a laboratory for the nurturing of souls through observing and replicating the exemplary behaviour of others.[69]

Monasticism was a process of *doing* as well as of reading and studying – as Peter Damian famously observed of his visit to Cluny in 1063. The nature of influences from observation is that it is rarely possible to demonstrate the mode of transmission. But just as Liutulf and the other Cassinese monks brought knowledge of contemporary Orthodox practices to Campania in the early years of the eleventh century, and Franks saw Orthodox monasteries in Syria at work during the first crusade,[70] so the Greek bishop Barnabas became a monk at the Benedictine monastery of Saint-Benigne, Dijon, before 1031, and Constantine of Trebizond was planting a vineyard as a monk at Malmesbury in the 1030s, while the Greek Sicilian Symeon, professed as a monk of Sinai, ended his life in Trier.[71] Exchanges from Orthodox monastic practice to the West are by their nature elusive, but they are implicit in both western and Orthodox sources. We might likewise pay closer attention to the kinds of shared practices implicit in the re-use or simultaneous use of the same spaces for monastic life by Orthodox and Latin monks, to the shared veneration of relics in regions where Orthodox and Latin monks came into contact, and especially to the introduction of eastern liturgical feasts in western monasteries.[72] In short, there is scope

---

[68] Michel Foucault, *Discipline and Punish. The Birth of the Prison*, trans. Alan Sheridan (Harmondsworth, 1979), 149.

[69] Caroline Walker Bynum, *Jesus as Mother. Studies in the Spirituality of the High Middle Ages* (Berkeley, 1982), 72–6.

[70] For an example of first crusaders at a Greek Orthodox monastery, 'Narratio quomodo reliquiae martyris Georgii ad nos Aquicinenses pervenerunt', *Recueil des Historiens des Croisades. Historiens Occidentaux*, V (Paris, 1895), 248–52; see also Charles H. Haskins, 'A Canterbury Monk at Constantinople c. 1090', *English Historical Review*, 25 (1910), 293–5; although there is no evidence that the monk in question spent time at a Constantinopolitan monastery, it would have been strange if he had not at least visited one; for another western visitor, Krijnie Ciggaar, 'Une description de Constantinople dans le *Tarragonensis* 55', *Revue des Études Byzantines*, 53 (1995), 17–40.

[71] *Vita S. Guillelmi Divionensis*, in *Acta Sanctorum ordinis S. Benedicti*, ed. L. D'Achery and J. Mabillon (9 vols., Paris, 1668–1701), VI, 302; William of Malmesbury, *Gesta Pontificum Anglorum*, V, 260–1, ed. Michael Winterbottom and Rodney M. Thomson (2 vols., Oxford, 2007), I, 620–1; *Vita S. Symeonis, Acta Sanctorum*, ed. J. Bollandus *et al.* (69 vols., Paris, 1643–1940), June I, 88–101; see also Michael Lapidge, 'Byzantium, Rome and England in the Early Middle Ages', in *Roma fra Oriente e Occidente*, Settimane di Studio del Centro Italiano di Studi sull'Alto Medioevo, 49 (2002), 363–400; Krijnie Ciggaar, *Western Travellers to Constantinople: The West and Byzantium 962–1204* (Leiden, 1996), 130–1.

[72] E.g. the feast of St Katherine in eleventh-century Canterbury, British Library Cotton MS Vit. E. XVIII, fo. 7r, and the early twelfth-century Cambridge Corpus Christi MS 270.

for a widening of the grammar of reform so as to include observation and imitation as valid agencies in determining monastic practice.

The monastic reform of the eleventh and twelfth centuries is now recognised to have been a complex, porous and malleable phenomenon. The variegated monastic scene inhabited by figures such as Dominic of Foligno in eleventh-century Italy, in which the Rule of Benedict was only one of a number of possible alternative ways of living a monastic life, makes for a picture of rich hues and textures.[73] Above all, historians have learned to be wary of the rhetoric of reform. Acute awareness on the part of reform-minded solitaries and communities of the ideals and practices of their forebears – the 'ancient fathers' whose costume Bartholomew of Farne tried to imitate – was honed by the study of the texts in which they were transmitted. But the range of such texts available to western monks of the eleventh and twelfth centuries was not only limited, but also skewed towards a particular type of early monasticism – that practised in Egypt. The *Institutes* and *Conferences* of John Cassian, Athanasius's *Life of Anthony*, Jerome's *Vitas patrum*, *Life of Paul the Hermit* and translation of one version of Pachomius's *Rule*, are all concerned primarily with Egyptian monasticism. Rufinus's translation of Basilian monastic regulations, and similar pseudo-Basilian material, were also known in some western monasteries, but this still left out of consideration a large corpus of monastic texts from Syria and Palestine. The monasticism described by Cyril of Scythopolis, John of Ephesus and Theodoret of Cyrrhus, to name only the most obvious examples, could scarcely have been known in the West from textual transmission. Yet, it is clear that some of the monastic practices and ideals of the Holy Land and to a lesser degree Mt Athos were known, however tenuously, in pockets of the West in the eleventh century, and known largely from personal experience and observation, through modes of transmission that are only implicit in the sources. These practices and ideals owed less to the Egypt seen through the lens of Cassian and Jerome than to the Holy Land. In this respect, Jerusalem stood at the heart of western monasticism during the period of reform.

Paul of Caen, abbot of St Albans (1077–93), is said to have adopted eastern monastic disciplinary norms, *Gesta abbatum sancti Albani*, ed. T. Riley (3 vols., 1867–9), I, 60. The Cistercian monastery of Vallis Lucens (Vaulvisant) owned a Latin translation of the liturgies of St Basil and St John Chrysostom in the twelfth century, now Paris Bibliothèque Nationale Nouvelles Acquisitions Latines 1791; A. Jacob, 'La traduction de la liturgie de S. Basile par Nicholas d'Otrante', *Bulletin de l'Institut Belge de Rome*, 38 (1967), 51–2.

[73] John Howe, *Church Reform and Social Change in Eleventh-Century Italy: Dominic of Sora and his Patrons* (Philadelphia, 1997); Graham Loud, *The Latin Church in Norman Italy* (Cambridge, 2007), 53–9; and the forthcoming book by Paul Oldfield, *Sanctity and Pilgrimage in Medieval Southern Italy (1000–1200)* (Cambridge); on Greek monasticism in Italy, S. Borsari, *Il monachesimo bizantino nella Sicilie e nell'Italia meridionale prenormanne* (Naples, 1963), 60–76; G. Vitolo, 'Les monastères grecs de l'Italie mériodionale', in *Moines et monastè res dans les sociétés de rite grec et latin*, ed. J.-L. Lemaitre, M. Dmitriev and P. Gonneau (Geneva, 1996), 99–113.

Transactions of the RHS 22 (2012), pp. 75–93 © Royal Historical Society 2012
doi:10.1017/S0080440112000072

NEGOTIATING THE MEDIEVAL IN THE MODERN: EUROPEAN CITIZENSHIP AND STATECRAFT

By Janet Coleman

READ 4 FEBRUARY 2011

ABSTRACT. What, if anything, do historians and theorists of international relations owe to the theories and practices of the Middle Ages? This paper traces a number of themes that were intensely debated by theologians during the fourteenth century, tracking especially two different approaches to 'the political' on the part of neo-Augustinian voluntarists on the one hand and neo-Aristotelian intellectualists on the other. In the scholastic attempts to answer the question: 'What are we presumed to be? And, in consequence, what is the scope of politics?', their different views concerning the consequences of what Christians call 'Original Sin' and 'the Fall' are highlighted. Especially, the position of the voluntarists is shown to have been taken up not least by *the* Master of the Modern: Hobbes. The neo-Augustinian voluntarists can thereafter be seen to have provided some of the same arguments that have recently been rehearsed by contemporary 'realist' critics of modern liberalism who, it is argued, are negotiating the medieval in the modern.

Some historians as well as theorists of international relations have recently expressed an interest in discovering whether medieval ideas and practices have survived, in some form or other, to penetrate later, modern political theories and practices of international relations. My having been invited to contribute to one of their workshops[1] inspired me to begin this paper by sharing some reflections that resulted from our discussions. But as I hope will become clear: 'in my beginning is my end'.[2]

There has been some serious reconsideration of chronological periodisation, of what is meant by the 'medieval' as a distinct period separate from, say, the early modern and the modern.[3] Those of us who are medievalists have long been aware of the tendency amongst some medieval historians to problematise the sixteenth-century Renaissance

---

[1] Workshop in the Department of International Politics, Aberystwyth University, Wales, organised by Dr William Bain: 'Will and Reason: Negotiating the Medieval in Modern International Relations', 1–2 Sep. 2010.

[2] T. S. Eliot, *Four Quartets*, East Coker (1944/59), 23.

[3] C. Fasolt, 'Hegel's Ghost: Europe, the Reformation and the Middle Ages', *Viator*, 10 (2007), 345–86; J. Coleman, 'Medieval Political Theory c. 1000–1500', in *The Oxford Handbook of the History of Political Philosophy*, ed. G. Klosko (Oxford, 2011), 180–205.

as a unique event, their insisting instead on an earlier twelfth-century Renaissance as a necessary precursor and forerunner so that the sixteenth-century version was not so 'new' or 'unique'.[4] As historians, we also know of concerns within the discipline as to where precisely the Middle Ages may be said to end and the Renaissance, or, indeed, the Reformation, to have begun. Our discipline is filled with publications entitled 'Forerunners' of something or other.[5] And Britain has had a famous and long-enduring legal fascination with retrieving and implementing an 'ancient constitution' by which was meant, of course, the medieval constitution.[6] So this paper tries to deal with 'continuities' within what might be considered a European tradition of thinking and acting 'as Europeans'.[7]

The very idea that the Middle Ages was left behind, 'thankfully', with the emergence not only of the sixteenth-century Renaissance, but certainly of the Reformation is, from an historian's perspective, an extremely interesting 'modern' ideological project that seeks breaks and new beginnings, engaging a wilful forgetting of yesterday and the past. Earlier in my career, I spent considerable time trying to investigate how 'the past' was construed, what remembering entailed and how the psychological 'faculty' of Memory was thought to function, according to classical Greek, Roman, medieval and early modern thinkers.[8] My aim was to discover the perspectives of those who bothered to address these issues in their pursuit of saying something about what they thought *history* to be, why they thought anyone bothered to write historical narratives and how these affected political thinking and practice. I came to the conclusion that in contrast to the variety of views of earlier thinkers, the 'modern' project was working with an underdeveloped understanding of what language is and how it works, over generations. Furthermore, the 'modern' project was seeking to locate the beginnings of ourselves *as* 'modern', and the consequence was that the centuries-long belief that *historia magistra vitae* – that history is the teacher of life – was thought no longer to be relevant to us. Moderns, it is said, ' make it new' and do

---

[4] *Renaissance and Renewal in the Twelfth Century*, ed. R. Benson, G. Constable and C. Lanham (Oxford, 1982).

[5] *Forerunners of the Reformation: Essays in Late Medieval and Early Reformation Thought*, ed. H. Oberman (Edinburgh, 1986), is only one example of many.

[6] J. G. A. Pocock, *The Ancient Constitution and the Feudal Law: A Study of English Historical Thought in the Seventeenth Century* (Cambridge, 1957).

[7] J. Coleman, 'Citizenship and the Language of Statecraft', in *Finding Europe: Discourses on Margins, Communities, Images ca. 13th – ca. 18th Centuries*, ed. A. Molho, D. Curto and N. Koniordos (Oxford, 2007), 223–52.

[8] J. Coleman, *Ancient and Medieval Memories: Studies in the Reconstruction of the Past* (Cambridge, 1992); J. Coleman, *A History of Political Thought from the Middle Ages to the Renaissance* (Oxford, 2000), esp. 203–7.

not repeat the past because 'the past' is now taken to be 'over-and-done with'.[9]

What it means to be a 'modern' person is defined according to one prevailing view as being a uniquely subjective, passion-driven, self-interested individualist, where individual choices to act in one way or another are guided by one's Will rather than by one's Reason. The 'modern' voluntarist person is then situated within a 'moral' frame that is relativist, in the sense that moralities are understood as having emerged from, and been modified by, our different states' conventional, positive, coercive laws. These laws are taken to have developed as responses to perceived threats to the security of the whole, i.e. responses to contingencies as historical emergencies. So over time, the laws can and do change and the specifics of the enforceable moral frame also change. Any citizen of a modern state is said to possess equal rights, of a certain kind, enshrined in his/her state's positive law. These rights, in law, are open to modification. The laws do not and cannot cover every action. Where momentarily the laws have nothing to say, each of us is left with permissions to act in ways that the laws remain silent about. All of this can and does change. But there is an underlying presumption that the changes are progressive and they alter the past in ways that are better in the present and will ensure an even better future for self-interested individualists as described.

The details of any moral order that is enforceable are said to have emerged as secondary conclusions from what is a primary 'logical' solution to everyone's problem, experienced everywhere and at all times: the problem is said to be that we are *naturally* competitive, envious and intolerant in our interpersonal relations.[10] A knowledge of history is

[9] Coleman, *Ancient and Medieval Memories*, 558–99, on the medieval and Renaissance sense of the past; on current historians' views on a Renaissance sense of the past, and on modern discourse concerning senses of the past: J. Coleman, 'The Uses of the Past (14th – 16th Centuries): The Invention of a Collective History and Its Implications for Cultural Participation', in *Cultural Participation: Trends since the Middle Ages*, ed. Ann Rigney and Douwe Fokkema, Utrecht Publications in General and Comparative Literature, 31 (Amsterdam, 1993), 21–37; R. Koselleck, *Futures Past: On the Semantics of Historical Time* (Cambridge, MA, 1985), trans. K. Tribe, from *Vergangene Zukunft. Zur Semantik geschichtlicher Zeiten* (Frankfurt, 1979), esp. 'Historia Magistra Vitae: The Dissolution of the Topos into the Perspective of a Modernized Historical Process', 21–38; G. W. F. Hegel, *Lectures on the Philosophy of World History: Introduction: Reason in History*, trans. H. B. Nisbet (Cambridge, 1975), 21: 'Rulers, statesmen and nations are often advised to learn the lesson of historical experience. But what experience and history teach is this – that nations and governments have never learned anything from history or acted upon any lessons they might have drawn from it. Each age and each nation finds itself in such peculiar circumstances, in such a unique situation, that it can and must make decisions with reference to itself alone.'

[10] J. S. Mill, *On Liberty*, in *J. S. Mill's On Liberty in Focus*, ed. John Gray and G. W. Smith (1991), 20: 'Yet so natural to mankind is intolerance in whatever they really care about, that religious freedom has hardly anywhere been practically realized, except where religious

thought simply to show examples of this 'fact' but history does not establish its truth. Rather, it is logic, a more general understanding of consequences, that reveals how men have always solved the problem about how we are, and have ever been, everywhere, non-cooperators, driven by what each of us takes to be individual self-interest and certainly not driven by some elusive and substantive common good. The logical solution to our problematic interpersonal relations is the founding of the body politic or commonwealth. History provides examples but its construction is always a product of logic, not of history. Humans uniquely show themselves to have established *artificial* (not natural) contracts which entail a mutual renunciation of the exercise of their individual, subjective judgements, and on the part of each voluntarist individual, the transference of his right or power to be an authority over himself to a representative third party. Union only in *this* artificial, representative actor or third party is achieved through the consent of every individual in a (non-unified) multitude to transfer his own power to make judgements to it. But the reason for seeking such union is that each individual aims at something else: peace and security, that is, an end to interpersonal conflict.

On this view, the political is conceived as a sovereign *artificial person*. We, however, as individuals, are *natural* and *not artificial*, persons. So the body politic that we construct through Reason is a *representative **persona*** not a *natural **persona***. In it alone is there a concourse of Wills that produces the desired, same *effect*: peace and security. Only in the modern sovereign state itself is there said to be a *union* which uniquely has the power to compel each of us to keep the peace should any of us be so foolish as to believe he can break laws with impunity. This 'modern' project establishes its own teleology: that the European citizen (and the statecraft which gave rise to it) was always implicit in the abstract and has finally come to be realised, indeed actualised, entirely by human Will and by the human capacity for deductive logic that understands consequences. Hence, it sustains a view that this is not simply Europe's history, but universal history although its truth has only recently come to pass, Europe having been the place of its most clear, rapid and rational emergence. To me this is bad history. In fact, as held by self-confessedly modern persons, it is not history at all.[11]

---

indifference, which dislikes to have its peace disturbed by theological quarrels, has added its weight to the scale. In the minds of almost all religious persons, even in the most tolerant countries, the duty of toleration is admitted with tacit reserves'; J. Coleman, *Ancient Greek, Modern and Post-Modern Agonisms: The Possibilities for Democratic Toleration*, the C.Th. Dimaras annual lecture, 2007, Institute for Neo-Hellenic Research, National Hellenic Research Foundation (Athens, 2008).

[11] Those familiar with the writings of Hobbes will recognise this scenario, although it is a truncated version. Indeed, the logical genesis of founding and legislating for commonwealths is not, for him, a 'modern' project, but, rather, is one that has universally been true, everywhere. Its logic does not dictate a type of constitution and can be monarchy (preferred

Those with some interest in and knowledge of European history and who tell this story of the emergence of our 'modern' selves sometimes begin with the fifteenth century as the ideal type of the 'late medieval' as 'forerunner', supposedly in the process of transforming itself into 'the modern'. There was, of course, a fifteenth-century shared range of languages, in law, in theological and social discussions, not least in using and abusing a classical Greek and Roman inheritance of ways of speaking about what politics is, what it is for and how the social is best to be arranged for the kinds of beings humans are presumed to be. But these are *the* questions. And my argument is that these are the questions that endure into 'the modern', allowing us to negotiate the medieval in the modern.

What are/ were we presumed to be? And what is the scope of politics? The answers to these very questions had been contested, certainly during the Middle Ages. The range of socio-political theories with which I am most familiar is heavily invaded by scholastic Catholic theology, which did not, in fact, hold to one view on these matters, most certainly not during the thirteenth and fourteenth centuries. Briefly, I want to demonstrate this. And scholastic Catholicism did not end either with the sixteenth-century Renaissance or Reformation. It did, however, come to be transformed by

---

by Hobbes) or a representative assembly of men, so long as the sovereign speaks with a single speech act. Hobbes, *Leviathan*, I.ix, observed that History is *not* what he calls (Civil) Philosophy. He says that there are two kinds of Knowledge: (1) knowledge of fact and (2) knowledge of consequences of one affirmation to another. Knowledge of consequences he calls 'science' and is *conditional*, being the kind of knowledge required in a philosopher who *reasons*. The register of science are such books as contain demonstrations of consequences of one affirmation to another: either consequences from accidents of natural bodies (natural philosophy); or consequences from the accidents of politic bodies, which is called politics and civil philosophy, i.e. the consequences from the institutions of commonwealths to the rights and duties of the body politic or sovereign; and the consequences from the institution of commonwealths to the duty and rights of subjects. Unlike 'modern' theorists who use Hobbes as a paradigm for the modern sovereign state, Hobbes himself is demonstrating that every first founder and legislator of bodies politic – those of the Gentiles, Jews and early Christians, Greeks Romans – were engaged in understanding the causes from which all men draw universal principles, everywhere, these being the natural fear of the future and ignorance of the causes of such future fears, *Leviathan*, I.xii. On persons natural and artificial, Hobbes, *Leviathan*, I.xvi; on a multitude comprised of individual men made one person, i.e. union, where the unity is in the representative artificial person, *Leviathan*, I.xvi; on the *difference* between Prudence and Reason, where Reason is reckoning, adding and subtracting of the consequences of general names *agreed on* for the marking and signifying of our thoughts, *Leviathan*, I.v. The use and end purpose of Reason is to *begin* with definitions and settled (not subjective) significations of names and proceed from one consequence to another. On Hobbes's view, man is unique in being able to reduce the consequences to general rules or theorems. Further, men reason alike *if* they have good principles. Note, however, that Reason is *not* born with us but is learned, through 'industry', i.e. being taught logical syllogisms; Reason is not got by experience as Prudence is. More will be said on Hobbes below.

the socio-political and theological debates of Reformers and in conflict with them.

Medievalists are familiar with the twelfth-century Cistercian St Bernard of Clairvaux's *De consideratione*[12] in which he spoke of the whole world, and not simply of 'Europe', as a Christian unity under the spiritual and material jurisdiction of the papacy, expressed in the Church's universal, canon law. Perhaps this may be considered, using modern jargon, to be some kind of Christian cosmopolitanism. This Pauline language of world evangelisation and conversion, of Gentiles first and Jews thereafter, did not, of course, begin in the Middle Ages, nor did it end with the Reformation. The shift away from a unified Catholic Christendom was not to some secular characterisation of Europe but, rather, to confessional divides as discrete objects of loyalty wherever one found religiously identifiable communities of practice within defined but ever-changing geographical borders. All such were Christian of one kind or another. The forging of Europe as a recognisable set of concepts over time was continuously undertaken *sub specie aeternitatis* and notably in socio-legal languages penetrated by doctrinal Christianity of one sort or another.

Nietzsche observed something that shocked me when I first came across it. He said that words in European languages were steeped in presumptions about Being. In *Human, All too Human*, he wrote:

> To the extent that man has for long ages believed in the concepts and names of things as in *aeternae veritates* he has appropriated to himself that pride by which he raised himself above the animal: he really thought that in language he possessed knowledge of the world. The sculptor of language was not so modest as to believe that he was only giving things designations; he conceived, rather, that with the words he was expressing supreme knowledge of things.[13]

But a fourteenth-century theologian, William of Ockham, whom we might call a philologist, as was Nietzsche, observed this well before Nietzsche, at least when he came to insist that spoken language was and ever had been *ad placitum*, a conventional means of signifying or referring. Language was *not* a mirror of the inner constitution of nature. Knowledge,

---

[12] Bernard of Clairvaux, *Five Books on Consideration: Advice to a Pope*, trans. J. D. Anderson and E. T. Kennan, Cistercian Fathers Series, 37 (Kalamazoo, 1976), esp. Book Three, 82.

[13] F. W. Nietzsche, *Human, All too Human*, trans. R. J. Hollingdale (Cambridge, 1996), 16. But see F. W. Nietzsche, *Twilight of the Idols and the Anti-Christ*, trans. R. J. Hollingdale (Harmondsworth, 1968), 48: 'Change, mutation, becoming in general were formerly taken as proof of appearance, as the sign of something which led us astray. Today, on the contrary, we see ourselves as it were entangled in error, necessitated to error, to precisely the extent that our prejudice in favor of reason compels us to posit unity, identity, duration, substance, cause, materiality, being; however sure we may be, on the basis of a strict reckoning, that error is to be found here ... I fear we are not getting rid of God because we still believe in grammar.'

for Ockham, is about the logical consistency of our propositions and, hence, we are living our lives in a realm of probabilities rather than certainty, beyond our immediate experience of things.[14]

Nietzsche did not, however, presume that the more humble position, as conventional designators, would solve any problems. After all, Europeans having been taught an attitude to their languages, to language itself, to the Word (St John's Gospel) as a reference to some inhering 'Being', had shifted to a view of language as designating or signifying by convention. And when they realised this, they learned to designate and then think themselves confronting enemies who signified differently, thereby ensuring their own presupposed fixity and self-identity. The very idea that language use and its designations were subjective opinions, habituated practices enforced by convention, already had been realised during the Middle Ages. And then the battle began as to whose conventions better approximated to the Truth.

It was military outcomes that determined subsequent, regional social systems and the varieties of Christian dogma practised therein: the sixteenth-century wars of religion and thereafter were based on the principle *cuius regio eius religio* which authorised rulers to establish in their own territories the doctrinal Christianity of their choice. Insofar as Europe is an *historical entity*, I am here suggesting that its historicity is in the *fact* of the on-going internecine spiritual/political warfare, the emergent conflicts between Catholics and Protestants, their mutual post-Tridentine absorption of the positions of their opposites, while nonetheless maintaining *distinct* attitudes to the following agenda, an agenda that was already set and debated during the Middle Ages. This agenda dealt with the following concerns:

What is a community as a *societas*, i.e. as a collective or corporate entity and what is its relation to individual members and their political governance?

What is considered justified/legitimate coercion of individuals on the part of 'state' authorities, and is justified rule to be by law or by force?

---

[14] William of Ockham, *Summae logicae*, ed. G. Gal (St Bonaventure, New York, 1974), *De suppositione impropria*, Pt I c. 77, 237: 'Et ideo multum est considerandum quanto terminus et propositio accipitur de virtute sermonis et quando secundum usum loquentium vel secundum intentionem auctorem et hoc quia vix invenitur aliquod vocabulum quin in diversis locis librorum philosophorum et Sanctorum et auctorum aequivoce accipiatur, et hoc penes aliquem modum aequivocationis. Et ideo volentes accipere semper vocabulum univoce et uno modo frequenter errant circa intentiones auctorum et inquisitionem veritatis, cum fere omnia vocabula aequivoce accipiantur.' Ockham was arguing even in this school textbook on logic that an author's intentions in his text could only be secured by *not* thinking that every term had one single, timeless and univocal meaning. J. Coleman, 'Using, not Owning – Duties, not Rights: The Consequences of Some Franciscan Perspectives on Politics', in *Defenders and Critics of Franciscan Life: Essays in Honor of John V. Fleming*, ed. M. F. Cusato and G. Geltner (Leiden and Boston, MA, 2009), 65–84, at 74.

What perspective should we endorse concerning man's rationality and capacity for disciplined *self*-governance?

When we consider what motivates men to act in one way or another, what is the role of the individual's Will, his desires, and their relation to his Reason?

What is the relation between the individual's good and the common good?

And in tackling this agenda, regional habitudes and conventions developed to determine who was 'in' and who was 'out'.

To oversimplify: the long-enduring debates from within Christianity itself concerned what were taken to be *different* consequences of the Fall and what Christians call 'Original Sin'. It is from the answers to questions on this agenda that I think we can trace the modern European, indeed Euro-American, debate over whether right is prior to the good or the good prior to right, a debate that is still on-going between modern liberals and communitarians.[15] In short, it is my view that those who study the evolution of law and politics from the Middle Ages to modernity need to study the theologies that underpinned them. And if one examines the theologies, one finds two positions that were vigorously debated during the thirteenth and fourteenth centuries precisely by men educated theologically and with remits to advance views on state and church governance. The debate was between those whom I have called neo-Augustinian voluntarists on the one hand, and neo-Aristotelian intellectualists on the other.[16] What was being examined was the source of human motivation to act in one way or another and the degree to which Reason could be expected to trump a contrary Will.

Neo-Augustinians held that we are first and foremost self-lovers, and lovers of the community only secondarily and in consequence of the *utilitas* of the community for beings whose primary love of self defines their fallen *status*.[17] Neo-Aristotelian intellectualists, on the other hand,

[15] J. Coleman, 'Pre-Modern Property and Self-Ownership Before and After Locke: Or, When Did Common Decency Become a Private rather than a Public Virtue?', *European Journal of Political Theory*, 4 (2005), 125–45.

[16] J. Coleman, 'Are There Any Individual Rights or Only Duties? On the Limits of Obedience in the Avoidance of Sin According to Late Medieval and Early Modern Scholars', in *Transformations in Medieval and Early-Modern Rights Discourse*, ed. V. Makinen and P. Korkman (Dordrecht, 2006), 3–36; M. Kempshall, *The Common Good in Late Medieval Political Thought* (Oxford, 1999).

[17] Henry of Ghent, *Quodlibeta magistra Henrici Goethals a Gandavo* (2 vols., Paris,1518; repr. Leuven, 1961); *Henrici de Gandavo Opera omnia*, ed. R. Macken (Leuven, 1979); Kempshall, *Common Good*, 161, 171–3; James of Viterbo, *De regimine christiano*, in *James of Viterbo: On Christian Government*, trans. R. Dyson (Woodbridge, 1995), 151; *The Cambridge Translations of Medieval Philosophical Texts*, II: *Ethics and political philosophy*, ed. A. S. McGrade, J. Kilcullen and M.

argued that naturally we love the community and neighbours *before* the love of self so that the common good always takes priority over the good of the individual which, in fact, derives from it.[18] My focus hereafter will be on some of the positions of neo-Augustinians because they reintegrated Augustine into their theories of knowledge to lasting effect. It is their views, not least on what after the Fall we are able to know, and how we know what we know, that came to exert a huge influence on the European future and its 'modernity'.

Fourteenth-century Franciscans like Duns Scotus[19] and William of Ockham[20] were concerned to sever the association of God and Necessity in order to replace a contemporary radical Aristotelian interpretation of a determined universe with a realm of contingency. Man could then understand God as free-willing in a realm of what was called His *potentia absoluta*, where His freedom was not limited by His commitments to the world as it now is, established *de potentia ordinata*. Our world as contingent led to an affirmation that God had committed Himself to this world rather than to possible other worlds, so that man was to look upon his world as issuing from a contract, a *pactum Dei*. But this was a very special kind of contract, and Hobbes would later correctly recognise it as covenant. According to fourteenth-century neo-Augustinians, the contingency of the world does not make it unreliable; but its creation and man's salvation were simply not to be viewed as ontologically necessary, so that God's free Will could remain in absolute freedom.

Already in the early fourteenth century we have the Franciscan theologian Duns Scotus asserting that after the Fall the natural law had been suspended,[21] and, hence, we no longer have access to its principles naturally, innately and intuitively to guide our behaviour, by which he meant that the philosophical order of rationality gives us no access to the other order of rationality, that of God and His absolute Will; that our rational capacities are now limited to a kind of non-judgemental, intuitive

Kempshall (Cambridge, 2001) (Kempshall trans.), 297; for specific *quodlibet* and other full references see Coleman, 'Are There Any Individual Rights', 13–24.

[18] Coleman, 'Are There Any Individual Rights', 11; Thomas Aquinas, *Summa theologiae*, ed. Leonina (Rome, 1888–1906), vols. IV–XII, at Ia 2ae, Q.90, a.4; Ia 2ae Q.94, a.5, ad 3; Coleman, *Ancient and Medieval Memories*, ch. 19, on Albert the Great, 416–21; and ch. 20 on Thomas Aquinas, 422–60; Coleman, *A History of Political Thought from the Middle Ages to the Renaissance*, ch. 2 on Thomas Aquinas, 81–117.

[19] Coleman, *Ancient and Medieval Memories*, on Scotus, 465–99.

[20] *Ibid.*, on Ockham, 500–37; Coleman, *A History of Political Thought, from the Middle Ages to the Renaissance*, on Ockham, 169–98.

[21] This post-lapsarian suspension of natural law meant that the once self-evident and immutable principle, *de iure naturae*, that of the communion of goods for common use, was revoked. Scotus, *Ordinatio*, IV d.15 q.2 n.3: 'istud praeceptum legis naturae de habendo omnia communia revocatum est post lapsum'. For a fuller discussion with citations and texts, see Coleman, 'Using, not Owning – Duties, not Rights', 65–84.

awareness of existents as here and now and this simply allows us to doubt something or be aware of thinking something. But this intuition does not give us knowledge of the individual in its singularity *ut hoc*. We do not now have the power to grasp individuating difference. Instead, the first object of our cognition is confused and indistinct, what Scotus called a 'species' above the individual and this is achieved by abstractive cognition which knows the *nature* of the individual but not its individuating difference; what *is* known distinctly by the intellect is the *concept* of the individual's being, its *haecceitas*, its more 'universal' 'thisness', and this is the intellect's own object as a *representation* of the individual. Mind now works through symbolic expressions *representing* the quiddity of the object, referring to the *intelligible* aspect, the essential, formal characteristics of things. What is emphasised is that the 'thisness' of a thing is not determined by its im-mattered existence; and against intellectualists like Aquinas, Scotus argued that man's intellection was not limited to concepts that were abstracted from sense experience, because if this were the case, we could not have the face-to-face vision of God that is promised to man in the afterlife. But for God's immediate presence to be an object of our intellection, this must be a result of *His free act, His* Will to be present to any created intellect in all the proper and essential meaning of divinity to be known intuitively. We cannot achieve this on our own in our present condition.

Scotus is concerned to underline the distinction between Nature and Will, between an unconscious biological determinism on the one hand, and conscious choice on the other. He is also concerned to argue that our intellect can be conceived as being separate from the material world as perceived by the senses. And in so doing, he opens up a realm of plausible mental fictions, a realm of mental possibilities divorced from empirical certainties. Furthermore, all that experience does for us is confirm the cognitive possibilities that are open to the human intellect concerning what God's Will does creatively. But there is no unconditional necessity in the natural world. Hence, a demonstrative deductive science – that of logic – must only be concerned with the *possible* in a world of contingents. We must *presume* that Nature functions in a regular manner, determined by a formal linking of causes up to God's Will. The finite created world is knowable to us only through the mediation of form and abstractively, and any created intellect now can reach *finite being* by virtue of causes which naturally move it, but, again, any individual finite being is *not* grasped *ut hoc* but rather by the *quiddity* of material things.

What has happened to the belief that the image of God is somehow in us and is what is best in our nature, even though fallen? Scotus insists that perfect intellection depends on *the divine exemplars* and cannot exist without the Word being there, *if* we have heard it. Drawing on Augustine, this means that *once evangelised*, the Word is somehow lodged in our memories.[22] Citing Augustine, he insists that we attribute to the memory everything that we know and it is *our will to remember* that causes a more perfect understanding especially of things spiritual. Scotus must affirm that man's end is salvation, an immediate union with God through an intuitive vision of God's essence, but unlike the intellectualists, it is not sufficient to say that through a rational contemplation of God by means of sensibles alone, man can achieve his end. Philosophical Reason is limited; it falls into the error of believing that there are rational means of attaining salvation and the vision of God. This would give no place to the *necessity* of God's *freely willed initiative* in man's salvation. It is the divine initiative that constitutes the radically contingent acceptance of man. Through God's free initiative to offer grace we see how this may allow a rational creature consciously to turn towards his final end, through an act of now enlightened Reason whereby Truth, the *summum bonum*, is willed for itself. What is occurring when a man as creature receives the free initiative of grace and wills to turn to God as the sovereign good is the *implementing* of a commandment, which is itself a duty to love God more than anything else. Although we possess a rational and natural love of God, and from which issues moral order, beyond that moral order is a radical divine initiative *ad extra*.

If our Reason is now so limited, then what were the consequences for our liberty to control our choices to act well or ill? If there is no rule, not even the Ten Commandments, to which right reason need conform in order to obtain the radical divine initiative, salvation, then could our free will, on its own, and unaided, as it were, voluntarily choose faith and to love God? But this itself could *not* be sufficient because Scotus sketches a radical distinction, indeed distance, between God's infinite, absolute, initiating Will and that of man. Absolutely, *God's Will cannot be held to any obligation to us*. Our condition here and now is one where neither God nor Nature is 'legible' merely through our own efforts.

William of Ockham, another Franciscan theologian who similarly sought to establish the radical liberty and autonomy of God, went further than Scotus to insist that cognitively we only have access to concrete existents, and that everything exists only in its own singularity.[23] This

---

[22] J. Coleman, *A History of Political Thought from Ancient Greece to Early Christianity* (Oxford, 2000), ch. 6, on St Augustine, 292–340; Coleman, *Ancient and Medieval Memories*, chs. 6 and 7, on Augustine, 80–111; J. Coleman, 'The Philosophy of Law in the Writings of Augustine', in *A History of the Philosophy of Law from the Ancient Greeks to the Scholastics*, ed. F. D. Miller, Jr, and C. Biondi (Dordrecht, 2007), 187–218.

[23] For one of the best discussions of Ockham's positions, see M. McCord Adams, 'William of Ockham: Voluntarist or Naturalist', in *Studies in Medieval Philosophy*, ed. J. F. Wippel (Washington, DC, 1987), 219–48. Henry of Ghent, Peter John Olivi, Duns Scotus and Ockham all wanted to establish how the human mind, now, can arrive at truth and certain knowledge without some direct, divine illumination that some thought was the meaning of

turns every universal, everything conceptualised *as* a collectivity, into nothing more than a name or grammatical term *signifying* the individuals within the collectivity, the collective having no *real* existence, it being only a name for singular existents of which it is comprised. This is what is called his nominalism. Furthermore, *relations between* individuals have *no reality*. There 'is' then, no common nature, which equates to there 'is' no common human nature. There are only singulars, individuals and our philosophical or logical Reason has no capacity to assert, with certainty, a common *telos* or common good. There is neither a common nature nor a universal as a direct object of our intelligence. Human intelligence, as created but now fallen, cannot be so perfect as to judge and understand with absolute certainty. Our intellect, now, has no innate knowing and therefore no *immediate* knowledge of Truth and therefore, of God. We are left with a capacity to suppose, logically, the *hypothetical* existence of a subject; we cognitively depend on sensible, exterior things that we perceive and experience, and we reason based on our experiences in the circumstances. We know moral precepts either as (logical) self-evident principles, *per se nota*, i.e. avoid evil, or we know them from and in experience: deductively, we reach conclusions as to further moral precepts, thereby discerning right from wrong in the circumstances. This moral knowing is *not* from authority. It comes from every individual having an intuitive notion that he is by nature free and by this Ockham means that each experiences a Will to do or not do what is rational. We possess as individuals a *libertas* and we know of it only by experience. We do have a natural liberty and Reason is central to its exercise. But Ockham separates *recta ratio*, a judgement of Reason, from what happens when we will, because he says that everyone from his own experiences can observe how he can and does will what is bad against precepts of Reason. Politically this has consequences: what we know we owe to others, what our moral obligations are, objectively, we also know from experience that we do *not* infallibly and necessarily will to do or perform.[24]

Augustine's texts, especially his *De Trinitate*, VIII, on whether we have direct knowledge of God through a particular intervention of divine truth. In Olivi's *Quaestiones in secundum librum Sententiarum*, III, ed. B. Jansen (Quaracchi, 1926), Appendix: *Quaestiones de Deo cognoscendo*, 455–554, he insisted that we establish epistemologically what it is possible for us to know, and how, now, *in statu isto*. Ockham rejected a literal interpretation of Augustine and instead argued that while God *is the principle* of our knowledge, He *is not the object* of that knowledge, now.

[24] Coleman, 'Using, not Owning – Duties, not Rights', 76–80; Ockham, Quodlibet, II, q. 14, in *Quodlibeta septem in Venerabilis Inceptoris Guillelmi de Ockham Opera philosophica et theologica ad fidem codicum manuscriptorum edita*, ed. P. Boehner, G. Gal, S. F. Brown *et al.* (17 vols., St Bonaventure, New York, 1974–88), the Quodlibeta in *ibid.* IX, 176–8; Ockham, *Opus nonaginta dierum*, ch. 14, in *Guillelmi de Ockham Opera politica*, ed. J. G. Sikes and H. S. Offler (Manchester, 1963), II, 435: on *recta ratio, ex dictamine rationis naturalis convincitur*; Ockham, *Dialogus*, the revised text, in H. S. Offler, 'The Three Modes of Natural Law in Ockham: A Revision of the Text',

Augustine plays a central role in the shaping of all of these arguments. Especially during the fourteenth century there was a huge effort to reexamine the texts of St Augustine. His texts helped fuel the debates just described, between intellectualists and voluntarists, not least in the voluntarists taking the view that the consequences of the Fall left our Reason insufficient to control the experienced exercise of our contrary Wills. *Contrary Wills*, the clear evidence of there being contumacious persons who would not be guided by Reason or authority, penetrated the theory and practice of procedures and justifications for *inclusion and exclusion* in the community, notably in excommunication, and in church inquisitorial trials mirrored in 'state' and city courts. It reflects pre-modern social mentalities and attitudes to the criteria that determined social inclusion and exclusion. Over the centuries, it raises issues of *intolerance and tolerance* concerning external behaviour in the *foro externo*, and by the sixteenth century, it has been shown that interior dispositions in the *foro interno* were to be 'read off' of external behaviour, including speech. As a consequence, the respective roles of both church and public authorities in maintaining communal discipline, peace and order became high priorities not only in discourse but in legal stipulation and enforcement. This reveals an evolving tradition of European discourses on the ways in which, depending on one's status in a hierarchy of citizenship, one was to be held responsible before the community for maintaining one's *fama*, i.e. one's public self or reputation in good order, in both Catholic *and* Protestant regions. This took the form of procedures for correcting one's sins for the public good, e.g. defamation by public rumour of individuals judged contumacious, either by communities *or* by representative authorities in their name.[25] Increasingly, what was considered 'the public good' was peace and security of the whole. How anyone might negotiate the private quality of his life was not a matter of politics but of private conscience, an intensely internal, personal and unmediated dialogue between his Maker and his private self that escaped juridical scrutiny. The problem, however, came to be acknowledged that so much of one's 'private' self was held to spill out, evidently, into the *foro externo*, being ripe for scrutiny as an expressed, usually disruptive, Will, that the private self's 'true' intentions could only and uniquely fully be known subjectively by oneself – and God.[26]

Franciscan Studies, 37 (1977), 207–18; Wilhelm von Ockham, Dialogus, German trans. and commentary J. Miethke (Darmstadt, 1992), III, Dialogus 2.1.15 on natural precepts.

[25] J. Coleman, 'Scholastic Treatments of Maintaining One's *Fama* (Reputation/Good Name) and the Correction of Private "Passions" for the Public Good and Public Legitimacy', *Cultural and Social History*, 2 (2005), 23–48.

[26] J. Locke, *An Essay concerning Human Understanding*, ed. P. H. Nidditch (Oxford, 1975), 2.25 and 2.27; Coleman, 'Pre-Modern Property and Self-Ownership', 135–6. Hobbes's version of this 'private conscience' is revealed as dealing with what has not yet come under the

In contrast, what one might call the earlier medieval conception of the self was a normative self. But it was not self-defining, subjective or unique. Rather, it was thought that the self's normativity had already been defined by God in whose image man was made and the self's responsibility for self-discipline or governance was through the deployment of right reason, *recta ratio*, available to *all* humans and in the *same* way. Hence, there were said to be powers given to each and every member of the species for exercise by individuals as self-governors in their living a morally constrained life. Moral rules were *a priori* obliging and to which men had access through rational comprehension of the natural law, supplemented by the divine law of the Decalogue. During the seventeenth and eighteenth centuries both Catholic and Protestant natural law theorists reveal that there still remained a confrontation between protagonists of a variety of recognisably scholastic and ancient ideas of morality and values as naturally *a priori* inherent in the structure of the world, and of God's providential ordering of human ethical normativity, accessible in *some way or other* to human Reason.

What this implied was that whatever was to be understood by humans having moral rights emerged from their prior grasp that there are natural duties to be fulfilled. These duties do not depend on the existence of particular personal or institutional ties based on convention, local contracts, themselves based on voluntary, local consent between a rights-holder and a duty-bearer. Natural duties to others of our kind are, on this view, said to go well beyond the duties of citizenship and derive from valid claims of need, requiring our acknowledgement, everywhere, of having natural duties of mutual assistance to the species. But the issue that was debated, especially from the fourteenth-century scholastics onwards, was not only *how* such duties come to be known by us but *whether* we can in fact voluntarily will to perform them even if they are known. If, as some held, following Augustine, God's wishes concerning the constitutional and legal specifics of the political may no longer be inferred by us, then the political is *not* some sacred ordering according to our knowledge of God's Will because we have no such knowledge. What politics actually is, is simply what we or our governors deem useful in the circumstances. The consequence is that moral rights cannot be thought to be substantively stable over time concerning what one must or must not do, other than: be obedient to sovereign rules, whatever they are, for peace and security. If, on this view, using *only* our natural faculties, we have no access to prior objective justice, and cannot implement a *lex* securely to ensure that our own willed acts with others of our kind will be obeyed in reciprocity, then the logic of understanding consequences gives us no option other than

consideration of the sovereign; otherwise, individuals must accept their own judgements as irrelevant.

to set up politics in a very distinctive way. Calvin in his Geneva made it quite clear what this was: natural law morality can only be accessed from grace and faith and not by Reason. For him it was *only* Christians under Christian political governance of the kind he instituted who could be positively induced to live according to the Ten Commandments.[27] What some had thought to be *praecepta certa*, certainly known precepts of natural law available to everyone and everywhere, and, hence, capable of implementation, were to be replaced by positive law and convention.

In his recent lecture on Cromwell and the protectorate, Blair Worden observed that the mistrust of Cromwell was largely inspired by his deployment of the beliefs and language of Puritanism for political ends.[28] Only recently, seventeenth-century historians have become more interested in the content of his religion, rejecting an earlier historical perspective that religion was simply the seventeenth-century's way of talking about something else, i.e. economics, political aspirations.[29] Worden is correct in saying that Cromwell's religion never turned away from the world it sought to transform. But from the Middle Ages onwards, religion never did turn away from the world it sought to transform. That there was always a religious dimension to political debates, admonitions against betraying the divine spirit, that politics was about not being blind to God's purposes, and the ways in which political calculation could be seen as congruent with the divine Will was at the heart of European Protestantism and the central place it held in Cromwell's 'heart'. Cromwell's programme of religious and moral reform at home was meant to create a commonwealth fit for God's eyes and to avert divine wrath.[30] Something was seen to be amiss in church and state, and to be rectified; lawyers and antiquarians went back to explore medieval parliamentary history to find forerunners and precedents for a vision of parliament as a great council of the realm and with ultimate authority, especially concerning where emergency powers legitimately lay. From whatever political 'side' preferring what they took to be either the ancient constitution or a republic, everyone knew that God permits mankind to alter the forms of rule for reasons of prudence and circumstance. Politics was up to us. Worden demonstrates that the debates concerned the site of authority (i.e. parliament), and were intended to counter the view that force or soldiers constituted legitimate authority. Parliament rules by law and not by the sword, whether the constitution be a monarchy resting

---

[27] M. Garcia-Alonso, 'Biblical Law as the Source of Morality in Calvin', *History of Political Thought*, 32 (2011), 1–20.

[28] B. Worden, 'Oliver Cromwell and the Protectorate', *Transactions of the Royal Historical Society*, sixth series, 20 (2010), 57–83.

[29] *Ibid.*, 59.

[30] *Ibid.*, 60.

on public consent, or a mixed government, similarly resting on public consent. No sword-government but law-government[31] with the sword backing the law for the non-compliant.

Enter Hobbes. When he developed what he thought was his original theory of political association in his *Elements of law*[32] and *De cive*,[33] he insisted that he was presenting something contrary to what he said the books penned by university dogmatics had proposed, because their views were incompatible with peace and security as the aims of government. For him, the *body politic* can *only signify* a situation in which the Wills of many concur and this *only to some one and same action, effect or consequence*.[34] This is not the same thing as saying that men do not continue to have conflicting ideas because they *will* be divided *after* they agree on the best way of coming together for security. For Hobbes, the natural causes of conflict, interpersonal envy and rivalry remain, so that men will not be willing to help each other or keep the peace unless they are compelled to do so by a common *fear*.[35] What, according to Hobbes, the old dogmatics had claimed to be a *societas* that was formed only for mutual aid does not, then, afford the parties of this association what they really and ultimately desire: security in their interpersonal relations. Something more needs to be done to prevent discord amongst individuals and what they take to be their private goods that override security. Politics, then, is about everyone directing their own actions to the same end, a *summum bonum* understood simply as the common peace, and this requires a *renunciation* of the *exercise* of private Will and desire, and judgements issuing from these. And this can only come about through the construction of a single Will concerning matters of peace and defence. To set up this single Will each must subject his own private Will to the Will of a single *representative* 'other' be it one man or an assembly. This general submission or subjection is called *union*. The *body politic* is not then simply equated to a summing of each citizen's Will in the creation of a *civitas* or commonwealth. Rather, the *body politic* is a *consequence* of many concurring about *one and the same effect*, and when unified is to be conceived as one *artificial, representative* **persona** whose Will, by agreement of several men, is taken to be the Will of them all.

---

[31] *Ibid.*, 83.

[32] T. Hobbes, *The Elements of Law Natural and Politic*, ed. F. Tonnies, 2nd edn (1969), II.8.5.

[33] T. Hobbes, *De cive*, Latin text (Paris, 1642); *De cive, the Latin Version*, ed. H. Warrender (Oxford, 1983).

[34] Hobbes, *Elements of Law*, II.8.7: 'The error concerning mixed government hath proceeded from want of understanding of what is meant by this word *body politic*, and how it signifieth not the concord, but the union of many men.' *Ibid.*, I.12.7, 8: 'when the wills of many concur to some one and the same action, or effect, this concourse of their wills is called consent; by which we must not understand one will of many men, for every man hath his several will; but many wills to the producing of one effect ... many wills in one or more [is] called union'.

[35] Hobbes, *De cive*, V.4.

I have written about how this replays only one of the two relevant corporation theories developed during the Middle Ages.[36] It is the nominalist theory that insists that collectives or corporations are *not* natural existents but are, rather, grammatical terms *signifying* something that does not itself have its own natural Will to engage in action. Instead, it is our concept, what Hobbes calls a mortal god that we set up, which draws its powers to act and to judge *from* the natural individuals who have *transferred the exercise of their own powers* to this artificial entity as a third, representative party that unites the Wills of all *only* in itself.

Similarly, for Ockham, public authority, the office of a sovereign ruler, is a legal *concept or* **persona**, created by a corporation of individuals who only come to be *a unified* collection of real persons *when represented* by something that is itself *not real* but is, rather, a *persona ficta, imaginaria et repraesentata.*[37] Fictive entities on their own cannot perform real acts or possess legal rights under law. It is only real, autonomous, rational individuals who are capable of renouncing or holding legal rights. Public authority must unify the wills of natural persons and have their powers or rights of exercise from the *populus* – a term signifying a collection of rational individual agents who unanimously constitute government.[38] Government then acts for the public utility, determining what is expedient in the circumstances. Ockham argued that a man is praised for what he wills rather than for what he understands, since man's cognitive acts are natural, but his power to perform or not, his power to act on what he knows, is what is to be judged. Ockham is, then, what I have called a rational voluntarist, in that he is not sceptical about human knowing but about our willing what we know.[39] Since no *individual's* Will can be represented, and since a collective Will is not a real thing, then it is not that an individual is alienating his moral autonomy and responsibility to some other individual, as neighbour. Instead, political authority is something else and once established certainly could be 'absolutist'. Ockham means by this that there need not be any regular participation of the people once sovereign public authority or government is established, nor need there be institutions to restrain the power of sovereign government that has been constituted by a unanimous consent of all rational individuals. Once established, it will be the circumstances that will dictate whether

---

[36] Coleman, *A History of Political Thought from the Middle Ages to the Renaissance*, 47, and throughout concerning the different ways of interpreting 'corporation' and the 'corporate will' on the part of authors including Aquinas, John of Paris, Marsilius of Padua, Ockham and these diverse positions compared with radical early modern constitutionalism, 166–8, 180.

[37] *Guillelmi de Ockham Opera politica*, ed. H. S. Offler (Manchester, 1956), III: *Tractatus contra Benedictum*, 189–91.

[38] Ockham, III, *Dialogus*, 2.2.27 and 2.1.16.

[39] Coleman, *A History of Political Thought from the Middle Ages to the Renaissance*, 190.

or not sovereign government acts according to its own positive laws that preserve public safety. The Fall has ensured that men conclude that they need to live under positive law because it is evident now that we are incapable of ruling ourselves by Reason. Ockham argued in his *Dialogus* that men know from experience that they are now inclined to conflict and to seeking their own interests, and precisely because they come to know this, not least from observing their contrary Wills, it is *they* who *conceive* the sovereign as an exit from such conditions.[40]

In Hobbes's version of this, we ask: what is left to the individual who thus transfers his power of judging others to an entity that now commands and requires obedience? His answer: a private conscience that only can be exercised in the public domain when the artificial *persona* has not spoken, made law or commanded, a position that is surely the same for the fourteenth-century voluntarist, neo-Augustinian, nominalist Ockham.

Conclusion

International relations has taken as its paradigm what is called 'realism'. Hence, I was particularly interested to find political realism to be engaging political theorists more generally in a recent special issue of the *European Journal of Political Theory*.[41] Some notable observations are made in the Introduction by Richard North about the several contributions published therein. The first is that liberal political philosophy *is* the philosophy of our times, although just whose liberalism is being endorsed – Rawls's, Dworkin's, Habermas's, Kant's – leads to confusions. Although liberalism has received criticism from communitarians, what is presented in this issue is a criticism of liberalism from a variety of political realisms. One of the major realist critiques (Glen Newey) proposes that justice is not the only consideration relevant to politics and, indeed, is not the first virtue of social institutions. Further, that there is no compelling reason to believe that morality trumps other kinds of reason of action. Instead, *if* we recognise that political authority, on the one hand, and morality, on the other, are *disparate* sources of normativity, rather than taking morality as fixed and politics as negotiable, then we can, it is asserted, have a more realistic practical political theory. Take as a 'fact' some 'cooperative' existence but put morality's standpoint and content as variable. Then we are told that political realism can appreciate the historical contexts in which political decision-making and action take place without reducing the study of politics to history (Philp). Politics, then, for realists is not overly concerned with justice, or morality, or indeed history. On this view,

---

[40] Coleman, 'Using, not Owning – Duties, not Rights', 76–83; Ockham, *Opus nonaginta dierum*, in *Guillelmi de Ockham Opera politica*, II, chs. 26–8, 88, 93.
[41] *European Journal of Political Theory*, 9.4 (2010) Special Issue: *Realism and Political Theory*, Richard North, Introduction, 381–4.

politics is largely about a focus on the conditions of peace and security, with a maintenance of social order that is somehow sufficient to enable the living of a minimally worthwhile life (Horton). So the thrust of much realism comes down to a desire, the need, to recognise the priority of politics over ethics, with politics defined as focusing exclusively on the conditions of peace and security.

North rightly asks: is this realism only another form of liberalism, of a Hobbesian or Lockeian variety? It focuses on preventing public harms rather than on realising moral goods. Politics on this view is nothing other than the securing of peace, security, stability and is not some Kantian (or other) moralised notion of autonomy.

How 'new' is this so-called modern and new, realistic, thinking? That it can be asserted that early modern thinkers, who can be called realists, broke with the ancients – as though the ancients spoke with one voice, which of course they did not – indicates an unfamiliarity even with the Master of the Modern: Hobbes. I have tried to indicate that Hobbes reflected on and used both Greek and Roman sources and especially the positions of medieval neo-Augustinian nominalists. And he argued against 'the other side', the Aristotelian 'intellectualists'. I have tried to indicate that there was already at the heart of medieval scholasticism of the neo-Augustinian kind a tendency to present a voluntarist, conflictual model of interpersonal relations; there is no doubt that other scholastics followed the Aristotelian intellectualist tradition, well into the nineteenth century and beyond. But it was because of the medieval neo-Augustinian answer to the question regarding what we may presume ourselves to be, that politics as a solution to our fallen status and problem came to be viewed as primarily about peace and security. Politics was not, for them, about any stable, moralised notion of actualised, individual autonomy. I suggest that modern political realism is a secularised version of one long-enduring interpretation of the consequences of Original Sin. Modern political realists, unbeknownst to them, are the heirs to medieval scholastic neo-Augustinianisms. They are negotiating the medieval in the modern.

Transactions of the RHS 22 (2012), pp. 95–110 © Royal Historical Society 2012
doi:10.1017/S0080440112000084

PEOPLE OF THE COVENANT AND THE ENGLISH BIBLE

By Naomi Tadmor*

READ 17 JUNE 2011 AT LANCASTER UNIVERSITY

ABSTRACT. The paper shows how the important theological and Anglo-biblical term 'Covenant' was formulated in the course of successive biblical translations, from the original Hebrew and Greek to the King Kames Bible. It suggests that the use of the term in English biblical versions reflected – and in turn propelled – the increasingly prominent Covenant theology. Once coined in the vernacular Scriptures, moreover, the term was applied to religious political alliances: from the Scottish Covenants of the 1590s to the English Solemn League and Covenant, 1644, studied in the paper.

On 5 February 1643/4, the English parliament assembled in Westminster and ordered a special oath to be 'solemnly taken'.[1] The 'Solemn League and Covenant', ratified by the Scottish Convention of Estates, and partially enacted in England since the autumn of 1643, was now to be enforced throughout the realm. The entire mechanism of the English state was to be put into action to facilitate the making of the oath.[2] Within six days, 'true Copies' of the document were to reach the provinces. Local committees were to receive them in the counties and the boroughs, and to dispatch them to the parishes. Each minister, churchwarden and constable within each and every parish was to be delivered a copy in person; a certificate was devised to attest for the receipt, and a clerk appointed in London to collect the records flowing from the provinces. At the next stage, all clergymen were required to read the 'said Covenant publikely', in their local churches and chapels, and prepare their congregations for

---

* I am very grateful to Mordechai Cogan, Colin Kidd, David Smith and Nili Wazana for their generous reading of the draft.

[1] 'Covenant to be taken throughout England and Wales', see 'February 1644: An Ordinance, enjoyning the taking of the late Solemn League and Covenant, throughout the Kingdom of England and Dominion of Wales', *Acts and Ordinances of the Inter-regnum, 1642–1660* (1911), 376–8. www.british-history.ac.uk/report.aspx?compid=55913& strquery=covenant accessed May 2011.

[2] For the relation between the centre and localities, see esp. e.g. A. Fletcher, *Reform in the Provinces: The Government of Stuart England* (New Haven and 1986); M. Braddick, *State Formation in Early Modern England* (Cambridge, 2000); S. Hindle, *The State and Social Change in Early Modern England, 1550–1640* (Basingstoke, 2000).

making the oath by the following Sunday. In the next days, the clergymen and local officers themselves were to travel to provincial centres and subscribe to the oath there, following which they were to return and complete the arrangements. On the designated Sunday, all men 'above the age of eighteen' were to assemble in the local church or chapel, including not only settled inhabitants but lodgers who happened to be in the place. A special sermon was to be delivered, and the full text of the Covenant was to be read 'distinctly and audibly' from the pulpit. During the entire time that the Covenant was read, the men were to stand on their feet, 'uncovered' (that is, their hats humbly removed), until the time came for them to pronounce the crucial words. Then, they were to lift their right hand – bare, with no glove to shield the flesh from God's sight and from one's neighbour's gaze. Having declared the oath, they were to subscribe to it, whether by 'writing their names' on a roll or in a book, or by placing 'their marks, to which their names were to be added'. Parishes were to deposit the written records for safekeeping, as they kept other important deeds and bonds. At the same time, they were to report in writing the names of those who refused to subscribe.

As Edward Vallance explained in 2001, this English 'Solemn League and Covenant' was much more than a marriage of convenience with the Scots during a time of trouble.[3] While the 'Covenant' rolls, still kept in archives, attest to the extent to which the order was carried out, personal records suggest that it was extremely seriously undertaken. The contractual individual obligation was binding. Breaking the oath was perjury.[4] The bond postulated a formal boundary around the community of faith, as well as the body politic, still couched at that stage firmly in terms of loyalty to the king. This was, moreover, a matter of confessional identity: a Protestant notion of Christendom was embedded in the very formulation of the oath, while copies were immediately dispatched to Protestant churches worldwide.[5] The alignment with the Scots swung the war in favour of parliament and against the king. From the religious perspective, it propelled the confessional landslide that marked the Godly revolt. The political and religious dimensions of the Solemn League and Covenant are widely studied. What were the broader cultural and ideological resonances, however, that helped it to achieve such purchase? This article investigates the provenance of these important notions.

---

[3] E. Vallance, '"An Holy and Sacramental Paction: Federal Theology and the Solemn League and Covenant in England', *English Historical Review*, 116 (2001), 50–75, and esp. 50; see also e.g. *The Scottish National Covenant in its British Context*, ed. J. S. Morrill (Edinburgh, 1990), and e.g. M. J. Braddick, *God's Fury, England's Fire: A New History of the English Civil Wars* (2008), esp. ch. 10.

[4] Vallance, 'The Solemn League and Covenant', esp. 72–4.

[5] *Ibid.*, 69.

One immediate context to mention is the preceding Scottish National Covenant (culminating in the Bishops' Wars, 1639–40) in which several strands had come together: objection to the religious policies of Charles I, defence against the English intruder, millenarian notions, as well as a strong notion of a special pact between 'God and his people in the Covenant of Grace' in Scotland, then in England.[6] Not less important was the notion of 'covenant' in the contemporary theology. Lexical evidence suggests its enhanced development from the first decades of the sixteenth century through the latter decades, and its propagation thereafter.[7] The first explicit formulation of a pre-fall 'covenant of works' dates to 1585.[8] The covenant theology then swiftly made its way in broadly disseminated tracts, such as catechisms, as Ian Green has shown.[9] By the 1640s, it had achieved prominence to the point that it was incorporated into the official Westminster Confession.[10] Yet another, and at that time closely related, idea concerns banding. The use of oaths to cement allegiances between peoples and leaders is both ancient and widespread; however, under the influence of the covenant theology it came to acquire a new revolutionary thrust.[11] On the Scottish side, the 'Covenant' was perceived as a renewal

---

[6] I. Green, *The Christian's ABC: Catechisms and Catechizing in England c. 1530–1740* (Oxford, 1996), 459. See also esp. S. A. Burrell, 'The Covenant Idea as a Revolutionary Symbol: Scotland, 1596–1637', *Church History*, 27 (1958), 338–50; C. L. Hamilton, 'The Basis for Scottish Efforts to Create a Reformed Church in England, 1640–41', *Church History*, 30 (1961), 171–8; S. A. Burrell, 'The Apocalyptic Vision of the Early Covenanters', *Scottish Historical Review*, 93 (1964), 1–24; J. B. Torrance, 'Covenant or Contract: A Study of the Theological Background of Worship in Seventeenth-Century Scotland', *Scottish Journal of Theology*, 23 (1970), 51–76; M. Steele, 'The "Politick Christian": The Theological Background to the National Covenant', in *The Scottish National Covenant*, ed. Morrill; J. D. Ford, 'The Lawful Bonds of Scottish Society: The Five Articles of Perth, the Negative Confession, and the National Covenant', *Historical Journal*, 37:1 (1994), 45–64, esp. 64.

[7] See in particular D. A. Weir, *The Origins of the Federal Theology in Sixteenth-Century Reformation Thought* (Oxford, 1990), esp. chs. 1, 4, 5.

[8] R. Letham, *The Westminster Assembly: Reading its Theology in Historical Context* (Pittsburgh, 2001), 112. Early reformed theologians such as Bucer, Musculus and Bullinger extensively considered Adam, yet not in terms of 'covenant' (perhaps owing to the absence of a literal mention of a covenant with Adam in Genesis). The theology of William Perkins (d. 1602) was influential in England in seeing Adam as bound by 'covenant' and representative of humankind, e.g.: 'he was the Father of vs all: and was not a pri|uate man as wee are now, but a publike person . . . what couenant God made with him, was made for him|self & vs': M. W. Perkins, *A Faithfull and Plaine Exposition vpon the 2. Chapter of Zephaniah by that Reuerend and Iudicious Diuine, M.W. Perkins. Containing a Powerfull Exhortation to Repentance: As Also the Manner hovve Men in Repentance Are to Search Themselues* (1609), p. 36; Green, *The Christian's ABC*, esp. 403–11.

[9] Green, *The Christian's ABC*, 403–5, *passim*; Vallance, 'The Solemn League and Covenant', 57.

[10] See esp. Letham, *The Westminster Assembly*, ch. 7.

[11] Green, *The Christian's ABC*, esp. 409, 459–60; Burrell, 'Covenant Idea'; J. B. Torrance, 'The Covenant Concept in Scottish Theology and Politics and its Legacy', *Scottish Journal of Theology*, 34 (1981), 225–43; Steele, 'The "Politick Christian"'; M. McGiffert, 'Covenant,

of earlier bonds made in 1572, 1581, 1590 and 1596;[12] from 1590, the term 'covenant' was explicitly employed in describing the renewed religious and political allegiance.[13] On the English side, the Solemn League and Covenant was heralded by the Protestation Oath, ordered in 1641, and the Vow and Covenant, taken by members of the two houses of parliament in June 1643.[14]

Lastly, two additional highly resonant notions to mention here – and which concern me in particular – are to do with the Bible and the language of the law. Both – I suggest – are also tied to the English literate culture, already touched upon while describing the making of the oath. At the point that the Scots and the English were discussing their covenant, they had already before them, for example, the canonical King James Bible, in which the word 'covenant' appeared more than 270 times in the Old Testament alone, designating an array of agreements, including not least the crucial agreements between God and His chosen people.[15] As well as that, they could find the term in the popular Geneva Bible, both in the text and copious notes; that Bible had appeared by then in at least 140 editions since its initial publication in 1557.[16] Scottish households were required to purchase a copy, if they had the means; in England, Bible ownership had increased tenfold between 1570 and 1630, proportionally the highest rate in Europe.[17] A brief glance at the Scottish and English documents reveals how resonant this biblical language of 'covenant' had become. Beyond the manifestation of the term in the very titles of the Scottish and English documents, the Scottish form was headed by four phrases

Crown, and Commons in Elizabethan Puritanism', *Journal of British Studies*, 20 (1980), 32–52; Vallance, 'The Solemn League and Covenant', esp. 50–60.

[12] Ford, 'The Lawful Bonds', esp. 49, 54–5, 64.

[13] Burrell, 'Covenant Idea', 341; Ford, 'The Lawful Bonds', 49.

[14] Vallance, 'The Solemn League and Covenant'.

[15] Electronic word searches with spelling variations in *Holy Bible Conteyning the Old Testament, And the New: Newly Translated out of the Originall Tongues & with the Former Translations Diligently Compared and Reuised by His Maiesties Speciall Commandment Appointed to be Read in Churches* (1611) (KJV), *The Bible in English 990–1970*, http://collections.chadwyck.co.uk/bie/htxview?template=basic.htx&content=frameset.htx accessed May 2011; machine-readable transcripts of cardinal English versions, quoted here, are taken from this database. The main spelling variations are: couenant, couenaunt, covenaunt and couenat.

[16] A. S. Herbert, *Historical Catalogue of Printed Editions of the English Bible, 1525–1961* (1968), 61–2, and, e.g., G. Milligan, 'Versions, English', J. Hastings *et al.*, *Dictionary of the Bible* (5 vols., Edinburgh, 1898–1904), IV, 858; S. L. Greenslade, 'English Versions of the Bible, 1525–1611', in *The Cambridge History of the Bible*, III: *The West from the Reformation to the Present Day*, ed. S. L. Greenslade (Cambridge, 1978; 1st edn 1963), 141–74, esp. 159; J. P. Lewis, 'Versions, English', *Anchor Bible Dictionary*, ed. D. N. Freedman *et al.* (6 vols., New York, 1992) (*ABD*), VI, 822. The first full edition of the Geneva Bible was published in 1560, the last was dated 1644. During this period, a number of revisions were also issued.

[17] N. Tadmor, *The Social Universe of the English Bible: Scripture, Society and Culture in Early Modern England* (Cambridge, 2010), 8–9, and references there.

from the Scriptures; the English by three, carefully edited, and from the Hebrew Bible alone. The first suggested that a 'perpetual covenant' was to be made (at this point the words 'to the Lord' had been subtly removed from the King James version of Jer. 50:5, which gave the impression that it was the present covenant that the text may have ordained). Another citation confirmed that 'all Judah rejoiced at the oath'.[18] The aim of the oath was indeed to make a covenant so that 'the Lord may be one, and His name one' not in 'all the land', as originally prophesised in Zach. 14:9, but, as paraphrased in the oath: in the 'three kingdoms'. The plea – again, paraphrasing Zach. 1 – was that the Lord 'may turn away His wrath and heavy indignation' and let the three kingdoms dwell in peace. One can hardly imagine a more integrated political manifestation of a scriptural notion of 'covenant', typical of the contemporary culture of the Bible, widely appreciated by scholars.

Yet, how did this language of 'covenant' become so dominant in the vernacular Bible? It is at this point that we reach the common law. The primary meaning of the term 'covenant', technically employed since the Norman Conquest, was indeed a legal contract, stemming from the Latin *conventio*.[19] While the term could historically be applied to general agreements or conditions within them (often relating specifically to leases and rents), it designated especially written contracts made under sign and seal, a usage dating back to the 1330s and undoubtedly known to the parliamentarians of the 1600s, who were educated and dealt habitually with matters of the law.[20] When the Restoration regime enacted the Statute of Fraud, the demand for any covenant to be written had become

---

[18] 2 Chron. 15:15. Several phrases were added at that point to the English version highlighting, among other things, that covenant is to obtain peace: 'and the Lord gave them rest among them'. Note also the second phrase 'Take away the wicked from before the King: and his Throne shall be established in righteousness', Prov. 25:5. The fourth citation from Gal. 3:15, which appeared in the Scottish document, was taken not from KJV but from the Geneva Bible, which still included the word 'testament' at that point, and where the words 'on the oath', were added.

[19] Oxford English dictionary online, s.v. 'covenant', www.oed.com.ezproxy.lancs.ac.uk/view/Entry/43328?rskey=wcq2HL&result=1&isAdvanced=false#eid accessed May 2011.

[20] 70 per cent of MPs in 1640–2 had attended either the Inns of Court or one of the universities, 55 per cent the Inns of Courts, and many who attended the universities also proceeded for a period at the Inns of Court, as the legal profession was expanding and the law was generally considered an important accomplishment for a gentlemen. Both the universities and the Inns of Court had by that time expanded to attract unprecedented numbers from among the gentry and middling ranks: see esp. L. Stone, 'The Educational Revolution in England', *Past and Present*, 28 (1964), 41–80, esp. table 8, 63; W. Prest, 'Legal Education of the Gentry at the Inns of Court, *Past and Present*, 38 (1976), 20–39; and see e.g. L. Stone, 'The Size and Composition of the Oxford Student Body 1580–1909', in *The University in Society*, ed. Lawrence Stone (2 vols., Princeton, 1974), e.g. I, 24–8, table 4.1, 93; F. Heal and C. Holmes, *The gentry in England and Wales, 1500–1700* (Stanford, 1994), esp. e.g. 133–4; R. O'Day, The professions in early modern England, 1450–1800 (Harlow, 2000).

a legal requirement, still valid today. In 1643/4, this was already a widely accepted practice.[21]

It was this legal concept, I suggest, that was increasingly applied over time not only in religious and political discourses, but in the very language of biblical translation. If the language of 'covenant' had become progressively more dominant in the theological and political vocabulary of our period, a similar process – I suggest – can be discerned in the English Scriptures themselves. One reason why the English Bible had become so popular – as I argued elsewhere – was because it was not simply translated, but also (to use a contemporary verb) 'Englished'. The term 'covenant' provides us with an interesting case of 'Englishing', which both preceded the widespread currency of the theological and political language of covenanting, and in time reflected it, if not propelled it. Indeed, one could even go as far as suggesting that the very notion of 'covenant', as it was coined in the British political and religious culture by the 1640s, was rooted not necessarily in the Bible itself, but in a unique interface that emerged through the processes of translation. An appropriate place to start, then, would be the translation history of the term 'covenant'. It is to this particular case study of translation and polemics that we now turn.

The word *berit* (or *berith, bᵉrit, bĕrît*,[22] plural *beritot*) appears in the Hebrew Bible to designate a range of treaties and pacts, whether between two equal parties who agree to support one another, or, most often, between unequal parties, as the weak agrees to serve the strong and the strong to protect the weak.[23] The biblical *beritot* include an alliance of friendship between individuals (e.g. the *berit* between David and Jonathan, 1 Sam. 18:3); symbolic treaties between larger parties (such as the *berit* between Abraham and Abimilech, Gen. 21:32; Isaac and Abimelech, Gen. 26:28; or Jacob and Laban, Gen. 31:44);[24] as well as treaties between heads of nations (e.g. Josh. 9:6,11), and even a treaty between the nation and its elected monarch (2 Sam. 3:21, 5:3; 2 Chron. 23:3). A range of biblical treaties are similarly contracted between God and humankind, and between God and his chosen people and select leaders amongst them. God's *berit* with Noah thus extended to a treaty with humankind following the Deluge (Gen. 6:18, 9:8–17), while several *beritot* enshrine the reciprocal commitment between God and the people of Israel, starting from the *berit* with Abraham and his seed, the *berit* for the possession of the land and

---

[21] 29 Ch. II c. 3, see the law with current amendments: www.legislation.gov.uk/aep/Cha2/29/3 accessed December 2011. See also e.g. A. P. Fox, *Oral and Literate Culture in England, 1500–1700* (Oxford, 2000), esp. ch. 5.

[22] ברית: my transliteration here as elsewhere follows the modern Hebrew pronunciation.

[23] E. S. Hartum, 'Berit', *Encyclopaedia biblica, thesaurus rerum biblicarum*, 9 vols. (Jerusalem, 1950–88) (in Hebrew), II, 347–51.

[24] *Ibid.*, 348.

the treaty surrounding the deliverance from the Egyptian slavery and the giving of the Law. God's commitment to the house of David is mentioned likewise as a *berit* (Pss. 89: 3–4, 26–37; 132: 11–18). Prophetic notions of deliverance are also coined in the language of *berit* (e.g. in Jer. 31), while the *berit* between God and Israel is seen as subject to renewal – such ideas became in time important in Christian readings.

At the heart of the various *beritot* is a solemn oath, which is uttered verbally. Another important feature concerns the manner of transaction. The biblical treaty, in its most usual form, is neither signed nor sealed (in the manner of the English covenant); nor is it imagined as a tied 'bond', let alone a bilateral written one. Rather, the biblical treaty is 'cut' (indicated with derivations from the root *k-r-t*). The sacrifice of animals is often implied or presented.[25] As well as that, the *berit* is signalled by tokens, some of which themselves invoke the notion of 'cutting': the dissection of animals, sprinkling blood and even cutting the flesh as in the act of circumcision (Gen. 15:9–11, 17; Gen. 17; Exod. 24:8; Ps. 50:5).[26] A curse or a sanction against the breaking of the treaty is manifested at times in the synonym *'alah*, which signified both a *berit* and the curse levied against its breach (Gen. 26:28; Ezek. 16:59, 17:18; Deut. 29:11, 13). The punishment for breaching the *berit* is conveyed with the use of the same root 'to cut' (*k-r-t*), indicating the removal of the transgressor from amongst the living.[27] The ritual of cutting and the sprinkling of the blood convey a threat – what might happen to the person who breaks the oath. Written documents mentioned in the context of *berit* contain principal testimonials and instructions (e.g. *sefer ha-berit*, 'the book of the covenant', in Ex. 24:7, *divrei ha-berit*, 'the words of the covenant' in 34:28; or *luḥot ha-berit*, 'the tables of the covenant', Deut. 9:9). Yet, the *berit* itself is rooted essentially in the rites and ritual of an oral culture, characterised by verbal oaths and agreements attested by symbolic deeds.[28]

---

[25] H. Tadmor, 'Treaty and Oath in the Ancient Near East: A Historian's Approach', in *Humanizing America's Iconic Book: Society of Biblical Literature Centennial Addresses 1980*, ed. G. M. Tucker and D. A. Knight (Chico, CA., 1982), 127–52; reprinted in H. Tadmor, *'With My Many Chariots I Have Gone up the Heights of Mountains': Historical and Literary Studies on Ancient Mesopotamia and Israel*, ed. M. Cogan (Jerusalem, 2011), 205–36. See esp. e.g. the cutting of animals Gen. 15:9; Jer. 34:18–19; Ps. 50:5. For a learned English historical exposition of the 'cutting' of the *berit*, see e.g. H. Ainsworth, *Annotations upon the Five Bookes of Moses, the Booke of the Psalmes, and the Song of Songs, or, Canticles VVherein the Hebrevv Vvords and Sentences, Are Compared with, and Explained by the Ancient Greeke and Chaldee Versions, and Other Records and Monuments of the Hebrewes* (1627), 42–3.

[26] Other tokens included commemorative stones (Gen. 31:44–54), extending the hand (Ezek. 17:18) or eating shared food (Josh. 9:14), which itself can form a part of the solemn ritual of contraction.

[27] E.g. *ve-nikhretah ha-nefesh*, Gen. 17:14.

[28] Tadmor, 'Treaty and oath'.

English translators struggled with this complex notion from the very outset. The range of terms employed by them to designate the biblical *beritot* include, among others, 'bond' or 'boond', 'bond of peace', 'token of a bond of pees', 'sign of a bond of peace', 'appointment' or 'pointment', 'testament', 'league', 'covenant' or 'covnenant of peace', and various others. The Anglo-biblical term 'covenant', as seen above to have been employed around the middle decades of the seventeenth century, was the outcome of decades if not centuries of translation and revision. An important source of complexity, moreover (in addition to the broad remit of the Hebrew *berit* and its cultural features) was the influence of the ancient Greek and Latin biblical versions, which continued to serve both as mediating texts and as sources for translation in their own right.

The first medieval English vernacular Bible, the Wyclifite Bible, closely followed the Vulgate, where *pactum* and *foedus* appeared interchangeably corresponding with the Hebrew *berit*: while the one could be rendered as 'bond' or 'bond of peace', the other was coined as 'covenant' or 'covenant of peace', and the two also appeared interchangeably. Beyond that, the term 'testament' was employed, corresponding with the Latin *testamentum*, which preceded and complemented the Vulgate's *pactum* and *foedus* (in line with the Greek *diathēkē*, first employed in the Septuagint to correspond with *berit* and subsequently in the Christian Scriptures, echoing *berit*); this usage remained habituated in Old Testament English contexts particularly in the language of the Psalms. *Zot beriti* (this is my treaty, Gen. 17:10) in the early and Latinate Wyclifite version (*c.* 1384), for example, was thus conveyed with the phrase 'covenant of pees', corresponding with *hoc est pactum meum*, while *le'ot berit* (as a sign of the treaty) in the next verse became 'token of a bond of pees' agreeing with *signum foederis*.[29] In Ps. 43:18 (Masoretic Text 44:17) *berit* was rendered as 'testament'. Similar usages remained in the later Wyclifite version (*c.* 1395) with some variations, and at times greater unity. The important allegiance between God and Abraham in Gen. 17, for example, remained 'bond of pees', otherwise unified as 'couenaunt'. God's contract with man following the Deluge was also named 'boond of pees',[30] as was the contract made by Abraham with Abimelech, or the crucial 'bond' between God and his chosen people in Deut. 5.[31] Elsewhere, the same

---

[29] Wyclifite Bible, Earlier and Later Versions, machine-readable transcript, reproducing *The Holy Bible Containing the Old and New Testaments, with the Apporcryphal Books, in the Earliest English Version Made from the Latin Vulgate by John Wycliffe and his Followers*, ed. J. Forshall and F. Madden (Oxford 1850) (Wyc. EV, LV).

[30] Wyc. LV, Gen. 9:12–17.

[31] Wyc. LV, Gen. 21:32; Deut. 5:2–3, 9:11, 15.

relation was described as 'covenant',[32] yet on the whole the mentions of 'covenant' in the revised Wyclifite text had declined.[33]

When William Tyndale came to translate the Pentateuch around the late 1520s[34] (in the spirit of the Reformation, not from the Latin Vulgate but from the original Hebrew), he thus faced a complex vernacular tradition. Although early notions of a covenant theology, which had developed in Zurich in particular, may have reached England through Tyndale,[35] he evidently did not readily endorse the biblical 'covenant' terminology in his translation work. One can only wonder what the reason might have been: perhaps the legalistic resonance of the term did not always strike the right note; perhaps the literary cadence interfered; perhaps he wished to distance himself from the Wyclifite Bible; perhaps he was disturbed by a possible association with a Latinate rendition; and perhaps he was concerned that 'covenant' was too removed from the crucial Greek term, *diathēkē*, employed since the dawn of Christianity, yet most simply meaning not treaty or pact but last will and testament.[36]

The *Oxford English Dictionary* suggests that 'the 16th c. English versions at length used covenant entirely in OT'. Examining Tyndale's rendition, the rule hardly applies. Tyndale employed the term 'covenant' sparingly, more in explanatory comments and notes than in the text itself. Within it, he preferred the terms 'pointment', 'appointment' and 'testament', as well as 'bond', which he employed alongside 'covenant'.[37] His glossary, which he appended to his first rendition of Genesis, explained: 'Testame[n]t here is an appoynteme[n]t made betwene god and ma[n], and goddes promyses. And sacrame[n]t is a signe representinge soch an appoyn[t]ment and promeses'.[38] In describing the *berit* between Abraham and God in Gen. 15, 17, for example, he thus used 'bond', 'covenant' and 'testament' alternately.[39] Interchangeability can be seen in the following passage

---

[32] E.g. Wyc. LV, Deut. 7: 9, 12, 8:18, 9:9, cf. 5:2–3; see also 'to couenaunt', Wyc. EV, Isa. 42:6.

[33] The Pentateuch of the LV shows a decline of about one third, the books of Joshua, Judges, 1–2 Samuel and 1–2 Kings show a decline of nearly a half.

[34] First printed 1530, New Testament fully printed 1526.

[35] See e.g. Green, *The Christian's ABC*, p. 404.

[36] See e.g. A. Schenker, 'Διαθήκη pour ברית: L'option de traduction de la LXX à la lumière du droit successoral de l'Égypte ptolémaïque et du Livre de la Genèse', in *Lectures et relectures de la Bible: festschrift P.-M. Bogaert*, ed. A. Wénin and J.-M. Auwers (Louvain, 1999), 125–31 (I am grateful to Jan Joosten for the reference); see also e.g. Weir, *The Origins*, 58–9.

[37] The term 'bond' was increasingly relegated to represent negative ties such as slavery and bondage, see Tadmor, *The Social Universe of the English Bible*, ch. 3.

[38] In *The Pentateuch*, trans. W. Tyndale (Antwerp, 1530), no page number.

[39] William Tyndale (Pentateuch, Jonah and New Testament), 1530–4: machine-readable transcript, reproducing *Tyndale's Pentateuch* (1530) (Tyn.), Gen. 15:18, 17:2, 4, 7, 9–11, 13–14. See e.g. Tyn. Deut. 7:9, 12; and 'appoyntment' and 'tables of appointment', e.g., Deut. 5:3,

from Lev. 26:42–5, where four terms are employed corresponding with the Hebrew *berit* (my accentuation):

> And I wil remember my **bonde** with Iacob and my **testamet** with Isaac, and my **testament** with Abraham, and will thinke on the londe ... I will not so cast them awaye ... that I will vtterlye destroye the[m] a[n]d breake myne **appoyntment** with them ... I will therfore remebre vnto the[m] the first **couenaunt** made when I broughte them out of the lond of Egipte.

Tyndale's rendition of important ecclesiastical words such as 'elder' rather than 'priest', or 'congregation' instead of 'church', was the subject of a great deal of public disputation.[40] His creative rendition of *berit* sailed with little notice, and was changed more by friends than by foes. However, while Tyndale's seminal rendition was absorbed into subsequent English versions to the point that 76 per cent of the King James Old Testament is still estimated to be based on Tyndale, his translation of *berit* was by and large revised.[41] By the time that the covenanters were lifting their right hand to the Lord, their heads bowed in reverence, it was the legal term 'covenant' that won the day.

In the first instance, however, the Tyndalian understanding of *berit* was in fact absorbed into the first vernacular Bible to be issued in England with the approval of Henry VIII, ironically less than a year after Tyndale's martyrdom: the 'Thomas Matthew' version, prepared by Tyndale's disciple, John Rogers. There, the term 'covenant' was employed more than 130 times in the text and the notes of the Old Testament.[42] Clearly,

---

9:9, 11, 15; and see also the different usages in Tyn. Deut. 28:69 or 29:1, and 29:11, 13, 20, 24–6.

[40] Tyndale's translation policies attracted controversy and were disputed in detail by Sir Thomas More, see T. More, *Dyaloge of Syr Thomas More Knyghte ... Wyth many othere thyngys touching the Pestylent Sect of Luther and Tyndale* (1529); W. Tyndale, *An Answere vnto Sir Thomas Mores Dialoge Made by Vuillyam Tindale* (Antwerp, 1531); T. More, *The Co[n]futacyon of Tyndales Answere Made by Syr Thomas More knyght* (1532); and see also, e.g., D. Daniell, *William Tyndale: A Biograohy* (New Haven, 1994), esp. 178–201, 250–80; Greenslade, 'English Versions of the Bible', 145–7; D. Rollison, *The Local Origins of Modern Society: Gloucestershire 1500–1800* (1992), 'Tyndale and all his sect', and esp. 90–2, 96. As Rollison explains, the term 'elder' reflects not only Tyndale's theology but the contemporary social structure of local communities. Following Tyndale, Coverdale employed 'congregation' for 'church', 'elder' for 'priest', and 'love' for 'charity', etc. (but used 'penance' explaining that what he meant by it was true repentance). The ecclesiastical words largely remain in the Bishops' Bible, but 'charity' is substituted where Tyndale had used 'love' (Greenslade, 'English versions of the Bible', 160–1; J. P. Lewis, 'Bible, Bishops', *ABD*, I, 719). 'Arguments about the language' erupted once more surrounding the publication of the Catholic Rheims-Douai version and were important in bringing about the commissioning of the King James Bible. For translation policies and debates, see especially D. Norton, *A History of the English Bible as Literature* (Cambridge, 2000), chs. 1–2, and on 35; M. Dove, *The First English Bible: The Text and Context of the Wycliffite Versions* (Cambridge, 2007), 37–46, and references there.

[41] See Tadmor, *The Social Universe of the English Bible*, p. 16, and references there.

[42] Electronic search in Thomas Matthew, 1549: a machine-readable transcript, reproducing *The Byble, that is to Say All The Holy Scripture: In Whych Are Cotayned the Olde*

the faithful pupil, Rogers, allowed himself to review the translation of *berit*, whether to gloss Tyndale's 'boke of the appointment' and 'blood of the appoyntment' in Exod. 24, to clarify the 'tabernacle of the witness' in Exod. 27, or to add three headings in the Book of Genesis, bearing the word 'covenant', that did not appear in Tyndale's early edition.[43] The key prophecy in Jer. 31 was introduced by him using the two significant terms together 'The newe Testament and couenaunt'. This terminology was incorporated in the next decade into the first English authorised version, the Great Bible, published in 1539, which therefore retained terminological diversity.[44] If the Tyndalian rendition of *berit* was revised, it was not for want of dissemination and recognition. However, by that time another disciple, Miles Coverdale, though strongly leaning on Tyndale, had raked over the semantic field of *berit* to produce a greater unity of the language of 'covenant'.

Scholars wonder to what extent the Yorkshire born clergyman, Miles Coverdale, had before him the Wyclifite text as he was preparing his version of the English Bible.[45] If so, his extensive use of 'covenant' may have been a discreet bow to the native Lollard tradition. Equally important may have been the influence of the reformer Heinrich Bullinger, one of the forefathers of covenant theology, with whom Coverdale corresponded, and whose work he translated and popularised in England.[46] Most important, however, was possibly the influence of

and New Testamente, Truely & Purely Translated into English, & Nowe Lately with Greate Industry & Diligece Recognised (1549) (TM).

[43] Gen. 9, 21 and 31. Daniell notes that Tyndale edited such usages in his 1534 version to reinforce the term 'covenant', having 'thought himself through into a more full-blooded Protestant covenant theology'. Yet, revisions remained inconsistent in Genesis and were not extended through the 1534 Pentateuch, where considerable variation was retained: Tyndale's Old Testament: Being the Pentateuch of 1530, Johan to 2 Chronicles of 1537, and Jonah, ed. D. Daniell (New Haven, 1992), xxii–xxiii, and references there; The Firste Boke of Moses Called Genesis Newly Correctyd and Amendyd by W[illiam].T[yndale]. (Antwerp, 1534).

[44] *Berit* was rendered alternately in the Great Bible at Gen. 17, for example, as 'bond', 'testament' and 'everlasting testament', and the TM prelude to Jer. 31 was reproduced, see the Great Bible, 1540: a machine-readable transcript, reproducing *The Byble in Englyshe, that is to Saye the Contet of Al the Holy Scrypture both of Ye Olde, and Newe Testamet, with a Prologe Therinto, Made by the Reuerende Father in God, Thomas Archbysshop of Cantorbury, This Is the Byble Apoynted to the Vse of the Churches* (1540) (GB).

[45] D. Daniell, *The Bible in English: Its History and Influence* (New Haven and London, 2003), 185; Dove, *The First English Bible*, 192–3.

[46] The several English editions (which contain adaptations) bear different titles, and vary in length: H. Bullinger, *The Christen State Of Matrimonye ...*, trans. M. Coverdale (Antwerp, 1541); Bullinger, *The Golde[n] Boke of Christen Matrimonye ... Set Forthe in English by Theodore Basille*, trans. M. Coverdale (1543; 1st edn 1541). The treatise was reissued in 1548, entitled 'The Christian state of matrimony: and how man and wife should kepe house together with love', within a three-part volume entitled *The Christen Rule or State of All the Worlde from the Hyghest to the Lowest and how Euery Man Shulde Lyue to Please God in Hys Callynge*, containing

Luther's Bible, which Coverdale employed as he was doing his translation work.[47] Be that as it may, Coverdale's Bible, issued in 1535, contained a large number of usages of 'covenant' in the Old Testament, with over seventy in the Pentateuch alone, more than sixfold their number in Tyndale. These largely corresponded with Luther's use of 'Bund' in the Old Testament (and 'Testament' in the New).[48]

When the Geneva Bible was issued by pious exiles (prepared, among others, by the same Miles Coverdale, by that time in his sixties), awareness of the Hebrew had considerably expanded and with it the theology of 'covenant'. The total mentions of 'covenant' in the Old Testament rose by that time overall, including nearly eighty mentions in the Pentateuch text itself, as well as numerous notes reinforcing the idea not only of covenant, but of covenant and grace.[49] A related transition, which took place at the same time, was the division of the semantic field of the Hebrew *berit* into 'covenant' and 'league'. Perhaps because of the increasing significance of 'covenant' in the religious discourse, as well as its solemn contractual resonance, translators felt that it was inappropriate for designating certain man-made *beritot*. The part-synonym 'league', first employed in two instances in the Great Bible (at Isa. 33), was applied in the Geneva Bible most notably in reference to problematic *beritot*, such as the *berit* between Joshua and the deceitful Gibeonites, which promised them protection under false pretences (Geneva Josh. 9: 6, 7 11, 14–16), or the

also chapters from Tyndale's 1528 tract. Bullinger's name does not appear on any of the English editions of his treatise. The name on the title pages of the first English editions is 'Translated by Myles Coverdale'. Some editions contain a second preface by the popular polemicist Thomas Becon. Two bear the name 'T. Basille', Becon's pseudonym. Becon, one of the most widely read English polemicists of the period, is claimed to have boasted that the publisher affixed his name to the Bullinger–Coverdale treatise so as to increase sales. See also references to Coverdale's adaptation of Bullinger's treatise in D. Cressy, *Birth, Marriage, and Death: Ritual, Religion and Life-Cycle in Tudor and Stuart England* (Oxford, 1997), 271, 277, 294, 297, 350–2.

[47] Coverdale's Pentateuch, New Testament and probably Jonah were based on Tyndale. Coverdale confessed that his command of the Hebrew was insufficient and that he therefore relied in his work on the remaining parts on other sources; these included the Vulgate and Luther's Bible, see Tadmor, *The Social Universe of the English Bible*, pp. 3–4 and notes there, and see esp. e.g. Daniell, *The Bible in English*, 174, 181–5, 193–7; Daniell, 'Miles Coverdale', *Oxford Dictionary of National Biography* (online), ed. L. Goldman, Jan. 2009 edn, Oxford, 2004–9, www.oxforddnb.com accessed December 2011, and references there; Norton, *A History of the English Bible as Literature*, pp. 29–34; Lewis, 'Versions, English', *ABD*, VI, esp. 820–1; Greenslade, 'English versions of the Bible', 147–51.

[48] Biola Unbound Bible, http://unbound.biola.edu/ containing, among others, Luther's Bible (1545); online-bibeln, www.bibelwissenschaft.de/online-bibeln including, among others, *Biblia Hebraica Stuttgartensia, Septuaginta, Biblia Sacra Vulgata*, KJV, accessed May 2011.

[49] Geneva Bible, machine-readable transcript, reproducing *The Bible: That is the Holy Scriptures Contained in the Olde and Newe Testament. Translated According to the Ebrew and Greeke, and Conferred with the Best Translations in Diuers Languages. With Most Profitable Annotations vpon All The Hard Places . . .* (1587) (Geneva).

'league' of enemies 'with craftie counsel' against God's people (Geneva Ps. 83:3, 5; Masoretic Text 83:4, 6).[50] In a note appended to Mat. 26, the phrase 'league and covenant' appeared for the first time. A similar logic was accepted, albeit restrictedly, in the next authorised version to be printed in England, the Elizabethan Bishops' Bible (BB), which set apart the 'temporall league' to designate, for example, the *berit* between Abraham and his confederates, Isaac and Abimelech, and Jacob and the crafty Laban.[51] In describing the *berit* between Joshua and the deceitful Gibeonites, 'agreement', 'covenant of peace', 'covenant' and 'league' were employed alternately (BB Josh. 9:6, 11, 15–16).[52] The division of the semantic field of *berit* was endorsed by the translators of the English Catholic version, the Rheims-Douai (RD) version, fully published by 1610 (ostensibly following the *Vulgate* yet with strong awareness of the Hebrew original), which considerably augmented the use of both 'covenant' and 'league'. Old Testament textual mentions of 'league' now increased to over fifty,[53] more than double their number in either the Geneva or the Bishops' Bibles to include a wide array of temporal *beritot*, such as the 'league of friendship' between David and Jonathan (RD 1 Sam. 18:3 and notes) and various international treaties (e.g. RD 2 Kings 3:5 and notes; 2 Chron. 16:3, 20:37). At Neh. 10:30, the key phrase 'leagues & couenantes' appeared where the renewal of the people's *berit* with God was described.[54] Indeed, at the same time, the number of textual mentions of 'covenant' rose more than in any of the contemporary cardinal Protestant versions to designate not only an array of binding 'covenants' before the Lord, but phrases otherwise translated in the Protestant Bible with the use of the thorny word 'congregation'.[55] The overall mentions of 'covenant' in the Old Testament text and notes thus shot up to about 350, including over 120 textual references in the Pentateuch alone, more than eleven times

---

[50] At 2 Chron. 16:3, the terms 'covenant' and 'league' were employed, subtly reflecting the speaker's emphasis on the 'covenant' with himself, as opposed to a mere 'league' with an opponent, in Hebrew both read: *berit*.

[51] Bishops' Bible, 1568: a machine-readable transcript, reproducing *The Holie Bible Conteynyng the Olde Testament and the Newe* (1568) (BB), Gen. 14:13 note, 26:28 and notes, 31:44 and notes.

[52] Rheims-Douai, 1582–1610: a machine-readable transcript, reproducing *Holie Bible Faithfully Translated into English out of the Authentical Latin. Diligently Conferred with the Hebrew, Greeke, and Other Editions in Diures Languages* (Douai 1609–10) (RD).

[53] Based on word search of 'league', and excluding eleven mentions in 1–2 Maccabees.

[54] Albeit to gloss *'alah* and *shevuʿah*, and with reference to *'amanah*, see: RD Neh. 9: 32, 38, 10:29, Masoretic Text Neh. 9:32; 10:1, 30.

[55] E.g. Num. 4:25, 30, 33, 6:10, 13, 18; 2 Chron. 1:3, *'ohel moʿed*, translated in RD as 'tabernacle of couenaunt', 'couenaunt of testimonie'; cf. e.g. Geneva, 'Tabernacle of the Congregation'; *'ohel moʿed mikhsehu*, RD Num. 4:25: 'roofe of the couenant'; see also *mishkan ha-ʿedut*; e.g. Ex. 38:21; Num. 1:50; 10:11: RD Geneva, 'tabernacle of testimonie'.

their number in the Thomas Matthew Pentateuch and about five times their number in the Great Bible's Pentateuch, based on Tyndale.[56]

When the King James translators combed the text with an eye to both fidelity and uniformity, the overall mentions of 'covenant' in the Pentateuch declined to a total of eighty-one. The number of textual references to 'league' was reduced to a total of twenty-two, endorsing both Geneva amendments and several Douai revisions.[57] As the semantic field of *berit* was adjusted and confirmed, the last remaining usages of 'testament' were weeded out of the Hebraic Scriptures, leaving this Latinate term in the title of the 'Old Testament', in the New Testament and in the liturgy.[58]

However, by that time, the broader understanding of 'covenant' had manifestly changed. The legal term, removed in part from the revised Wycliffite version, sparingly employed by Tyndale, and corrected by Coverdale not necessarily in agreement with the Hebrew but with the German, had been incrementally naturalised in the vernacular language of the Bible, as well as in the broader religious discourse of the time. By the 1590s, as scholars note, this notion was enshrined in learned treatises and lexicons and was making its way in more widely disseminated catechisms and tracts. While debates about salvation increasingly divided believers, the notion of 'covenant' moreover emerged as a relatively neutral scriptural terrain, which could be shared – at least to an extent – by Calvinists and non-Calvinists alike. Not only ardent puritans but non-predestinarians, such as one of the translators of the King James Bible, Lancelot Andrewes, were able to incorporate the notion of 'covenant' in their work.[59] Indeed, even the translators of the Catholic Rheims-Douai version, as seen here, had no difficulty in employing the term – profusely, with more textual mentions than any of the cardinal Tudor and Stuart Protestant versions, while confirming both its sanctity and its contractual force by splitting the semantic field of *berit* between 'covenant'

---

[56] Or about 330 excluding Tobit, Ecclesiasticus and 1–2 Maccabees, based on an electronic searches and additional comparisons in RD, TM and GB.

[57] E.g. KJV Josh. 9; 2 Sam. 3: 12–13, 21 and 5:3, confirming that the deposition of Saul and the anointment of David by his people was a 'league', rather than a 'covenant', as in RD.

[58] BB Deut 31:9; Josh. 3:3, 3:6, 4:9; Jer. 3:16. See also Green, *The Christian's ABC*, 404, and the disappearance of 'testament' from theological tracts by the 1590s, Weir, *The Origins*, 58. Note the increased use of 'covenant' in KJV NT.

[59] For Andrewes, see Green, *The Christian's ABC*, 406. The avowed anti-Calvinist Thomas Jackson, for example, embraced the notion of 'covenant' while highlighting the mystery and prophecy embedded in the Greek *diathēkē*, and criticising those who argue otherwise: T. Jackson, *An Exact Collection of the Works of Doctor Jackson ... Christ Exercising his Everlasting Priesthood ...* (1654), 3259. Compare, e.g., the learned exposition reconciling *berit* and *diathēkē* in A. Willett, *Hexapla, that is, A six-fold commentarie vpon the most diuine Epistle of the holy apostle S. Paul to the Romanes* (1611), 2–3, *passim*.

and man-made 'leagues', and moreover expanding the use of the term to include disputed expressions.[60] This, which stretched the use and meaning of 'covenant' well beyond the contractual discourse, differed from the policy of the King James version, which largely unified the contractual terminology.

Scholars highlight the ways in which conceptions of the law had become central in the theology of 'covenant', since the 'Covenant of Works' (itself formulated around the same time, as mentioned above) emphasised notions of Law, associated with *berit*.[61] The biblical term 'covenant', grafted from a long-standing legal tradition, was evidently well positioned for conveying the idea, albeit while accentuating a formal and literate dimension rather than the oral and ritualised one, and often the individual conscience rather than the collectivity. As happened in many cases of 'Englishing', this was a reciprocal exchange: while the legal term became habituated in the vernacular Scriptures, contemporary legal concepts acquired an air of sanctity.[62] The collocation 'league and covenant', borrowed from the Geneva Bible and reinforced in the Catholic Douai Bible, was also naturalised by association as both a temporal and divinely sanctioned pact, with legal and literate overtones, as seen in the Solemn League and Covenant, with which we started, and its biblical thrust and legal and administrative enforcement.

And so we return to the English Solemn League and Covenant. Contrary to its professed aim, peace was not restored to the land. Nor was the 'the King's Majesty's, person, and authority' augmented as a result.[63] No sooner was Charles I's son restored to his English throne than an order was issued by his loyal parliament 'That the Instrument or Writing, called The Solemn League and Covenant, a copy whereof is hereunto annexed, be burned by the Hand of the Common Hangman.'[64] The administrative mechanism of the state was put into action once more, this time to ensure that 'all other Copies' of the said covenant should be taken out of all the public places where they had once been stored. In the course of the forthcoming decades, scholars and theologians increasingly moved to question the 'covenant' theology itself, by that time tainted in England in the eyes of many owing to its association with the revolt, and fostered primarily in Scotland and in the colonies across the Atlantic. Once again,

---

[60] Above, n. 54.

[61] See in particular, for example, how words such as 'precepts', 'law' and 'conditions' have crept into contemporary lexicons to explain biblical passages such as Jer. 31:33–4: Weir, *The Origins*, e.g. 55–8; Letham, *The Westminster Assembly*.

[62] Tadmor, *The Social Universe of the English Bible*.

[63] Solemn League and Covenant, *Journal of the House of Commons: Volume 3: 1643–1644* (1802), 25 Sept. 1643, item III URL: www.british-history.ac.uk accessed May 2011.

[64] *Journal of the House of Commons: Volume 8: 1660–1667* (1802), 254. URL: www.british-history.ac.uk accessed May 2011.

the boundaries of the community of faith were re-drawn, and, alongside them, political identities. Before long, the entire debate shifted once more owing to new critiques and enlightenment thought. The biblical language of 'covenant', once enshrined in the King James version, however, was there to stay. The Tyndalian 'appointment' or 'pointment' disappeared, and 'bond' was largely relegated to a different semantic field. Select usages of 'league' remained and were replaced in revised versions.[65] As for 'testament', as modern reference books indicate, see 'covenant'.[66]

[65] Usages of 'league' corresponding with *berit*, e.g. Josh. 9:6, 11; 15, 16; Judge 2:2; and 2 Sam 5:3, mentioned above, were frequently changed in revised versions to 'covenant', as indicated, for example, in the standard A. Cruden, *Cruden Complete Concordance of the Old and New Testaments* (Peabody MA, n.d.; 1st edn 1869), s.v. 'league'.

[66] See e.g. *The New Bible Dictionary* (1962), e.g. s.v. 'Testament', 1253; In *ABD*, for example, there is no entry for 'Testament'.

Transactions of the RHS 22 (2012), pp. 111–39 © Royal Historical Society 2012
doi:10.1017/S0080440112000096

THE MORAL GEOGRAPHY OF BRITISH
ANTI-SLAVERY RESPONSIBILITIES*
The Alexander Prize Essay

By Richard Huzzey

ABSTRACT. By examining British anti-slavery debates across a longue durée –
before and after West Indian emancipation – the basis of moral responsibility for
political action may be reassessed. Recent interest in humanitarian or transnational
compassion may have underappreciated the geographical limitations of the moral
responsibility Britons assumed for slavery and the slave trade. The notion of national
complicity was crucial in mobilising individual Britons to petition, abstain from slave-
grown produce or otherwise pressure parliament. While the peculiar aftermath of
the Napoleonic Wars created a British responsibility for other nations' slave trading,
there was little comparable appetite for the internationalising responsibility for the
slave-labour origins of traded goods. This meant that transnational obligations to
police the slave trade did not translate into concern about the slave production
behind overseas trade. By tracing these national debates over time, it is possible to
discern the dominant and recessive arguments for how and when moral revulsion
should translate into political action by Britons and the British state. This suggests
a need to revisit scholarly conclusions about abolitionist campaigning, the basis
of moral responsibility for slavery, and the antecedents of modern consumer
responsibility.

Examining the anti-slavery pronouncements of Britons across two
generations, it is easy to imagine that the children of the first abolitionists
had much harder hearts than their parents. In 1823, the earnest
campaigner Zachary Macaulay insisted that 'every Englishman who loves
his country should dedicate his whole life, and every faculty of his soul, to
efface this foul stain from its character'.[1] A mere twenty-two years later, his
son, the MP and historian Thomas Babington Macaulay, argued that his
'especial obligations in respect of negro slavery ceased when slavery itself
ceased in that part of the world for the welfare of which I, as a member
of this House, was accountable'. The younger Macaulay seemed to give
voice to many Victorians' hardening distaste for 'busying ourselves about

---

* Thanks must go to Seymour Drescher, Margot Finn and Jay Sexton for their comments
on the argument advanced here, though they are blameless for any remaining infelicities.
[1] Zachary Macaulay, *Negro Slavery, Or A View of the More Prominent Features of that State of
Society as it Exists in the United States of America and in the Colonies of the West Indies* (1823), 33.

matters which we do not fully understand, and cannot efficiently control'.[2] The apparent contrast between these declarations of father and son – one rousing and one defeatist, one inspiring activity and the other advocating apathy, one assuming responsibility for slavery and the other shirking it – may actually be misleading.[3] While their views on slavery and empire differed in many important ways, both men emphasised Britons' moral responsibility for slavery within their own nation's territories.[4]

The idea of national guilt was one of the main ingredients in popular campaigns against the slave trade and slavery, and it structured subsequent disagreements about how international policies against slavery should be decided. To understand the dynamics of national guilt requires investigating the moral geography of British anti-slavery politics over a long period of time. The phrase 'moral geography' may seem peculiar or even pretentious, but it is an efficient way to describe the problem of how Britons considered the spatial dimensions of their responsibilities regarding slavery; a 'moral geography' is a study of how place shapes people's feelings of moral responsibility for an evil.[5] Such an approach can investigate the role of place in the humanitarian politics of anti-slavery, which confronted complicated networks of national, imperial and transnational commerce. In particular, it is useful to consider why the Victorian state focused on slave-trade suppression rather than encouraging foreign emancipations or why British consumers abstained from West Indian slave-grown sugar before the Emancipation Act yet proved such untroubled customers of slave-grown produce from foreign parts after 1833.

For more than two centuries, slaving may have been seen by some as distasteful, but it was by no means a sin requiring legislation to ban it. In the sixty years after 1776, abolitionists redefined first the slave trade and then slaveholding as national rather than personal sins, obliging legal interdiction by the state.[6] The morality of slavery moved from the frontiers of individual conscience to the chambers of the houses of parliament,

---

[2] The 1845 speech is reproduced in Thomas Babington Macaulay, *Speeches of Lord Macaulay, Corrected by Himself* (1866), 169.

[3] For interpretations of the younger Macaulay's treachery, see Eric Williams, *Capitalism and Slavery* (1964 [1944]), 193–4; Howard Temperley, *British Antislavery 1833–1870* (1972), xv; Robert E. Sullivan, *Macaulay: The Tragedy of Power* (Cambridge, MA, 2010), 259–60.

[4] For a close reading of the differences between the two men see Catherine Hall, 'Troubling Memories: Nineteenth-Century Histories of the Slave Trade and Slavery', *Transactions of the Royal Historical Society*, sixth series, 21 (2011), 147–69, esp. 162–9, and Catherine Hall, *Macaulay and Son: Architects of Imperial Britain* (New Haven, 2012).

[5] For varied uses of this phrase by geographers, see David Matless, 'Moral Geographies', in *Dictionary of Human Geography*, ed. R. J. Johnston, Derek Gregory, Geraldine Pratt and Michael Watts, 4th edn (Oxford, 2003), 522–3.

[6] The best recent account is Christopher Leslie Brown, *Moral Capital: Foundations of British Abolitionism* (Chapel Hill, 2006).

revising the boundaries of individual, national and local sovereignty. For slavery to shift from a matter of personal behaviour to national concern would require British responsibility for the actions of others. Sympathy for the suffering of others is qualitatively different to assuming a moral duty and personal agency in stopping that suffering.[7] Delineating the geographical limits of this externalisation of guilt and presumption of responsibility for slavery, therefore, becomes an important task.[8]

Historians have previously examined the emergence of humanitarian anti-slavery sentiment as part of 'a momentous turning point in the evolution of man's moral perception and thus in man's perception of himself' or as 'revolutions in moral responsibility' resulting from 'shifts in the conventional boundaries of moral responsibility'.[9] While attitudes about the proper spheres of British power and responsibility changed over time, there were also perpetual differences when it came to calculating Britons' moral responsibilities. These ethical divisions consistently existed in the anti-slavery movement. Particular post-emancipation crises threw these distinctions into sharper relief but did not create them. Studying the moral geography of anti-slavery consciences will highlight some challenges for those scholars, such as Thomas Haskell, Adam Hochschild and Michael Barnett, who are impressed by British abolitionists' role in an internationalist humanitarian awakening.[10]

National and consumer sins

By the middle of the eighteenth century, moral objections to slavery and the slave trade impressed many religious communities in the British Atlantic world. Following the lead of individual Quakers, meetings affiliated with the Society of Friends in North America started to fear the polluting influence of slaveholders as members of their religious communities. John Woolman, a Pennsylvanian Quaker, went further and decided also to abstain from purchasing goods produced by the enslaved.[11] These two models of proto-abolitionism, one shunning slave ownership

[7] On differences, see Thomas Haskell, 'Capitalism and the Origins of the Humanitarian Sensibility, Part 1', as reprinted in *The Antislavery Debate: Capitalism and Abolitionism as a Problem in Historical Interpretation*, ed. Thomas Bender (Berkeley, 1992), 107–35. On the ways sentiment could be deployed in a national campaign, see Brycchan Carey, *British Abolitionism and the Rhetoric of Sensibility: Writing, Sentiment, and Slavery 1760–1807* (Basingstoke, 2005).

[8] Haskell, 'Capitalism . . . Part 1', 132–5.

[9] *Ibid.*, at 113 (quoting David Brion Davis) and 133 (Haskell himself).

[10] *Ibid.*; Adam Hochschild, *Bury the Chains: Prophets and Rebels in the Fight to Free an Empire's Slaves* (New York and London, 2005), 5; Michael Barnett, *Empire of Humanity: A History of Humanitarianism* (Ithaca, 2011), 57–62. For caution over the relationship between human rights and emancipation in world history, see Robin Blackburn, *The American Crucible: Slavery, Emancipation and Human Rights* (New York, 2011), 178–88.

[11] Thomas P. Slaughter, *The Beautiful Soul of John Woolman, Apostle of Abolition* (New York, 2008), 106–17.

and the other shunning all derivative products of slave labour, shared a fear that the sinfulness of slavery was polluting, whether the contagion stemmed from communion or consumption. While both possibilities relied on assumptions of sin, Woolman's moral geography – his sphere of responsibility – was far more expansive that those Friends of the Society who merely condemned slave dealing by co-religionists. He assumed personal responsibility for avoiding the fruits of slavery, becoming anxious at his consumption of sinful products. He shared with other Quakers an expanding assumption of moral responsibility for slavery that was founded on fears that the opening defeats of the French and Indian Wars in 1754 were linked to Pennsylvania's violent association with slavery.[12] However, Woolman's position on consumer goods was radical and unusual, based on pollution through participation in the market rather than the pollution of religious communion with slaveholders.

Intellectually, Woolman's unbounded personal responsibility, which presumed a global moral canvass, was radically different from his peers. In practice, so long as the slave-grown produce he rejected originated in Britain's West Indian or American colonies, he shared with others a moral geography constrained by the borders of the British Empire. Thomas Haskell takes Woolman as an empirical example of his theory that growing marketisation in the modern world transformed individuals' 'operative sphere of responsibility'. Transnational commerce, he posits, made a man like Woolman 'attentive to the remote consequences of his acts and familiar with the intricate web of mutual dependencies that the market establishes between buyers and sellers'.[13] Haskell quotes his subject's view that 'unrighteousness to the injury of men who live some thousands of miles off is the same in substance as ... the injury of our neighbours' and Woolman made arguments about the suffering of slaves on Africa's distant shores that would be echoed by later abolitionists.[14] However, while the Quaker's moral geography ranged over great distances, its implied radicalism in disrespecting the political boundaries on a map was largely undeveloped and untested. Distinguishing between the radical individualism of Woolman's particular practices and the national political campaigns of later anti-slavery activists is vital to understanding the political dimensions of abolitionists' moral geography.[15]

[12] Blackburn, *American Crucible*, 150–2, 161–3; Slaughter, *Beautiful Soul*, 123–4, 131–3, 150–1, 162, 245–9, 279, 287–8, 292–3. On Quaker antecedents, see Ruth Ketring Nuermberger, *The Free Produce Movement: A Quaker Protest Against Slavery* (New York, 1944), 4–8.

[13] Haskell, 'Capitalism ... Part 1', 133; Thomas Haskell, 'Capitalism and the Origins of the Humanitarian Sensibility, II', in *The Antislavery Debate*, ed. Bender, 136–60, at 159.

[14] As quoted by *ibid.*, 158.

[15] This develops a point made by David Brion Davis, 'The Perils of Doing History by Ahistorical Abstraction: A Reply to Thomas L. Haskell's *AHR Forum* Reply', in *The Antislavery Debate*, ed. Bender, 290–309, at 297, 307–8.

In Britain, the Somerset and Knight cases of the 1770s safely insulated the home country from the legal institution of slavery by ruling that it belonged in the colonies alone.[16] The physical distance between the West Indies and Britain was the same as it always had been; what changed, by the last decades of the eighteenth century, was the moral distance – the political conception of Britons' responsibility for slavery.[17] Even if arguments drawing on natural rights and Christian doctrine could be used to establish the sinfulness of making slaves of other peoples, the success of a political campaign against slavery rested on nationalising this sin. Making slavery the sin of a nation, rather than of individuals, would align the moral motive and legal authority for action against human bondage. Anthony Benezet, in his 1767 writings, alluded briefly to this idea, developing the American Quakers' steps in this direction.[18] Within a decade, Granville Sharp advanced the argument that the guilt of slavery fell collectively on Britons, not just on slave traders or slaveholders. He did so by appealing to popular notions of 'the immediate Interposition of DIVINE PROVIDENCE, to recompence [sic] impenitent NATIONS according to their Works'.[19] Every Briton might have an obligation to act once the millstones of guilt had been distributed through nationality and subjecthood. Moreover, a transatlantic war of words during the American Revolution had the unintended consequence of discussing national blame for slavery and the slave trade. As Christopher Brown suggests, this offered individuals, sects and nations the prize of 'moral capital' for their abolitionist virtue and, consequently, guilt for their sinful inaction.[20]

After 1787, mass petitioning and popular support urged the nation's parliament to act against a barbaric trade supplying a debased colonial society.[21] It is beyond the scope of this paper to determine whether

[16] Brown, *Moral Capital*, 95–101; Dana Rabin, '"In a Country of Liberty?": Slavery, Villeinage and the Making of Whiteness in the Somerset Case (1772)', *History Workshop Journal*, 72 (2011), 5–29; William R. Cotter, 'The Somerset Case and the Abolition of Slavery in England', *History*, 79 (1994), 31–56.

[17] Seymour Drescher, *Capitalism and Antislavery: British Mobilization in Comparative Perspective* (Oxford, 1987 [1986]), 22–4; James Lee Ray, 'The Abolition of Slavery and the End of International War', *International Organization*, 43 (1989), 405–39, at 434. For earlier metropolitan concern about colonial bondage, see John Donoghue '"Out of the Land of Bondage": The English Revolution and the Atlantic Origins of Abolition', *American Historical Review*, 115 (2010), 943–74.

[18] Anthony Benezet, *A Caution to Great Britain and Her Colonies* (Philadelphia and London, 1767), 42; Blackburn, *American Crucible*, 152.

[19] Granville Sharp, *The Law of Retribution, or A Serious Warning to Great Britain and Her Colonies* (1776), title page. Capitalisation follows the original.

[20] Brown, *Moral Capital*.

[21] See John Oldfield, *Popular Politics and British Anti-Slavery: The Mobilisation of Public Opinion against the Slave Trade, 1787–1807* (Manchester, 1995); Carey, *British Abolitionism*; Drescher, *Capitalism and Antislavery*; Clare Midgley, *Women Against Slavery: The British Campaigns 1780–1870* (1992).

God-fearing Britons expected punishments for inaction in this world or the next but both fears could be found in countless references to 'the mercy of Providence ... from Heaven for those enormous evils we have committed', as William Pitt begged.[22] The nation's collective responsibility for the morality of British merchants and British colonists was a dominant idea throughout the anti-slavery campaigns. Political sovereignty created obligations for the conduct those engaged in the British slave trade.

A distinct reformulation of moral responsibility emerged after 1791 when parliament had rejected a bill to abolish Britain's slave trade for the first time. A proposed abstention from sugar – anachronistically, we would call it a consumer boycott – was radical in method, intent and theory, as Clare Midgley argues.[23] Practically, an individual or family disavowal of slave sugar placed significant new power into the hands of women. Politically, self-denial promised to let consumer power do what parliament should have done: stop the traffic in slaves from Africa to the sugar colonies. Intellectually, this tactic identified Britons' active consumption of slave-grown sugar as a new reason to take a similarly active role in abolitionism. A pamphlet on the topic, written by William Fox and promoted by his publisher Martha Gurney, enjoyed swift sales, amassing twenty-six editions, with perhaps 130,000 copies printed in London and many more again in provincial and piratical printings.[24] Fox instructed readers that 'if we purchase the commodity, we participate in the crime'. He reasoned that, '[w]ere an hundred assassins to plunge their daggers into their victim' then 'every one of them would be guilty of the intire [sic] crime'.[25]

Such a doctrine anticipated later transnational consumer movements in connecting the moral responsibility of consumers and the means by which their purchases were being produced. In the late eighteenth century, however, this argument was still strongly infused with the moral geography of empire and with national identity. While the consumption of slave-grown produce transferred guilt from the West Indian planter to the British consumer, it did so within a closed market of protective

---

[22] *The Debate on a Motion for the Abolition of the Slave-Trade in the House of Commons, on Monday the Second of April, 1792* (1792), 172.

[23] Clare Midgley, *Feminism and Empire: Women Activists in Imperial Britain, 1790–1865* (Abingdon, 2007), 41–64.

[24] Anon. [William Fox], *An Address to the People of Great Britain, On the Utility of Refraining from the Use of West India Sugar and Rum*, 5th edn, corrected (1791); Timothy Whelan, 'William Fox, Martha Gurney and Radical Discourse of the 1790s', *Eighteenth-Century Studies*, 42 (2009), 397–411, at 397; Timothy Whelan, 'Martha Gurney and the Anti-Slave Trade Movement, 1788–94', in *Women, Dissent and Anti-Slavery in Britain and America, 1790–1865*, ed. Elizabeth J. Clapp and Julie Roy Jeffrey (Oxford, 2011), 44–65.

[25] [Fox], *Address*, 3–4.

tariffs. The monopoly granted to the British West Indies meant that the 'laws of our country ... prohibit us the sugar cane, unless we will receive it through the medium of slavery'.[26] Moreover, when Fox asserted that 'the offices of humanity and functions of justice' should universally protect the 'rights of men' of any race, he did not suggest that fellow-Britons opposed abuses everywhere. Anchored in his own experience of anti-slavery and West Indian monopoly, Fox never argued that British consumers would be morally responsible for the way a foreign commodity, such as cotton, was produced. This scenario earned barely any contemplation while British sugar enjoyed a protected monopoly in the home market. Rather, he specified direct action against the suffering of Africans perpetrated by *British* planters at a distance from the metropole and *British* slave traders even when beyond the boundaries of the empire.[27] Fox attacked the violation of the 'common law' (of Britain) when 'fellow subjects' (by which he meant slaves born on British soil) were held in slavery.[28] His moral outrage was defined by nationality rather than 'by geographical boundaries' of distance. Much of the universalist language surrounding 'all nations of one blood' reflected an eighteenth-century conflation of race with 'nation'.[29] In this light, Fox condemned racial slavery perpetuated by Britons, rather than offering a moral mandate for transnational action.

Finally, we should observe that this consumer responsibility for sugar production came as an instrument for abolishing the slave trade; while abolitionists ultimately expected this to transform West Indian slavery into a freer form of labour, sugar would still be made by slaves, even if it was less polluted by the blood of Africans killed in the middle passage. Elites including William Wilberforce were troubled by Fox's appeal to popular economic power precisely because it sought to circumvent a proper political decision for parliament. If abstention had targeted some foreign produce of slavery, manufactured in territories outside the sovereignty of the crown, then it would have been utopian but unthreatening. The constitutionality of the abstention campaign was in question precisely because it usurped the responsibility of parliament by promising to overturn a determination of MPs.[30]

When Elizabeth Heyrick revived the tactic to press for immediate emancipation after 1824, she still wanted to 'have purified the nation from the foulest of its corruptions' alongside the promise 'of possessing "*clean hands*"' through boycotting West Indian goods. Like Fox, she emphasised

[26] *Ibid.*, 2.
[27] *Ibid.*, 11.
[28] *Ibid.*, 8.
[29] Hall, 'Troubling Memories', 167–8.
[30] Esther Copley, *A History of Slavery and its Abolition*, 2nd edn (1839), 295.

that planters and consumers were 'the thief and the receiver of stolen goods'.[31] Heyrick mentioned foreign slaveholding states only to note that 'we must purge ourselves of these pollutions' in order 'to persuade them to follow her [England's] example'.[32] Like her, T. S. Winn celebrated the ambiguity of deriving guilt through both one's nation and one's consumption. He admitted in 1825 that 'it may seem hard that the Nation should be bound by the unjust acts of its Government' but it was fair enough given that 'every man, woman and child, in Great Britain, have for centuries been, and still actually are, abettors of, and participators in, the iniquitous system, by being purchasers and daily consumers of the guilt produce of Slavery'.[33] Before emancipation, the captive market for sugar consumption made consumer and imperial responsibilities identical.

Such a formula helped abolitionists rouse individuals' sense of duty to escape a guilt devolved on them by their country, and this idea was easily revived as late as 1838 during agitation against the 'apprenticeship' imposed on freed West Indians. In this campaign, the Ladies' Anti-Slavery Association in the North declared that '[t]he crimes of our country have lain heavy on our hearts; we could not bear to partake of the guilty produce, to leave the legacy of unexpiated sin for our children'.[34] Until their victory over planters in the British Empire, anti-slavery rhetoric could pair together imperial and consumer identities, since their sugar came from one of their own colonies.[35]

Given the political challenges facing anti-slavery campaigners in their attacks on British slave trading or West Indian slavery, it is hardly surprising that theoretical differences were ignored so easily. However, as the foregoing examples suggest, arguments for abstention from slave-produced sugar or rum contained the kernel of a radical proposal for individual consumer responsibility. While circumstances did not test how many abolitionists would expand this concept from imperial produce to foreign, slave-grown goods, this question would confront Britons after emancipation. In order to trace the ways in which British anti-slavery politics transcended or respected national borders now requires analysis of the imperfect distinctions contemporaries drew between slave-trade suppression and foreign slaveholding. In turn, the next two parts of this paper will consider the moral geographies of responsibility for the slave trade and slavery beyond the borders of the British Empire, before

---

[31] Elizabeth Heyrick, *Immediate, Not Gradual Abolition: Or, An Inquiry into the Shortest, Safest, and Most Effectual Means of Getting Rid of West Indian Slavery* ([Boston, MA, 1838] 1824), 4, 12, 35.

[32] *Ibid.*, 3.

[33] T. S. Winn, *A Speedy End to Slavery in Our West India Colonies: By Safe, Effectual, and Equitable Means for All the Parties Concerned* (1825), 50.

[34] *The British Emancipator*, 16 May 1838, 94.

[35] See too Samuel Kingsford, *Duty of Individuals, As It Respects the Slave Trade* (1792), 3–5.

drawing conclusions about the contours and causes of the boundaries on Britons' consciences.

International suppression of the slave trade

The Slave Trade Abolition Act of 1807 banned British subjects from engaging in slave trading anywhere in the world; while the prohibition extended beyond the borders of the empire, it only sought to regulate the actions of Britons or those trading in British territories. So, while the geography of anti-slavery responsibility extended to any foreign port where British slave traders operated, this derived from the authority and responsibility of parliament. However, in reality, this ban was impossible to enforce if British slave traders had recourse to the flags of other countries. During the Napoleonic Wars, the royal navy intercepted hostile foreign shipping and readily checked the flags of neutral shipping visiting European ports or colonies. In 1814, one MP told the House of Commons that 'it had come to his ears, that there were persons in this country base enough to wish for the return of peace, on account of the facilities it would afford for carrying on this detestable traffic under another flag'.[36] As the conflict ended, the British government faced one of the first dilemmas presented by the transformation into an anti-slave-trading nation: how would abolition be enforced in times of peace? It was this practical difficulty, as much as fears of economic disadvantage, which led British foreign policy to push for foreigners to abolish their slave trades and cooperate in mutual naval interdiction.[37]

Rather than presenting French abolition as a condition of peace imposed by the victors on the vanquished, Wilberforce and others insisted that the French would be abolishing a trade that had been suppressed by the ravages of war.[38] Abolition became a legitimate area for international meddling since a peace treaty's 'legal permission to carry it on would practically be a new establishment of it'.[39] It was precisely because Britain held preeminent sway over peace negotiations that subjects felt responsible and legitimate in directing foreigners to act against the slave trade. Abolitionists objected to their country signing a treaty 'creating

[36] *Hansard*, first series, 2 May 1814, XXVII, 646.

[37] See David Eltis, *Economic Growth and the Ending of the Transatlantic Slave Trade* (Oxford, 1987); Paul Michael Kielstra, *The Politics of Slave Trade Suppression in Britain and France, 1814–48* (New York, 2003); Jenny S. Martinez, *The Slave Trade and the Origins of International Human Rights Law* (Oxford, 2012).

[38] William Wilberforce, *A Letter to His Excellency Prince of Talleyrand Perigord &c. on the Subject of the Slave Trade* (1814), 48–9, 54, 64.

[39] *Hansard*, first series, 2 May 1814, XXVII, 642; *British and Foreign State Papers*, III, 903–5: Wellington to Prince de Benevent, 26 Aug. 1814. For the reality of the situation, see David Eltis, 'Was Abolition of the U.S. and British Slave Trade Significant in the Broader Atlantic Context?', *William and Mary Quarterly*, 3rd series, 66 (2009), 715–36.

it anew' given that 'the war had practically abolished it for many years past'.[40] For abolitionist petitioners, a victorious Britain could not claim neutrality at a time when French merchants planned, 'with the aid of British Capital, to carry on the Trade on the Coast of Africa'. Once more, a cry raised by Wilberforce insisted that 'all who would not be partakers of the guilt' their country would 'protest against it'.[41]

A response duly emerged from the provinces; in Plymouth, for example, 'a very numerous and respectable' assembly bemoaned that Britain might 'confederate in the Revival' of the slave trade, bringing down 'Divine Vengeance' on 'all those who shall either carry on or be wanting in their utmost exertions, to prevent, the Continuance of so odious and detestable a Traffic'.[42] Between a fifth and a third of Britain's adult male population signed such a petition during the peace negotiations.[43] Amongst these anti-slavery supporters in the country, there were a variety of attitudes towards the defeated French, both vindictive and altruistic, when it came to imposing abolition as a condition of peace.[44] In the British cabinet, quite aside from national calculations of realpolitik, politicians were under pressure from sporadic bursts of petitioning, as Seymour Drescher convincingly shows. The mass mobilisation of 1814–15 demanded that slave-trade abolition should be a priority in peace negotiations; it was one of a handful of occasions when large numbers of Britons campaigned for anti-slavery measures in foreign, rather than imperial, policy.[45]

In negotiations surrounding the Treaty of Paris, Wellington offered Prince Talleyrand's government 'a sum of money or an Island in the West Indies, in order to obtain from them the immediate abolition of the Slave Trade'.[46] Ironically, the restored Bourbons held out in 1814 for a five-year delay in abolition, but found themselves stomaching an immediate ban in 1815 when Napoleon issued one at the start of the Hundred Days in a cynical appeal to British public opinion.[47] More appreciated was the abolition of the Dutch slave trade, undertaken to thank Britain for the

---

[40] *Hansard*, first series, 2 May 1814, XXVII, 638.

[41] *British and Foreign State Papers*, III, 901–2: Wellington to Castlereagh, 25 Aug. 1814; Wilberforce as quoted by Betty Fladeland, 'Abolitionist Pressures on the Concert of Europe, 1814–1822', *Journal of Modern History*, 38 (1966), 355–73, at 358.

[42] 1/669/4, Plymouth and West Devon Record Office, address to the prince regent, 1814.

[43] Seymour Drescher, 'Public Opinion and Parliament in the Abolition of the British Slave Trade', in *The British Slave Trade: Abolition, Parliament and People*, ed. Stephen Farrell, Melanie Unwin and James Walvin (Edinburgh, 2007), 42–65, at 64.

[44] Kielstra, *Politics*, 28–33; Seymour Drescher, 'Whose Abolition? Popular Pressure and the Ending of the British Slave Trade', *Past and Present*, 143 (1994), 136–66, esp. 160–2.

[45] *Ibid.*, 159–64. The distinction between 'foreign' and 'imperial' anti-slavery policy deserves further development, but will have to wait for a separate treatment.

[46] *British and Foreign State Papers*, III, 907–9: Wellington to Castlereagh, 4 Oct. 1814.

[47] Fladeland, 'Abolitionist Pressure', 362–6.

freedom of the Netherlands.[48] In the case of the monarchs of the Iberian nations, economic recapitalisation provided by British loans had to be tied to abolition in the case of Spain or restriction for Portugal. As Castlereagh concluded, 'the present temper of Parliament and of the Nation' would not permit a loan to establish security for a regime that promoted the slave trade as a national interest.[49]

British popular support for international slave-trade suppression had dramatic consequences for the shape of nineteenth-century British foreign policy beyond the practical need to prevent Britons hiding under the flags of slave-trading nations. Without the particular opportunities and challenges presented to British abolitionists during the construction of a new Concert of Europe, the national right and national obligation to meddle in others' slave trades would have been far weaker. In the decades following the Napoleonic Wars, British legal recognition of new South American states was tied to their abolition of the slave trade.[50] British arbitration of Spanish decolonisation was framed by a popular abhorrence of complicity in restoring regimes that would sponsor the slave trade and Canning promised in 1822 that 'no state in the New World will be recognized by Great Britain which has not frankly and completely abolished the trade in slaves'.[51] Having sought local abolition laws, declarations or constitutional articles, British diplomats pursued a new round of Latin American treaties guaranteeing mutual search at sea between the royal navy and the Argentine Confederation, Uruguay (both 1839), Mexico (1842), Bolivia, Chile (both 1842) and Ecuador (1847); the Foreign Office showed particular urgency in securing the right of search from nations with flags abused by slavers and not from others, such as New Granada, whose flags the slave traders adopted less often.[52]

The transnational basis of slave-trade commerce did not respect the political boundaries of nineteenth-century empires. As early as 1810, the philanthropic African Institution erroneously briefed the royal navy that a ship was only Portuguese – and therefore permitted to supply slaves to Brazil – if it was built, owned and crewed by Portuguese men. Such

---

[48] Holger Lutz Kern, 'Strategies of Legal Change: Great Britain, International Law, and the Abolition of the Transatlantic Slave Trade', *Journal of the History of International Law*, 6 (2004), 233–58, at 241.

[49] *British and Foreign State Papers*, III, 923–6: Castlereagh to Sir Henry Wellesley, 30 July 1814. See also Drescher, 'Whose Abolition?', 163–4; Bernard H. Nelson, 'The Slave Trade as a Factor in British Foreign Policy 1815–1862', *Journal of Negro History*, 27 (1942), 192–209, at 197–200.

[50] Leslie Bethell, *The Abolition of the Brazilian Slave Trade: Britain, Brazil and the Slave Trade* (Cambridge, 1970), 27–61.

[51] As quoted by James Ferguson King, 'The Latin-American Republics and the Suppression of the Slave Trade', *Hispanic American Historical Review*, 24 (1944), 387–411, at 391.

[52] *Ibid.*, 400–9.

ambiguities in treaties were regularly used to expand Britain's legitimate responsibilities and powers throughout the next century.[53] In 1839 and 1845, Palmerston and Aberdeen redesigned – or, more accurately, twisted – international law to authorise the royal navy to enforce more completely slave-trade abolition against Portuguese and Brazilian shipping. The governments of these nations were not meeting the obligations that Britain understood to have been contracted in bilateral treaties. If these powers did not enforce abolition, then both Whigs and Tories were willing to police these foreigners' merchants as if they were British. This was not without controversy amongst parliamentarians, since it pushed the boundaries of Britain's powers under bilateral treaties; Aberdeen himself was critical of Palmerston's actions and anxious about his own when he followed a similar course.[54] Later attempts to secure an international ban on slave trading actually underlined the fact that most Britons assumed the need for national consent from other 'civilized' countries, given the problems arising from unilateral or serial bilateral suppression regimes.[55] The impossibility of enforcing British abolition without powers over foreign flags created a national moral interest in other nations' sins. The expense, bloodiness and violence of the campaign did not escape criticism from pacifists and penny-pinchers, particularly in the 1840s. Rather than defending the slave trade, however, *laissez-faire* MPs such as William Hutt, Richard Cobden and William Gladstone argued that the naval campaign was ineffective in suppressing illegal traffickers and only succeeded in causing greater suffering. They challenged whether legal, diplomatic and military bullying by Britain undermined the cultivation of domestic anti-slavery sentiment.[56]

What is striking is how this expansive, ambitious approach to slave-trade diplomacy contrasted with a meek and weak policy in pushing foreigners to abandon slavery altogether. In the same period, activists from the British and Foreign Anti-Slavery Society had hoped that British recognition of the Republic of Texas, together with loans, could be tied to emancipation. By contrast, Palmerston and Aberdeen focused almost exclusively on a slave-trade suppression treaty in return for recognition, leaving slaveholding to internal Texan politics.[57] While some thought

[53] Kern, 'Strategies', 237–8.

[54] Bethell, *Abolition*, 242–66.

[55] Edward Keene, 'A Case Study of the Construction of International Hierarchy: British Treaty-Making against the Slave Trade in the Early Nineteenth Century', *International Organization*, 61 (2007), 311–39.

[56] Richard Huzzey, 'Gladstone and the Suppression of the Transatlantic Slave Trade', in *William Gladstone: New Studies and Perspectives*, ed. Roland Quinault, Roger Swift and Ruth Clayton Windscheffel (Aldershot, 2012), 253–68.

[57] David Turley, 'Anti-Slavery Activists and Officials: "Influence", Lobbying and the Slave Trade, 1807–1850', in *Slavery, Diplomacy and Empire: Britain and the Suppression of the Slave Trade*,

recognition of a new, slaveholding nation constituted active complicity on the part of Great Britain, establishment opinion concluded that slaveholding would not be encouraged and anti-slave-trade interests would be advanced.[58] Such questions of where foreign policy should draw a line between tolerating slavery and pushing for slave-trade suppression would resurface in the American Civil War. The United States had long resisted permitting Britain a right of search.[59] There was wisdom, not eccentricity, in Lincoln's calculation that the 1862 Lyons–Seward Treaty would confirm his administration's humanitarian credentials in British eyes.[60] While Britons fiercely disagreed over the rights or wrongs of the conflict and the extent to which slavery lay at the heart of the war, Palmerston's government was safe in the knowledge that the Confederate constitution banned the slave trade. On this point, the Southerners converged with the consistent priority of Britain's anti-slave-trade foreign policy, aware it was a precondition for their much-desired diplomatic recognition.[61] On both sides of the Atlantic, however, those pro-Union partisans who saw the recognition of a slaveholding power as inconsistent with Britain's anti-slavery policies were introducing a novel and controversial proposition.

Rather than using foreign policy to promote emancipation alongside slave-trade suppression, British governments used moral suasion with other 'civilised' powers. This reflected a preference for making foreign populations aware of their own national guilt rather than assuming for Britons the responsibility of acting against slaveholding in other societies. Before the unique circumstances surrounding the Congress of Vienna, Henry Brougham had argued that '[n]o great reform has ever taken place in one part of the international and intercolonial systems, without

---

1807–1975, ed. Keith Hamilton and Patrick Salmon (Eastbourne, 2009), at 87–91; David Turley, *The Culture of English Antislavery, 1780–1860* (1991), 205–11; Bertram Wyatt-Brown, *Lewis Tappan and the Evangelical War against Slavery* (Baton Rouge, 1997 [1969]), 248–56.

[58] *Edinburgh Review*, Apr. 1841, 266–8; N. Doran Maillard, *The History of the Republic of Texas, from the Discovery of the Country to the Present Time and the Cause of Separation from the Republic of Mexico* (1842), 75–90.

[59] Steven Heath Mitton, 'The Free World Confronted: The Problem of Slavery and Progress in American Foreign Relations, 1833–1844' (Ph.D. dissertation, Louisiana State University, 2005); Harry E. Landry, 'Slavery and the Slave Trade in Atlantic Diplomacy, 1850–1861', *Journal of Southern History*, 27 (1961), 184–207; Donald L. Canney, *Africa Squadron: The U.S. Navy and the Slave Trade, 1842–1861* (Washington, DC, 2006). Look for Mitton's forthcoming work on 'the Ashburton capitulation'.

[60] Howard Jones, *Blue & Gray Diplomacy: A History of Union and Confederate Foreign Relations* (Chapel Hill, 2010), 122–3; Howard Jones, *Abraham Lincoln and a New Birth of Freedom: The Union and Slavery in the Diplomacy of the Civil War* (Lincoln, NE, and London, 1999), 65–6.

[61] *The Southern Confederacy and the African Slave Trade: The Correspondence between Professor Cairnes, AM, and George McHenry, Esq*, ed. George B. Wheeler (Dublin, 1863); W. E. B. Du Bois, *Suppression of the African Slave-Trade to the United States of America, 1638–1870* (Boston, MA, 1896), 188–9.

a similar change being soon effected in all the other parts'; Britain could rely on setting 'an example of reformation'.[62] British abolitionists such as Thomas Clarkson and Zachary Macaulay took it upon themselves to develop popular anti-slavery movements in other countries precisely because they recognised the limitations of British foreign policy in spreading their principles abroad.[63] This concern for foreigners' self-determination weighed far more heavily in public opinion and political action concerning slavery than it did regarding the slave trade. As we shall see in the next section, these differences can be illuminated more clearly by now considering why Britons proved so deferential to the political geography of slaveholding when framing their anti-slavery duties.

Anti-slavery in one country?

While a combination of practical and contingent circumstances meant that abolition of the slave trade dragged British consciences abroad, politicians could adopt a more distant approach to foreign slaveries. Continuing slave trades depleted and devastated the African continent or disrupted abolitionist nations' efforts but the perpetuation of slaveholding within other countries was more readily ignored. This division was not simply natural but a contentious development framed by the national basis of British anti-slavery guilt before the West Indian emancipation of 1834–8. In the decades following 1838, some abolitionists hoped to see their government take moral responsibility for the porous commercial or financial relationships which still fed New World slaveries; they wished to embrace the potential global market responsibility left undeveloped and untested in earlier radical abolitionism. That the British population ultimately accepted international trade and national consumption of slave-grown goods and the export of capital or equipment for foreign slaveholders deserves careful explanation. Had the 'moral geography' of British anti-slavery supporters shrunk, relieving political pressure on statesmen?

In fact, as we have seen, political boundaries mattered as much as distance in determining Britons' sense of moral responsibility for slaves' suffering. While the differences between a bounded social responsibility of national or church community and an unbounded individual responsibility to all humanity had been present in mid-eighteenth-century ideas, there had been little tension or testing of which model of moral responsibility would win out in practice. After the termination of apprenticeship in 1838, conflicts multiplied in number,

---

[62] As quoted by David R. Murray, *Odious Commerce: Britain, Spain and the Abolition of the Cuban Slave Trade* (Cambridge, 1980), 22.

[63] Kielstra, *Politics*, 43–4; Fladeland, 'Abolitionist Pressures', 356–7, 360, 370.

size and importance as subjects invested in foreign businesses profiting from a form of labour now prohibited in the British Empire, as domestic dependence on slave-grown sugar and cotton grew, and as escaping slaves sought sanctuary on the 'free soil' of the United Kingdom. In these three spheres of complicity, arguments for apathy and inaction ultimately won out and it is necessary to explain why.

The 1807 Slave Trade Act had banned Britons from financing the trafficking of Africans to other nations' colonies, but British proved even more difficult to police than subjects. Moreover, following West Indian emancipation, the British government acted slowly, gradually and unconvincingly to implement similar restrictions on capital in slaveholding industries. While Britons were ordered not to own slaves or invest in businesses using them, the huge commercial investment in the slave-infused economies of Latin America suggests many breaches of the law's letter and spirit. The case of the Cata Branca slaves, where Brazilian abolitionists presented evidence of a London-based company's fraudulent working of slaves, was an unusual occasion when illegality was caught. For many years, British mining businesses, such as the St John d'el Rey Company, maintained the fiction that they hired slave workers rather than owning them.[64] When tangible public examples were exposed, the British government was embarrassed into investigation and action. It seems that the rarity and difficulty of these cases bred official fatalism rather than duplicity, since the state was poorly equipped to untangle practical circumstances on the ground and secure convictions.[65]

Where British subjects directly owned slaves and the government faced incontrovertible evidence, action followed for fear of public anger. This was a politics of 'clean hands', desperately avoiding moral responsibility or complicity rather than seeking or seizing opportunities to interfere in foreign slaveries. Loans or investments where British subjects did not assume personal responsibility for slaveholding could be accepted as the price of doing business in a world still suffused with slavery. The moral geography of British anti-slavery extended to subjects' overseas property but not to their dividend cheques. This apathy mirrored political resignation towards British involvement in slave-related imports and exports – but the latter situation was less the product of weary consensus than a turbulent political contest.

---

[64] Matt D. Childs, 'A Case of "Great Unstableness": A British Slaveholder and Brazilian Abolition', *The Historian*, 60 (1998), 717–40; Marshall G. Eakin, 'Business Imperialism and British Enterprise in Brazil: The St. John d'el Rey Mining Company, Limited, 1830–1960', *Hispanic American Historical Review*, 66 (1986), 697–741.
[65] For an alternative view, see Marika Sherwood, *After Abolition: Britain and the Slave Trade since 1807* (2007).

While abolitionists pioneered mass abstention from West Indian sugar and rum during the period stretching from 1791 to 1833, they were consuming increasing quantities of slave-grown cotton. With a series of advances in cotton-gin technology, the slave agriculture of the American South boomed in response to the unending demand of the industrial mills of northern England.[66] By the turn of the nineteenth century, imports of cotton from the United States dominated the British market and, despite the disruption of the war of 1812, swelled the profitability of plantations. Annual cotton cultivation in the slave states increased from around 2 million to 182 million pounds of cotton between 1791 and 1823, strengthening Southerners' attachment to their 'peculiar institution'.[67] Clarkson himself denied the need, in 1792, to extend British anti-slavery abstention campaigns to slave-grown cotton, not least because that 'might take away the bread of a million of our fellow subjects, the innocent poor of this country'.[68] The limited scope of abstention, targeting imperial sugar, suggests that it was a tactical obligation for British abolitionists, rather than an imperative for all forms of slave-grown imports. It is hard to credit Elizabeth Heyrick or the Liverpool merchant James Cropper, both advocates of abstention from West Indian sugar in the 1820s, with ignorance or imbecility in their apparent inconsistency. Instead, their sense of moral responsibility was attuned to the political geography of the British Empire, rather than simply the physical breadth of the Atlantic Ocean.

Before 1833, one of the only people to propose economic sanctions for foreign sins abroad was not a radical abolitionist but a very conservative foreign secretary. In the midst of his desperate attempts to balance the demands of Britain's anti-slavery conscience and French national pride in 1814–15, Lord Castlereagh suggested 'a League against the import of Colonial produce grown by States, dissentient from the general policy' of abolishing the slave trade. This clearly struck him as a neat way to appease popular pressure through British commercial policy rather than French politicians, but it seems not to have met with enthusiasm by his peers.[69] No such trade penalty was applied to states resisting abolition and, even if it had, the Castlereagh proposals would not have penalised the produce of slavery *per se* since all European nations including Britain itself retained slavery after banning the slave trade. This germ of an idea

[66] Angela Lakwete, *Inventing the Cotton Gin: Machine and Myth in Antebellum America* (Baltimore, 2005).

[67] Michael M. Edwards, *The Growth of the British Cotton Trade, 1780–1815* (Manchester, 1967), 89–96, 105.

[68] Drescher, *Capitalism and Antislavery*, 217.

[69] *British and Foreign State Papers*, III, 905: Castlereagh to Bathurst; *British and Foreign State Papers*, III, 901: Castlereagh to Wellington, 6 Aug. 1814; Fladeland, 'Abolitionist Pressures', 362, 365.

fell on stony ground, in all likelihood, because Britain's existing system of duties excluded foreign sugars, making a 'League' against French exports a fairly hollow threat.

Until emancipation, the long-standing policy of West Indian protection rewarded slave cultivation. However, growing anxieties about the price of sugar led some politicians by the 1840s to propose free trade in sugar. In general, free traders vilified emancipated black Britons as undeserving of special protection, resisting the claims of protectionists that the illegal slave trade would prosper from the measure.[70] This question exposed differing views of the moral geography of Britain's anti-slavery responsibilities. While Bishop Samuel Wilberforce suggested that the consumption of slave-grown commerce would 'plunge this country again into the guilt of this great crime', he was soon disappointed to discover that the rest of the country did not feel the same way.[71] Some of the cleric's allies supported an imperial preference for wholly non-humanitarian motives, but the arguments that they employed still bear study since these shaped the national debate beyond the houses of parliament. As Milner Gibson argued, '[t]hey must confine their attention to their own country' rather than 'making their trade depend upon the municipal laws of foreign nations, and the abolition of slavery in other lands' when the 'two things were distinct'.[72] British authority, legitimacy and responsibility for slave production, he and his peers suggested, was confined to British soil, and the development of abolitionist movements in other nations would only be hampered by the isolation, rivalry and hostility of protectionism.[73]

Some protectionists reasoned that the principal beneficiaries of an open sugar trade would be the Brazilian and Cuban slaveholders still buying illegally imported slaves from Africa whereas the cotton-exporting United States enforced a largely effective ban. However, defending the Whig preference for freer trade in 1845, Thomas Macaulay insisted that this distinction was sophistry, given that a domestic slave trade thrived between the 'breeding States' of the upper South and 'the sugar and cotton States' down the Mississippi where enslaved Africans were in the highest demand. By this measure, America's exports were 'the fruits, not only of slavery, but of the slave trade'.[74] Since the exclusion of slave-grown sugar was morally inconsistent with the embrace of slave-grown cotton, Macaulay suggested that the nation's anti-slavery conscience, which his

[70] Richard Huzzey, 'Free Trade, Free Labour and Slave Sugar in Victorian Britain', *Historical Journal*, 53 (2010), 359–79.

[71] *Hansard*, third series, 13 Aug. 1846, LXXXVIII, 666.

[72] *Hansard*, third series, 8 July 1846, LXXXVIII, 122.

[73] Huzzey, 'Free Trade', 368–9.

[74] Macaulay, *Speeches of Lord Macaulay*, 164–6, 168.

father had played so significant a role in cultivating, had to keep out of the customs house.

Philosophically, this argument demanded the consistency of a universal rule that would place the guilt of consuming any and all slave produce either inside or outside the proper moral duties of the British nation. This type of argument met short shrift from particularly clever protectionists such as Benjamin Disraeli, who in 1846 told his Whig opponents that he had 'no wish to argue the question abstractly'. He denied the 'abstract principle, that a man, because he is obliged to wink at a certain evil, is bound to commit a greater one' and so defended the poorly mapped moral geography of the *status quo* against their 'flashy plea'. His distinction between 'an abstract or a concrete position' analysed the terms of debate more rigorously than other clashes inside the Palace of Westminster or without. Disraeli actually noted that the inconsistency now derided by free traders was consistency with the fact that slave-trade abolition 'was supported by men who patronized slave-grown cotton and slave-grown tobacco'; indeed, 'when Clarkson, and at a subsequent period, Wilberforce addressed those districts of the north of England which originated the great movement against slavery', the industry of those areas had been 'fed with cotton the produce of slave labour' and British subjects had 'been smoking, snuffing, and chewing slave-grown tobacco' long before and after they petitioned parliament. Far from being ignorant of this, 'a practical people knew how to deal with circumstances' and 'must put an end to those abominations we can control, and shut our eyes to those we cannot control'.[75]

In Disraeli's hands, the protection of sugar was not a hopeless attempt to seal British society in a moral vacuum from the practicalities of a fallen world. Rather, he drew a distinction between an established dependency 'we cannot control' and a rejection of a novel reception of slave-grown sugar, which would mean allowing new 'abominations we can control'.[76] Therefore, while he declined to draw indelible boundaries between moral responsibility for slavery in Brazil and slavery in the United States, he still emphasised national limits of responsibility: in this case, Britain had a duty not to slide backwards into greater dependency on slave produce, even if he agreed that it was impossible to break the addiction entirely. Hence, the slavery of foreign nations became the business of the British legislature if parliamentarians were going to create a new field of fortune rather than accept the inevitability of existing market forces. If other protectionists had stuck to such a clever rationalisation of existing trade policy, they may have had rather more luck than they did.

---

[75] *Hansard*, third series, 8 July 1846, LXXXVIII, 157–8.
[76] *Ibid.*

In 1841, Sir Robert Peel had developed a similar argument: 'I do not recognise that principle' that 'there is some overpowering moral obligation which compels us to abstain altogether from the consumption of the produce of slavery'. Rather, 'after attempting to adjust this balance of good and evil', he came down 'in favour of this continued exclusion of sugar, the produce of slave labour'.[77] And while he did not support abstraction, he compared Britain to Rome in a poem of Dryden's, arguing that while Britons did not 'rule the world, and make mankind obey' as the Romans had done, there was still 'a sway, an "awful sway", which we could still exercise – that there was in our hands not a material but a moral power, enabling us to "rule the world", and, through the influence of high principles and of glorious sacrifices, to "make mankind obey"'.[78] That Peel, the son of a cotton merchant, found slave-grown cotton unobjectionable was unremarkable, but his line of logic was interesting. Like his future tormentor Disraeli, he rejected any hint of extending the moral geography of British anti-slavery responsibility indefinitely, preferring to focus on the agency of the British government in changing existing market conditions. Such a theorem diverged from the free traders on the question of whether a novel importation of sugar would implicate Britons in foreign guilt but accepted the more general notion that Britain was not responsible for the way their raw materials were cultivated abroad. The question of the sugar duties was so controversial because it required an active choice on the part of the government and so presented an unusually clear example of British trade policies' responsibility for slavery overseas.

If some parliamentarians for or against the sugar duties could happily agree that the moral geography of anti-slavery conscience did not extend to foreign produce, then what had happened to the radical, unbounded implications of John Woolman, William Fox and Elizabeth Heyrick's consumer responsibility? Some abolitionists did attempt to revive the general principle that purchasers of slave-grown articles became participators in the tyranny of slavery. However, following the sugar debacle, which had split the British and Foreign Anti-Slavery Society, the Birmingham Quaker Joseph Sturge and his comrades hoped to promote individual, consumer choice where national tariff barriers did not exist – and this was an option that even Richard Cobden could condone, as hopeless as he thought the effort was.[79] A transatlantic 'free produce' movement promoted free-labour goods on just this basis.[80] Sturge went so

---

[77] *Hansard*, third series, 18 May 1841, LVIII, 616.

[78] *Ibid.*, 626.

[79] *Harriet Beecher Stowe in Europe: The Journal of Charles Beecher*, ed. Joseph S. Van Why and Earl French (Hartford, CT, 1986), 118–19: entry for 23 May 1853.

[80] Nuermberger, *Free Produce Movement*; Lawrence B. Glickman, '"Buy for the Sake of the Slave": Abolitionism and the Origins of American Consumer Activism', *American Quarterly*,

far as securing special underwear for all his family, removing the faintest stain of slavery from his intimates.[81] An aged Thomas Clarkson now championed abstention from all slave-grown produce, where fifty years earlier he had limited the principle to West Indian exports.[82] Doubtless, early Victorians who patronised free-labour repositories did believe that their consciences were tied to the means of production rather than their national responsibilities as Britons. However, they were few in number and represented a surprisingly small minority of abolitionists and an even smaller proportion of the public.

Recalling his former life as a slave, the black abolitionist John Brown insisted in 1854 that if British women witnessed 'the infliction of what are called slight punishments on these unfortunate creatures, they would, I am sure, never in their lives wear another article made of slave-grown cotton'.[83] Yet, as one advocate for East Indian cotton complained after the American Civil War, 'it may safely be affirmed that, if the annihilation of slavery had depended upon the people of this Christian land paying knowingly one farthing per yard extra for free-labour calico, slavery would have gone on for ever'.[84] Ironically, during that conflict, those Britons who advocated 'interfering in the affairs of a nation three thousand miles away' to reopen the cotton trade were the same ones who considered the slave production of that commodity as none of their business.[85] Far from being a decline or betrayal of the principles underlying the imperial boycotts of the 1790s and 1820s, Victorian dilemmas over sugar and cotton presented starker distinctions over the limits of individual consumer and national responsibilities. Given that earlier pamphleteers had offered both engines of guilt as operating in parallel, it is not clear how many abstainers in the earlier period really supported a principle of individual consumer responsibility given that they did not extend the rule to foreign cotton or tobacco.

If the vast majority of Britons voted with their shopping baskets and accepted the foreign produce of slavery in their homes, they could get far more exercised when slaveholding foreigners brought their human

---

56 (2004), 889–912; Carol Faulkner, 'The Root of the Evil: Free Produce and Radical Antislavery, 1820–1860', *Journal of the Early Republic*, 27 (2007), 377–405.

[81] Stephen Hobhouse, *Joseph Sturge, His Life and Work* (1919), 111; Louis Billington, 'British Humanitarians and American Cotton, 1840–1860', *Journal of American Studies*, 11 (1977), 313–34.

[82] *Howitt's Journal*, 27 Nov. 1847, 338–9; *Hansard*, third series, 27 July 1846, LXXXVIII, 4–27. For fabrication of his consistency, see *Anti-Slavery Reporter*, 2 Apr. 1860, 88–9.

[83] John Brown, *Slave Life in Georgia: A Narrative of the Life, Sufferings, and Escape of John Brown, a Fugitive Slave, Now in England*, ed. Alexander Chamerovzow (1854), 172.

[84] John Watts, *The Facts of the Cotton Famine* (London and Manchester, 1866), 116. He did go on to suggest significant numbers would accept such privations if the trade in free cotton had survived long enough in the market.

[85] As noted by *ibid.*, 116.

property directly on to British soil. As David Turley has charted, the geographical proximity of the West Indies and Canada to the United States led to numerous controversies concerning American slaves on British soil. When slaves from the United States arrived in British colonies during a storm, piloted seized vessels to British ports or marched across the Canadian border, slavery could not be dismissed as the sovereign responsibility of another nation.[86] While the Foreign Office acceded to demands for an article of extradition in cases where fugitives were accused of crimes, anxious abolitionists were reassured by Lord Aberdeen that in practice this would never happen – and, indeed, it did not.[87]

The messy realities of anti-slavery policy on the spot threw up still more difficulties, however. British officials and naval officers stationed in slaveholding countries had for many years been given individual discretion in balancing respect for local sovereignty with their occasional instincts to aid escaping slaves. In 1874–5, a series of Fugitive Slave Circulars caused a major political controversy. With approval by Disraeli's Conservative administration, the Admiralty explicitly banned British officers from obstructing the capture of fugitive slaves seeking asylum on their vessels. While respectful of international law, which placed ships under local jurisdiction while in port, the judgement outraged moral sensibilities since it seemed to require the navy's active complicity in the upholding of slave ownership.[88] Scrambling to contain the scandal, the government ultimately retreated behind a Royal Commission after issuing an equally controversial second order, depicted by one cartoonist as binding the hands of a sailor, humiliatingly restraining him from his national responsibility to hate slavery (Figure 1).[89] The circulars were not such dramatic departures from military, legal and political opinion as the press imagined, since British dedication to slave-trade suppression had always coexisted with respect for the domestic slaveholding laws of foreign countries. However, the circulars violated the boundaries of moral responsibility for many circulation-conscious editors whose readers could find active complicity rather than resigned distance in the government's position on abandoning stowaways.

---

[86] David Turley, '"Free Air" and Fugitive Slaves: British Abolitionists versus Government over American Fugitives, 1834–61', in *Anti-Slavery, Religion and Reform: Essays in Memory of Roger Anstey*, ed. Christine Bolt and Seymour Drescher (Folkestone, 1980), 163–72; Sharon A. Roger Hepburn, 'Following the North Star: Canada as a Haven for Nineteenth-Century American Blacks', *Michigan Historical Review*, 25 (1999), 91–126.

[87] Turley, 'Anti-Slavery Activists'; Paul Finkelman, 'International Extradition and Fugitive Slaves: The John Anderson Case', *Brooklyn Journal of International Law*, 18 (1992), 765–810.

[88] William Mulligan, 'The Fugitive Slave Circulars, 1875–76', *Journal of Imperial and Commonwealth History*, 37 (2009), 183–205.

[89] *Punch*, 4 Mar. 1876, 79.

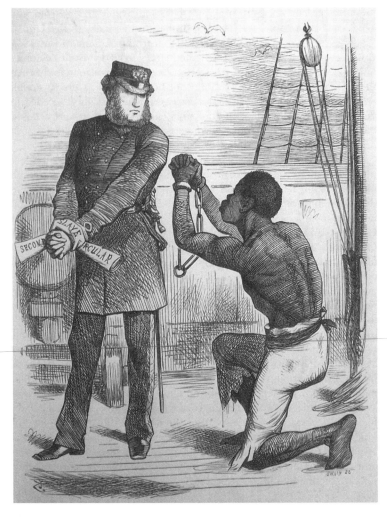

Figure 1 (Colour online) 'Men and Brothers!!', *Punch*, 4 Mar. 1876, 79. Fugitive Slave. 'Take these off!' Captain, R.N. 'How can I? – With *this* on?'

Just as Northerners in the United States objected to the Fugitive Slave Law making them complicit in Southern slaveholding, it seems likely that a majority of the British public, comprising supporters of both parties, felt that their nation should not transform their sailors into slave catchers. The treatment of slavery in African communities under later nineteenth-century British colonial rule is too large a topic to discuss here, but some basic facts may illustrate that imperial officials' selective blindness was largely consistent with the 'moral geography' of earlier foreign relations. Because protected countries were not technically British colonies, their domestic affairs were often considered as 'foreign' as those of sovereign states so long as British institutions and personnel did not become overtly complicit in slavery. When such compromising occasions were highlighted in parliament, ministers eagerly assured MPs that officials would not intervene to return slaves. In 1896–7, for example, the Tory attorney general, Sir Richard Webster, insisted that it would be illegal to detain slaves for being fugitives in British East Africa but quite proper to return them to be tried for incidental crimes. An opposition MP chastised him: 'it was a shock to find that in any legal sense the status of slavery was recognised under British influence'; the scandal of 1874–5 showed that 'if slaves were to be treated by English officers different from free men, a strong feeling in the country would rise against it'.[90]

Under the legal innovation of protectorates, the British government avoided complicity in slaveholding while permitting intra-African slaveries to continue within 'uncivilised' communities. This practice echoed the linguistic and legal abolitions in 1840s India, where 'traditional' slavery was denied the sanction of the courts and Anglo-Indians rechristened their slaves as 'servants'.[91] What British policy continued to attack was inter-racial slave trading, at least in theory – there were plenty of examples of officials on the spot hiding information from Whitehall. This was partly the result of a desire for stability – external slave trades caused disruptive slave raiding while tolerating 'traditional' domestic slaveries made for an easier life – but the combination was politically and culturally viable because of the nature of British anti-slavery thinking.[92] As Arthur Balfour insisted, this caution did not mean 'that they regarded it as part of the permanent policy of this country

[90] *Hansard*, fourth series, 11 Aug. 1896, XLIV, 481–2; *Hansard*, fourth series, 24 June 1897, L, 534–7. See also Jan S. Hogendorn and Paul E. Lovejoy, 'Keeping Slaves in Place: The Secret Debate on the Slavery Question in Northern Nigeria, 1900–1904', in *The Atlantic Slave Trade: Effects on Economies, Societies, and Peoples in Africa, the Americas, and Europe*, ed. Joseph E. Inikori and Stanley L. Engerman (Durham, NC, 1992), 49–76.

[91] Margot Finn, 'Slaves out of Context: Domestic Slavery and the Anglo-Indian Family, c. 1780–1840', *Transactions of the Royal Historical Society*, sixth series, XIX (2009), 181–203.

[92] On this vast subject, see Paul Lovejoy, *Transformations in Slavery: A History of Slavery in Africa*, 2nd edn (Cambridge, 2000); *Slavery and Colonial Rule in Africa*, ed. Suzanne Miers and Martin A. Klein (1999); *The End of Slavery in Africa*, ed. Suzanne Miers and Richard Roberts (Madison, 1988); *Slavery in Africa: Historical and Anthropological Perspectives*, ed. Suzanne Miers and Igor Kopytoff (Madison, 1977); Suzanne Miers, *Britain and the Ending of the Slave Trade* (1975); Kevin Grant, *A Civilised Savagery: Britain and the New Slaveries in Africa, 1884–1926* (New York, 2005).

to maintain in any district under our control an institution so alien to our traditions, our wishes, and our whole habits of thought, as the institution of slavery'.[93] Both parties found comfort in a system that denied a legal status to slavery under the British flag but permitted it to continue amongst protected peoples. Drawing parallels between these practices and earlier British policies does not excuse colonial heartlessness but rather acknowledges the long-standing flaw in the anti-slavery mould that shaped many Britons' consciences across generations. The upheavals of external slave trades justified international concern in the way that slavery within other societies could not.

Tensions over the boundaries of moral responsibility informed a famous *Punch* cartoon of 1865. At a time when politicians debated the purpose of expensive West African colonies, the artist John Tenniel suggested that Britain owed Africa nothing and should redirect humanitarian sentiment closer to home (Figure 2). An accompanying comic poem developed his theme that an overextension of national responsibility left London's pauper urchins asking,

> Ain't I black enough to be cared for?
> I'm not a black nigger, 'tis true,
> As armies and fleets is prepared for,
> And missionaries is sent to.[94]

The image was dedicated to the Conservative Lord Stanley, who had recently argued that 'thirty years after the extinction of slavery, and sixty years after the legal extinction of the slave trade, I think we may fairly hold that whatever debt we owed to the people of Africa has by this time been paid off'. The son of the colonial secretary who oversaw the Emancipation Act, Stanley proposed that anti-slavery obligations should not extend to colonial, military or missionary establishments in West Africa, maintaining that 'it is constantly assumed that in some way or other we are responsible for the fortunes and destiny of the African race' when 'I am afraid we had better first look at home'.[95] This scepticism that missionary or philanthropic projects exploited Britain's anti-slavery conscience to further their own ends, ignorantly or mischievously, had a long heritage.

The title of Tenniel's cartoon, 'telescopic philanthropy', came from the chapter in Charles Dickens's *Bleak House*, published a decade earlier. That novel's mockery of Mrs Jellyby, the misguided philanthropist, matched

[93] *Hansard*, fourth series, 24 June 1897, L, 533.

[94] *Punch*, 4 Mar. 1865, 87–8. Many thanks to Anthony S. Wohl's 1999 students at Vassar College for stirring my interest in this image: 'Punch Cartoons', Vassar College, 1997–9, http://projects.vassar.edu/punch/ accessed 11 Apr. 2012.

[95] *Hansard*, third series, 21 Feb. 1854, CLXXVII, 551.

Figure 2 'Telescopic Philanthropy', *Punch*, 4 Mar. 1865, 89. Little London Arab. 'Please, 'M, ain't we black enough to be cared for?' (with Mr Punch's complements to Lord Stanley).

Dickens's pessimism for British anti-slavery obligations to Africa.[96] Reviewing a book about Thomas Fowell Buxton's Niger Expedition of 1840, Dickens commented on anti-slavery exertions more generally:

[96] Charles Dickens, *Bleak House* (1853), ch. 4; Harry Stone, 'Charles Dickens and Harriet Beecher Stowe', *Nineteenth-Century Fiction*, 12 (1957), 188–202; Grace Moore, *Dickens and Empire: Discourses of Class, Race and Colonialism in the Works of Charles Dickens* (Aldershot, 2004), 67–70.

'[g]ently and imperceptibly the widening circles of enlightenment mist stretch and stretch, from man to man, from people on to people' but 'no convulsive effort, or far-off aim, can make the last great outer circle first, and then come home at leisure to trace out the inner one'. Instead, 'work at home must be completed thoroughly, or there is no hope abroad'.[97] This critique of abolitionist plots to undermine African participation in the European slave trade summed up the notion of the 'telescopic philanthropy' Tenniel's cartoon would later illustrate. Far from defending slavery, pessimists such as the author, the politician and the illustrator suggested that Britons were powerless to speed 'the mighty revolutions of the wheel of time' in dismantling foreign slave trading or slaveholding and so should focus on tangible and immediate calls on their philanthropy.[98]

Whether Britons surveyed the moral geography of world slavery with the help of 'telescopic philanthropy' or not, most suffered from anti-slavery myopia – and many abolitionists before 1833 had done so too. While Victorian Britons clearly differed over the extent to which they could control and the means by which they might undermine slavery abroad, it is striking how limited their differences were. Brief abolitionist attempts to force the state's import tariffs to discriminate between slave- and free-labour produce faded quickly, while opposition to expenditure on naval suppression of the slave trade was always expressed in terms of efficacy rather than amorality. While the public could be enraged by evidence of active complicity, they were still content to let more expansive responsibility for anti-slavery stop where the writ of British law ended.

Clean hands

In deciding when foreigners' slave trading or slaveholding touched British consciences, the mainstream of anti-slavery opinion followed Pontius Pilate and focused on keeping blood off their hands. Heyrick had explicitly promoted abstention from West Indian sugar not only as a method to pressure parliament but also as a way of guaranteeing 'clean hands' from the stain of national guilt.[99] Her own strictures did not dictate whether 'clean hands' required abstention from foreign slave-grown products, though it seems likely she would have embraced such radicalism if she had lived beyond 1831. Regardless, 'do no evil' became the rule of official anti-slavery policy, even if there could still be political and public quarrels over what constituted active rather than passive acquiescence in the evils of foreign slavery.

---

[97] *Examiner*, 19 Aug. 1848, 531–3.
[98] *Ibid.*, 533.
[99] On this emphasis in Heyrick's work, see Faulkner, 'Root', 381.

Whether slave-trading in international waters or owning slaves on British soil, the sins of fellow-Britons clearly triggered national obligations; slaveholding violations of British sovereignty in Canada, the Caribbean or the deck of a docked ship did too. The reconstruction of post-war Europe gave Britons a causal responsibility for the revival of slave trading and consequent treaty engagements, required to police illegal British slave traders, provided extra-territorial rights and responsibilities over foreign slavers. There may have been practical or material incentives for British assumption or abrogation of particular responsibilities, but the ideological divisions assumed a life of their own in determining what future politicians could or could not get away with. An emphasis on national identity spreading slaveholders' polluting sin to all Britons had justified political action before 1833; afterwards, it hobbled radical interpretations of responsibility for foreign slavery.

This article opened by noting how Zachary and Thomas Macaulay placed similar stress on national responsibilities to address imperial sins, though they spoke in different contexts. The younger man likely differed from his father in the conclusions he drew from the maxim that, 'to every individual and every society, Providence has assigned a sphere within which benevolence ought to be peculiarly active' and in consequence 'it is not true that we are bound to exert ourselves to serve a mere stranger as we are bound to exert ourselves to serve our own relations'.[100] However, in discriminating between one's responsibility for slavery depending on its location – and its political location rather than its geographical proximity – both Macaulays reflected intergenerational British consistency. This conclusion has implications for the histories of consumer morality, the expansion of humanitarian sympathy and the causes of abolitionism, which will be addressed in turn.

First, while historians have been right to point to the political radicalism of consumer abstention practised by British abolitionists, particularly given the implicit rejection of parliamentary sovereignty and the political agency accorded to women, the moral logic behind such acts was incredibly complex. It was not the same moral consumerism that drives many twenty-first-century shoppers to feel causally responsible for the means by which their food or clothes are manufactured. The link between anti-slavery and ethical consumption has been noted in recent years as abolitionist abstention is examined as a predecessor to the modern fair-trade movement. In 2007, to mark the bicentenary of slave-trade abolition, Britain's Westerham Brewery launched 'William Wilberforce Freedom Ale',

[100] Macaulay, *Speeches of Lord Macaulay*, 164–6, 168.

made with fair-trade sugar from Malawi.[101] Local fair-trade groups and the BBC's History webpages continue to draw such parallels.[102] Scholars have, similarly, been impressed by the extent to which British anti-slavery saw consumption as the source of guilt and a weapon to erase it, drawing parallels with the contemporary anti-sweatshop movement.[103] However, while the language of 'clean hands' and the guilt of the buyer suggest similarities with 'fair-trade' consumerism, individual responsibility was inflected with national responsibility for ending slavery in Britain's own colonies before 1833. After this, the principle of abstaining from foreign produce was an innovative addition to abolitionist debates about what it meant to be an anti-slavery empire. A fuller consumer responsibility for the means of production developed in the later nineteenth and twentieth centuries.

Given that it is interdependent, international commerce that Haskell credits for creating a sense of humanitarian obligation to slaves (albeit as an unintended side effect), it seems unconvincing that these connections were so weak in establishing personal responsibility for foreign slavery. If agency was more often refracted through national rather than individual responsibility, then Haskell's model is both a poor description of Britain's moral revolution and a poor explanation of its causes.[104] Although abolitionists spoke of common humanity and international brotherhood in establishing sympathy, these reflected uncertainties about the nationality of slaves and contemporary elision of 'race' and 'country'. While humanitarian sympathy could extend over political borders, humanitarian action stuck within very clear lines. The idea of the political nation and the power of the state played a pivotal role in creating agency and responsibility over such transnational market institutions as the Atlantic slave trade or New World slavery. It was not an expansion of responsibility for far-away suffering that permitted the rise of abolitionism but a new responsibility for suffering inflicted by the British state, under its laws or by its subjects. The political geography of moral responsibility expanded to include colonists and international traders under the British

[101] '"William Wilberforce Freedom Ale" launched by Westerham Brewery Co. to mark the 200th anniversary of Abolition of Slave Trade in England', Stop the Traffic, Feb. 2007, www.stopthetraffik.org/news/press/press0207.aspx accessed 22 Dec. 2011.
[102] 'Fairtrade and the Slave Trade Abolition Campaign', Garstang Fairtrade, www.garstangfairtrade.org.uk/slave-trade-fairtrade/index.html accessed 7 Jan. 2012; Mike Kaye, 'The Tools of the Abolitionists – Mobilising the Public', BBC History, Feb. 2011, www.bbc.co.uk/history/british/abolition/abolition_tools_gallery_07.shtml accessed 7 Jan. 2012.
[103] Michelle Micheletti, 'The Moral Force of Consumption and Capitalism: Anti-Slavery and Anti-Sweatshop', in *Citizenship and Consumption*, ed. Kate Soper and Frank Trentmann (2007), 121–36.
[104] For similar objections, see David Eltis, *The Rise of African Slavery in the Americas* (Cambridge, 2000), 80–4, 274–84.

flag, suggesting that answers will lie in the study of late eighteenth-century political culture rather than the determinations of economic culture.

Finally, in explaining the sudden emergence and rapid triumph of anti-slavery ideas in modern Britain, this argument confirms a recent turn away from macroeconomic explanations for a revolution in political culture. While Drescher long ago demonstrated that abolition was 'econocide', the following decades saw scholars retreat towards models based on unintended capitalist acculturation rather than deliberate capitalist calculation.[105] As Christopher Brown and Srividhya Swaminathan, amongst others, have suggested, religious and political ideas created the terms of the anti-slavery debate and were, in turn, reshaped by it.[106] Material changes in modernising Britain may have created new gaps in the market for public campaigning, informing, abstaining and pamphleteering. However, the adoption of anti-slavery campaigners relied on the individual talents and agency of cultural entrepreneurs and political activists, not to mention the receptivity of a public able and willing to accept and propagate these ideas. A study of 'moral geography' suggests that ideas of national responsibility trumped market responsibilities throughout Britain's anti-slavery campaigns. Given the stress abolitionists laid on establishing personal guilt and sin in mobilising individual activists, David Brion Davis is right to redirect our attention to the religious content of popular anti-slavery, just as political contingency has displaced material determinism in the work of recent decades.[107]

While the conflicts over Britain's responsibilities reflected different 'strands and sources of anti-slavery thought that had co-existed before 1838', the two strands or sources were not simply 'eschatological evangelicalism and utilitarian political economy'.[108] The distinction was rather more complex, turning on understandings of national agency or the balance between national and consumer guilt. These varied interpretations hinged on different plans of the moral geography of British anti-slavery, defining to what extent responsibility was tied to individuals' transnational consumption of produce or to individuals' political responsibility for their own nation. And those moral geographies drawn in the wake of emancipation had, long before, been traced by the first generation of abolitionists.

---

[105] Seymour Drescher, *Econocide: British Slavery in the Era of Abolition* (Chapel Hill, 2010 [Pittsburgh, 1977]); Seymour Drescher, review of *The Antislavery Debate: Capitalism and Abolitionism as a Problem in Historical Interpretation*, ed. Thomas Bender, in *History and Theory*, 32 (1993), 311–29.

[106] Brown, *Moral Capital*; Srividhya Swaminathan, *Debating the Slave Trade: Rhetoric of British National Identity, 1759–1815* (Farnham, 2009).

[107] David Brion Davis, 'The Universal Attractions of Slavery', *New York Review of Books*, 56 (2009), 72–4.

[108] Embarrassingly, this quotation is from Huzzey, 'Free trade', 373.

Transactions of the RHS 22 (2012), pp. 141–69 © Royal Historical Society 2012
doi:10.1017/S0080440112000102

THE *CHALLENGER*: HUGH HAMILTON LINDSAY AND THE RISE OF BRITISH ASIA, 1832–1865[*]

By Robert Bickers

READ 23 SEPTEMBER 2011

ABSTRACT. This paper explores the life and activities of Hugh Hamilton Lindsay (1802–81), an East India Company official who worked at Canton from 1820. Lindsay's is a key voice in the challenge to the Company's policies in China on the cusp of the abolition of its monopoly, and to British policy on the eve of the first 'Opium War' with the empire of the Qing. Lindsay first made his mark on Sino-British relations by leading a covert East India Company foray north along the Chinese coast in 1832 in the ship *Lord Amherst*, and in widely disseminating his bullish conclusions and policy recommendations in publications and reports that followed. He is known as a bellicose pamphleteer, but a more complex picture emerges if we follow Lindsay and his commercial activities as the British fanned out from Canton into the Chinese 'treaty ports' opened after 1842, and across Britain's wider developing empire in Asia. His field of operations developed to include the British colony of Labuan and led him into a heated public conflict with Sir James Brooke in the early 1850s. Lindsay was never happy with the *status quo*: he lobbied and hectored, and in business he innovated, and pushed hard on the frontiers of British power and influence. Commercial opportunity drove him, but so did a specific vision of the 'English character', and notions of pride and national and personal honour.

By most accounts it was not broken, so why did it need fixing? The old China trade, the 'Canton trade', was efficient and predictable in its charges and procedures, and it was well regulated. It serviced what was for the British an increasingly important exchange, which produced revenues from monopoly opium sales for British India, and tea duties for the British exchequer, delivered silver for the East India Company at Canton and shipped tea to British drinkers. We have recently been learning a good deal more about this trade and its global position, and getting away from Anglophone perspectives which have dominated accounts to date. Ranged across the Pearl River delta, the trade was headquartered at the Portuguese colony of Macao, active in the foreign 'factories' at

---

[*] The author would like to thank Sir William Young for alerting me to the existence of George Chinnery's portrait of Lindsay, and for allowing me to reproduce it here.

Canton; ships (and men) were serviced at Whampoa, and opium hulks were moored at Lintin. It was a polyglot, cosmopolitan and profitable arrangement. It served the Qing court, to which was funnelled directly revenue from the Canton customs; it was profitable for the East India Company which shipped out tea, and for the private or country traders, Parsees, Scots, English and the Americans, who shipped in opium; and it was lucrative too for the 'cohong' (*gonghang*), the Chinese official merchant monopoly at Canton, and for the Chinese traders all down the illicit supply line which funnelled deep into China the fast-rising dark-star of the wider Canton trade: opium.[1]

Until the late 1830s, there was a tiny little foreign colony on the riverbank on the south-west side of the great walled city of Canton. Although only formally allowed to lodge there during the trading season, the few-score foreigners were able to do their business, and use this window on China to great effect: as well as commodities – principally tea and silk – information about the empire of the Great Qing dynasty poured out, and not just information gleaned from Chinese books and the court's official news record, but botanical and geological specimens, wildlife and material objects. It was a pretty cosy life, its cellars well stocked, servants attentive and luxury cheap. Members of the Cohong entertained the foreigners well, banqueting them in style, showing them the city's great gardens, serving their varied needs. The foreigners were largely left to regulate themselves, for this was efficient, and was in the general pattern of Qing administrative practice. We have some fine memoirs of this period. American William Hunter's is the most well known. *The 'Fan Kwae' ['Foreign Devils'] at Canton before treaty days* is an affectionate portrait of his years working there for Russell & Co., and in later years, Hunter can be spotted regaling youthful companions on P&O steamers all the way to China with tales of his twenty years in the east, his 'manner too of imparting information is so very pleasing & his views of everything display so much good sense that you never tire of listening to him'.[2] Hunter had

---

[1] W. E. Cheong, *The Hong Merchants of Canton: Chinese Merchants in Sino-Western Trade* (Richmond, 1997); Paul A. Van Dyke, *The Canton Trade: Life and Enterprise on the China Coast, 1700–1845* (Hong Kong, 2005); Paul A. Van Dyke, *Merchants of Canton and Macao: Politics and Strategies in Eighteenth-Century Chinese Trade* (Hong Kong, 2011). The Anglophone perspective was established most firmly by the five volumes of H. B. Morse, *The Chronicles of the East India Company Trading to China* (Oxford, 1926–9). See also *China Trade and Empire: Jardine, Matheson & Co. and the Origins of British Rule in Hong Kong, 1827–1843*, ed. Alain Le Pichon, Records of Social and Economic History, New Series, 38 (Oxford, 2006).

[2] Knowledge: Fa-ti Fan, *British naturalists in Qing China: Science, Empire and Cultural Encounter* (Cambridge, MA, 2004); Canton: Jonathan A. Farris, 'Thirteen Factories of Canton: An Architecture of Sino-Western Collaboration and Confrontation', *Buildings and Landscapes*, 14 (2007), 66–83; Hunter: James Dow papers, private collection, diary (hereafter Dow diary), 20 June 1851. As well as *The 'Fan Kwae' at Canton before Treaty Days, 1825–1844* (1882), Hunter published *Bits of Old China* (1885).

everything he needed, and he left China in 1842 with a $200,000 fortune: not bad for eighteen years work, worth a tyro listening to.

This Canton compromise was a peculiar arrangement, but it worked, and it certainly worked for William Hunter. But then along came the Scots, Hugh Hamilton Lindsay and his cohort, and they wrecked it, smashing it beyond repair, and they led Britain to take its 'place' in Asia, an ordained place in their eyes, not one subservient to the Qing, or dependent on Portuguese whims. Their impatience brought twenty years of disorder and conflict to south and east China, rebellion as well as war, and brittle stand-offs that passed for peace.[3] This paper explores the world of this man, Hugh Hamilton Lindsay, the world he helped fashion and the tools with which he helped make change happen. He was an East India Company official, a pamphleteer, trader and MP; he was an innovator, and a risk taker who challenged the *status quo*. The nephew of the sixth earl of Balcarres, his father, Hugh Lindsay, was eighth son of the fifth earl – which was not exactly an auspicious start in life. But Hugh Lindsay senior was an East India Company mariner, who joined its court of directors in 1814, and was sometime chairman of the company. He would have retired financially comfortable from the maritime service. This elder Lindsay is remembered, if at all, for so strongly opposing the introduction of steamships to the maritime service that the first steamer built in India, in 1829, for running experimentally on the Suez–Bombay run, was mockingly named after him.[4]

The son proved less conservative and as radical in fact as that steamer. Hugh Hamilton Lindsay arrived in Canton in late 1821 as a writer with the East India Company's select committee there. He left the company in 1833, later setting up a business in Canton. With the expansion of the British presence across south and east China after the First Opium War, Lindsay & Co. became one of the most prominent of British firms, riding high and aristocratic, living extravagantly, investing in new markets, pushing hard at the apparent limits to British enterprise in China and later in Japan. Lindsay also directed attention at the developing British presence in Southeast Asia, particularly Borneo. That was to prove a disaster for Lindsay, but a telling one. And his eponymous firm, Lindsay & Co., went bankrupt, spectacularly, in 1865, the highest-profile early victim of the bursting of the great Shanghai bubble as a result of the disastrous outbreaks of peace in both the United States and in China,

---

[3] Frederic Wakeman Jr, *Strangers at the Gate: Social Disorder in South China, 1839–1861* (Berkeley, 1966).

[4] Sir Evan Cotton, *East Indiamen: The East India Company's Maritime Service*, ed. Sir Charles Fawcett (1949), 37, citing Capt. John Innes: average profit per voyage by early 1830s: £6,100; Daniel R. Headrick, *The Tools of Empire: Technology and Imperialism in the Nineteenth Century* (New York, 1981), 135–6.

with the ending of their respective civil wars.[5] Jardine, Matheson & Co.'s continuing contemporary success and inescapable historical notoriety has obscured the tale of the failures, Dent & Co., and Lindsay's, who formed with the 'Princely Hong' the key British commercial triumvirate in early treaty port China.

Lindsay served the East India Company in Canton in the last decade of its formal China trade monopoly, which ended at the close of 1833, so by necessity he had to look to, and shape his own future.[6] He is routinely noted amongst the advance guard of belligerent British lobbyists clamouring for war with China, and for breaking down the closed door of the Qing. First, in 1832, he led a clandestine East India Company reconnaissance of the southern and eastern ports of China, most famously landing at Shanghai and harassing officials there.[7] He lectured them on the actual meaning of a term they used when dealing with him, which he insisted on interpreting as 'barbarian', when they assured him it simply meant 'foreigner'. They were being disingenuous: foreigners were barbarians, they were outside the pale of civilisation. This debate about the meaning of 'yi' – 'barbarian' or 'foreigner' – rumbles on yet, but the British later fixed their interpretation in treaty, forbidding its use by Qing officials.[8] Lindsay also distributed wherever and whenever he could a pamphlet, in bad Chinese ('pidgin Chinese' concluded one reader), containing an 'Account of the English character'.[9] Sometimes officials forbade people to accept it, but generally those who came to look at or meet the Britons eagerly took copies away. Secondly, Lindsay published in

---

[5] Robert Bickers, *The Scramble for China: Foreign Devils in the Qing Empire, 1832–1914* (2011), 182–3.

[6] Anthony Webster, *Twilight of the East India Company: The Evolution of Anglo-Asian Commerce and Politics, 1790–1860* (Woodbridge, 2009).

[7] He published his own account of the expedition as *Report of Proceedings on a Voyage to the Northern Ports of China, in the Ship Lord Amherst* (1833). This was a republication of the official report to the Company by Lindsay (1–267), with Karl Gützlaff's journal appended (269–96). The report was itself printed as a parliamentary paper *Ship Amherst* (House of Commons 410 (1833)).

[8] Recent analysis of the debate: Song-Chuan Chen, 'The British Maritime Public Sphere in Canton, 1827–1839' (Ph.D. thesis, Cambridge University, 2009), 100–25 (Lindsay at 103–5), and Lydia H. Liu, *The Clash of Empires: The Invention of China in Modern World Making* (Cambridge, MA, 2004), 31–69 (on Lindsay at 40–6).

[9] *Da Yingguo ren shilü shuo.* A copy of the original pamphlet is held in The National Archives: FO 1048/32/8, 'Copy of a printed paper landed by the Lord Amherst at Ningpo. Received at Macao, for translation, July 1832'. The original English text was printed in the *Canton Register*, 18 July 1832, 68–9. This text is in all but a couple of instances identical with the English original, composed by Charles Marjoribanks, outgoing president of the select committee at Canton, transcribed in British Library, Asia, Pacific and Africa Collections, India Office Records (hereafter BL, APAC), IOR/10/30, Secret Consultations of Select Committee of Supercargoes, fos. 123–31. It was translated by the missionary Robert Morrison, who served as the East India Company's translator. The assessment of Morrison's work comes from Arthur Waley, *The Opium War through Chinese Eyes* (1958), 228.

1840 in London a starkly titled pamphlet: *Is the War with China a Just One?* It hardly needs adding that his answer was 'yes', and in this way Hugh Hamilton Lindsay gifted himself to historians and commentators looking for evidence of British warmongering at the onset of Commissioner Lin's opium imbroglio at Canton. And on the basis of his account of the 1832 voyage he already had form: he was a warmonger's warmonger, the foremost of the 'war hawks'.[10] Lindsay even has a walk-on role in Amitav Ghosh's 2011 novel, *River of Smoke*, as the 'rubicund', 'genial', president of the British chamber of commerce at Canton. So he is a fixture of the Canton coast in the run up to confrontation and war, in histories of it and in fictions.

This paper first explores the life and character of this 'courtly', violent man. It then outlines his activities and assesses his significance in three up-to-now separate spheres in which he or his firm have been discussed: in pre-Opium War Canton, in treaty port China after 1842 and in the 'Eastern Archipelago', and more precisely Labuan, on the island of Borneo. Significantly, his operations in the latter two spheres were directed from London, for Lindsay was to retire from Asia in 1839 when he left Canton to lobby for war, although he did not retire from the Asian fray. This is a story of the man on the spot, and what he can do to further imperial expansion, but it also reinforces the point that London remained a key spot, for the men in the East, and a site of British China. And Lindsay never actually saw in person the China opened to wider foreign residence that he had lobbied so long and forcefully for.

Canton and the coast

The Lindsay family – there are scores of them, with a fairly narrow repertoire of Christian names – is hardly obscure, and like Emma Rothschild's Johnstons, it was tightly woven into the fabric of Britain's global empire. Lindsay's aunt, as Lady Anne Barnard, has outshone her husband, mere colonial secretary at the new Cape Colony, with her now well-mined letters and journal, and through acting as hostess for the governor, Lord Macartney. Volume III of the 1849 *Lives of the Lindsays* contains her memoir alongside accounts of his great-grandfather, fourth earl, governor of Jamaica; the 1780 battle of Conjeveeram (two Lindsays amongst those captured by Tipu Sultan); and the defence of St Lucia against the French in 1779 (uncle Colin), and an escapade of his own father at Canton. Lindsays saw the Cape, India, the Caribbean and China.[11] And the family was embedded in domestic public life: there

---

[10] Gerald S. Graham, *The China Station: War and Diplomacy, 1830–1860* (Oxford, 1978), 69–71.

[11] Emma Rothschild, *The Inner Life of Empires: An Eighteenth-Century History* (Princeton, 2011); Lord Lindsay, *Lives of the Lindsays, or A Memoir of the Houses of Crawford and Balcarres*, III (1849).

were prominent cousins, at various removes, but actively intertwined in his business and private life: Coutts Lindsay, founder of the Grosvenor Gallery; Alexander Lindsay, bibliophile and art historian. When Lindsay & Co. defaulted in 1865, Lindsay turned to the wider family for private support to attempt to prevent official bankruptcy and family embarrassment.[12] The company itself was then led by his nephew, Robert Crawford Antrobus. So family and business are intertwined: no surprise there. Lindsay as we shall see lived in two overlapping worlds of business, that of familial relations, credit and trust, and that of the still-evolving world of the joint stock company, and a business world in which expectations were changing.

Lindsay's early years are obscure but it seems that he did not graduate from any of the Scottish universities, and possibly studied at Vienna. He certainly knew the university, and spoke German.[13] His appointment was approved by the East India Company directors in late March 1821, upon the nomination of his father (at the cost of all other patronage rights for the season), and a month later he was on the company ship *Windsor* heading out east. He arrived in China in September 1821, his first job 'to assist generally in the office, and weigh and receive teas'. Lindsay served initially as a salaried writer, and from 1829 as a Supercargo earning commission, earning an additional allowance as a student of Chinese.[14] He seems to have been attentive to this, fancying himself a Sinologist, and speculating about making a future name for himself in 'Chinese affairs and politics'.[15] At this point, very few Britons knew any Chinese, or thought of learning it. Lindsay went home on leave in 1825, returning in 1827, and in 1829 he made a visit to Java, which 'much inchanted' him, with two Company colleagues.[16] He left the Company in 1833, part-travelling back on that steamship named for his father, and returned to Canton in 1836 to trade on his own account, as Lindsay & Co.[17] There he became chairman of a new chamber of commerce (it was his 'child' one correspondent noted), and in May 1839 he was one of those who hurried back to Britain to

---

[12] Staffordshire Record Office (hereafter SRO), D(W)1920/5/4/8, Coutts Lindsay and Lindsay to Hugh Hamilton Lindsay, 17 Sept. 1865.

[13] *The Rev. Joseph Wolf . . . in a series of letters to Sir Thomas Baring, Bart. Containing an Account of his Missionary Labours . . .* (1839), 322–3.

[14] BL, APAC, IOR, H/398, resolution of 21 Mar. 1821, IOR, G/12/223 (factory diary), 3, 4, 8 Sept., 2 Oct. 1821; *East India Register and Directory* (1825–32).

[15] SRO, D(W)1920, 4/1, Hugh Hamilton Lindsay to mother, (draft), from Amoy, Apr. 1832.

[16] Leave: on the *General Harris*, leaving Canton on 1 Jan., arriving on 11 May 1825: *Oriental Herald*, 5:18 (June 1825), 755–7; Java: via the *Marquess of Camden*, leaving Canton on 16 Feb. 1829, *Oriental Herald*, 22:68 (Aug. 1829), 382–4; enchanted: Hugh Hamilton Lindsay to Harriet [Low?], from Samarang, 25 Apr. 1829, SRO, D(W) 1920/4/1.

[17] With William Wallace: *Chinese Repository*, 5:9 (Jan. 1837), 430.

lobby the government to take action against China when Commissioner Lin launched his campaign to stamp out the opium trade.[18]

Personally he seems to have been as genial as Ghosh's fictional recreation, described as 'droll', and a 'pleasant person of courtly and polished manners'. He was tall, and handsome in his youth, before China, sickness and perhaps youthful 'dissipation' took their toll. (The suspicion is that of an ambivalent admirer's in 1833.) Courtly polish notwithstanding, Lindsay's key contributions are violent, disruptive and challenging. But then he was also seen as 'always ready, for *adventures* of any kind'; he 'has the spirit of adventure most fully developed'.[19] The artist George Chinnery communicated some of that spirit in his portrait, which seems to date to *c.* 1827–33 (Figure 1). Lindsay enters history actively in 1832 when together with Karl Gützlaff, a Lutheran missionary from Pomerania, and with the connivance of the outgoing select committee president, Charles Marjoribanks, he ventured east and then north along the Chinese coast in a chartered ship, the *Lord Amherst*. They stopped at Xiamen (Amoy), Fuzhou and Ningbo, before reaching Shanghai, where they stayed some weeks. Then they sailed north touching the Shandong coast, before sailing across to Korea, and back south via the Ryukyus to Canton. They were away for six months, and the British at Canton were able to chart their progress, for the efficient administrative reporting system of the Qing was frantic with information and reports about the mysterious appearance at the various ports of a British ship, name unknown, those in charge of which included 'Hu Xiami' (Lindsay), and Jia Li (Gützlaff) – who spoke good Chinese (and was often thought to be Chinese) – claiming to have come from Bengal and been blown off course.[20]

At each port, Lindsay parlayed in Chinese, seeking permission to trade (they carried a large stock of sample products), and all the while distributing their little pamphlet on the British. Local officials tried to blockade them from entering ports, ordered them to leave and generally sent along to Peking somewhat hazy reports about their success in getting the foreigners to go. The ship undertook an 'experiment' (Lindsay's term) in violence, in order to get its way at one or two points when war junks were being used to block them. At Shanghai, they lingered longest, and argued most hotly about language and status. Qing officials laughed when

[18] *Chinese Repository*, 6:1 (May 1837), 44–7; various items of correspondence in SRO, D(W)1920/4/2, notably James Innes to H. H. Lindsay, 20 Dec. 1836.
[19] *Lights and Shadows of a Macao Life: The Journal of Harriet Low, Travelling Spinster*, ed. Nan P. Hodges and Arthur W. Hummel (Woodinville, WA, 2002), I, 204, 589–90 (20 July 1833), 557 (28 May 1833), 639 (12 Oct. 1833).
[20] Chinese accounts of the progress of the ship are analysed in Immanuel C. Y. Hsü, 'The Secret Mission of the *Lord Amherst* on the China Coast, 1832', *Harvard Journal of Asiatic Studies*, 17:1/2 (1954), 231–52. Originals of the documentation, located in the Bodleian Library, were printed in *Dazhong ji* (Arriving at the inner truth), ed. Xu Dishan (Shanghai, 1931).

Figure 1 (Colour online) Portrait of the Hon. Hugh Hamilton Lindsay, by George Chinnery, *c.* 1827–33, reproduced by kind permission of Sir William Young.

Lindsay said or wrote that they came from 'Great' Britain – '*Da Yingguo*' – for the Qing was referred to as the Great Qing (*Da Qing*), but the Scotsman would object and harangue his generally unfailingly polite hosts with his notions of his own and Britain's status.[21]

[21] Bickers, *Scramble for China*, 18–45.

Lindsay refused to stand such slights, literally in fact: he refused to stand in the presence of Qing officials if they – conforming with their own notions of their status – sat and did not allow him to do so as well. There was much storming out of meeting rooms, and palaver over physical dispositions in encounters over tea and snacks. The ostensible reason for the voyage, in Lindsay's formal instructions, was 'to ascertain how far the northern posts of this empire may gradually be opened to British commerce'.[22] In fact, there were other aims. Lindsay and his supporters were trying to outflank the authorities at Canton, by getting their views about what they saw as British difficulties at that port transmitted to Peking by other officials. Secondly, and related to this, he was disseminating positive information about the British, in Chinese, wherever he could. A copy of the pamphlet did in fact make its way to Peking – but hardly had the desired effect for the emperor found it quite unintelligible. But Lindsay was also attempting to outflank his more conservative elders in the Company, by taking the initiative and heading out of confined Canton along the coast. This was also the twilight of the Company's monopoly operation in China, so Lindsay and his 'country trade' supporters were clearly also scouting out opportunities that might be opened in the new era to come. This mystery ship was treated with somewhat surprising restraint, and in the records of the voyage compiled by Lindsay and by Gützlaff it is clear that what violence there was, in words, and in actions, came from the British side.

Those records took the form of Lindsay's official report for the Canton select committee, which was printed too as a parliamentary paper, and then as a book. Gützlaff provided a supplementary account, which he also republished in a later volume containing three such memoirs of voyaging along the closed Chinese coast.[23] The voyage made Lindsay's name, for it was the subject of much debate in the periodical press, and very strongly informed British and other discussions in the 1830s of the potential of the China market, especially in the north at Shanghai.[24] It had its critics, who thought Lindsay bombastic, if not at times ridiculous

[22] BL, APAC, IOR/R/10/30, 'Secret Consultations of Select Committee of Supercargoes', committee to H. H. Lindsay, Esq., 12 Jan. 1832, fos. 297–300.

[23] *Ship Amherst*, Parliamentary Papers, 1833 (410); *Report of Proceedings on a Voyage to the Northern Ports of China, in the Ship Lord Amherst*. This is the official report with Karl Gützlaff's journal appended. BL, APAC, IOR/R/10/70, contains 'Journal by Hugh Hamilton Lindsay of voyage of the "Lord Amherst"', a manuscript of the Lindsay text, identical with that published, except that some Chinese characters have been inserted where names, ranks or places are mentioned. Gützlaff's account was published separately (and more fully) in *The Journal of Two Voyages along the Coast of China in 1831 & 1832* (New York, 1833) and *The Journal of Three Voyages along the Coast of China in 1831, 1832 & 1833* (1834).

[24] Reviews include: 'Chinese Voyage of the Lord Amherst', *Literary Gazette*, 24 Aug. 1831, 530–2, 31 Aug. 1833, 550–2; 'Documents relating to the Voyage Recently Undertaken by the Ship Amherst, to the North-East Coast of China', *Athenaeum*, 302, 10 Aug. 1833, 521–2;

as he sat on his dignity in meetings with officials. They deprecated the episodes of violence, and argued that forcing China further open would be counter-productive. And the whole episode was deceitful and contrary to the laws of the Qing, and led by a man whose argument was that the Chinese were deceitful and ignored the laws of the Qing. For some critics, the hypocrisy was self-evident, and disabling. But Lindsay launched some of the longest-running of British beliefs about what to do in China: that a little bit of violence could go a long way to unpick problems (a navy frigate, or a few Indiamen would do), and that the British needed to assert their dignity and standing to the haughty and arrogant Chinese. And he also reported privately that he could have sold any amount of opium if he had had it to trade.

Lindsay's report and other work, and his private correspondence, was suffused with anger. But why so angry, if the Canton trade could, objectively, work well and smoothly as most observers thought it did? The British, at least a vocal core of them, were angry at being confined to and in Canton, in a tiny trading colony where a man could easily count the width in steps of the only ground allowed for exercise (except a few times a month, when they were permitted to use a garden along the river). They were angry at other personal restrictions, which were intermittently applied with vigour, and they were angry at the seeming obtuseness of their erstwhile hosts, who would not officially recognise them, and would not allow them to communicate directly and formally with officials. Aside from bluster, the only 'weapon' the British had was to suspend trade, obviously a double-edged sword. In one dispute in 1829, the committee had moved its ships to Kowloon, opposite the island of Hong Kong. (Lindsay was with them, and concluded that 'a more advantageous spot for a settlement could not easily be found'.)[25] In 1831, during another stoppage, Lindsay was ordered back to Canton from Macao to hand over symbolically to the Chinese authorities the keys to the Company's quarters: in a humiliating public spectacle, these were refused.[26] The committee capitulated as it had in 1829. This was not how Britons expected to be treated, and increasingly for Lindsay and others, asserting British status meant being prepared to do so by force.

Back in England from 1833, Lindsay followed up his Lord Amherst book with a published *Letter to . . . Viscount Palmerston on British Relations with China* in March 1836. This was part of a concerted broadside of pamphlets fired by the British China traders aching for action, and sparked by the

'Experiment to Open an Intercourse with China', *Monthly Review*, 4:1 (Sept. 1833), 30–43; John Crawford, 'Voyage of the Ship *Amherst*', *Westminster Review* (Jan. 1834), 22–47.
[25] SRO, D(W)1920/4/2, Hugh Hamilton Lindsay to mother, 15 Nov. 1829.
[26] Morse, *Chronicles of the East India Company Trading to China*, IV, 278–92, Lindsay at 282–3.

'Napier affair'.[27] The first post-Company British superintendent of trade in China, the bumptious Lord Napier, had tried on his own initiative (though his orders were contradictory and ambiguous) to assert his office and status in Canton, and to secure recognition from the Qing officials. He was stonewalled, pilloried in proclamations pasted on Canton walls, placed under house-arrest and so retreated, ignominiously, his health broken in addition, to Macao, where he promptly died. Lindsay and other belligerents penned angry denunciations of the Chinese, and urged action on the British government. He argued for 'direct armed interference to demand redress for past injuries and security for the future', and continued to be precise about the limited means that need be committed: a battleship, two large frigates, six corvettes, three or four armed steamers and 600 men would do. And a 'lithographic press': they would blockade, and they would publish explanations of their actions to secure the support of the ordinary Chinese populace.[28] At the very least, the British should terminate what official presence they had in China, it was expensive to maintain, and insultingly ignored.

As we know, after 1839 the Canton British got their war; the warships (and the printing press) sailed. Lindsay had arrived in China just as the balance of trade was about to tip in favour of the foreign traders. Silver flowed out of the Qing, first slowly, then at rapidly greater and greater volumes, to widespread and destabilising effect. The combined effects of silver outflow and drug smuggling forced the Qing to take action, and that action led to war.[29] Lindsay churned out pamphlets once he got to London which lobbied for conflict and supported it once launched. All delivered his trenchant view of the violent path to putting relations on an equitable footing, and lobbying hard for compensation for the confiscation of British opium surrendered by Napier's successor to the Qing authorities.[30] The Canton British got that compensation, and they got out of their tiny reservation on the Pearl River. The road to China itself

[27] On which: Bickers, *Scramble for China*, 45–48; Glenn Melancon, *Britain's Opium Policy and the Opium Crisis: Balancing Drugs, Violence and National Honour, 1833–1840* (Aldershot, 2003), 35–40.

[28] H. Hamilton Lindsay, *Letter to the Right Honourable Viscount Palmerston on British Relations with China* (1836), 4, 13–14, 17.

[29] Lin Man-houng, *China Upside Down: Currency, Society, and Ideologies, 1808–1856* (Cambridge, MA, 2006). On the war and its aftermath: Hsin-pao Chang, *Commissioner Lin and the Opium War* (Cambridge, MA, 1964); Peter Ward Fay, *The Opium War, 1840–1842: Barbarians in the Celestial Empire in the Early Part of the Nineteenth Century and the War by which They Forced her Gates Ajar* (New York, 1975); Graham, *The China Station*; Mao Haijian, *Tianchao de bengkui: Yapian zhanzheng zai yanjiu* (Collapse of the Celestial Empire: A Reanalysis of the Opium War) (Beijing, 1995); James M. Polachek, *The Inner Opium War* (Cambridge, MA, 1992).

[30] A Resident in China, *The Rupture with China and its Causes . . . in a Letter to Lord Viscount Palmerston* [31 Oct. 1839] (1840), and A Resident in China, *Remarks on Occurrences in China since*

had already been opened: the Anglo-Dutch Treaty of London in 1824 had secured the status of Singapore, and passage through the straits.[31] But now, the British acquired bridgeheads within the realm of the Qing. Under the 1842 Treaty of Nanjing, the British acquired Hong Kong island and the Kowloon peninsula in perpetuity, as well as the right to reside and trade in five ports: Canton, Amoy, Fuzhou, Ningbo and Shanghai. Lindsay had seen all of these for himself back in 1832. And there was no Company now. China opened, however narrowly, to all Britons on an equal footing: those already prepared to jump in best placed to seize the opportunity. Lindsay & Co. was ready. The firm now leapt into opened China, acquiring plots in Hong Kong and Shanghai. They constructed what are thought to be the first buildings in the new colony, the Albany Godowns, and secured a good large plot in Shanghai, not on what became the bund, but at the heart of the new settlement nonetheless. In 1845, Lindsay & Co. – its Chinese name given in English as 'Quong Loong' (Guanglong) – had three partners, and six foreign staff. In 1859, in Hong Kong alone it had two partners, and nine foreign staff, an office at Fuzhou and a partner and five foreign staff at Shanghai.[32]

Lindsay & Co.

Lindsay & Co. took off in the newly opened treaty ports and the colony at Hong Kong. This was a classic merchant house of this era. It dealt in everything: opium, cotton piece goods, tea and held a share of an insurance company. A look at the company's activities through reports in the Shanghai press for a single year, 1852, when the firm was riding high, provides details of its global connections and its concerns. Quang Loong's opium hulk at Shanghai, the *Swallow*, was moored with the others outside the harbour limits, flying its blue, white and blue house flag. Lindsay had commissioned a London shipbuilder, Richard Green, to build him an American-style clipper, the magnificent, 700-ton, 174-foot long *Challenger*, which arrived on its maiden voyage in June, 108 days out from London, loaded with cottons. On 27 July, it sailed for home, with 625,000 pounds of tea and a thousand bales of silk.[33] This turned into one of the first of the famous clipper races, as the American *Challenge* and Lindsay's *Challenger* raced each other back from Anjer point. With Captain James Killick at the helm, Lindsay's vessel won by two days (under Killick's command,

the *Opium Seizure in March 1839 to the Latest Date* (1840); H. Hamilton Lindsay, *Is the War with China a Just One?* (1840).

[31] Jean Sutton, *The East India Company's Maritime Service, 1746–1834* (Woodbridge, 2010), 268.

[32] *An Anglo-Chinese Calendar for the Year 1845* (Hong Kong, 1845); *The Hongkong Directory with List of Foreign Residents in China* (Hong Kong, 1859).

[33] *North China Herald* (hereafter *NCH*), 31 July 1852, 212.

it was regularly two weeks swifter than under his successors).[34] *Challenger* was never the fastest of the clippers, but its innovative design set the pace, prefiguring the great ships to come: *Thermopylae, Sir Launcelot, Ariel*, great names from the triumphant age of sail. The Suez Canal opened in 1869, and until then, and for years afterwards, although the steamers steadily improved, sail carried this intensifying global trade.[35]

Such exchanges continued for Lindsay & Co. throughout 1852 at Shanghai: cotton goods from London; nearly two million pounds of tea to Liverpool, London and Sydney (via Manila); 3,000 bales of silk to London; cottons and opium from India. This was the licit trade, opium apart, which though illicit (hence the hulk moored outside the harbour limits) was effectively tolerated. But even with the licit trade, Lindsays and their staff, like all the British China companies smuggled and bribed their way through Chinese regulations, as the first inspector general of the foreign-staffed Chinese maritime customs outlined in a report in 1862: sixty hogsheads of coal shipped by Lindsays turned out to contain specie, whose export was forbidden, and the coal hid more treasure boxes: all were confiscated.[36] They and others denied the charges, and blamed individual wrong-doers, perhaps with good cause. But the culture of British and other foreign business in China was not amenable to Chinese restriction, and it was a commercially brave firm that played strictly by the rules.[37]

This was the China trade at Shanghai. But what did Lindsay himself do with his new-found freedom of movement in China? He stayed in Britain: Lindsay had entered parliament for the Tories in May 1841, although he did not do much there: twelve contributions to ten debates over the next two years, and half of those about compensation for opium seized, or justifying that trade. He spoke for the borough of Sandwich,

---

[34] Basil Lubbock, *The China Clippers* [1914], 5th edn (Glasgow, 1922), 118–19. Killick later bought the ship, and founded a shipping firm: David R. MacGregor, *The China Bird: The History of Captain Killick and the Firm He Founded Killick Martin & Company* (1961).

[35] Gerald S. Graham, 'The Ascendancy of the Sailing Ship 1850–85', *Economic History Review*, n.s. 9:1 (1956), 74–88.

[36] *NCH, passim*, 1852; 'Memorandum by Mr. Lay, Chinese Inspector of Customs, on the Complaints of the Hong Kong and Shanghai Chambers of Commerce', 11 Jan. 1862, in *Further Papers relating to the Rebellion in China*, Parliamentary Papers, 1863 (3104), 177–9, and Alex Perceval, chairman of the Hong Kong general chamber of commerce, to Lord John Russell, 26 Aug. 1861, in *ibid.*, 161–3. The companies hit back, denying these charges, Lindsays not least of all, but they protested rather too much: Lay certainly thought that they did: *China. Correspondence respecting Statements in Mr. Lay's Memorandum Dated January 11, 1862*, Parliamentary Papers, 1864 (3240).

[37] Though it could pay off, Rathbones, a start-up house that entered the China fray in the aftermath of the 1842 treaty avoided smuggling and opium as policy, and survived: S. G. Checkland, 'An English Merchant House in China after 1842', *Bulletin of the Business Historical Society*, 27:3 (1953), 158–89.

but, as he later put it, entered the House 'to advocate and support the interests of my brother merchants in China', and from 1843 until he stood down in 1847, he was silent.[38] Newspapers provide some glimpses of his life in Britain, public committee activity, presentation at court, hunting gossip, an estate near Chichester, taking a lease on a grouse moor: the life of a man who has repatriated his China trade profits and assumed a place in British public life. But China still needed lobbying for at the centre and a China house needed a British base. China remained distant, and exotic, and British China was too distant from power, and too much in the shadow of British India and its Southeast Asian satellites. Commercial considerations aside, British China needed a China lobby, or, as lobby is perhaps yet too concrete a description here, it needed settled visibility in London if it was to retain effective channels to power, and the ability to support 'brother merchants in China'. And there in the heart of the empire Lindsay also advertised himself as agent for vessels heading east: shippers to Batavia, Bombay, Hong Kong, Calcutta, Amoy and Shanghai were enjoined to contact his office in East India Chambers on Leadenhall Street. While he had long left John Company, he kept close to its central city location.[39] At Shanghai and in London, the personal stature of the partners, and their connections into the city, into Indian and into other markets were crucial to the high regard in which they were held.

By 1865, the firm had diversified further, and extended its geographical reach. Lindsay ostensibly withdrew in December 1856, as his private debts by then 'prejudiced the credit, and interests' of the firm, although he retained significant capital in the company, and owned its Shanghai property, and was soon in fact back in an influential position within it.[40] By 1865, Lindsay & Co. had steamers serving the new Yangzi trade, the thousand-ton *Fire Cracker* and the equally huge paddle-steamer *Fire Queen*, both built for the company in New York to take advantage of the newly opened river.[41] The senior partner was their registered owner. There was an office at Niuzhuang, new-opened in the north, property at Hakodate in Japan, a hulk at Hankou, interest in a cargo boat company at Shanghai and more. They shipped sugar, coal, rice, pepper and peas

---

[38] Hugh Hamilton Lindsay letter to the *Times*, 23 July 1847, 6. The election is described in detail in the *Standard*, 11 May 1841, 1, and the *Morning Post*, 12 May 1841, 5.

[39] Regular advertisements can be found in the *Times*, for example, between 15 Apr. 1840 and 22 Sept. 1864: office address, 8 East India Chambers, Leadenhall Street.

[40] SRO D(W) 1920/5, H. H. Lindsay to Lindsay & Co., 10 Dec. 1856, and 'Partnership Dissolution Agreement', 10 Dec. 1856; [illeg.] to R. C. Antrobus, 21 Jan. 1863.

[41] Edward Kenneth Haviland, 'American Steam Navigation in China, 1845–1878, Part II', *American Neptune*, 16:4 (1956), 252; and *idem*, 'American Steam Navigation in China, 1845–1878, Part IV', *American Neptune*, 17:2 (1957), 302–4.

in the coastal and river trade.[42] Much of this was trade within China, the coastal trade into which such firms inserted themselves, or it was a Southeast Asian country trade, where again the British were well-equipped interlopers. It was not all trade *with* China. However much the Chinese lapped up foreign manfactures – they loved revolvers and eyeglasses for example – markets for foreign goods remained difficult to access directly. Foreign trading interests diversified their operations, interpolating themselves structurally into existing markets by using their technological and treaty positions (their steamers and privileged tax status) to secure advantages in carrying trades.

The China trade required constant reinvention. Those who failed to change, to leap into newly opened ports or who failed to experiment with different business, soon suffered and fell. With the opening of the Yangzi to foreign navigation, new opportunities were also thrown open, and foreign enterprises leapt in. The early 1860s were gold-rush years. The Second Opium War of 1856–60 threw open new ports. *The Times* talked up Shanghai as 'the new El Dorado of commercial men'; clerks in London were impatient to get out there believing on appointment that their fortunes were made – if they lived out their terms in the East.[43] Lindsay and his firm proved steady and dramatic innovators. The 'enterprising spirit' of the man who pushed to get the *Lord Amherst* up the coast in 1832, led the firm first in to Hong Kong, to invest in the *Challenger* – the first of the great British clippers – to have it tugged straight to Hankou (Hankow) in 1863 to sail direct from there with the new season's tea crop – at significantly higher freight rates – and to commission the *Fire Cracker*.[44] Lindsays were not always first, of course, and they had strong competition, but they were prominent.

Reinvention and innovation were also needed because for all their new advantages – notably extraterritoriality, and the treaty-set low tariff – the foreign firms constantly found themselves outflanked by Chinese merchants who had more capital, knew their markets, knew good technology when they saw it (they loved the steamers too) and constantly edged the foreigner out of his new markets. Jardines, for example, steadily diversified. By 1872, they had largely left the opium trade and the cotton business, moving instead firmly into shipping and insurance and banking (the firm later made private loans to the imperial household). Tea exports would also eventually face debilitating competition from Indian teas,

---

[42] SRO D(W) 1920/3/3, 'Cash Memos', D(W) 1920/3/5, 'Memorandum of Position' Shanghai, Apr. 1865.

[43] *Times*, 12 Sept. 1864, 6; E. C. M. Bowra: diary, *c.* 7 May 1863, School of Oriental and African Studies, Library Special Collections, PPMS 69, box 2; Charles M. Dyce, *Personal Reminiscences of Thirty Years' Residence in the Model Settlement Shanghai, 1870–1900* (1906), 3.

[44] Spirit: SRO, D(W) 1920/5, [illeg.] to R. C. Antrobus, 21 Jan. 1863.

and Jardines switched to providing services for other exporters of tea, as well as silk, as the markets changed.[45] Change was not forced on the 'Princely Hong' by business failure as it was on smaller China fry, such as Little Brothers (who moved out of commerce and into treaty port utilities, and local journalism), or Dow & Co., but the continuing difficulties of competing against Chinese merchants dictated shifting to operations in which the British might have structural or other advantages. New treaty ports were quickly 'lost' to Chinese trade dominance. So the British and other foreign traders were always looking for new advantage. Where once they had railed against Chinese and East India Company restriction, now they lobbied hard for protection of their treaty 'rights', and for the advantages that this new form of shelter provided them.

So Lindsay & Co. were a key player in British-opened China. And they had flair: the *Lord Amherst*'s reconnaissance set an example that was still pursued three decades on in 1859, when the company's Shanghai partner Alexander Michie took a ship to explore new ports designated for opening in the north, Niuzhuang and Yantai, before the 1858 Tianjin Treaty had been ratified, and before, it turned out to his alarm, the war had actually concluded. Michie had to hop back to safety pretty swiftly. In 1861, he led a Shanghai chamber of commerce foray along the Yangzi.[46] The shifting topography of China opened to foreign trade demanded this readiness to jump ahead, scout out the land, make new contacts, bag a lot from the consul in the still just-marked-out new British concession, pitch for a wharf site and set to work.

The firm also had style and status. The stately *Challenger* itself epitomised that for Michie, on his maiden voyage east to join the firm in 1854 as his mail steamer spoke to the clipper in the Straits of Malacca, its 'shapely back hull and white sails reflecting the morning sun'.[47] Michie joined a firm in the thick of foreign public life in Shanghai: the chamber of commerce, council, all the public committees, the race club. Lindsay's nephew Antrobus was commander of the Shanghai volunteer corps, and in 1864–5 council chairman. Lindsays also lived well in China: Antrobus had his beagle pack at Shanghai, and made sure he secured a cricket

[45] On this see Thomas G. Rawski, 'Chinese Dominance of Treaty Port Commerce and its Implications, 1860–1875', *Explorations in Economic History*, 7:1–2 (1969), 451–73, and Jerry S. L. Wang, 'The Profitability of Anglo-Chinese trade, 1861–1913', *Business History*, 35:3 (1993), 39–65. See also Yen-p'ing Hao, *The Commercial Revolution in China: The Rise of Sino-Western Mercantile Capitalism* (Berkeley, 1986), and his *The Comprador in Nineteenth-Century China: Bridge between East and West* (Cambridge, MA, 1970). On Jardines: Edward LeFervour, *Western Enterprise in Late Ch'ing China: A Selective Survey of Jardine, Matheson & Company's Operations, 1842–1895* (Cambridge, MA, 1968).

[46] Alexander Michie, *The Englishman in China during the Victorian Era: As illustrated in the Career of Sir Rutherford Alcock* . . . (1900), I, 220–3.

[47] *Ibid.*, I, 238.

ground (he was no mean bowler). Quaker landowner Thomas Hanbury was shocked at the extravagance of their living at Shanghai: a reputed, and staggering, £16,000 annual housekeeping budget in 1865. Ernest Bowra sailed east in 1863 with Antrobus, 'the great China merchant', a gentleman 'in birth and by position'.[48] Such panache and gentlemanliness was also good credit-worthiness, and for getting company bills accepted. The property at Shanghai was 'a magnificent house. All the furniture &tc sent out from England.' There was no roughing it for Lindsays with their pillared drawing room, which could comfortably host a dance for sixty in 1851.[49] Everybody was extravagant before the great bust of 1865, though Lindsays seemed to have stood out even from that competitive pack right up until the crash.

The Eastern Archipelago Company

But as Shanghai's small elite community danced in his drawing room, Hugh Hamilton Lindsay in London was battling in court, pamphlet and press to save other investments, and later his own reputation. The focus now needs to turn to Borneo, away from the luxury of Shanghai, to the contrasting difficulties of a start-up mining operation on the island of Labuan. The British enterprise in China was coalescing into a firmer network of port cities. An offshoot of Indian resource, power and trade, it was secured by the Nanjing Treaty and by the Southeast Asian gains of Singapore and Penang, and the London Treaty. It was an increasingly sophisticated operation on the ground. It was headquartered at Hong Kong until the 1860s, after which the commercial centre of balance shifted to Shanghai; indeed, Lindsays relocated their headquarters there in 1861, while the diplomatic focus switched to now-open Peking and the new British Legation.[50] In 1860/1 the British China presence rapidly expanded into north China and along the Yangzi. After 1859, Japan had been an off-shoot; little copy-cat British concessions had been established there and staffed from China.[51] Holding all of this together were the treaties, the 'vigilance' of British officials and military power, and those

---

[48] Cricket: *NCH*, 6 Apr. 1861, 55; *Letters of Sir Thomas Hanbury* (1913), 3 Aug. 1865, 124; Bowra: 'Copy of his Diary Describing his Voyage to China in 1863 . . .', p. 8, Special Collections, School of Oriental and African Studies Library, PPMS 69, box 2.

[49] Dow letters, 16 Nov. 1851, 6 Jan. 1852, describing dinners at 'Hoggs': Hogg was the Shanghai partner, and would have been living at the house. On the persistence of social status as 'a proxy for directorial integrity' even as company structures and law evolved, see Paul Johnson, *Making the Market: Victorian Origins of Corporate Capitalism* (Cambridge, 2010), quotation from 205.

[50] *China Express and Telegraph*, 27 June 1861, 340.

[51] Pär Cassel, *Grounds of Judgment: Extraterritoriality and Imperial Power in Nineteenth-Century China and Japan* (New York, 2011); J. E. Hoare, *Japan's Treaty Ports and Foreign settlements: The Uninvited Guests 1858–1899* (Folkestone, 1994).

ships. And although this was the heyday of sail, it was also clear that steam would be king. P&O secured its mail contracts, and chuffed reliably to Hong Kong and on to Shanghai.[52] And steam needed coal.

By March 1848, Hugh Hamilton Lindsay was a director, and by the summer chairman, of the Eastern Archipelago Company (EAC), granted a Royal Charter in July 1847 for twenty-one years to develop the resources of the new British colony at Labuan in Borneo.[53] In March 1848, the company advertised a share issue. Their key interest was that necessity coal: coal for the royal navy, coal for the P&O (whose directors publicly supported the new company), coal for Singapore, coal for Hong Kong, coal for the ocean highway to Australia. Coal, in fact, for the world: in a telling map published in one of its later annual reports showing the 'advantageous position' of Labuan as a coaling station, the island was pictured at the centre of a global network of steamship routes (Figure 2), and such maps mesmerise.[54] That slow old bucket the *Hugh Lindsay* (which could carry coal for five days' travel) was now an antique, and though its successors ate their coal more efficiently, there were many more of them, moving more regularly and swiftly. The company had secured the charter, although its founder Henry Wise – former East Indiaman and London agent and publicist of Sir James Brooke, the 'White Rajah' – had secured the Labuan coal concession in his own name. Wise, who is widely credited with having made Brooke's reputation in Britain through his publicity efforts and lobbying, assembled a board of prominent directors, including Lindsay. The two men had known each other for some thirty years. Wise was placed within the new company as managing director (on a fine salary) and was largest shareholder, but now there developed a very tricky situation. Not only did matters proceed very slowly on the ground, for the company was undercapitalised and did not provide sufficient resource to its agents who confronted steep logistical and environmental challenges in Labuan, but a spiralling and multifaceted dispute between Wise and Brooke proved crippling. Brooke had first arrived in Borneo in 1839, and by 1842 had secured the governorship of the territory of Sarawak from the sultan of Brunei in return for his armed intervention

---

[52] Freda Harcourt, *Flagships of Imperialism: The P & O Company and the Politics of Empire from its Origins to 1867* (Manchester, 2006).

[53] Except where noted, I have drawn on this section from John Ingleson, *Expanding the Empire: James Brooke and the Sarawak Lobby, 1839–1868* (Nedlands, 1979), especially 57–64; Graham Irwin, *Nineteenth Century Borneo: A Study in Diplomatic Rivalry* ('S-Gravenhage, 1955), principally 134–8. An early notice of the Company's formation appeared in the *Morning Chronicle*, 25 Feb. 1848, 6, and 2 June 1848, 3, and its prospectus in the *Morning Post*, 20 Mar. 1848, 1. Each side in the controversy used parliamentary connections to secure publication as House of Commons papers of significant amounts of documentation, also used below.

[54] P&O: *Steam Navigation Gazette*, 3 June 1848, 369; map: frontispiece to *Sixth Annual Report (Year Ending 30th June 1854) of the Directors of the Eastern Archipelago Company* (1855) (hereafter *EAC Report, 1854*).

Figure 2 (Colour online) Labuan at the centre of the steamship world.
Source: frontispiece to *Sixth Annual Report (Year Ending 30th June 1854) of the Directors of the Eastern Archipelago Company* (1855).

to suppress rebellion. The Briton had parlayed promises of position into a perpetual personal grant of territory, and then used it to lever official British support for his gains. While Brooke, as even one of his friends admitted, had 'as much idea of business as a cow has of a clean shirt', he knew a potential threat to his new-consolidated position in Borneo when he saw one: a chartered company that he did not control.[55]

In the aftermath of the railway crash, and other joint stock company scandals, and the 1847 financial crisis, 1848 was a very bad year for a new company to try and raise funds.[56] Its charter had already provoked opposition from two chambers of commerce which opposed this seeming new grant of colonial monopoly, an East India Company in the making. Only a chartered company could manage this major task of colonial development, countered the Board of Trade.[57] But by November 1851, the EAC had shipped out barely 8,000 tons of coal, half to Singapore, a little to Hong Kong, the rest to navy ships at Labuan, and these had mostly to load it on their ships' boats from the beach and scull it out and haul it aboard.[58] One of their managers at Labuan, James Motley, rather more involved himself in the island's natural history than its coal, to notable scientific effect it might be said; the other (his brother) paid the staff with cloth, to his alleged private profit. Labuan's potential remained hypnotic; the island 'appears one immense coal field', reported one of the company's agents from the island. The seam the EAC had begun mining was pictured ranging across the entire northern peninsula of the colony (Figure 3). But excavating this black gold was proving a 'beastly' process.[59]

---

[55] The judgement was Admiral Sir Henry Keppel's in an 1849 letter to Wise, quoted in Irwin, *Nineteenth Century Borneo*, 137. On the structural challenge the EAC presented to Brooke see also Howard Cox and Stuart Metcalfe, 'The Borneo Company Limited: Origins of a Nineteenth-Century Networked Multinational', *Asia Pacific Business Review*, 4:4 (1998), 55–8. On Brooke's Borneo, see Irwin, *Nineteenth Century Borneo*; Ingleson, *Expanding the Empire*; and Nicholas Tarling, *The Burthen, the Risk, and the Glory: A Biography of Sir James Brooke* (Kuala Lumpur, 1982).

[56] H. M. Boot, *The Commercial Crisis of 1847* (Hull, 1984).

[57] *Eastern Archipelago Company. Copy of the Charter of Incorporation . . .*, Parliamentary Papers, 1847–8 (227).

[58] H. H. Lindsay to Sir John Parkington, 12 Mar. 1852, *Eastern Archipelago Company. Copies or Extracts of All Correspondence . . .*, Parliamentary Papers, 1852 (357), 32.

[59] 'Extract from Mr. Robert Coulson's letter to Thomas Brown, Esq., 20 June 1851', in *Eastern Archipelago Company. Copies or Extracts of All Correspondence . . .*, Parliamentary Papers, 1852 (357), 116; 'Map of Labuan island', copy of sketch enclosed in despatch from the officer administering the government of Labuan to Earl Grey, 2 July 1850, in *Eastern Archipelago Company. Copies or Extracts of All Correspondence . . .*, Parliamentary Papers, 1852 (357), facing 95; James Motley and Lewis Llewellyn Dillwyn, *Contributions to the Natural History of Labuan, and the Adjacent Coasts of Borneo* (1855); A. R. Walker, 'James Motley (1822–1859): The Life Story of a Collector and Naturalist', *Minerva*, 13 (2005), 20–37.

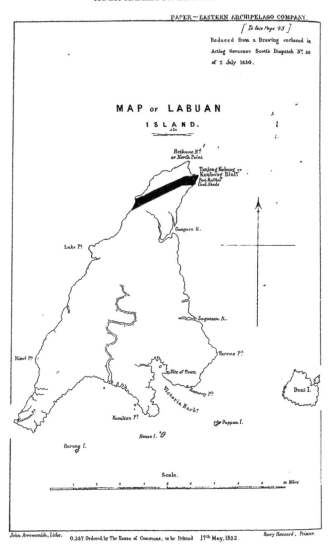

Figure 3 Labuan, island of coal.
Source: 'Map of Labuan island', copy of sketch enclosed in despatch from the officer administering the government of Labuan to Earl Grey, 2 July 1850, in *Eastern Archipelago Company. Copies or Extracts of All Correspondence . . .* , Parliamentary Papers, 1852 (357), facing 95.

James Brooke proved Lindsay's undoing. Having tried and failed at the China trade himself, Brooke had made his name and way in Borneo, and was 'rajah' of Sarawak. He had also now secured British recognition, rode high in public esteem and was governor of Labuan from 1847, and Borneo consul general. He and Wise comprehensively fell out by the middle of 1848, and Brooke attacked Wise through the EAC, which, besides being a vehicle which clearly enriched Wise before a single piece of coal had been lifted, also presented that clear political challenge to Brooke's authority. The company's slow progress in Labuan proved bad enough, for Brooke as governor moved to get it stripped of its charter on those grounds in various official dispatches starting in January 1850, though the Colonial Office saw no need and rebuffed him in January 1852.[60] But Brooke had an ace up his sleeve, and he then played it, for he knew that the directors had taken a risky short-cut in July 1848 by certifying to the Board of Trade that the Company had capital of £51,000 paid up as required under the terms of its charter. It had not: the money market in early 1848 had not delivered. Lindsay later commented on 'the utter horror and suspicion with which the public look at all joint-stock companies since the great railway crash; hence the utter impossibility of getting the public generally to take shares and advance money'. So, they 'purchased' Wise's existing plant at Labuan, against his future salary, royalties and shares, and presented that debt to Wise, for it was nothing but that, as capital. This was not desperately unusual for its time, but such creative accounting proved the charter's undoing.[61]

Lindsay was the public butt of the scorn that came to be directed at this certificate, news of which sparked a prominent debate highlighting anxieties about the morality of joint stock enterprises which were already under intense scrutiny as a result of the railway crash.[62] Despite consistently asserting that they had Board of Trade approval for this measure (which its legal assistant, later chancellor of the exchequer, Sir Stafford Northcote, did to an extent attest to), Lindsay and his colleagues were widely criticised in parliament, initially at Brooke's instigation through MP Henry Drummond, and the press.[63] Two withering commentaries in *The Times* in the summer of 1852 inflicted grievous wounds. Lindsay appealed to its editor, 'as one gentleman to another', to read the voluminous documentation justifying their action that the Company published, and to undo these 'unjust attacks upon

---

[60] *Eastern Archipelago Company. Copies or Extracts of All Correspondence . . .*, Parliamentary Papers, 1852 (357), 85–6, 98–101.

[61] Lindsay to Brooke, 24 July 1850, in *EAC Report, 1854*, 182. This report contains voluminous documentation covering the history of the company and its controversies.

[62] Johnson, *Making the Market*; Timothy Alborn, *Conceiving Companies: Joint-Stock Politics in Victorian England* (1998).

[63] Northcote's affidavit: 4 Mar. 1854: *EAC Report, 1854*, 71–4.

private character', but to little avail.[64] In return, Wise and others attacked Brooke, and he and his supporters attacked them and their staff in Borneo. Lindsay had tried to get personality out of the dispute in meetings and in correspondence with Brooke. 'Well, you advise arbitration', Brooke wrote to him, as he did, but there was nothing to arbitrate: 'Mr Wise has behaved ill and [for] that he will pay the penalty.'[65] Lindsay delivered the last of his pamphlets, assailing Brooke for abuse of his government office in attacking the company.[66] But Lindsay's reputation was hammered, and, equally to the point, so was his pocket, to the tune of at least £12,000 by the summer of 1851, and probably a great deal more by 1854.[67] It all came out, and as news of their sleight of registration hand was made public in 1851–2, the court cases began: a shareholder demanded his money back (he failed); the crown moved to annul the charter. Brooke appeared as a witness. The legal struggle lasted two years, reputations were technically restored, but the removal of the charter was confirmed in 1854.[68]

Brooke nonetheless proved a vulnerable opponent, for the allegations launched against him in this struggle led to his dismissal as governor of Labuan in 1852 and surrender of his other official appointments, which he had clearly abused, and more seriously to an 1854 commission of enquiry in Singapore, at which Wise provided damaging testimony, returning the earlier favour in London.[69] Brooke survived this, but not without humiliation and lingering questions about his actions and character. He was attacked as a tyrant, who had executed indigenes without due process, and who had with royal navy support massacred 'pirates' at the 1849 'Battle' of Batang Marau, when the royal naval steamer *Nemesis* (which had made its devasting debut during the Opium War in the waters around Canton) confronted and destroyed a large fleet of Dyak 'pirate' canoes.[70] He slapped back that his accusers were exploiting labour, were simply incompetent and had lied to secure confirmation of their charter. This personal quarrel between Wise and Brooke became a public dispute about slavery, freedom and tyranny. British empire in Asia had opened

[64] *Times*, 28 June 1842, 4, 21 July 1852, 4; *EAC Report, 1854*, preface, v.

[65] Brooke to Hugh Hamilton Lindsay, 7 Oct. 1850, SRO, D(W) 1920/4/2.

[66] H. H. Lindsay, *The Eastern Archipelago Company and Sir James Brooke* (1853).

[67] Calculated from data in *EAC Report 1854*, and detail from the EAC share register published in Sir James Brooke, *A Vindication of his Character and Proceedings in Reply to the Statements Printed and Circulated by Joseph Hume, Esq. M.P. Addressed to Henry Drummond, Esq M.P.* (1853), 29. Lindsay held 713 out of the 2,000 shares in Aug. 1851. Wise held 728.

[68] *Times*, 21 Apr. 1852, 7, 21 June 1852, 7; law reports in *The Queen on the Prosecution of Sir James Brooke, K.C.B. against the Eastern Archipelago Company; Containing, the Judgements of the Queen's Bench and the Exchequer Chamber, Together with Two Articles from the 'Times' Newspaper on the Merits of the Case* (1853).

[69] Ingleson, *Expanding the Empire*, 80–4; Irwin, *Nineteenth Century Borneo*, 149–50; Alex Middleton, 'Rajah Brooke and the Victorians', *Historical Journal*, 53:2 (2010), 381–400.

[70] Ingleson, *Expanding the Empire*, 64–72.

up routes for free and unfree migration: Chinese poured out of the empire of the Qing in the hungry 1840s to what they called 'Old Gold Mountain' (San Francisco) and 'New Gold Mountain' (Australia/Melbourne). British 'Coolie traders' – often conveniently badged as Spanish, and so at a technical remove from the reach of British officials – turned a blind eye to the press-ganging of men by their contractors into the 'Barracoons' at Xiamen, to be shipped off to Peru, Chile or Cuba. The new British infrastructure – laws, colonies and concessions, steamer routes – facilitated this fast-developing movement of people. The EAC recruited labourers from Bombay and Malaya; and we can always easily get a thousand Chinese, reported Lindsay to one Company meeting.[71] Officials moved to contain and regulate the trade as new press networks disseminated accounts of abuses and alleged abuses. But such anxieties and scandals of empire provided a further layer to the EAC dispute.

Brooke won the initial battle, comprehensively. The charter was removed, and without it the Company could not long survive. And Welsh coal proved cheaper at Hong Kong than Labuan's. In early 1857, it went into voluntary liquidation. Lindsay had thrown in good money after bad and lost out.[72] Wise did alright. In the midst of the crisis Lindsay surrendered his China partnership, temporarily it turned out, leaving a substantial amount of capital in the firm but clearly separating Lindsay & Co. liabilities from his own.[73] However, as noted, he seems swiftly to have regained an influential role within it. This Labuan episode was a disaster, but Lindsay had actually made the right call. His vision of British Asia was joined up: Labuan, Singapore, Hong Kong, Shanghai, hubs and out-stations of an integrated system. Lindsay & Co. acted as agents for the EAC in China, his nephew Antrobus attesting in 1855 to the strong demand from steamers at Hong Kong that the company could profitably meet.[74] But the EAC showed that while a entrepreneur like Henry Wise might work a joint stock company to his own signal advantage, it also proved that the Lindsay style, the old China coast style, of impulsive adventuring, would no longer suffice. It could not adequately serve the furnaces of the P&O and royal navy steamers: that needed smart, careful and efficient management, and technical expertise on the ground that did not overly dally with 'shells insects and birds' as Motley had; it needed

---

[71] *Nautical Standard*, 17 Aug. 1850, 524; *EAC Report, 1854*, 17.

[72] Lindsay retained involvement in a rump successor, the China Steamship and Labuan Coal Company, however, *Times*, 17 Aug. 1867, 4. The Company was active from 1861, at least, registered as a joint stock company on 8 June 1865, and formally struck off in 1883: *London Gazette*, 23 Jan. 1883, 403. Although it had been voluntarily wound up in 1866/7: see *Law Times*, 6 Feb. 1869, 667–9. See also Cuthbert Collingwood, *Rambles of a Naturalist on the Shores and Waters of the China Sea . . .* (1868), 157–60.

[73] See documents in SRO, D(W) 1920/5.

[74] *EAC Report, 1854*, 317–18.

resource. It certainly needed inspiration and imagination, but that was not enough. We start to move into the era of British consolidation in Asia, although China remains a shifting imperial frontier for a decade yet, and Lindsay himself does not fare so well.

Conclusion

The 1850s proved up and down years for Lindsay & Co., but in 1865 like many others, they were caught as the Shanghai bubble popped. It should have been too big to fall, or at least too grand: 'When houses like Lindsays' fail & Dents' retrench, . . . nobody can consider himself safe', wrote one smaller player on the China scene as the firm crashed.[75] Lindsay sold his horses, fired his servants and tried to salvage what he could. Coutts Lindsay and Lord Lindsay declined to throw him a family lifeline, and the bankruptcy was a public affair. There was a lingering taint of impropriety in the last days of the company – 'accusations of fraud and dishonesty'; bill transactions which were 'the common talk of the city' – which caused family rupture as Lindsay distanced himself from Antrobus, who had the 'entire management of the firm' in his hands. Thereafter, Lindsay's was a quieter life. He is listed as a registered broker in London in 1866, and remarked on as such in 1873, operating at Lloyds, but I find little else before his largely unremarked death in 1881: unremarked in China; unremarked in Britain except in *The Times* as the former member for Sandwich. There was nothing there on China, or on Labuan.[76] Lindsay slid out of the China trade world that he had so contributed to shaping. His last public China contributions that can be documented were in February 1860, and in 1863. Just elected a fellow of the Royal Geographical Society, on the nomination of John Crawfurd who had in fact long before mocked his *Lord Amherst* report, Lindsay delivered a paper sent by Alexander Michie about the abortive foray to the Gulf of Bohai in 1859, and the attention of the meeting was drawn to Lindsay's own long-ago foray into China *incognita*, but there was really little he could usefully now add to any discussion.[77] And in 1863, he proposed a motion calling for cuts in tea duties at a public meeting in London, but otherwise there seems to have been silence.[78]

[75] R. W. Little to parents, 17 May 1865, Little family papers, private collection.

[76] SRO D(W) 1920/5/4, Lindsay and Coutts Lindsay to Hugh Hamilton Lindsay, 17 Sept. 1865, Hugh Hamilton Lindsay to Sir Edmund Antrobus, 24 Sept. 1865; *Times*, 16 Oct. 1873, 6, 2 June 1881, 6.

[77] Sixth meeting, Monday, 13 Feb. 1860, *Proceedings of the Royal Geographical Society of London*, 4:2 (1859–60), 58–63; the original report is in the Royal Geographical Society archives, JMS/10/15, 1860, Alexander Michie, 'Notes of a Cruise in the Gulfs of Pechele and Leo-tung from April to August 1859'; Robert A. Stafford, 'Scientist of Empire: Sir Roderick Murchison', in *Scientific Exploration and Victorian Imperialism* (Cambridge, 2002), 138–9.

[78] *Commercial Daily List*, 28 Feb. 1863, 4.

Silence seems strange after his decades of shouting. The British struggle in China was partly a war of words, fought on the walls of Chinese cities, in pamphlets handed out from the 'Lord Amherst', or from naval boats, and fought across the globalising world of the Anglophone public. The installation of the Canton select committee's new Chinese-language printing press at Canton, it was remarked in 1831, 'may be regarded as forming a new era in our connections with China'. 'We have the means if we have the inclination', they claimed, 'to throw off in a few hours, any number of copies of any document in the Chinese language.'[79] So they did: the British threw off broadsides from their armed steamers, and then rowed to shore and handed out leaflets explaining why. Their pamphlets, handbills and posters were aimed to bypass local officials, notably at Canton, in order to reach ordinary city people and merchants, as well as higher officials. They tried to create a public debate, by breaking the Qing monopoly on information about the British. Lindsay was a self-conscious actor in this struggle, and knew the importance of words. He pamphleted in London, broadsiding the peacemongers, old John Company, the Chinese and later Sir James Brooke. He knew this was a struggle about representation, in the field, and at the centre, and he played his role. Words also followed deeds: reports, letters, delivery of the intelligence that he had garnered in the form and with the conclusions he wanted, of course. Lindsay worked to make China visible in texts and to sketch out his vision of a better and more secure British position in China, and he also contributed to the representation of China with exhibits at the Great Exhibition and then the Crystal Palace at Sydenham.[80] Words marked deeds too. He renamed parts of the landscape: Gützlaff Island, Marjoribanks Bay were inscribed on the charts the *Lord Amherst* brought back from the coast. And there is also a spotted kingfisher named for him, a memorial of his 1829 trip to Java.

Lindsay also stands out for the force of his anger, and for the argument that the British problem with and in China lay not simply in Qing 'obduracy', but in the fact (as he saw it) of British 'degradation'. National honour, he argued, was demeaned by British acceptance of Chinese restriction. Lindsay and his allies sought to make the Chinese understand who they were dealing with, who the British actually were: and when words alone failed, those should be joined with violence.

---

[79] BL, APAC, IOR/G/12/287, Secret Department, Select Committee to Court, 7 Nov. 1831.

[80] At the Great Exhibition in 1851 he provided sea slugs, swallows' nests (including display), silk and china, and was commended his contributions; at the Sydenham Crystal Palace in 1855 'a Chinese homestead'; he had earlier sent back Manila birds, one of which was named for him; *Reports by the Juries on the Subjects in the Thirty Classes into which the Exhibition Was Divided* (1852), 66; *Observer*, 7 May 1855, 6; *Philosophical Magazine*, 10:58 (1831), 302–4, report of Zoological Society meeting of 28 June 1831.

For only then, it seemed, would the pacific character of the British – who had 'no thirst for conquest' as Marjoribanks's pamphlet put it – be understood.[81] 'Our object in China is commercial intercourse, not territorial aggrandizement', Lindsay reiterated in 1840. He is not the last of the angry men in the history of Sino-British relations, nor was he the most damaging; that was probably the villain of the Arrow War, Harry Parkes, but he remains a prominent and noisy voice all the same. Lindsay's vision of a British China was one in which there was armed security for 'free and liberal' commercial intercourse. An 'insular possession' – an island seized from the Chinese – might be necessary, if the Chinese would stand it, another Gibraltar might be developed, although he argued that if the British 'planted our flag', then 'our career of British India would be repeated in China'. Perhaps there was glory to be had there, perhaps if 'light shines upon them from abroad' then

> how bright a page would such a consummation emblazon for us in the history of nations! To see so many millions of our fellow-creatures, now wrapt in darkness, pursuing the onward march of improvement in morality, science, and arts, but, beyond all, adopting the pure tenets of Christianity, would be a triumph indeed.[82]

Others toyed with this view. And there was a moment in the early mid-1860s when it seemed as if the flag would be decisively planted, and some talk of how much better a British China would be than a British India, but the moment passed, and the Qing state re-strengthened itself. The bloody horrors of the Anglo-French occupation of Canton in 1858–61 proved for some, such as H. N. Lay's successor Robert Hart, that 'cooperation' was the only course.[83] But what Lindsay mostly and steadily aimed at was not possession but security, a commerce placed on an 'equitable footing' in which the British 'dictate the terms', and always he lobbied for the prohibition of those opprobrious and insulting epithets that he discoursed about repeatedly.

Lindsay operated at the cusp of wide-ranging structural changes: change in the China trade, change in Sino-foreign relations, technological change, the spatial reorganisation of British power in East and Southeast Asia, changes in the organisation of capital and of legal frameworks. The British dictated most of the terms of that change. He was operating in advance of change too, and at least in times in advance of societal consensus on the propriety of innovative new structures and practices, and

---

[81] 'Brief Account of the English Character', BL, APAC, IOR/10/30, Secret Consultations of Select Committee of Supercargoes, fo. 125.

[82] Lindsay, *Is the War with China a Just One?*, 36–7, 140; *Rupture with China*, 26; *Remarks On Occurrences in China*, 41–2, 103.

[83] Bickers, *Scramble for China*, 187–229; Steven A. Leibo, 'Not So Calm an Administration: The Anglo-French Occupation of Canton, 1858–61', *Journal of the Royal Asiatic Society Hong Kong Branch*, 28 (1988), 16–33.

as entrepreneurs like him seized opportunity and courted controversy as law and governance struggled to keep up with the consequences of the new order in Asia. Controversy could not but follow. Lindsay had entered the fray through the old world patronage system of the declining East India Company, but he proved to be a modern. For Lindsay, unlike William Hunter, there was no good life at Canton. The trade was not efficient and predictable, but even if it was, his understanding of the British character, and his performance of it, meant that he could not tolerate the restrictions placed on the foreigner at Canton, accepted by his superiors, and on Britons generally though subservience to the old company monopoly. He attacked India House as he attacked the viceroy's Yamen at Canton. For Lindsay, this was the 'period of our degradation': opportunity motivated him, but anger and pride shaped his actions, infused his language and stoked his anger.[84] Lindsay saw Asia, saw it whole, and interconnected, and saw a new place in it for Britain, and through war and commerce set out to make it a British Asia. He fought both Qing and East India Company monopolies, substituting in their place a free-trade enterprise that smashed laws and customs. He is in some ways a gift for fictions.

It is worth comparing Brooke and Lindsay briefly. Both were sons of the Company. Brooke, the younger by a year, was born in it, and served it in India. Raised in England from the age of twelve, he entered the Company military in 1919, two years before Lindsay sailed east. Lindsay was better born, and certainly better educated. Both made their way in Asia as the East India Company declined, and both went forward beyond the accepted frontiers of empire, scouting out the territory beyond. They were young men in a hurry at the close of monopoly and the opening of a region that could be Britain's, with flag or traders planted, and that they intended to stake their own claims within. Brooke sailed in his armed schooner *Royalist*, Lindsay on the *Lord Amherst*. Both were also self-publicists, publishing manifestoes and apologias, sketching out grand visions of how Asia could and ought to be changed by Britain. Obviously, there was a world of difference between Shanghai in 1832 and the Borneo James Brooke first saw in 1839, but both men sought post-Company roles in the new spheres in Asia that British power was opening up, and lobbied for that deployment of British power, arguing in words and showing in deeds what might be done, and in both cases they were happy with necessary murder, with the use of the *Nemesis* and its like, whether against Dyak 'pirates' or the recalcitrant Qing.

Brooke's sultanate and interventions in Borneo proved an easy target for political radicals, and his is the more flamboyant contribution to British imperial history. But Lindsay was arguably a more important figure: the 1832 foray put north China on the British map – literally, for

[84] SRO, D(W)1920/4/1, H. H. Lindsay to mother, draft, 'Amoy', Apr. 1832.

their surveys of harbours and estuaries provided pioneering charts, used by the British war fleet in 1840–2. And he then put deeds to words. There were other lobbyists and warmongers, and other firms leapt in, and lasted. But with Hugh Hamilton Lindsay, we have the angry vision of an Asia that needs transformation, and a voice demanding change and detailing how to effect it; a voice challenging Chinese law and British weakness, challenging the Chinese language, even, a voice for violence. He was a man out for his fortune, and on the make, but a man powerfully driven by notions of what it was to be a Briton when faced with Asia, and how Asia was to be reshaped on 'British terms', and British assumptions and practices reshaped too, and driven to deliver a true account of the British character. That specific vision of the British character, angry, violent, visionary even, might then stand as his legacy, given its impact overall on the history of British relations with China.

Transactions of the RHS 22 (2012), pp. 171–97 © Royal Historical Society 2012
doi:10.1017/S0080440112000114

AFTER 1848: THE EUROPEAN REVOLUTION
IN GOVERNMENT

By Christopher Clark

READ 6 MAY 2011

ABSTRACT. This paper revisits the question of the impact of the 1848 revolutions on governance and administration across the European states. Few historians would contend that the immediate post-revolutionary years saw a 'return' to pre-1848 conditions, but the transitions of the 1850s are usually presented as episodes within a narrative that is deemed to be specific to the respective nation-state. This paper argues that the 1850s saw a profound transformation in political and administrative practices across the continent, encompassing the emergence of new centrist political coalitions with a distinctively post-revolutionary mode of politics characterised by a technocratic vision of progress, the absorption into government of civil-society-based bodies of expertise, and changes in public information management. In short, it proposes that we need to move beyond the restrictive interpretation implied by the tenacious rubric 'decade of reaction' towards recognising that the 1850s were – after the Napoleonic period – the second high-water-mark in nineteenth-century political and administrative innovation across the continent. The paper argues, moreover, that these transitions took place on an authentically European basis and that they only come fully into focus when we survey the spectrum of governmental experiences across the European states. The paper closes with some reflections on the broader implications of this reappraisal for our understanding of European history in the middle and later decades of the nineteenth century.

It is a commonplace in the historiography of nineteenth-century Europe that the failure of the revolutions of 1848 ushered in a 'decade of reaction'. It is not difficult to see why. In many parts of Europe, the collapse of the revolutions brought harsh repressions and concerted efforts to erase the memory of insurrection from public awareness. During the decade that followed, police forces were consolidated and their sphere of responsibility extended. It is perhaps in part a consequence of this grim scenario of repression and political stagnation that the 1850s remain, for most of the continental states, the least-researched decade of the century. For this decade falls, as it were, into a crevasse between the revolutions of 1848 on the one hand and the era of liberal revivals and national unifications on the other. It tends to be seen, moreover, through the eyes of those whose hopes were dashed when the revolutions collapsed. While few historians would contend that the immediate post-revolutionary years saw a 'return' to pre-1848 conditions, most narratives of the era proceed

from the assumption that this was a period of political stasis, in which the
historical forces mobilised by the revolutions of 1848/9 were temporarily
dammed up. It goes without saying that this idea has had a deep impact
on the historiographies of modern Europe.

Over the last twenty years or so, a process of revision has been
underway – my own interest in this project was sparked by a piece called
'The Austrian Experiment' published in 1994 by Robert Evans, which
argued for a radical reappraisal: the post-revolutionary decade, Evans
argued, was 'not restorative at all, but innovative, on a broad front, with a
clear and ambitious programme'.[1] But although there have been parallel
revisions in many of the European historiographies, there has to date been
no attempt to draw together their implications for the political history
of Europe as a whole.[2] Indeed, one of the most striking features of work
on this era has been the reluctance of scholars working within specific
nation-state traditions to look sideways at the experience of governments
in other parts of Europe. Instead, the transitions of the 1850s are presented
as episodes within a narrative that is deemed to be specific to the respective
nation-state. Thus, studies of Louis Napoleon focus on the emperor's effort
to recapture the legacy of the first Bonaparte or, alternatively, identify him
as the inaugurator of a distinctively French Gaullist tradition characterised
by a pragmatic policy blend that transcends the left-right divide, or of a
distinctively French mode of 'providential politics'.[3] The innovations of
the Cavour government in Piedmont are likewise set in the context of

---

[1] R. J. W. Evans, 'From Confederation to Compromise: The Austrian Experiment,
1849–1867', *Proceedings of the British Academy*, 87 (1994), 135–67, here 137.
[2] For discussions of the vast literature on the Second Empire, see J. F. McMillan, *Napoleon
III* (Harlow, 1991), 1–6; A. Plessis, *The Rise and Fall of the Second Empire, 1852–1871*, trans.
Jonathan Mandelbaum (Cambridge, 1979), 1–11; the quotations are from R. Sencourt,
The Modern Emperor (1933), and Plessis, *Second Empire*, 3; D. Barclay, *Friedrich Wilhelm IV and
the Prussian Monarchy 1840–1861* (Oxford, 1995); R. J. Bazillion, *Modernizing Germany. Karl
Biedermann's Career in the Kingdom of Saxony, 1835–1901* (New York, 1990); A. Green, *Fatherlands.
State-Building and Nationhood in Nineteenth-Century Germany* (Cambridge, 2001); R. J. Evans,
Rituals of Retribution. Capital Punishment in Germany, 1600–1987 (1997), 284; the same point is
made in R. J. Evans, *Tales from the German Underworld* (New Haven, 1998), 109, 218; H.-H.
Brandt, *Der Österreichische Neoabsolutismus: Staatsfinanzen und Politik, 1848–60* (2 vols., Göttingen,
1978) – a vast compendium on governmental practice in the post-revolutionary era; George
Barany, 'Ungarns Verwaltung 1848–1918', in *Die Habsburgermonarchie*, II: Verwaltung und
Rechtswesen, A. Wandruszka and P. Urbanitsch (Vienna, 1975), 306–468, esp. 328–38; G.
Szabad, *Hungarian Political Trends between the Revolution and the Compromise* (1977); N. Durán de la
Rua, *La Unión Liberal y la modernizacion de la España Isabelina. Una convivencia frustrada, 1854–1868*
(Madrid, 1979), esp. 339–46; Maria Filomena Mónica, *Fontes Pereira de Melo* (Lisbon, 1998);
A Caracciolo, 'La storia economica', in *Storia d'Italia*, III: *Dal primo Settecento all'Unità* (Turin,
1973), 509–693; N. Nada, 'Il regime di Vittorio Emanuele dal 1848 al 1861', in P. Notario
and N. Nada, *Il Piemonte sabaudo. Dal periodo napoleonico al Risorgimento* (Turin, 1993), 343–442,
here 364–7 (both with references to the historiography).
[3] Plessis, *Second Empire*, 4–6; Jean Garrigues, *Les hommes providentiels: histoire d'une fascination
française* (Paris, 2012); Francis Choisel, *Bonapartisme et Gaullisme* (Paris, 1987).

Italy's 'pre-unitarian' situation – the innovative politics of its leader are deemed to prefigure the specifically Italian tradition of pragmatic cross-partisan alliances known as 'trasformismo'.[4] The administrative reforms enacted in Hungary after the revolution are placed within a tradition that culminates in the modernising Hungarian police state of the later twentieth century.[5] In the case of the German states, the older writing on the 1850s noted that the period was marked by an historic compromise between the forces of liberalism and the conservative elites of the old regime, but this analysis was generally framed within the more protracted narrative of a German (or Prussian) *Sonderweg* defined by the 'failure' of the bourgeoisie to fulfil its emancipatory mission. The effect of this paradigm was not merely to highlight the specifically 'German' character of the compromise reached after 1848, but also to set it in a negative moral light.[6] Among the many historians who have set about demolishing the thesis of the 'special path' are a few who have focused specifically on the 1850s. David Barclay, James Brophy, Günther Grünthal and Abigail Green, for example, all highlight from different perspectives the dynamism and potential for change within the political systems established in the wake of the revolutions of 1848 and reject the teleology implicit in the *Sonderweg*.[7] But these studies are concerned with specific territories; the challenge they offer to the 'special path' pertains to the teleological distortions of the paradigm, not to its national focus.

In this paper, I propose an alternative view. I argue that the 1850s saw a profound transformation in political and administrative practices across the continent, a European 'revolution in government'.[8] The new politics

---

[4] Sandro Rogari, *Alle origini del trasformismo. Partiti e sistema politico nell'Italia liberale, 1861–1914* (Rome, 1998); Carlo Tullio-Altan, *La nostra Italia: clientelismo, trasformismo e ribellismo dall'unità al 2000* (Milan, 2000); Giovanni Sabatucci, *Il trasformismo come sistema: saggio sulla storia politica dell'Italia unita* (Rome, 2003); on this tendency in the Italian historiography, see also S. J. Woolf, 'La storia politica e sociale', in *Storia d'Italia*, III: *Dal primo Settecento all'Unità* (Turin, 1973), 5–510, here 472.

[5] Barany, 'Ungarns Verwaltung', 344.

[6] For a critical analysis of this historiographical tradition, see J. M. Brophy, *Capitalism, Politics and Railroads in Prussia 1830–1870* (Columbus, 1998), 1–18.

[7] Barclay, *Friedrich Wilhelm IV and the Prussian Monarchy*; Brophy, *Capitalism*; G. Grünthal, *Parlamentarismus in Preussen 1848/49–1857/58: preussischer Konstitutionalismus, Parlament und Regierung in der Reaktionsära* (Düsseldorf, 1982); Green, *Fatherlands*. The classic demolition of the *Sonderweg* thesis, D. Blackbourn and G. Eley, *The Peculiarities of German History. Bourgeois Society and Politics in Nineteenth-Century Germany* (Oxford, 1984), points suggestively at the need for a trans-national approach to the problem of nineteenth-century revolution and political change; see esp. 83–5 (Eley) and 173–5 (Blackbourn).

[8] Cf. G. R. Elton, *The Tudor Revolution in Government. Administrative Changes in the Reign of Henry VIII* (Cambridge, 1969), which deals of course with a very different subject matter, but speaks of a period 'when the needs of good government prevailed over the demands of free government' and 'order and peace seemed more important than principles and rights' (1) and perceives in administrative innovation a process of 'controlled upheaval' (427).

of the decade was characterised by the dominance of pragmatic, centrist coalitions whose rhetoric and outlook marked a clear departure from the ideologically polarised positions of left and right in the pre-March era.

The European governments of the 1850s sought to legitimate themselves, furthermore, by reference to their capacity to stimulate and maintain economic growth. They launched public works projects on a scale that exceeded anything attempted during the Restoration era. These projects were driven by the conviction that government had a crucial role to play in creating the preconditions for growth, and that growth, in turn, would ultimately neutralise the 'social question' that had haunted the 1840s. The intensified interest in infrastructural investment also signalled a transition from the *ad hoc* crisis-management characteristic of the pre-March regimes to a more systematic approach to the formulation of economic policy. Moreover, in the economic sphere, as in other areas of policy formation, the revolution dramatically accelerated the 'professionalisation' of government through the integration into the policy-making process of groups and organisations representing various forms of technical expertise.

The years following the revolutions of 1848 also saw, I argue, fundamental changes in the relationship between government and its public. The rigid and unimaginative governmental press regimes of the Restoration – with their cumbersome pre-publication censorship and drastic sanctions – gave way to a more flexible, collaborative and systematic approach to the press and more broadly to the problem of public opinion which had loomed so large in the pre-March era. In short, I would contend that we need to move beyond the restrictive and one-sided interpretation implied by the tenacious rubric 'decade of reaction' towards a recognition that the 1850s were – after the Napoleonic period – the second high-water-mark in nineteenth-century political and administrative innovation across the continent. The new political synthesis achieved in these years set a pattern for politics whose imprint can still be discerned in the political cultures of our own day.

In what follows, I first of all expand my claims about the salient features of European politics in the post-revolutionary decade, arguing that all were consequences, more or less directly, of the revolutionary upheaval and the crisis of legitimation that gave rise to it. I should stress, moreover, that my aim is not merely to establish that such a transformation took place, but to argue that it occurred on an authentically European basis, that it cannot be captured from the perspective of nation-state history; indeed, that it only fully comes into focus when we survey the spectrum of governmental experiences across the European states. The paper closes with some reflections on the broader implications of this reappraisal for our understanding of European history in the middle and later decades of the nineteenth century.

New constellations

How different was the political life of the European states after the revolutions of 1848? The revolutions brought about the promulgation of a number of new constitutions, but it is only relatively recently that historians have taken a concerted interest in assessing the impact of these important documents on the conduct of politics in individual states.[9] Yet, it is clear that in several states, the concession of a constitution created an entirely new point of departure for political developments. The Prussian constitution of 1849 was imposed by the crown, not drawn up by an elected assembly, yet it was extremely popular with the great majority of liberals and the majority of the moderate conservatives.[10] The political climate in post-revolutionary Württemberg was marked by the more confrontational style of the conservative first minister, Freiherr von Linden, but here too, as in Saxony, a gradual decline in the intensity of oppositional sentiment and a willingness among many of the liberals to collaborate with the government ensured that the administration could generally count on a majority during the early post-revolutionary years (1851–5).[11]

In Piedmont, likewise, the constitution granted in 1848 and retained thereafter (the *Statuto Albertino*) proved a more dynamic and open-ended compromise than most contemporaries could have predicted. The contradictions in the new settlement were gradually exploited to prune back the powers of the monarchy. What emerged in Piedmont, as in Prussia, was a completely new constitutional and political reality. The tone was set throughout most of the 1850s by a pragmatic coalition within the fledgling parliament of conservative and moderate liberal interests. In 1852, after a brief era of conservative hegemony, Count Camillo di Cavour, who had been known in the mid-1840s for his eccentrically reactionary and confrontational politics, entered into an alliance, known as the *connubio*, with the bourgeois liberal leader Urbano Rattazzi. The ideologically flexible 'governmental coalition' that resulted

---

[9] A useful comparative survey of constitutional innovation across Europe is *Verfassungswandel um 1848 im europäischen Vergleich*, ed. M. Kisch and P. Schiera (Berlin, 2001); see esp. the introductory essay by M. Kisch, 'Verfassungswandel um 1848 – Aspekte der Rezeption und des Vergleichs zwischen den europäischen Staaten', 31–62.

[10] Barclay, *Friedrich Wilhelm IV and the Prussian Monarchy*, 183; H. Wegge, *Die Stellung der Öffentlichkeit zur oktroyierten Verfassung und die preußische Parteibildung 1848/49* (Berlin, 1932), 45–8; Grünthal, *Parlamentarismus*, 185.

[11] H. Brand, *Parlamentarismus in Württemberg (1819–1870). Anatomie eines deutschen Landtages* (Düsseldorf, 1987), 654–5; for an important study that reaches some analogous conclusions for Saxony, see Andreas Neeman, *Landtag und Politik in der Reaktionszeit. Sachsen 1849/50–1866* (Düsseldorf, 2000).

allowed Cavour to secure parliamentary support for a wide range of modernising initiatives.[12]

In Spain and Portugal, allowance has to be made for the rather different historical and political setting. In both countries, politics was structured by the existence of two competing dynastic factions, one constitutional, the other reactionary (carlistas in Spain, miguelistas in Portugal). In both countries, the reactionary option had been (temporarily) banished by mid-century as a result of conflicts in which the moderate and radical liberals had joined forces to defeat the common enemy on the right. As a consequence, the key fault-line in Iberian politics during the middle decades of the century was not that between liberals and conservatives, but that between conservative/authoritarian and radical brands of liberalism (moderados and progresistas). There are, moreover, some variations in chronology: only in 1854 was there an upheaval in Spain whose scope and violence compares with those of 1848 in the rest of Europe.[13] The peak of the unrest during that year saw the construction of over 500 barricades across Madrid and fighting more intense than anything before the Civil War of the 1930s.[14]

The Spanish administrations that emerged after the upheavals in Madrid conformed to the European post-revolutionary pattern. First, there was the period of unstable coalition government known as the 'Bienio Progresista' (1854–6). When this collapsed in the political crisis of 1856, it was succeeded by a new force in Spanish politics. Known originally as the 'parliamentary centre' and later as the Unión Liberal, it was led by moderados, but built around a pragmatic coalition of left-wing moderados (known as puritanos) and pragmatic progresistas (known as resellados), supplemented by a cohort of younger political figures with 'eclectic and centrist attitudes'.[15] It developed a composite programme, in which the traditional social and constitutional conservatism of the

[12] Caracciolo, 'Storia economica', 612–17; D. Mack Smith, Victor Emanuel, Cavour and the Risorgimento (Oxford, 1971), 56–76; idem, Cavour (1985), 94–106; Giacomo Perticone, Il regime parlamentare nella storia dello Statuto albertino (Rome, 1960); Carlo Ghisalberti, Stato, nazione e costituzione nell'Italia contemporanea (Naples, 199); Rosario Romeo, Vita di Cavour (Rome, 1984); idem, Dal Piemonte sabaudo all'Italia liberale (Turin, 1963); Stefano Merlini, 'Il governo costituzionale', in Storia dello Stato italiano, ed. Raffaele Romanelli (Rome, 1995), 3–72, here 3–10, 13–15, 17–19.

[13] There were a number of separate uprisings in Spain in 1848, but they represented diagonally opposed interests and their impact was muted by the repressive measures adopted by the Narvaez government. J. M. García Madaria, Estructura de la Administración Central (1808–1931) (Madrid, 1982), 124.

[14] M. Espadas Burgos, 'Madrid, centro de poder politico', in Madrid en la sociedad del siglo XIX, ed. L. E. Otero Carvajal and A. Bahamonde (Madrid, 1986), 179–92, here 188.

[15] M. Cruz Seoane, Historia del periodismo en España (3 vols., Madrid, 1983), II: El siglo XIX, 241–2; V. G. Kiernan, The Revolution of 1854 in Spanish History (Oxford, 1966), 6; J. R. Urquijo Goitia, 'Las contradicciones politicas del Bienio Progresista', Hispania, 57 (1997), 267–302;

moderados were juxtaposed with progressive reformist impulses (especially in the sphere of economic policy). A very similar picture can be discerned in neighbouring Portugal – here too an episode of acute upheaval, the Revolution of Maria da Fonte in 1846 followed by the *Patuleia* of 1846–7, set the scene (after vain efforts by Costa Cabral to locate and occupy an elusive political 'middle ground') for the emergence in 1851 of a new regime under Field Marshal Saldanha. Saldanha adopted the name 'Regeneração' for his government, whose ministry was composed of a 'strange coalition' of prominent centrist figures from both camps and liberalised the old conservative constitution by incorporating some of the demands of the opposition (including direct elections and the abolition of the death penalty).[16] The political system thereby established was known as *rotativismo* because it involved the rotation of power between the two main political factions.[17] There followed a period of political stability unparalleled in Portugal between the Napoleonic invasion and the later twentieth century.[18]

Even within the highly authoritarian setting created by Louis Napoleon's *coup d'état* in France, it has become increasingly clear that that the stability of the regime depended upon its success in constructing a consensus from the post-revolutionary remnants of moderate republicanism and constitutional monarchism. In this respect, the 'Bonapartism' of the post-revolutionary period was quite distinct from its pre-revolutionary predecessor – it was a more 'composite' entity, in which leftist elements flowed together with forces of order seeking firm government.[19] Even in Austria, where for historical reasons options were more narrowly limited and counter-revolutionary measures especially severe, the policies adopted by the neo-absolutist administrations of the 1850s reflected a new order of priorities – more on this below – that took

C. J. Esdaile, *Spain in the Liberal Age. From Constitution to Civil War, 1808–1939* (Oxford, 2000), 109–22; José Ramón de Urquijo y Goitia, *La revolución de 1854 en Madrid* (Madrid, 1984),

[16] For contemporary British comment on Saldanha's 'strange coalition', which seemed to fly in the face of Portuguese political tradition, see the *Times*, 31 May 1851, 4, col. F, also 11 June 1851, 4, col. b. On the Patuleia and the Maria da Fonte insurrection, see Maria de Fátima Bonifácio, *História da guerra civil da patuleia, 1846–47* (Lisbon, 1993); Padre Casimiro, *Apontamentos para a história da revolução do Minho em 1846 ou da Maria da Fonte*, ed. José Teixeira da Silva (Lisbon, 1981), Jose Brissos, *A insurreição miguelista nas resistências a Costa Cabral (1842– 1847)* (Lisbon, 1997). For a brilliant study of the Regeneração, see José Miguel Sardica, *A regeneração sob o signo do consenso: a política e os partidos entre 1851 e 1861* (Lisbon, 2001). On Costa Cabral's vain efforts to inaugurate a centrist politics before the new regime, see Mari Fátima Bonifácio, 'Segunda ascensão de Costa Cabral', *Análise Social*, 32 (1997), 537–56, esp. 541.

[17] J. L. César das Neves, *The Portuguese Economy: A Picture in Figures. XIX and XX Centuries* (Lisbon, 1994), 45.

[18] Durán de le Rua, *Unión Liberal*, 345–6; for interesting reflections on the parallels between Spanish and Portuguese developments, see Ignacio Chato Gonzalo, 'Portugal e Espanha em 1856: a dispar evolução politica do liberalismo peninsular', *Análise Social*, 42 (2007), 55–75.

[19] B. Ménager, *Les Napoleon du peuple* (Aubier, 1988), 355–7.

account of a much broader range of social and economic interests than the policies pursued by Austrian administrations before 1848. In short, the precise form taken by the new political constellation varied according to constitutional conditions, but across the European states the agenda was set by a post-revolutionary *rapprochement* that proved capable of answering to the aspirations both of the more statist and moderate elements of the old liberalism and of the more innovative and entrepreneurial elements among the old conservative elites.[20]

So effective was this new constellation in controlling the middle ground of politics that it successfully marginalised both the democratic left and the old right. In Spain, the accommodationist *resellados* of the Progressive movement joined the Unión Liberal, while the left-wing *puros* were left sulking on the margins.[21] The same fate awaited those *setembristas* in Saldanha's Portugal who refused to make their peace with the new dominant coalition. In France, the radical elements of the old republicanism were marginalised – along with the legitimists – as the post-revolutionary regime consolidated its popular base.[22] In Piedmont, Prussia and Austria, conversely, the old aristocratic right – the *Hoch-* or *Altkonservativen*, or the *codini*, as they were known in northern Italy – were displaced, set aside, even denounced, by the state power. Cavour's *connubio* with Ratazzi set the Piedmontese government on a course that alienated and isolated the old aristocratic right of which he had once himself been an intermittent representative. In Spain, the 'astonishing feebleness' of the Carlist rebellion of 1855 merely demonstrated how isolated the extreme right now was.[23] The politics of the traditional conservatism, with its pious legitimism and its attachment to corporatist structures now appeared narrow, self-interested and retrograde. It was unthinkable, the Prussian minister-president, Otto von Manteuffel, pointed out to the conservative rural opponents of fiscal reform, that the Prussian state should continue to be run 'like the landed estate of a nobleman'.[24]

Regeneration

The programmes and rhetoric adopted by the post-revolutionary governments naturally varied from state to state in accordance with

[20] For an excellent comparative discussion of 'conservative-liberal modernisation' in Prussia and Austria, see A. Schlegelmilch, 'Das Projekt der konservativ-liberalen Modernisierung und die Einführung konstitutioneller Systeme in Preußen und Österreich, 1848/49', in *Verfassungswandel*, ed. Kisch and Schiera, 155–77.

[21] Seoane, *Historia del periodismo*, 244; Kiernan, *Revolution of 1854*, 5.

[22] H. C. Payne and H. Grosshans, 'The Exile Revolutonaries and the French Political Police in the 1850s', *American Historical Review*, 68/4 (July 1963), 954–73.

[23] Kiernan, *Revolution of 1854*, 5.

[24] Grünthal, *Parlamentarismus*, 476.

specific circumstances and traditions. But even a very cursory comparison reveals a number of common features that distinguish these regimes from their Restoration-era predecessors. Of these, the most significant are concerned with the making of economic policy. First, there was a transition from profit or revenue-oriented policies towards those aimed at the stimulation of medium- and long-term economic growth. This transition was achieved in part through permissive reforms – such as the abolition of regulations preventing the formation of joint stock companies – whose aim was to dismantle the various old-regime laws and regulations that obstructed capital concentration and investment.[25] But the state was also involved in more proactive ways in encouraging growth. Across Europe, there was a substantial expansion in public spending on various forms of domestic investment. At the centre of this public spending boom was a new concern for those forms of territorial infrastructural investment that – because they were likely, in the first instance, to be un-profitable – only the state could be entrusted to undertake. In Saldanha's Portugal, a new ministry of public works launched a vast programme of public building financed by lending on a huge scale. In 1850, Portugal had lacked railways or telegraph connections of any kind and disposed of fifty-three steam engines in all, generating a total of 777 horsepower. By 1856, when Saldanha's 'Gabinete Largo' came to an end, Portugal possessed the beginnings of a railway and telegraph network, a substantially improved road system and an array of government-sponsored credit institutes specialising in the investment needs of the farming sector.[26]

In Spain, the abortive uprisings of 1848 prompted an almost immediate shift within the *moderado* regime towards a more proactive and consistent approach to economic policy – a new ministry of commerce, education and public works was founded in the autumn of 1851, whose task would be the provision of infrastructure; 'the construction of public works, roads and railways, canals, ports and lighthouses is a necessity that none will contest, because it constitutes the routes of circulation, the single open avenue to the future for our producers'.[27] These trends were further reinforced during the Bienio Progresista and under the Unión Liberal, which in 1858 created an 'extraordinary budget' of 2 billon reales, funded by the secularisation of church properties, for 'a general plan, to be realised

[25] C. Trebilcock, *The Industrialization of the Continental Powers* (Harlow, 1981), 152; R. Price, *The French Second Empire. An Anatomy of Political Power* (Cambridge, 2001), 228, on Spain: P. Martin Aceña, 'Development and Modernization of the Financial System, 1844–1935', in *The Economic Modernization of Spain*, ed. N. Sanchez-Albornoz, trans. K. Powers and M. Sañudo (New York, 1987), 107–27, here 110; Durán de la Rua, *Unión Liberal*, 162–3; on Germany and Austria: J. J. Sheehan, *German History 1770–1866* (Oxford, 1989), 734; Brandt, *Neoabsolutismus*, 231–438.
[26] Durán de la Rua, *Unión Liberal*, 345; Mónica, *Fontes Pereira de Melo*.
[27] Royal Decree of 20 Oct. 1851, cited in Garcia Madaria, *Estructura*, 129.

within eight years of refurbishment, completion and new construction of roads, canals, ports, lighthouses and other works of this kind'.[28] Between 1854 and 1863, thanks to consistent investment and support from the government, an electric telegraph network was constructed that linked Madrid with all the provincial capitals, including the Balearic Islands and Ceuta in northern Africa.[29] As a consequence of this new commitment to the stimulation of growth, public investment came to constitute a higher proportion of total investment in Spain during the years of the Unión Liberal than at any time (leaving aside a brief upsurge in 1912) until the early 1930s.[30] The result was an improvement and expansion of infrastructural networks that established – for the first time – an integrated national market and made possible the gradual modernisation of traditional sectors of production over the following decades.[31] Far from starving other industrial sectors and thereby hindering growth, as some analysts have suggested, the infrastructural investments realised under the Unión Liberal broke the bottleneck in the mid-century Spanish transport system and triggered a substantial growth in national income.[32]

The role of the state in stimulating economic growth in France is well known and needs no detailed treatment here: it has often been observed that a 'technocratic romanticism' was at the heart of the regime's economic policy and the emperor's commitment to economic development is beyond doubt. The Second Empire was, as Alain Plessis has put it, 'the first regime in France to have given such distinct priority to economic objectives'.[33] In Prussia, too, there was a

---

[28] Royal decree of 10 Dec. 1858, cited in: Durán de la Rua, *Unión Liberal*, 137–8; on economic reforms of the Bienio, see Urquijo Goitia, 'Bienio Progresista'.

[29] E. Otero Carvajal, 'El telégrafo en el sistema de comunicaciones Español 1800–1900', in *Antiguo Regimen y liberalismo. Homenaje a Miguel Artola*, ed. J. M. Donézar and M. Perez Ledesma (3 vols., Madrid, 1994), II, 587–98, here 593.

[30] A. Carreras de Odriozola, 'Gasto nacional bruto y formación de capital en España 1849–1958: primar ensayo de estimación', in *La nueva historia economica en España*, ed. P. Martin Aceña and L. Prados de la Escosura (Madrid, 1985), 32–3.

[31] Durán de la Rua, *Unión Liberal*, 151.

[32] A. Gomez Mendoza, 'Los ferrocarriles en la economia Española, 1855–1913', in *La nueva historia economica*, ed. Martin Aceña and Prados de la Escosura, 101–16, here 113. Gomez Mendoza estimates that national income (excluding earnings that reverted to foreign investors) would have been between 6.5 and 12 per cent lower by 1878 without the infrastructural programme launched in the 1850s. This conclusion is broadly supported in N. Sanchez Albornoz, 'Introduction: The Economic Modernization of Spain', in *Economic Modernization*, ed. *idem*, 1–9, here 5. The contrary view is set out in G. Tortella Casares, *Los orígenes del capital financiero en España* (Madrid, 1972), esp. chs. 5–6; see also Esdaile, *Spain in the Liberal Age*, 113–14; there is a broadly analogous debate on France, see A. Mitchell, 'Private Entrepreneurs or Public Service? The Eastern Railway Company and the French State in the Nineteenth Century', *Journal of Modern History*, 69 (1997), 18–41, esp. 18–21.

[33] Trebilcock, *Industrialization*, 152; Price, *Second Empire*, 211; Plessis, *Second Empire*, 62; Éric Anceau, *Napoléon III. Un Saint-Simon à cheval* (Paris, 2008), 343–66; Pierre Milza, *Napoléon III*

heightened emphasis on the right of the state to deploy public funds for the purpose of modernisation.[34] Such arguments benefited from the congenial climate of contemporary German economic theory, which underwent a reorientation during the middle decades of the nineteenth century away from the stringently anti-statist positions of the German 'free trade school' towards the view that the state had certain macro-economic objectives to fulfil that could not be achieved by individuals or groups within society.[35]

In Piedmont, after Cavour's accession to the ministry of finance in 1851, measures were taken by the government to promote industry and agricultural credit, encourage joint stock companies and reduce various overheads, such as grain and navigation duties. By 1854, Cavour, now prime minister, had spent more than 200 million lire on railways alone.[36] In Hanover, Saxony, Württemberg, Piedmont and the Austrian empire, projects sustained by heavy borrowing were launched under state supervision – tunnels through the Alps, railways, canals, port facilities, schools, administrative buildings, bridges.[37] They served to bind peripheral regions to the metropolitan centres, and to legitimate state authority in a general sense; they also constituted a new form of state patronage: in France, for example, a railway terminus might be offered in return for a favourable vote in the plebiscite; under Franz Joseph in Austria, public works became an instrument of nationalities policy.[38] For the first time, as one historian of nineteenth-century France has noted – though it applies across the continent – 'the state was seen to give, not simply to take'.[39]

These policies were a direct consequence of the centrist constellation forged by the revolutions, in the sense that their realisation reflected the marginalisation of those conservative political groups whose political influence had previously prevented or delayed the implementation of

(Paris, 2004), 464–99; Antoine Olivesi and André Nouschi, *La France de 1848 a 1914* (Paris, 1993), 49–70; Dominique Barjot, Jean-Pierre Chaline and André Encrevé, *La France au XIXe siècle 1814–1914* (Paris, 1995), 377–405.

34 C. Tilly, 'The Political Economy of Public Finance and the Industrialization of Prussia 1815–1866', *Journal of Economic History*, 26 (1966), 484–97, here 492; Grünthal, *Parlamentarismus*, 476.

35 H. Winkel, *Die deutsche Nationalökonomie im 19. Jahrhundert* (Darmstadt, 1977), 86–7, 95; on this view as an instance of the German engagement with 'Smithianism', see E. Rothschild, *'Smithianismus' and Enlightenment in Nineteenth-Century Europe*, King's College Cambridge: Centre for History and Economics, Oct. 1998.

36 R. Cameron, 'French Finance and Italian Unity: The Cavourian Decade', *American Historical Review*, 62 (1957), 552–69, here 556–61.

37 On infrastructural investment in Hanover, Saxony and Württemberg, see Green, *Fatherlands*, 223–66.

38 Evans, 'Austrian Experiment', 138–9.

39 R. P. Tombs, *France, 1814–1914* (Harlow, 1996), 107.

such liberalising measures.[40] In Prussia, the major public expenditures of the 1850s would have been impossible without the revolutions of 1848, which enabled the administration to escape from the shackles of the 'State Indebtedness Law' that had limited public spending in the Restoration era. As one deputy of the Prussian Landtag declared in March 1849, the previous administration had 'stingily refused' to provide the sums necessary to develop the country. 'However', he added, 'we now stand at the government's side and will always approve the funds required for the promotion of improved transport and for the support of commerce, industry and agriculture.'[41] Neither the new income tax introduced in 1851 (whose legitimacy was perceived as deriving from the suffrage) nor the reform of the old land tax in 1861 (which redressed the traditional fiscal imbalance in favour of the eastern provinces), would have been possible before the revolution.[42]

The economic interventions of the post-revolutionary governments were distinctive not merely for their greater ambition and generosity with state resources, but also for their insistence upon the need to develop administrative measures in accordance with an over-arching pre-conceived plan. Whereas railway construction in Saxony and Württemberg before 1848 had proceeded in a more or less haphazard and fragmented way, administrators after 1848 insisted that railway policy must be focused on the creation of a unified and rational territorial network: 'The state can and must see its state railways as a whole', wrote the Saxon foreign minister, Friedrich Beust, in 1857.[43] In France, too, after 1848, the government encouraged a more coordinated approach to the laying of tracks and the framing of policy at a regional rather than a local level.[44] During the business crisis of 1846–8, some prominent Prussian liberals had called upon the state to take over the administration of the kingdom's railways and unite them into 'an organic whole'.[45] In the 1850s, the Prussian finance minister, August von der Heydt, himself a liberal entrepreneur, presided over a gradual 'nationalisation' of the Prussian railways, motivated by the conviction that only the state was capable of ensuring that the resulting system was rational

---

[40] Plessis, *Second Empire*, 62, stresses the influence of Saint-Simonianism on the emperor; McMillan, *Napoleon III*, 138–9, is sceptical. On the Orleanist sympathies of the old financial establishment, see Plessis, *Second Empire*, 76.

[41] Tilly, 'Political Economy of Public Finance', 490.

[42] *Ibid.*, 494.

[43] Cited in Green, *Fatherlands*, 251.

[44] M. Blanchard, 'The Railway Policy of the Second Empire', trans. J. Godfrey, in *Essays in European Economic History 1789–1914*, ed. F. Crouzet, W. H. Chaloner and W. M. Stern (1969), 98–111, here 104.

[45] David Hansemann, cited in Brophy, *Capitalism*, 50.

in terms of the state as a whole – private interests alone would not suffice.[46]

These efforts to tie individual railway concessions into a larger policy framework reflected a more general shift in governmental rhetoric. The 1848 revolutions marked a transition from the *ad hoc* management of specific revenue sources that had been typical of the pre-March administrations towards the concerted generation by government of an economic 'policy' informed by holistic perspectives. The organic connectedness of economic systems was the fashionable commonplace of the era. In a letter of 15 January 1860 to his minister of state, Achille Fould, Napoleon III expressed his conviction that 'the mediums of exchange must be increased in order for trade to flourish; that without trade, industry stagnates and maintains high prices that hamper the growth of consumption; that without a prosperous industry that ensures capital growth, even agriculture remains in its infancy'.[47] Measuring and improving the performance of this living entity required the collation of consistent statistical information, and it is no coincidence that the post-revolutionary decade saw the establishment or consolidation in a number of states of centralised statistical offices, whose task was to get the measure of the 'national economy'.[48]

The emergent technology of national statistics – many of whose most prominent exponents had long been active in the cause of political and social reform – in turn became a platform for the cooption by the post-revolutionary state of reformist forces within civil society.[49] In Germany, 'statistics as an autonomous science' had been a predominantly progressive cause and the new statistical bureaus established after the revolution became important agents of administrative modernisation.[50] In Spain, too, the ministers of the Unión Liberal insisted on the formation of a new statistical administration, on the grounds that without the

---

[46] *Ibid.*, 56. The quotation (from David Hansemann) is on 50. Von der Heydt's policy of nationalisation was reversed in the 1860s.

[47] Cited in Plessis, *Second Empire*, 62.

[48] Ian Hacking, *The Taming of Chance* (Cambridge, 1990), 33–4; T. Huertas, *Economic Growth and Economic Policy in a Multinational Setting: The Habsburg Monarchy, 1841–65* (New York, 1977); W. Goldinger, 'Die Zentralverwaltung in Cisleithanien – Die Zivile Gemeinsame Zentralverwaltung', in *Verwaltung und Rechtswesen*, ed. Wandruszka and Urbanitsch, 100–89, here 135, 177; Bazillion, *Modernizing Germany*, 268.

[49] This process is well known for Britain, thanks to Lawrence Goldman's work on the early and mid-Victorian statistical movement and its increasingly intimate relationship with government; L. Goldman, 'Statistics and the Science of Society in Early-Victorian Britain: An Intellectual Context for the General Register Office', *Social History of Medicine*, 4 (1991), 415–34; *idem*, 'The Social Science Association 1857–1886: A Context for Mid-Victorian Liberalism', *English Historical Review*, 101 (1986), 95–134. This kind of work is yet to be done for most of the continental states.

[50] Bazillion, *Modernizing Germany*, 268.

'investigation and knowledge of the fiscal and moral conditions of a nation', no government would be able to facilitate the 'germination of the seeds of prosperity' or remove 'the obstacles that oppose the progress and well-being of peoples'.[51] The coalition cabinets of the Unión Liberal facilitated a merger of *moderado* and *progresista* statistical approaches: whereas the *moderados* tended to see statistics as an instrument of societal control and centralisation, the *progresistas* saw it as an instrument for supporting the state's progressive intervention in the economy – the former preferred to place statistics within the remit of the Ministerio de la Gobernación – in effect, the ministry of the interior, the latter in the Ministerio de Fomento. In the event, it was not until 1861 that a new unionist statistical administration was created in the form of the Junta General de Estadística – a structure that would remain in place until 1945.[52]

In France, the responsibilities of the Statistique Générale de la France (founded in 1833) were greatly expanded in 1852 to allow for the integrated compilation of national data on an independent basis. Moreover, the long-standing rivalry between the official 'administrative statisticians' and the progressive, extra-governmental circles of 'social investigators' and 'moral statisticians' was resolved by the foundation, in 1860, of the 'Statistical Society of Paris', a voluntarist grouping that sought and obtained official endorsement from the ministry of trade.[53] I am not suggesting here that the preoccupation with statistics was something new – the European statistical movement was well underway by the 1830s, when the Italian poet Giacomo Leopardi (1798–1837) complained that his era was an 'age of statistics' whose needs were measured in the growing number of 'markets and offices'.[54] What was distinctive about

[51] Presidency of the council of ministers, preamble to royal decree founding a statistical commission, 3 Nov. 1856, in: *Colección legislativa de España (segundo trimestre de 1856)*, vol. 68 (Madrid, 1856), 194–6.

[52] Juan Pro Ruiz, 'Statistics and State Formation in Spain (1840–1870)', working paper produced as part of the research project PB97–0056 of the Dirección General de Investigación Científica y Técnica of Spain, viewed online at: citeseerx.ist.psu.edu/viewdoc/download?doi=10.1.1.202. For a good example of the *moderado* view of growth and development, which acknowledged the need for state intervention but defined the task of the state in terms of the need to contain and minimise the impact of change, see the 1848 *prospecto* of the ministry of commerce, education and public works in *Boletín Oficial del Ministerio de Comercio, Instrucción y Obras Públicas*, 1 (1848), 1–3.

[53] A. Desrosières, 'Official Statistics and Medicine in Nineteenth-Century France: The Statistique Générale de la France as a Case Study', *Social History of Medicine*, 4 (1991), 515–37.

[54] On the statistical movement, see Silvana Patriarca, *Numbers and Nationhood: Writing Statistics in Nineteenth-Century Italy* (Cambridge, 1996); Laurence Goldman, 'The Origins of British "Social Science": Political Economy, Natural Science and Statistics, 1830–1835', *Historical Journal*, 26 (1983), 587–616; Hacking, *Taming of Chance*; Michael John Cullen, *The Statistical Movement in Early Victorian Britain: The Foundations of Empirical Social Research* (Hassocks, 1975); for an anthology of contemporary treatises, see *Comparative Statistics in the Nineteenth*

the 1850s was the transformation in the relationship between statistics and the state. This period witnessed – across much of the European continent at least – the transition from a purely governmental to a civil-society-based statistical regime in which assumptions that had gained ground within reformist circles before the revolution could be brought to bear directly upon government. The resulting administrative effects were not confined to the uppermost tiers of government; rather, they penetrated deep into the regional and local management structures in the form of demands for information, which was to be tabulated in accordance with detailed instructions on newly designed, standardised forms.[55]

Even if the talk of an economic 'policy' was sometimes little more than a mask for pragmatic muddling through, the new emphasis on the formulation of 'policy' as a crucial dimension of domestic administration was itself significant. It was connected with a growing tendency to conceptualise the state as distinct from society.[56] In Portugal, the Maria da Fonte uprising, which was provoked by government efforts to introduce a new and more efficient system of taxation, stirred panic among the political elites. The conclusion was drawn that the government must henceforth do more than appeal to 'order' and provide the population with prior knowledge not only of the intentions of the government, but also of what it planned to do to realise them. From this moment onwards, one historian has argued, we see not just the emergence, but the swift diffusion of the concept of a political 'programme'.[57] The insistence on a more or less coherent and binding programme could even generate alterations in the structure of government.[58]

Century, ed. Richard Wall (Farnborough, 1973), cited in Emma Rothschild, 'The Age of Insubordination', *Foreign Policy*, 119 (Summer 2000), 46–9.

[55] See, for example, the efforts of the ministry of justice in Spain to improve its crime statistics through the circulation of a new standardised form (*hoja*) and the 'instrucción para llenar con exactitud las hojas de la estadistica civil creada por Real decreto de Diciembre de 1855' which insists that respondents reply 'in uniform fashion to the questions that the form contains' – an injunction strongly suggestive of the novelty of this procedure for the functionaries obliged to carry it out. *Colección legislativa de España (primer trimestre de 1856)*, vol. 67 (Madrid, 1856), 109.

[56] P. Nolte, *Die Ordnung der Gesellschaft* (Munich 2000), 52–3.

[57] José Borges de Macedo, 'O aparecimento em Portugal do conceito de programa politico', *Revista portuguesa de História*, 13 (1971), 396–423.

[58] On efforts to unify the structure of government in Spain, see Garcia Madaria, *Estructura*, 128; royal decree of 29 Feb. 1856, cited in Garcia Madaria, *Estructura*, 142; cf. the 'Instrucción para promover y ejecutar las obras publicas de Caminos, Canales, Puertos y demas análogos aprobada por Real Decreto de 10 de Octobre de 1845', Archivo Histórico Nacional Madrid, FC OP, leg. 2; on Austria: Evans, 'Austrian Experiment', 138; Barany, 'Ungarns Verwaltung', 329–62.

Post-ideological politics

A corollary of these developments was the growing prestige of ministries of finance and of the men who led them. In Piedmont, control of the finance ministry was pivotal to Cavour's exercise of power. The Spanish finance minister, Manuel Alonso Martinez, exercised a dominating influence in the cabinets of the Bienio Progresista, and in Portugal the former revolutionary and sometime minister of finance and public works, António Maria de Fontes Pereira de Melo, became the most prominent representative of the Regeneração. The term *fontismo* was coined to denote the dramatic expansion of government investment and promotion that took place after 1851.[59]

Economic policy came to occupy a central place in the efforts of the various post-revolutionary regimes to legitimate themselves in the eyes of the public. The use of 'developmentalist' arguments as such was not new, nor was the concept of unitary transport networks or the employment of circulatory metaphors;[60] what was distinctive about the post-revolutionary era was the prominent place such topoi now occupied in government pronouncements and propaganda. Once again, it is France that provides the most extravagant example: Napoleon III's appeals to the French public consistently foregrounded the economic achievements of the regime, and sought to legitimate it in terms not of a higher moral order, but of the material betterment of the French.[61] For the Murillo and O'Donnell governments in Spain, the 'appeal to material interests' became a recurrent theme. In Saldanha's Portugal, 'Regeneração' became the buzz-word of the decade, encapsulating as it did the fashionable preoccupations of the new regime. Official statements on economic policy were couched in a celebratory, propagandistic language that promised all things to all men.[62] The financial and

[59] Urquijo Goitia, 'Bienio Progresista', 282–3; César das Neves, *Portuguese Economy*, 46–7; in general, see the important recent study by Mónica, *Fontes Pereira de Melo*.

[60] On the use of developmentalist arguments in relation to canal building before the advent of the railways, see J. M. Hernandez and J. Vidal Olivares, 'Infraestructura viaria y ferrocarriles en la articulación del espacio economico Valenciano, 1750–1914', *Hispania*, 51 (1991), 205–43, here 225; on continuity in public infrastructural planning in France, with specific reference to the dirigiste tradition of the Corps des Ponts et Chaussées, see C. O. Smith, 'The Longest Run: Public Engineers and Planning in France', *American Historical Review*, 95 (1990), 657–92; Smith stresses long-term continuity of statist construction projects in France, but also notes that the early 1850s saw a restructuring of railway development marked first by the consolidation of the twenty-eight French railway companies into six regional monopolies and secondly by highly successful government stimulation of private investment (677).

[61] McMillan, *Napoleon III*, 137–41.

[62] See Urquijo Goitia, 'Bienio Progresista', 270, citing the Acta del Consejo of 19 Dec. 1854: '[our objective is] to open the springs of civilisation, to bring them to our country by means of those mighty vehicles [i.e. steam trains] that constitute the glory of modern

economic managers of this era were elevated to the status of gurus, technocratic saviours entrusted with the redemption of humanity. In the sessions of the Conseil Général of the Département du Nord of 1858, there is a 'Report on Domestic Water Transport' in which we find extraordinary but entirely characteristic panegyrics on the subject of engineers and planners: 'Honorons les hommes auxquels l'État a confié le soin de réaliser les biefaits que cette admirable création de l'esprit humain nous promet; [esperons] que leur activité, que leur intelligence [trouvera] une large remuneration.'[63]

What underlay this emphasis on material achievement was the belief – highly characteristic for the post-revolutionary era – that material 'progress' (the word was often used in this connection) would ultimately do away with the need for the ideologised, confrontational politics of the old regime. In Spain, it was the Fomento, the ministry of development, that took responsibility in 1851 for creating a commission tasked with 'harmonising the reciprocal interests of the factory owners and textile workers of Barcelona' – conceptualising 'the economy' as a network of interdependencies encouraged legislators to believe that sage government provision could bridge the social divide.[64] 'Peace, order and contentment reign throughout the country', Marshal Saldanha told Queen Maria II in the summer of 1854. 'The people renounce politics in order to busy themselves with their own affairs'; the country was so prosperous, he told another correspondent, that it was 'beyond the power of any individual or party to disturb the public tranquillity'.[65] A report of 1856 by the French ministry of agriculture, commerce and public works made the link between economic growth and political tranquillity explicit: at the time of the February Revolution, it pointed out, there had been 3,600 km of railways in France. But the three years of political turmoil that followed had seen total stagnation – not a single track had been laid. Only since the Bonapartist seizure of power had there been a surge in construction of an asset which 'in our modern civilisation has become an essential condition of prosperity, indeed for the very existence of a country'.[66] The point is that this was not just about what Hans Ulrich Wehler once

civilisation, to reinforce our political unity by facilitating communication among all the provinces; to bestow movement and value upon our products'.

[63] Conseil Général du Département de Nord, session de 1858, rapport par M. F. Kuhlmann, Archives Nationales, F/12/6848/B, 14.

[64] Ministerio de Fomento, 'Real decreto, creando una comisión para que proponga los medios de armonizar los intereses recíprocos de los fabricantes y trabajadores de Barcelona', 10 Jan. 1851, in *Colección legislativa de España (primer cuatrimestre de 1851)*, vol. 64 (Madrid 1855).

[65] Cited in *Memoirs of Field-Marshal the Duke of Saldanha with Selections from his Correspondence*, ed. J. A. Smith, Conde da Carnota (2 vols., 1880), I, 315, 326.

[66] Ministry of agriculture, commerce and public works, report to the emperor, Paris, 30 Nov. 1856, Archives Nationales Paris F/14/8508A.

called 'counter-revolutionary innoculation', namely pursuing prosperity as a means of muting the forces of revolution; more and more it was the other way around: political peace was valued for the sake of prosperity and progress. It was material progress itself that came to constitute the ultimate public and political good. The reordering of priorities after 1848 was reflected in the 'economisation' of political discourses, as liberals, disillusioned ex-democrats and government administrators alike sought in economic liberalisation and the promotion of growth the remedy for all social ills and thus, ultimately, for all political conflict.[67]

Urban improvement

The management of urban space is one area in which the challenge posed by revolutionary upheaval, the new emphasis on infrastructural improvement and a readiness to embrace substantial programmes of public spending combined to generate closely analogous initiatives across the capital cities of the European states. Paris, Berlin and Vienna had all seen street-fighting and the erection of barricades in 1848, and the same occurred in Madrid on an unprecedented scale during the disturbances of 1854. All four cities saw substantial programmes of improvement during the 1850s. The best-known case is of course Paris, where the local prefect, Baron Haussmann, launched a massive programme to restructure the centre of the old city, extend and modernise its sewerage system and provide it with clean running water. A central concern was the perceived need to clear away the obstacles posed by the old inner city to the circulation of persons and goods – 'circulation' was as resonant a concept to the urban planners as it was to liberal economic theorists.[68] Madrid witnessed a restructuring programme that displayed many similar features – the laying down of broad avenues, the clearance of slums, the clarification and embellishment of key junctions (the Plaza del Sol is the best-known example), the standardisation of building regulations and first halting efforts at the construction of salubrious working-class housing. The most ambitious project of these years was the construction of a system of dams, syphons, aqueducts and reservoirs to bring clean fresh water to the city. Launched in 1851 and upgraded after financial difficulties in 1855 with the help of a huge public loan, this innovation transformed the

[67] Sheehan, *German History*, 734.

[68] N. Papayanis, *Horse-Drawn Cabs and Omnibuses in Paris. The Idea of Circulation and the Business of Public Transit* (Baton Rouge, 1997), 92–5. On the same obsession in a British context, see M. Daunton, 'Introduction', *Cambridge Urban History of Britain*, III: *1840–1950*, ed. *idem* (Cambridge, 2001), 1–56, esp. 1–13. There is now a vast literature on the restructuring of Paris under Haussmann; among those studies I found most useful are D. H. Pinkney, *Napeoleon and the Rebuilding of Paris* (Princeton, 1958), and A.-L. Shapiro, *Housing the Poor of Paris, 1850–1902* (Madison, 1985).

prospects of the city, sweeping away one of the most important obstacles to its expansion. Here, as in Paris, the rationalisation of the inner structure of the city went hand in hand with municipal expansion. The expansion of the outer borders of Madrid was promoted above all as a means of bringing the largely improvised and under-serviced new quarters on the city's periphery under the control of the municipal authorities, of imposing order, in other words, upon a process of spontaneous expansion that was already well underway. Urban planners aimed to create a rational and hygienic urban civic space, characterised by a salubrious blend of air and light, harmoniously proportioned apartment houses, parks and tree-lined avenues, as well as the various other necessities of city life – marketplaces, slaughterhouse, hospitals and prisons.[69] Madrid may never have achieved the kind of dramatic transformation that reshaped the city of Paris, but the enhanced prominence and political voice of urban planners testified to a new sensitivity on the part of the state authority to the needs of the city as a living system. What was distinctive about the projects of planners such as Mesonero and Castro in Madrid was a 'global conception of the city' that aimed to heighten its 'socio-spatial homogeneity' while at the same time accommodating the exigencies of the urban class structure.[70] In Haussmann's writings, one finds, similarly, a 'global and systematic approach to the urban problem and a conception of the totality of methods appropriate to its treatment'.[71]

Vienna was not subjected to the kind of structural reform that transformed Paris, mainly because it was felt that the city's spacious baroque centre already provided a serviceable urban environment. Here, as in Paris and Berlin, the debate focused on the 'lessons' of the revolution. Should specific quarters be created for the various nationalities, so that visitors and immigrants from all corners of the *Vielvölkerstaat* would develop a positive attachment to the capital, as one politician suggested in 1858? Outlandish as it sounds, this proposal actually exercised a brief influence on planning policy for the city: the *Dogenhof* in the Praterstraße, for example, was constructed with a view to developing the Lepoldstadt into

[69] Santos Juliá, D. Ringrose and C. Segura, *Madrid. Historia de una capital* (Madrid, 1994), 288–313.

[70] Fernando Roch, 'Reflexiones sobre le reordenación urbanistica en el Madrid de mediados del siglo XIX', in *Madrid*, ed. Otero Carvajal and Bahamonde, 89–96, here 92–3.

[71] F. Choay, 'Pensées sur la ville, arts de la ville', in *La ville de l'âge industriel: le cycle haussmannien*, ed. M. Agulhon (Paris, 1983), 159–271, here 168; Jeanne Gaillard, *Paris. La ville 1852–1870. L'urbanisme Parisien à l'heure d'Haussmann* (Paris, 1976); on similar developments in Berlin, see Barclay, *Friedrich Wilhelm IV*, 75, 237–8; Frank Joseph Thomason, 'The Prussian Police State in Berlin 1848–1871' (Ph.D. thesis, University of Baltimore, MD, 1978), 185. Although it is formulated within the framework of the older 'decade of reaction' school, this study remains useful as the only detailed study of Hinckeldey's policies for Berlin; the best interpretative discussion of Hinckeldey is in Barclay, *Friedrich Wilhelm IV*, esp. 237–44, 273–5.

a kind of Italian quarter.[72] Of particular concern, however, was the future of the ring of fortifications that surrounded and enclosed the inner city. On this issue, the lessons of the revolution were difficult to read. During the upheavals of 1848, the insurgents had themselves scaled the fortifications and used them as firing positions against the troops deployed to restore order within the city. It was also argued by some that the retention of walls would have the effect of splitting the garrison into ineffectual units who would have difficulty working together. But the military leadership, whose authority in security matters was paramount during the immediate post-revolutionary years, took the view that the walls offered an indispensable line of defence against a potential uprising from without, and argued that the early modern line of fortification should in fact be further extended and strengthened. Only in 1857 was the debate resolved in favour of those who favoured the dismantling of the walls and the use of the resulting space for the construction of a broad ring road flanked by representative buildings, green areas and high-quality housing.[73] The result was the laying out of the spacious Ringstraße that still runs around the inner city of Vienna.

The desire for a more ordered urban setting was hardly a product of the revolution – both in Paris and in Madrid the improvement of the urban fabric had been a theme of public discussion for much of the first half of the century. In Vienna, there had been calls for the opening up of the inner city for at least fifty years. But the revolution changed the situation in a number of ways: first, it further reinforced the association between overcrowding, poor sanitation, disease and political upheaval.[74] And a further consequence of this concern was the increasing involvement in urban management of extra- or semi-governmental committees of hygiene experts, whose advisory role was now formalised under new legislation.[75] In this area, as in various other 'technical' spheres of administration, governments drew increasingly on the expertise accumulated within progressive circles of civil society. Secondly, the revolution shifted the balance of power between the state

---

[72] M. Masanz and M. Nagl, *Ringstraße. Von der Freiheit zur Ordnung vor den Toren Wiens* (Vienna, 1996), 66.
[73] W. Wagner, 'Die Stellungnahmen der Militärbehörden zur Wiener Stadterweiterung in den Jahren 1848–57', *Jahrbuch des Vereins für die Geschichte der Stadt Wien*, 17/18 (1961/2), 216–85, here 223; Masanz and Nagl, *Ringstraße*, 65–71.
[74] C. Díez de Baleón, 'Barrios obreros en el Madrid del siglo XIX: solución o amenaza para el orden burgués?', in *Madrid*, ed. Otero Carvajal and Bahamonde, 117–34; R. H. Guerrand, *Les origines du logement social* (Paris, 1967). On the association of disease with political unrest, see R. J. Evans, *Death in Hamburg. Society and Politics in the Cholera Years 1830–1910* (1990), 118–19.
[75] Shapiro, *Housing the Poor of Paris*, 16–28.

and the municipal authorities, enabling the former to override the entrenched opposition of municipal elites to major public expenditure.[76]

Press and publicity

The years following the revolutions of 1848 also saw a renegotiation of the relationship between government and its public. In many continental states, the revolutions of 1848 triggered a transition towards a more organised, pragmatic and flexible handling of the press than had been the norm in the Restoration era. A central feature of this transition in many states was the abandonment of censorship. Censorship – in the sense of the vetting of printed material for political content prior to publication – had been an important instrument of government power in the Restoration era and the call for its abolition was one of the central themes of liberal and radical dissent before 1848. In the course of the revolutions, censorship regimes across Europe were dismantled and the freedom of the press enshrined in laws and constitutions. To be sure, many of the permissive press laws issued in 1848 did not survive the reimposition of 'order'. On the other hand, this did not imply – in most states – a return to pre-March conditions. The focus of press policy in the German states, for example, shifted from the cumbersome pre-censorship of printed material to the surveillance of those political groups that produced it. A substantial component of the liberal programme thus survived the debacle of the revolution.[77]

This was an important shift, because the transition from 'preventive' to 'repressive' measures brought governmental measures into the open. Newspapers and journals could only be penalised after they had begun to circulate, that is, after the 'damage', as it were, had been done. The administration was thus under increasing pressure to find other, less direct means of influencing the press. At the same time, differences between the police authorities, the judiciary and responsible ministers as to what constituted an illegal printed utterance meant that efforts by the former to deploy repressive measures to the full were often thwarted.[78] In Spain,

---

[76] Papayanis, *Horse-Drawn Cabs*, 96–7; E. Bendikat, *Öffentlicher Nahverkehrspolitik in Berlin und Paris 1890–1914: Strukturbedingungen, politische Konzeptionen und Realisierugsprobleme* (Berlin, 1999), 66–70; Santos Juliá, Ringrose and Segura, *Madrid*, 288–313; on the same phenomenon in Berlin: B. Schulze, 'Polizeipräsident von Hinckeldey', *Jahrbuch für die Geschichte Mittel- und Ostdeutschlands*, IV (Tübingen, 1955), 81–108, here 93–4.

[77] D. Fischer, *Handbuch der politischen Presse in Deutschland, 1480–1980. Synopse rechtlicher, struktureller und wirtschaftlicher Grundlagen der Tendenzpublizistik im Kommunikationsfeld* (Düsseldorf, 1981), 60–1, here 65; Kurt Koszyk, *Deutsche Presse im 19. Jahrhundert* (Berlin, 1966), 123; F. Schneider, *Pressefreiheit und politische Öffentlichkeit* (Neuwied, 1966), 310.

[78] K. Wappler, *Regierung und Presse in Preußen. Geschichte der amtlichen Pressestellen, 1848–62* (Leipzig, 1935), 94; R. Kohnen, *Pressepolitik des deutschen Bundes. Methoden staatlicher Pressepolitik nach der Revolution von 1848* (Tübingen, 1995), 174.

the constitution of 1856, one of the foundational documents of the Unión Liberal, also explicitly prohibited (art. 3) the confiscation of newspapers before their distribution to the public had commenced.[79] Just as in Prussia, where press controls were tightened in 1851, stiffer regulations (the *Ley Nocedal*) were introduced in Spain in 1857, during the brief return to power of the *moderado* leader Narváez. This law was not abandoned by the unionist government that succeeded Narváez, but it was not rigorously applied. Whereas in Prussia, ideological divisions within the administration undermined the effectiveness of repressive legislation, the same effect was achieved in Spain by the tug-of-war between *moderado*, *progresista* and unionist factions within the post-revolutionary political elite. As a consequence, the dramatic expansion of political print brought about by the revolution of 1854 proved irreversible: the number of periodicals published in Madrid tripled and the size of the editions also increased.[80]

In France, the *coup d'état* of Louis Napoleon in December 1851 was followed by severe measures against the oppositional press; many journalists were arrested and a number of journals simply disappeared. The republican press in the provinces virtually vanished altogether and only eleven newspapers remained in operation in Paris.[81] Small wonder that the conservative Prussian minister-president, Otto von Manteuffel, contrasted the high-handedness of French policy with the relative liberty enjoyed by press organs in Prussia.[82] But the severity of the new legislation should not be exaggerated. Once the new regime had established itself, the suspension of journals, though permitted in theory, became very rare in practice. Far more common were official police warnings to dissenting editors, but even these became much less frequent from the summer of 1853, with the accession of Persigny and later of Billault to the ministry of the interior.[83] More importantly, perhaps, the overall circulation of newspapers as a whole went up sharply as these were sold at lower prices (subsidised by advertising) in the railway stations rapidly proliferating across the country.[84] In France, then, as in Spain, Prussia and a number of the lesser German states, the expansion of political print and of the politicised reading public proved irreversible.

[79] Seoane, *Historia de periodismo*, 228.

[80] M. Kossok and Mauricio Pérez Saravia, 'Prensa liberal y revolución burguesa. Las revoluciones en Francia y Alemania en 1848 y en España en 1854', in *La prensa en la revolución liberal: España, Portugal y America Latina*, ed. A. Gil Novales (Madrid, 1983), 390–444, here 433–4.

[81] P. Guiral, 'La presse de 1848 à 1871', in C. Bellanger, J. Godechot, P. Guiral and F. Terron, *Histoire générale de la presse française* (Paris, 1969), 207–382.

[82] Wappler, *Regierung und Presse*, 94.

[83] Guiral, 'La presse', 252; R. Bellet, *Presse et journalisme sous le Second Empire* (Paris, 1967), 11.

[84] Bellet, *Presse et journalisme*, 284–5.

Governments dealt with this expansion by adopting a more supple and coordinated approach to the business of shaping public attitudes. On 23 December 1850, the coordination of press policy in Prussia was for the first time given a secure institutional basis in the 'Central Agency for Press Affairs' (Zentralstelle für Pressangelegenheiten). The Agency's responsibilities included the administration of funds set aside for the purpose of subsidising the press, the supervision of subsidised newspapers and the cultivation of 'relationships' with domestic and foreign papers, in the hope that this would inaugurate 'an organic exchange [Wechselwirkung] between all arms of the state and the press'.[85] The new agency thus oversaw the transition from a system based on censorship to one based on news and information management.

Analogous transitions can be observed in many of the other continental states. In the more authoritarian climate of the early Bonapartist regime in France, Interior Minister Persigny argued that repressive measures ought to be supplemented by 'energetic intervention on the part of the administration in favour of good social principles', and added that such intervention could best be accomplished by means of 'publications and pamphlets encouraged and, if need be financed, by the administration'.[86] In France, too, the advent of the new regime brought a more proactive and coordinated approach to the management of public opinion, which in some respects militated against the use of repressive measures. As Pierre Latour-Dumoulin, founder and chief of the new Directorate for Publications (Direction générale de la Librairie) observed in a report to the emperor in 1856, official warnings and prosecutions had a negative effect on public opinion. It was therefore preferable to 'prevent the excesses of newspapers in order not to have to repress them' and to 'temper the rigors of the law by moderating its enforcement'.[87]

A survey of press policy elsewhere in Europe reveals many parallels.[88] In any case, even the non-governmental press was very substantially penetrated by government sponsorship – throughout the states of the German confederation, almost all major newspapers accepted material from journalists and correspondents in the pay of the various press offices.[89] Less work has been done on the press policy of the Unión Liberal after 1856, but here too there were efforts to cultivate what was

---

[85] Wappler, *Regierung und Presse*, 16–17, 5.

[86] Cited N. Isser, *The Second Empire and the Press* (The Hague, 1974), 15–16.

[87] Cited in Price, *Second Empire*, 172.

[88] Green, *Fatherlands*, 148–88; Guiral, *La presse*, 250; Isser, *Press*, 16. For an account of the 'offiziöse Presse' in the German states that comes to less sanguine (but also in my view less persuasive) conclusions on the success of such journals, see E. Naujoks, 'Die offiziöse Presse und die Gesellschaft (1848/1900)', in *Presse und Geschichte. Beiträge zur historischen Kommunikationsforschung*, ed. E. Blühm (Munich, 1977), 157–70.

[89] Kohnen, *Pressepolitik*, 150.

called the 'good governmental press' under a relatively liberal system of controls; this in itself amounted to a substantial advance on the approach of their predecessors, the conservative *moderados*, whose leader Narváez remarked that 'it is not enough to confiscate papers. To finish with bad newspapers you must kill all the journalists.'[90]

Conclusions

What difference will a study of this tableau of political realignment and administrative innovation make to the way we think about the history of Europe's nineteenth century? I think it is important for three reasons. First, it makes us think again about the impact of the revolutions of 1848. These upheavals may have ended in failure, marginalisation, exile, imprisonment, even death, for some of their protagonists, but their momentum communicated itself like a seismic wave to the fabric of the European administrations, changing structures and ideas, bringing new priorities into government or reorganising old ones, reframing political debates. In any case, it is also important to remember those 'men of 1848' who did not fall or fail, but passed into the structures of authority. One of the curious characteristics of the post-revolutionary regimes is how prominently they were served by men of 1848: Rattazzi and his liberal ministerial colleagues in Piedmont, the Piétrie brothers, Rouher and de la Guérronière in France; Alexander Bach, the Krauss brothers, Kleyle, Meyer, Pipitz, Hock and many others in Austria, or formerly radical figures within the Spanish Progressive movement.[91] The prominence of former democrats in the post-revolutionary police structures is particularly noteworthy.[92]

Re-reading the 1850s in this fashion also has the potential to change the way we think about the era of national unifications. The attractiveness of the Piedmontese model to the southern and central Italian elites cannot be understood without reference to the distinctive compromise achieved after 1848. Indeed, one could take this argument further and argue that the very different constitutional settlements reached in the wake of the unifications of Italy and Germany – the former unitary, the latter federal – can be explained in part by the impact of 1848. In Germany, the modernising compromise forged after 1848 enabled Prussia to overcome, or at least reduce, its 'constitutional deficit' and allowed a number of the lesser territorial states both to master the challenge of revolution and further to consolidate their domestic legitimacy. In Italy, by contrast, the same transition merely widened the political and

[90] Cited in R. Carr, *Spain 1808–1975*, 2nd edn (Oxford, 1982), 240 n. 2.
[91] Evans, 'Austrian Experiment', 146–7; Durán de la Rua, *Unión Liberal*, 345.
[92] Ménager, *Les Napoléon du peuple*, 128–9.

economic 'modernisation gap' between Piedmont and the lesser Italian states, accentuating the leadership role of Turin and ruling out a genuine compromise with the forces of traditional provincial authority.

Third, there is the European dimension of the argument. I stressed at the outset that my aim was not merely to establish that a significant re-alignment of political forces took place within specific post-revolutionary political cultures, but to argue that this occurred on an authentically European basis. The 1848 revolutions were European revolutions in a sense that does not apply to the great upheavals of 1789–99, 1830–1, 1871 or 1917. For all the diversity of context, occasion, ethnicity and language, the rhetoric and political demands of those liberals who challenged traditional authority in 1848 were remarkably consistent across the cities of Europe. In the light of this fact, it is perhaps unsurprising that the process of accelerated adjustment and accommodation that followed took such analogous forms across the continent. Perhaps we need to modify to some extent the notion that the revolution, in opening the Pandora's box of na-tionalism, divided the continent against itself. After all, the developments we have considered suggest that the revolution had a homogenising, or 'Europeanising' impact on the continental administrations.

What we need in order to understand this process is not the kind of comparative history that ends up by reenacting narratives of national or ethnic difference. We need instead to work towards a better understanding of the international networks and the routes of transmission that made such simultaneity possible. Some valuable work has been done on Europe-wide radical and liberal networks before the revolutions of 1848, but much less is known of the inter-state networks that informed policy-making in the era of counter-revolution. How exactly did the free-trading model overcome its detractors to achieve such dominance within the European political elites during the decades after 1848? Where did the arguments and legislative models for reformist initiatives come from and through which agencies or individuals were they conveyed? How exactly was the 'English model' – often encapsulated for continental politicians in the person of Peel – transferred, interpreted and received across the European states and how did it feed into the assumptions guiding the formulation of policy?

How did the international congresses and exhibitions of professionals that proliferated so dramatically during this era – hygienists, penal reformers, statisticians – interact with policy cultures in the individual states? It is clear, to take just one example, that the statistical movement was from its beginnings a trans-national affair, involving the exchange of ideas and techniques across an informal network of enthusiasts that encompassed Belgium, France, the German states and Great Britain.[93]

---

[93] Goldman, 'The Origins of British "Social Science"', esp. 594–5.

Those exponents of 'political economy' or 'moral statistics' who sought to enter into a partnership with specific administrations were also positioned within their own trans-national networks, both through the exchange of individual and corporate correspondence and through attendance at professional jamborees, such as the International Congresses of Statistics that began in 1851 and continued into the mid-1870s.[94] Though little is yet known of the precise impact of such organisations upon policy formation in specific national centres, it is clear that they opened new and capacious conduits for knowledge transfer, and that they encouraged policy-makers to conceive of their tasks in comparative/competitive, trans-national terms.[95] The weekly 'Scientific Review' published by the ministry of development in Madrid printed numerous articles bristling with statistics on 'industrial progress in Belgium', 'English industry and the expansion of London', 'revenues of the English and French Railways', 'wool imports to England' and so on.[96] Of course, we have to beware of overstating the case: in the files of the ministry of development in Madrid, I found copies of the *Mittheilungen aus dem Gebiet der Statistik* issued by the Directorship of Administrative Statistics in the Austrian empire's ministry of commerce and dutifully forwarded to Madrid by the Spanish embassy in Vienna, but closer inspection revealed that the pages were uncut![97]

Nevertheless, the existence of such networks, and of the emergent European 'administrative intelligentsia'[98] that sustained them, is important to the argument set out in these pages, because it helps to explain the striking simultaneities that can be observed in the post-revolutionary accommodations of the European states. We are accustomed to thinking of the clock of European history as geared in accordance with the variable geometry of relative backwardness. While this is doubtless true for broader processes of societal modernisation, it has less bearing on those educated trans-national elites whose culture and learning were in many respects genuinely European.

---

[94] On the 'transfer function' of international exhibitions and the paucity of work in this area, see W. Kaiser, 'Inszenierung des Freihandels als weltgesellschaftliche Entwicklungsstrategie. Die "Great Exhibition" 1851 und der politischer Kulturtransfer nach kontinentaleuropa', 2. I am grateful to Professor Kaiser for allowing me to see a copy of this essay before publication.

[95] On these and other dimensions of the still only nascent history of international networks, see *The Mechanics of Internationalism*, ed. M. H. Geyer and J. Paulmann (Oxford, 2001), esp. the introductory essay by the editors, 1–25.

[96] 'El progreso industrial en Bélgica', 'Importación de lanas en Inglaterra', 'La industria inglesa y la expansión de Londres', 'La industria algodonera en Alemania', 'Ingresos de los ferro-carriles ingleses y franceses', in *Revista Científica del Ministero de Fomento*, 2 (1863), 28–9, 50–5, 60–1, 193–211, 225–34, 250–1.

[97] Archivo Histórico Nacional, Madrid, FC OP (Fomento) leg. 236.

[98] I borrow this term from Goldman, 'Social Science Association', 100.

Lastly, we might ponder on the historical location of the political synthesis that emerged after 1848: we know the coalitions that sustained the politics of the 1850s eventually frayed and came undone under the pressure of internal divisions and an increasingly inauspicious economic climate. The 'Social Question' returned in an even more challenging form. The 'end of politics' was not in sight for them and it is not in sight for us. But the idea itself feels familiar, perhaps because this was an idea whose appeal has been felt more than once. There are suggestive parallels between the transitions of the 1850s and the authoritarian reformism of the Napoleonic era, another moment in which states were reshaped to absorb and lend institutional expression to the waning energies of a revolution. And the realignments of the 1850s might also prompt us to consider contemporary resonances. The tendency to place economic policy at the centre of government and to assume (or hope) that growth will bring the answer to our problems, the inclination to respect public opinion while seeking proactively to manage it, a certain tiredness and disappointment with the great slogans and categories of left and right and an enthusiasm for technical solutions – these aspects of the post-revolutionary settlement remind us that the statesmen of the 1850s were in some respects our contemporaries.

Transactions of the RHS 22 (2012), pp. 199–221 © Royal Historical Society 2012
doi:10.1017/S0080440112000126

AUDITORY SNAPSHOTS FROM THE EDGES OF EUROPE

By Michael Beckerman, Jessica Schwartz,
Roland Huntford, Roger Buckton, Michael Cwach,
Kevin C. Karnes, Timothy J. Cooley, Bret Werb,
Petra Gelbart and Jeffrey A. Summit*

READ ON 17 JUNE 2011 AT THE UNIVERSITY OF LANCASTER

Sound recordings available at

http://dx.doi.org/10.1017/S0080440112000126

ABSTRACT. This article presents thirty 'auditory snapshots' from a wide variety of geographical locations and contexts in order to elaborate several points. First, we believe that the study of history cannot be separated from the study of sound, whether in the form of 'soundscapes' or pieces of music. Second, we find that considerations of edges, into which we fold such things as provinces, peripheries and frontiers, can be greatly enriched by looking at a broad range of musical phenomena, from the liturgy of Ugandan Jews to reggae-infused Polish mountain songs and from the sounds of Mozart's Black contemporary Saint-Georges to *Silent Night* on the Southern Seas. Finally, drawing on certain ideas from James C. Scott's *The Art of Not Being Governed*, we argue that paradoxically, in music, the middle often has unusual properties. In other words, musical structure mimics the ongoing battle between those in positions of authority and those who wish to evade that authority. Beginnings and endings, then, tend to be sites of power and convention, while middles attempt to subvert it. While culturally and geographically we may contrast centres and peripheries, in music the centre is often the edge.

1. England's edges and the estuary
[Example 1: Lune Estuary]

If things had held to plan this article would never have been written. James C. Scott would have given the keynote address at a conference on

* This article is based on the keynote lecture given by Michael Beckerman at the Royal Historical Society (RHS) Symposium *Edges of Europe: Frontiers in Context* held at Lancaster University on 16–17 June 2011. The co-authors above have provided general comments on the entire article, and several have devoted themselves to co-authoring a section with Michael Beckerman. In that case, the names of the individual authors appear in parentheses before that section. Absent these, the central work was done by Michael Beckerman. Special thanks to Derek Sayer, Chair of History at Lancaster University, and Yoke-Sum Wong, Paolo Palladino, Naomi Tadmor, Nathaniel Tadmor, Christopher Jotischky, Madeline Stanich, Anna Beckerman, Isabel Shaida and Julia Foote for their assistance.

the Edges of Europe, and would have spoken on the subject of 'The Art of Not Being Governed.' If his talk had been published in this journal, the readers, no doubt, would have heard about the Zomia, those areas in Southeast Asia and South China above 500 metres where, as Scott argues, the gravitational pull of the State exerts itself in unusual and uneven ways. While we do invoke mountains here from time to time, we have begun and will end in the flattest possible places. But the constellation of ideas we draw upon will have certain family resemblances to Scott's approach. First, we will suggest that Culture, writ large, may unfold differently in metaphorical Zomias, into which we shall fold such things as edges, provinces, peripheries and frontiers; and second that listening to the sonic traces of these places in a variety of ways, from the ephemeral to the analytical, is revealing, and raises questions essential to any broader inquiry of a historical or political nature.

Almost all the following examples you will hear (available at http://dx.doi.org/10.1017/S0080440112000126) are things we call *music*, but the first example is a soundscape made on 15 June at the Lune Estuary near the Stork Club (where, speaking of European edges, they now feature a South African menu).

As recently as the 1950s it was almost impossible to collect the ambient sounds of a place and most early recordings were restricted to sounds that lay 'within the horn' to invoke the cone-shaped microphones that flourished in past times. It may seem cruel to add to the historian's already daunting task, but we follow the lead of many working within the field of sound studies and declare that without attempting to imagine the concrete sounds of the past, our reconstructions will be blindingly incomplete. So we start with the literal sound of England's edges and the estuary, where, more than most places, the sounds of wind and nature mix with the evidence of human converse and the distant whoosh of the mechanical.

Let us go further out on the sea.

2. *Silent Night* on the Southern Ocean (Roland Huntford) [Example 2: Glade Jul]

On 9 August 1910, Roald Amundsen sailed from an island near Kristiansand, on the Skagerrak, with a crew of men and dogs aboard the *Fram* – a vessel made famous earlier by Fridtjof Nansen – and left the coast of Norway for the open sea. The crew believed they were going to try to gain the North Pole, but Amundsen had other plans, since both Frederick Cook and Robert Peary had claimed that prize a few months earlier. It was just before the ship left Madeira on the evening of 9 September 1910 that he informed everyone of his true intention to reach the South Pole. The stable but ungainly vessel made its way south through the trade winds, doldrums and the roaring 40s. By Christmas

Eve they had reached 150°W 56°S, about 900 miles from the Great Ice Barrier in the Antarctic, and had encountered 'finer weather'.

This is how Amundsen described Christmas Eve aboard the *Fram* in his book *The South Pole*:

> I slipped behind the curtain of my cabin for an instant and set the gramophone going. Herold sang us 'Glade Jul'. The song did not fail of its effect; it was difficult to see in the subdued light, but I fancy that among the band of hardy men that sat round the table there was scarcely one who had not a tear in the corner of his eye.

Just a few years earlier, Mark Twain had concluded his humorous but moving *Eve's Diary* with what is thought to be a tribute to his own, recently deceased, wife, 'Wherever she was, there was Eden.' And we might say in that spirit: wherever the *Fram* was, there was the edge of Europe, like the phonograph itself and the singer of this recording, portable and intrepid.

One can only think of those men heading off to Antarctica alone on the seas before radio connections, more inaccessible than any Zomia, and how they might have listened to what to them was a technological marvel; especially the second repetition with the bells [Example 3: Glade Jul, bells].

Paradoxically, Amundsen literally had to sneak out of Norway because of the enormous debts he had accrued setting up his expedition. So he was simultaneously a kind of outcast on the edge and a complicit part of the imperial competition for a geographical prize.

The recording heard in Example 3 was made a year before Amundsen's voyage, it was a 'new hit' by Vilhelm Herold, a famous Danish tenor from Amundsen's generation. We may end this snapshot with a thought. Although *Silent Night* has crept into the mainstream and may be as close to an international Christmas anthem as anything, it was a piece written at the last minute in a provincial Austrian town by two amateurs for Christmas Eve in 1818, and first performed on guitar. It is somehow fitting that it is this quintessential creation from the Austrian mountains that was played by Amundsen ninety years later on a flat sea, and, further, that *Silent Night* achieves its greatest power by having its own edge appear only at the very end of the song's middle, paradoxically on the words, 'Sleep in heavenly peace.' There will be more on middles to come as we get closer to the middle of this study.

3. Accordions of Puhoi (Roger Buckton and Michael Cwach) [Example 4: Finger Polka]

Some 2,000 nautical miles north of Amundsen's Christmas position lies the small village of Puhoi, New Zealand. In the 1860s, a group of German-speaking Bohemians from the Plzen region were tempted by glowing – and ultimately somewhat misleading – reports of a paradise across the sea. Expecting flat, arable land, they instead found Zomia-like hills and impenetrable bush. But they stayed, worked with enormous determination and have remained as an intact community for 150 years. They have also tried to keep their musical traditions alive.

The recording featured in Example 4, for three accordions, bagpipe and fiddler, is called the Finger Polka by the Puhoi natives. There are many kinds of edges, and many things go on in these edges, but one of them is preservation. While the political authority of a mainstream may become dissipated as a result of emigration (and Puhoi was inaccessible by anything but packet boat until the 1950s), the cultural authority of the former centre becomes greater as communities seek to prevent change. Actually, the process is twofold. On the one hand, there must be change, because performance forces will always be arbitrary – if a piper does not arrive with pipes there are no bagpipes – and can never be identical to those back home. The combination of three accordions, violin and bagpipe is not to be found today in Bohemia; on the other hand, there is a psychological mandate, an imperative to sustain the remembered past. Ethnomusicologist Roger Buckton reports that the performers felt that this Finger Polka was a special Puhoi heritage work.

Yet this is a common tune that is heard in many different places. Example 5 is taken from a Czech folk festival [Example 5: Finger Polka from Czech Folk Festival], and Example 6 from the Elektra Soft Polka Humour Album, hardly Czech [Example 6: 'Annie in the Cabbage Patch']. There are slight differences, and in the end no algorithm can inform us as to whether the changes are things misremembered, or things too well remembered. But they are certainly different. We may remember that when Dvorak visited Spillville, Iowa, in 1893, a Czech colony established in the 1840s, he felt as if we was speaking with his own grandparents. Here the rough and ready sounds played by octogenarian and nonagenarian musicians allow us to hear a polka in amber.

4. Latvia, edges and masses (Kevin C. Karnes) [Example 7: Latvia]

Already at 'sunrise' (it had never gotten fully dark), strange sights began to appear. Women and men and children, alone and in groups, walking below my hotel window, dressed head to toe in traditional garb: black and red skirts and crisp white blouses, all elaborately trimmed with bright abstract patterns, most of murky pagan origins . . . every now and then, most stunning of all, a monstrous, extra-large-pizza-sized crown of oak branches and leaves worn proudly by an elderly man or woman.

These are the words of Kevin C. Karnes who recorded the example you just heard at the All-Latvian Song Festival in 2008, a once-every-five-years event that has continued largely uninterrupted since 1873. All the regional choirs march through the city to the big, specially built festival amphitheater, in traditional costume, with Latvian flags waving from every window above the parade route. A massed-choir concert itself features thousands of singers rotating on and off of the stage. The whole thing runs for hours and hours, well into the night.

The piece heard in Example 7, titled *In Latvia*, was composed by Andrejs Jurjans – onetime head conductor of the song-festival choir – in 1913, and has been a staple in the repertoire ever since. Written by Auseklis, poet-hero of the 'National Awakening' of the late nineteenth century, pen-name of Mikelis Krogzemis, it is a heady brew of over-the-top nationalist symbols, mixing warlike and pastoral images:

> On Latvia's hills, in Latvia's meadows,
> the spirit of freedom revives in my heart.
> There I see men, powerful as oaks,
> maidens blossoming like lindens.
> I hear the ancient songs of bards,
> composed in the shade of divine trees.
> They fill the heart with heavenly joy,
> and raise the spirit to the divine.

Karnes describes the scene:

> There were choirs from every city and town in the country, and choirs from all those corners of the globe to which Latvians had emigrated at the end of the war (from Germany, North America, Australia, Brazil). There were choirs from schools and cultural centers and neighborhoods and all sorts of social groups. There was a 'Fireman's Choir' from Ventspils in the east. And there was an enigmatic 'Bees' Choir' from who knows where.

Later in the evening they all assembled, filling the stage from one side to the other. Karnes writes: 'Here, all those choirs of five and fifty combined into one extraordinary mass, with individual singers – and individual choirs – simply disappearing into the whole. The program book listed over 20,000.'

Example 8 is taken from a tourist ad for Latvia, contrasting the singing of one with the sound of thousands [Example 8: Tourist Advertisement]. This kind of mass singing appears to be unique to Estonia, Latvia and Lithuania, going back to the first song festivals in the 1870s. It came to international attention in the early 90s when people spoke of Estonia's 'Singing Revolution', as if these geographical and political edges of Europe were trying, literally, to sing their nations into existence. Here, song represents simultaneously the urge to escape from one kind of State authority – the Soviet – and perhaps unwittingly mandate another.

5. *Mit hjerte*: the edges model the centre
[Example 9: *Mit hjerte*, opening]

Listeners familiar with French twentieth-century music might sense there is something familiar about this melody heard in Example 9, and others might recognise it as a slowed-down version of Ravel's *Tombeau de Couperin* [Example 10: Ravel's *Tombeau*].

If that was all there was, perhaps it might not be worth our interest. But in this case, the passage serves as the introduction to a Scandinavian Christmas song *Mit hjerte Altid Vanker* played by the group Bukkene Bruse on their album, *Den fagrasta rosa* [Example 11: *Mit hjerte* vocal]. The introduction based on Ravel is not just a little slower than the source, but so slow that it virtually seems to change the very nature of the original, far more so than any intermediate tempo might. In confronting the way the northern edge imagines the mainstream we not only must deal with issues of tempo, but also of structure and ornamentation. In Ravel's original, the ornament is on the downbeat, in Example 9 a beat later. Even more significant is the issue of structure and meaning because the opening of *Mit hjerte* was not taken from the opening of the *Tombeau de Couperin*, or even the opening of one of its movements. Rather, it comes from one of the middle movements of Ravel's *Tombeau*. Further, this seeming 'introduction' to the carol is almost a minute and half long, as if obscuring the nature of what is edge and what is centre.

The idea of borrowing from Ravel came from Arve Moen Bergset, the singer and fiddle player in Bukkene Bruse. He is a classically trained violinist, and is now playing first violin in the Oslo Philharmonic Orchestra. According to Bjørn Ole Rasch, the group's arranger and a Professor of Music at the University of Agder,

> the group saw it as a challenge to combine these, but it became so much easier when we discovered the beauty and simplicity of Ravel's composition which went so easily with both versions of the carol. I have always liked the idea of combining different styles of music and this was one of the few possibilities to combine folk music with classical which has not been done very often in Norway. (Except for Grieg of course . . .)

So, by taking Ravel's sprightly tune, a creature of the middle if there ever was one, and reconfiguring it as an elegiac two-voiced Norwegian fiddle *introduction* by altering harmonies and displacing ornaments, it is a pristine example of what happens when the edges seek to process the centre. Like Van Gogh trying – and failing – to be even a competent draughtsman, the periphery tends to distort the centre. But to what end? Bukkene Bruse's change is obviously distortion with a purpose.

Many have remarked that considering Ravel's avowed purpose to honour friends who had been killed in the First World War (the Forlane, for example was dedicated to the memory of the Basque painter Lieutenant Gabriel Deluc), the *Tombeau* is conspicuously bright and airy. In this case, though, it may be a matter of the periphery discovering a way of listening overlooked by the centre. For despite its brightness, when we revisit Ravel through the scrim of the Norwegian fiddle version, the passage in question is heartbreaking. Here, the middle has become beginning, and the song

Mit hjerte, usually performed without an introduction, has become the expressive middle. The edge has taught the centre how to listen to itself.

Incidentally, this piece provides yet another example of the fictions of 'national culture', for this 'Norwegian' carol is based on a Swedish folk song and a Danish text.

6. Of music and fencing [Example 12: Sinfonia Concertante in E Flat]

He was by all accounts among the finest swordsmen in France. John Adams, in a diary entry from 17 May 1779, called him 'the most Accomplished man in Europe in riding, running shooting, fencing, dancing, music', and said that he could 'hit a crown piece in the air with a pistol ball'. Probably the greatest violinist in France at the time of the Revolution he was also an important composer and inventor of the genre of the Sinfonia Concertante. Though there is no documented meeting between him and Mozart during the latter's visit to Paris in 1778, it is unlikely that Mozart's famous and quite original Sinfonia Concertante for Violin and Viola, K.364, composed the following year, could have come into existence without such a model.

He, in this case, is the Chevalier de Saint-Georges, born Joseph Bologne, the son of a minor French aristocrat and a former Senegalese slave from Guadalupe. Example 12 features part of his own Sinfonia Concertante in E Flat. In the years before the Revolution he took Paris by storm as perhaps the most conspicuously accomplished, admired and envied physical personality in France – a kind of cross between Michael Jordan, Mozart and Pushkin.

Example 13 contains another example of the Chevalier's work, this time from the Violin Concerto in D [Example 13: Violin Concert in D Major]. Here, the Chevalier's style marks a directness and conspicuous virtuosity of a type not previously familiar in France and it might be tempting to regard this sound as the sound of the edge taking over the centre. For, after all, no matter what one thinks of middles, they are almost always the very site of virtuosity. Whether in bebop or Mozart, rock guitar or the Chevalier's concerto, technical fireworks almost always reside in the centre. But there are other kinds of transformations as well.

7. Trebunie-Tutki – Twinkle Brothers: Górale from the Zomia (Timothy J. Cooley) [Example 14: Pierso Godzina, *Don't Betray My Love*]

Finally, we reach Scott's literal Zomia of elevated highlands, specifically the Polish Tatras, where Muzyka Podhale, or 'Górale' music has flourished for more than a century – though certainly its antecedents go back much further. Whether or not mountain isolation has traditionally resulted in the evasion of some kind of centralised 'musical authority', Górale music has been recognised and discussed by many scholars as a distinctive style. In *The Art of Not Being Governed*, Scott suggests that after about 1950, and especially with satellite photography, GPS and new modes of transportation, the Zomia may be fast losing any special status it might ever have had. And, of course, Górale music has somewhat famously ceded aspects of identity and forged new connections with other groups, some of them seemingly quite random.

Example 14 is a brief clip from the collaboration between the Trebunie-Tutki family group who still live in the Podhale mountain region and people closer to the sea. While the Górale rhetoric sounds nationalist and isolationist in their own third-person description, 'they have to be close to the sky-touching mountains, dark forests and green valleys, to hear the wind whistling and to feel an air vibration during a thunderstorm. And all those things you can find in their music', they have forged a notable collaboration with the Twinkle Brothers of Jamaica. Of course, things are not always as they seem. While they are a traditional reggae band, one of the Twinkle Brothers lives in London and the other in Oakland, and the project itself was the brainchild of a Warsaw DJ.

That there was such a crossover between mountain and sea islands, between vodka and reefer, if you will, may be of interest, but more compelling is the organisation of the song, and the way the process unfolds. As we heard, the opening features what sounds like traditional Górale music, until the electronics and the reggae rhythm mysteriously interject themselves. And yet this music itself is on the edge of Polishness, since the tune is really from the Slovak side of the mountains. The Tutki family plays along its own national edge.

This recording of the song works to undermine its roots. Once we 'get' the reggae beat, it seems that the Trebunie-Tutki band will simply use it as an accompaniment as heard in Example 15 [Example 15: Pierso 1]. But in the very middle of the song – and as we get nearer the middle of this talk study will further accentuate the importance of middles – there is a striking change [Example 16: Pierso 2]. We find a kind of reggaeisation of the original; with a literal translation but an altered accent pattern. But by the end, the Twinkle Brothers have moved away from the Polish original, and created something like their own song, but based on 'mountain' echoes [Example 17: Pierso 3]. Here we might say that two edges have met – Górale and Rasta – and fashioned something that never could have come from the centre.

8. The Muselmann sings (Bret Werb)
[Example 18: Muselmann]

Example 18 presents a song you might have heard at the Bologna Theater Communale in the mid-1960s performed by a man dressed in a concentration camp uniform. We know little of his audience at that time, but we have some information about the show and the showman. The piece was originally composed in the Sachsenhausen concentration camp between 1940 and 1943 by Alexander Kulisiewicz, a Catholic who had been a law student in Poland. In 1939 he was arrested for making derogatory remarks about the Nazis (supposedly he wrote something like, 'Forget Hitler, heil Butter!'). For this, he was sent to Sachsenhausen where he spent the next six years.

While in Sachsenhausen, Kulisiewicz became a kind of secret troubadour, over the years writing more than fifty songs based on his experience, and ultimately collecting hundreds of songs from other inmates of other camps. As he wrote, 'In the camp, I tried under all circumstances to create verses that would serve as direct poetical reportage.'

He first sang *Muselmann* for his friends in Cell Block 65 toward the end of July 1940. (Like Kulisiewicz, the protagonist of *Muselmann* was a political prisoner whose uniform, as noted in the song, was branded with a 'red triangle badge.') Kulisiewicz added further verses during the fall of 1943, including the final verse.

The word describes those 'emaciated walking corpses, on the threshold between life and death'. The figure of the Muselmann has had the dubious honour of becoming a player on the world stage, at least of Holocaust literature and criticism. Works by such figures as Agamben, Cicioux, Todorov, Žižek, Langbein and especially Primo Levi have delineated the classic 'limit' figure on the edge, and understood the concentration camp as the ultimate edge between the real and unreal, life and death, aesthetics and ethics, and their nullification.

The Muselmann and the song about him raise questions that cannot be readily answered. Primo Levi raised them first with his almost offhand formulation of the powerful paradox that the Muselmann was the real witness to the Holocaust, but was unable to witness because of his condition. Other vexing issues remain: how is it that the lowest of the low came to be called 'Moslems'? In terms of our auditory snapshots, we might wonder how or why a Yiddish/Polish *orientalist* song with the name of the Mauritanian Princess 'Zulejka' became the source composition for 'The Muselmann'?

[Example 19: Zulejka] As Bret Werb points out, even stranger is that Kulisiewicz probably did not even know Zulejka, but rather a parody of it called 'Shanghai' he picked up while performing in the circus. But there is no doubt of the changes that ensue when the chorus of Zulejka is somehow transformed into one of the most powerful indictments of Nazi horror.

[Example 20 a and b: Zulejka and Muselmann] In hearing the voice of the Muselmann as something between agony and *orientalism*, and in our acknowledgement that the figure himself actually hears nothing, the Muselmann may be the ultimate creature of the edges.

9. Gypsiness and the Uhrovska Manuscript C298 (Petra Gelbart) [Example 21: C298]

In the 1950s, an extraordinary manuscript was discovered. Called today the 'Uhrovska Rukopiesne' it is a compendium of popular musical styles from the 1730s. Marked with the names of local dance types, many of which are still around today, the collection is considered a kind of eighteenth-century fake book, probably for use by the primas, or first violinist of a band.

The recording in Example 21 is a realisation of the short snippet from that manuscript in an album titled 'Telemann: The Baroque Gypsies', by Ensemble Caprice, directed by Matthias Maute. The accompanying notes make the argument that the manuscript somehow represents the musical practice of the 'gypsies', here with a potentially de-ethnicising lower case 'g'. We have looked at edges on the periphery, but the phenomenon of Gypsy or Romani music engages edges that are *in* the centre, rather than above or outside it.

Although Roma were partly subject to state-sanctioned slavery, extra taxes or capital punishment based simply on their origin, James Scott rightly considers them to be one of the groups that have sometimes eluded the authority of the State. The ways in which this independence from governance has been imagined, in reference to the laws of State, religion or culture, has almost always betrayed more about the author than about the people in question. The Ensemble Caprice wishes to present an unfettered version of Baroque music by channelling what one might believe to be Romani culture, even if the only currently verifiable 'Gypsy' element of our sound example is the attack of the bow in combination with gritty string timbres, with neither technique being exclusive to Roma.

Yet, despite the certainties of the Ensemble Caprice about the Gypsiness of the Uhrovska Manuscript, a lengthy recent article about the manuscript lacks even a single mention of Gypsies or Roma, and rather it speculates about whether the manuscript represents Slovak or Hungarian culture; additionally, the introductory essays accompanying the facsimile shed no light on the subject. And yet the Ensemble Caprice seems so sure. How can that be?

In order to approach this question it is important to understand that there are four fundamental aspects to the way the Roma fit into history. First, and perhaps most conspicuous, is what we call *the vacuum*. Since Roma were for the most part not literate, almost all their actual utterances from before the twentieth century, other than song texts, have vanished. If the Roma do exist, it is almost always in the documents of others, characterised by outsiders. The second mode is that of *contestation*, as Hungarians, Slovaks, Russians, Czechs or Spaniards dispute whether or not particular contributions (anything from cimbalová hudba to flamenco) represent Romani musicianship, or are simply reflections of a local or national style, played and sometimes 'distorted' by the Roma as hired hands. The third mode is the one many are familiar with, which we call *Gypsiness*, a complex realm of overwrought fantasy, where the Roma become repositories for all those things the surrounding culture either wishes to intensify or cannot own up to; usually, though not entirely, having to do with sex, with illogical ideas of freedom thrown in for good measure. It is a version of the classic relationship between so-called dominant and subaltern groups, and, as such, paradoxically, this third mode involves something we might call 'observing by looking away'. That is, the purveyors of Gypsiness essentially do not want to know the truth about the Roma and whatever 'they' are really doing 'over there'. And whether 'over there' means Gypsies, the Baltics (who can keep those countries straight?) or 'the Orient', knowledge is meant to be laced with both fantasy and a passionate desire *not* to know. Finally, there is a *pernicious* mode, illustrated most recently by travesties like the television series *My Big Fat Gypsy Wedding* and involving defamatory representations of Romani people.

For better or for worse, as all historians know, faith cannot be removed from historical writing. We do not *know* with any certainty the role Roma played in the development of Western so-called 'common musical practice', but most of those who have studied the evidence believe there was an important connection. Thus, a group that has always formed a discursive periphery was actually at the centre of attention at certain times and for certain historical figures. While the most notable of those was Franz Liszt, Example 22 gives us a snapshot of Georg Philip Telemann listening in *some* way to the Roma, in a hyper-virtuosic passage from his 'Gypsy' Sonata in D minor [Example 22: Telemann 'Gypsy' Sonata].

It might be as convincing a sample of 'Gypsiness' as the Ensemble Caprice's recording of the anonymous snippet from the manuscript. But buyer beware! Believing in Gypsiness, the ensemble fulfils that prophesy in its performance choices which, though seductive, involve a certain amount of historical fantasising. Despite its sensuous power, listening should not be a matter of confirming our views, but of challenging them.

But there is some firm evidence of Roma in the Uhrovska Manuscript that we might mention. One short passage, numbered 230 in the catalogue, is marked 'Czigany'. It is an ungainly piece, perhaps so odd that Ensemble Caprice overlooked it.

We do not know what the designation means; whether it is a piece called 'The Gypsy Dance', or something notated after the compiler heard a Gypsy perform. The Roma are difficult to locate in the eighteenth century; they do not always stand still for our historicising. But they offer an inner edge that helps to shape the mainstream.

10. Some sexy moments in a Fibich Quintet or when the edge is in the structural centre [Example 23: Fibich Quintet Trio#2]

We are still not through with the idea of the centre. The passage featured in Example 23, with its 'Czech' accents, drones, syncopations, arabesques, unanticipated interjections and air of mystery is taken from the inner part of the Scherzo from Zdenek Fibich's *Quintet for Winds* written in 1893, the same year as Dvorak's 'New World' Symphony. One of the reasons Fibich is far less popular today than he was when he, rather than Dvorak, was considered by many to be the proper heir to Smetana, involves his reluctance to buy into the display of conspicuous Czechness (his most substantial works are three full-length stage melodramas on Greek themes). And, indeed, most of his Quintet sounds far more like Schumann than any of his Czech contemporaries, especially the opening of the Scherzo [Example 24: Fibich Scherzo, opening].

Interestingly, Fibich gives his Scherzo two Trios. The first is more like a simple ballad, while the second is the passage from Example 23. If by the edge we invoke Scott's notion of that which evades the authority of the State, in musical terms, the edge is frequently the centre, which evades the standardised authority of beginnings and endings. In the middle, composers are free to do whatever they want – either because no one cares what they do in the middle, no one notices or listeners are so secure they do not even understand the fact the rules have changed. Fibich, a buttoned up internationalist at the start and finish of the work, hides a strong statement about sexy Czechness as a kind of anti-rationalist substance, bowing to no precedent or force. And he places it in the very middle.

11. Musical change in the liturgy of the Abayudaya (Jewish people) of Uganda (Jeffrey A. Summit) [Example 25: *Lekhah dodi*]

There are times when the edges of Europe touch other cultures and that contact results in unexpected outcomes. Such is the case with Semei

Kakungulu, a powerful military leader of the Baganda people, who self-converted to Judaism in 1919. In the 1890s, Kakungulu was recruited by the British to fight against Muslims and Roman Catholics in the battles to take control of Uganda. He was evangelised by the Anglican Church and allied himself with the British in the hope that he would be recognised as *kabaka* (king) of the eastern region of Uganda. He was sorely disappointed when the British reneged on their promises. Kakungulu's disillusion with the British and his close reading of the Bible led him to reject the Anglican Church and call for stricter adherence to the Torah, the Five Books of Moses. When he began to teach that the Torah requires circumcision for all males, and for boys to be circumcised on the eighth day, he was told that only Jews practised that ritual. Kakungulu reportedly replied, 'If this is so, then from this day on, I am a Jew.' According to Abayudaya elders, Kakungulu followed the example of the patriarch Abraham and circumcised himself and his sons. Soon afterwards, about 3,000 of his followers were circumcised in the largest mass conversion to Judaism on record. At first, they practised a form of proto-Judaism that focused on Biblical ritual observance, incorporating aspects of Judaism with Protestantism. Today, the Abayudaya, a community of approximately 1,000 people living in villages surrounding the town of Mbale in Eastern Uganda, are practising Jews. Many members scrupulously follow Jewish ritual, observe the laws of the Sabbath, celebrate Jewish holidays, keep kosher and pray in Hebrew.

The Abayudaya's first contact with mainstream Judaism occurred in 1926 when Kakungulu met a Jewish trader, Yusuf (Joseph), in Kampala. Yusuf taught the community leaders elementary Hebrew, certain prayers and blessings and the basics of kosher slaughtering. Since the community's self-conversion and through the difficult period of Idi Amin's rule, the Abayudaya's Jewish observance has been shaped by their commitment to follow mainstream Jewish practice, an approach that has been amplified since their increased contact with Jews from North America, Europe and Israel since the mid-1990s. They understand their developing Hebrew literacy and selective adoption of Jewish musical traditions from North America as a way to authenticate their Jewish expression and affirm their status as members of the world Jewish community. Here, we consider recent developments in the music of the Abayudaya liturgy and examine how various global factors – the education of their rabbi in an American institution and the increase in ethno-tourism to their relatively isolated community in Eastern Uganda – have impacted the development of the musical realisation of their Shabbat (Sabbath) worship.

In 1983, Amnon Shiloach and Eric Cohen examined the dynamics of change in Jewish Oriental Ethnic Music in Israel and wrote that 'Less change can be expected in religious music than in social and recreational music', explaining that 'The degree of stability of music is closely related to its function.' Yet, in the case of the Abayudaya, the change in religious music has been considerable and following Shiloach's and Cohen's understanding, this change *is* propelled by functional issues. The first change we consider is the product of personal agency on the part of the community's leader and a strategic desire to bring their musical practice in line with what they understand to be mainstream Judaism.

Importing authenticity

On Rabbi Summit's first research trip to Uganda in 2000, members of the community stressed that one of their largest problems was their isolation from 'their Jewish brothers and sisters' around the world. These young leaders spoke about how their parents had read about the formation of the State of Israel in local newspapers in 1948 and had sat in open fields expectantly waiting for airplanes to arrive to Mbale to bring them to Israel 'on the wings of eagles', as prophesied in the Torah. They lamented, 'We are Jews but no one knew we existed.' In the 1960s, when Israel was involved in development work in Uganda, the Abayudaya built a relationship with the secretary at the Israeli embassy in Kampala who arranged to have prayer books and other educational material sent to the community. Gershom Sizomu had developed a strong Jewish background but his dream was to study in rabbinic school and Summit had the contacts at the Hebrew Union College-Jewish Institute of Religion in New York to arrange for him to be a visiting student for a semester in 2001.

When Summit began his research in Uganda in 2000, most of the community's liturgical music consisted of psalms sung in Luganda to the community's own compositions. Abayudaya musicians had also composed their own melodies for popular Hebrew hymns such as *Lekhah dodi* (Come, My Beloved) and *Adon Olam* (Master of the Universe). Gershom and his brother J. J. Keki had heard examples of nusach (traditional Ashkenazi Jewish chant) on their visits to the ex-pat Jewish congregation in Nairobi, as well as from the occasional visitor from North America, but chant was not used for many prayers in their service. Apart from the well-known melody for the *Shema* (Listen! [Israel]), they used few melodies that would be recognisable to North American worshippers.

The community decided to affiliate with the Conservative Movement. In their practice, they were more traditional than most Reform Jews and even as they reached out to Orthodox institutions, the Orthodox questioned their Jewish status. Gershom attended the Conservative Movement's Ziegler School in Los Angeles. In the notes to a CD Gershom recorded in 2007, he wrote that he 'chose to attend rabbinic school to better understand ancient and modern Judaism and bring the Ugandan community into mainstream Judaism'. Now, many tunes familiar in

Conservative congregations, such as the Hatzi Kaddish chanted in traditional nusach, have been integrated into the service.

These musical changes, together with the adoption of various melodies well known in American Conservative congregations, create a strong bond with Jews who visit from North America. Rabbi Summit spoke to one woman active in her Conservative congregation who visited the community in 2009. She said, 'There I was in Uganda, but I felt so at home in the service! We really are one people.' It should be obvious that the life of a Ugandan subsistence farmer and an upper-middle-class American business woman have less, rather than more, in common. Yet, these shared musical traditions undergird a powerful sense of peoplehood felt by both communities when these Jews meet. This sense of connection, strategically created by changes in the congregation's music, has practical implications as well. When this woman returned to Boston, she became actively engaged in raising money to support Abayudaya students attending college in Uganda.

Introducing musical instruments in Friday night worship

Up to the year 2004, following the traditional halachic (Jewish legal) prohibition that instrumental music was not to be played on the Sabbath, the Abayudaya did not use musical instruments in the Friday night service. Gershom's composition of *Lekhah dodi*, a signature tune for the community, was sung a cappella as you heard in Example 25. However, when Gershom worked as a rabbinic intern at Congregation Shomrei Torah in West Hills, CA, he was introduced to the Conservative Movement's growing practice that allowed the use of instruments during *Kabbalat Shabbat*, the first part of the Friday evening service, when, technically, it was not yet Shabbat. With this halachic imprimatur, the Abayudaya on Nabugoye Hill introduced guitars and drums before sundown in the *Kabbalat Shabbat* service to, in Gershom's words, 'increase participation.'

While the authority to use instruments in the service comes from Gershom's experience with the Conservative Movement, the Abayudaya have a history of using music to increase community participation in worship. Many members of the Abayudaya had left the community during the difficult years of Idi Amin's rule in the 1970s when synagogues were closed and the Abayudaya were forbidden to gather for worship. Beginning in 1979, the young leaders of the community set the psalms of the service in Luganda to melodies they both composed and adapted from local Christian worship in order to make Jewish prayer more accessible and draw their community back to Jewish practice. Today, Abayudaya leaders continue to be strategic in their musical choices both to shape the worship experience and increase community participation. To intensify this participation, the community has also introduced a dance around the reader's stand during the singing of *Lekhah dodi*. Often, half the congregation will leave their seats to participate as members and visitors clap their hands, sing and circle the reader's stand at the front of the synagogue.

The addition of instrumentation and the dance during *Kabbalat Shabbat* intensifies worshippers' participation on several levels. For the Abayudaya, this is a point in the service for heightened participation by the community's women. While younger women are literate in Ludanda, English and increasingly Hebrew, older women know parts of the Hebrew service by memory and primarily add voice during the singing of the psalms in Luganda. Their singing and prominent participation in the dance during *Lekhah dodi* bring these women centre stage during this portion of the service. At the same time, the addition of instruments has given a role, and training opportunity, to the next generation of the Abayudaya's musicians and much of the music during this section of the service is played by the community's youth.

The inclusion of instrumental music and dance also has an impact upon visitors to the community who often speak about their experience at *Kabbalat Shabbat* as a high point of their visit to the Abayudaya. Visitors are drawn into the dance and the combination of the drumming and community's melodies for these psalms and hymns code the Abayudaya worship experience as 'African'. In *Ma'ariv*, the main section of the evening service, tunes and nusach familiar to North American Jews code the service as Jewish. We should stress that there is not a strict delineation placing all of the African elements in *Kabbalat Shabbat* and North American musical and linguistic elements in *Ma'ariv*: there are syncretic elements in both sections of the service. Yet, together the two sections of the service create a Jewish experience that resonates authentically with both community members and visitors, rich in *minhag hamakum*, local tradition, while providing a serviceable bridge to mainstream Judaism, both real and imagined.

Conclusions

Rabbi Summit spoke with Gershom about how he understood the process of looking to America for melodies for Abayudaya worship and gently observed, 'You know, Gershom, some might comment that this foreign influence on your worship traditions could be equated with Colonialism?' Gershom countered and replied, 'I think that Colonialism occurs when we change from what is Abayudaya and adopt the foreign. In this case, we use our own compositions for *Lekhah dodi* and other hymns. We do not yet have Ugandan tunes for the *Ma'ariv* service. So as soon as we compose those tunes, we will switch and use our own compositions.' Musical changes in Abayudaya worship over the past twelve years have been strategic and functional as the community negotiates the boundaries between mainstream Judaism and their developing local practice.

12. Go down Moses and other examples of direct speech [Example 26: Go Down Moses]

When Antonín Dvořák arrived in the United States in September of 1892, there were many voices trying to teach him about American music, or, more to the point, what American music was or should be. Many of these voices believed that the only true source for American music was Black. These included Dvořák's employer at the National Conservatory, Jeannette Thurber, the noted critic Henry Krehbiel and Mildred Hill who, under the pseudonym Johann Tonsor wrote an article urging the 'Messiah of American music' to use African American song as a foundation for national style, and wrote her own hit song, *Happy Birthday* under the influence of that mandate.

Of all these, we may argue that the most influential figure was Henry Thacker Burleigh, an African American singer and the grandson of a slave who both worked and studied at the National Conservatory. In his own reminiscences, and those of others such as Victor Herbert, it is made clear that while Dvořák may have discovered the 'bones' of African American melos through notation and description, he grasped the 'flesh' from Burleigh.

The snapshot from Example 26 is the only known record of Burleigh's voice (he hated recording), made in 1919 by George Broome in New York. He is singing his own arrangement of the spiritual *Let My People Go*, perhaps the most political and activist of the spiritual texts, a classic example of Scott's hidden transcripts.

In this context we would like to make some observations about expression, middles and what we may call 'direct musical speech'. The song vacillates between narrative and direct speech. The words 'When Israel was in Egypt land' have a 'Once upon a time' quality, while the words 'Let my people go!' are a personal interjection. But in the middle of the song the direct speech, the 'command' takes over entirely ('Go Down Moses!'); the slightly fragmented phrases become whole and powerful.

By now we have suggested that in many different kinds of music the edge is found in the middle. Dvořák chose Black songs as a source for an American school of composition because he felt they were the most expressive of those available to American composers. It is no wonder that a movement modelled on the emotional depth of Black music forms the centre, and the most popular part of Dvořák's 'New World' Symphony [Example 27: 'New World' Largo]. And perhaps this particular dialogue between edge and centre would not be complete without noting that the wordless Largo (actually inspired by an episode from Longfellow's *Song of*

Hiawatha) was given a specifically Black voice by Dvořák's student Willam Arms Fisher in his famous arrangement called *Goin' Home* [Example 28: *Goin' Home*].

With this excursion to the United States we have headed west from Europe and we shall continue in that direction for our final snapshot:

13. Marshall Islands (Jessica Schwartz) [Example 29: Moriba.1]

Juae, dipukae,	currents close to the island,
kab jeḷat	currents further from the island
jeḷatae (2x)//	currents furthest from the island

This returns us to the seas, pulled by currents to the furthest point from where we began, arriving at the low-lying coral atolls in the central Pacific Ocean that comprise the Republic of the Marshall Islands. Recorded on land literally on the other side of the world (the longitude of Lancaster, UK is 2°W and Majuro, RMI, is 171°E), the choir heard in Example 29 is comprised of Bikinian men and women. The song is called *Ñe ij kememej tok aeloñ eo aò* (When I Remember My Atoll).

It was recorded in 2009 at a church on Ejit Island, a land mass the size of a football field in the capital atoll of Majuro, where approximately 300 displaced Bikinian people live. You may remember that Bikini Atoll was the site of the first post-war, and, nine years later, the most powerful, nuclear weapons test. Given the persistence of radiation on their islands, Bikinians remain in exile. The song you have just heard blurs the boundary between edges and middles by sonically representing the way indigenous populations and their lands became central to expansionist projects. As Americans sought access to more people and resources, the Bikinians customary lands and practices became edges, of America and of Europe as well.

The four-part harmonies echoing in the resonant space of the church share the central fixtures on Ejit Island: community, church and loss. Loss permeates the song. The beginning and ending lyrical gestures speak of a homeland lost and, with it, an agency lost [Example 30: Moriba.2].

Anij ekajoor, tōl in wōnake wōt kōj//	God is strong, leads us and protects us
Men otemjej	Everything is
rej ilo bein (2x)	in his hands

It is in the middle of the elegy where our hearing of the first encounter with Americans is amplified. In addition to the musical space – the sound of the four-part harmonies of the hymnal in the physical space of the church – we confront the core lyrics: 'God is strong, leads us and protects us/Everything is in his hands.'

As missionaries banned traditional cultural practices and silenced aspects of local oral and musical cultures, European musical traditions routed through American Protestant hymnody became central. It was this very missionary project that established the ethical link and ideological foundation for the US nuclear testing programme. In an act that mirrored the missionaries' arrival on the vessel known as *Morning Star*, the US navy sailed into Bikini on a Sunday morning and told the Bikinians that it was in God's will that their island be used 'for the good of mankind', that is, to test nuclear weaponry.

The lyrics, 'God is strong . . . ', 'Everything is in his hands', references what has become the Bikinian motto, 'Men otemjej rej ilo bein Anij' ('Everything is in God's hands'). These words were spoken by King Juda, the leader of the Bikinians, to United States Commodore Wyatt in 1946 as he ceded Bikinian land to the United States for nuclear testing.

Some listeners might find the musical expression strange, and, indeed, to our western ears, the song does not seem to convey what one might expect from people whose homeland has been irradiated and partially vaporised by the US. However, we may identify one of Scott's 'hidden transcripts' of resistance in this middle passage. The narrative continues to 'thank the chief and elders', presumably King Juda and all those who had to leave Bikini and travel to an island with inadequate food supplies, for 'overcoming the currents' as they went further and further away from their homeland. Here, the Bikinians do not thank God directly, they remark on the strength and leadership, but they thank their elders. This contrasts many of the speeches that begin, 'First, I would like to thank God for allowing us all to be here today.' *Not* giving thanks is potentially taboo, but the Bikinians are using 'God' and referencing their motto as a reminder to the United States of its ethical obligation to return them home.

The imagery of the elders struggling, being pulled by currents that are further and further away from their homeland of Bikini is somehow not confirmed by the tonal structure of the song as we might expect, resolving instead on the tonic with the words, 'jelat, jelatae' (currents furthest from the island). For Bikinians, original home provided everything they needed to survive – food, shelter, for example, and more broadly, culture. Though they are not far away from Bikini in geographical terms, we may agree that living in a place where their subsistence is completely dependent on the United States situates them as far as possible from their homeland.

This as much as anything explains why Bikinians utilise the agency they do have by keeping the memories of their homeland alive in songs and stories, waiting and wondering if they will ever be able to return to Bikini. And we must recognise them as happenstance denizens of a place selected to maintain, somehow, the edges of Europe in the Cold War – both by containing communism in the Soviet Union and expanding American and European markets.

Conclusions

In the end, let us return from the central Pacific to the sounds of the Lune estuary and note that, along with edges, estuaries have their own symbolic power. In the audio snapshots accompanying this article, you may hear traces of pasts invisible to the historical record that both affirm and contest the notion of an edge, whether it is *Silent Night* resonating in the great empty sea spaces or Jamaicans high in the Polish hills. You will have encountered echoes from middles in Fibich and Kulisiewicz that cannot be assimilated with our commonplace understanding of them.

Now we have only our own endings to deal with, and so we conclude with the basic question posed by the conference that gave rise to our musings, an ultimately messy and impossible one: what does it mean to be an 'edge of Europe'? To answer such a question, we must know precisely what we mean by 'edge' and what exactly 'Europe' might be. As difficult a task as that might be, we note that any answers we can muster will have enormous historical and geopolitical significance, especially in a fractal world of infinite edge. For however we imagine reality we might agree that every centre has an edge, and every edge a centre, and the dialectic of edges and centres proceeds even down to the most minute levels.

Putting some of our ideas in Scott's terms, we believe that the power of musical works often lies in tensions between the authority of beginnings and ends and the relative anarchy of the middle Zomias. Unable to resolve this contest, we cannot let the music go; it lives within us through the conflict. We conclude that these same forces persist in whatever we call culture, or politics, or history. And because history is rarely silent, the study of sound is not separate from the study of history. Thus, one who wishes to know more about 'how the wheels run' will use any possible practice, including listening to and imagining both musical and non-musical sound, as part of the attempt to grasp the rich, dynamic, tormented and ongoing percolation between the edge and the rest [Example 1: Lune Estuary.2].

General bibliography

Benton, Lauren, *A Search for Sovereignty: Law and Geography in European Empires, 1400–1900* (Cambridge, 2010).
Power, Daniel and Naomi Standen, eds., *Frontiers in Question: Eurasian Borderlands 700–1700* (1999).

Rumford, Chris, 'Theorizing Borders', *European Journal of Social Theory*, 9:2 (2006), 155–69.
Scott, James C., *The Art of Not Being Governed: An Anarchist History of Upland Southeast Asia* (New Haven, 2009).
Domination and the Arts of Resistance: Hidden Transcripts (New Haven, 1990).

England's edges and the estuary

Erlmann, Veit, ed., *Hearing Cultures: Essays on Sound, Listening and Modernity* (Wenner Gren International Symposium Series, Oxford, 2004).
Hewitt, Martin and Rachel Cowgill, eds., *Victorian Soundscapes Revisited* (Leeds, 2007).
Picker, John M., *Victorian Soundscapes* (Oxford, 2003).
Schafer, R. Murray, *The Soundscape* (Rochester, VT, 1977, 1994).
Smith, Mark M., *Listening to Nineteenth Century America* (Chapel Hill, 2001).
Sterne, Jonathan, *The Audible Past: Cultural Origins of Sound Production* (Durham, 2002).
Thompson, Emily, *The Soundscape of Modernity: Architectural Acoustics and the Culture of Listening in America 1900–33* (Boston, MA, 2002).

Silent Night on the Southern Ocean

Amundsen, Roald, *The South Pole* (New York, 2001), 160.
Huntford, Roland, *The Last Place on Earth* (New York, 1985), originally published under the title *Scott and Amundsen*.
Race to the South Pole: The Expedition Diaries of Scott and Amundsen (New York and London, 2010).

Of music and fencing

Banat, Gabriel, *Chevalier de Saint-Georges: Virtuoso of the Sword and the Bow* (Stuyvesant, 2006).
Guede, Alain, *Monsieur de Saint-George: Virtuoso, Swordsman, Revolutionary* (New York, 2003).

Trebunie-Tutki – Twinkle Brothers: Górale from the Zomia

Cooley, Timothy J., *Making Music in the Polish Tatras: Tourists, Ethnographers and Mountain Musicians* (Bloomington, 2005).

The Muselmann sings

Agamben, Giorgio, *Remnants of Auschwitz: The Witness and the Archive* (New York, 2002).
Amery, Jean, *At the Mind's Limits* (Bloomington, 1980).
Anidjar, Gil, *The Jew, the Arab* (Stanford, 2003).

Langbein, Hermann, *People in Auschwitz* (Chapel Hill, 2004), especially 'The Muselmann', 89–105.
Levi, Primo, *The Drowned and the Saved* (New York, 1989), especially 'The Gray Zone', 36–69.
Sofsky, Wolfgang, *The Order of Terror: The Concentration Camp* (Princeton, 1999).

Gypsiness and the Uhrovska Manuscript C298

Telemann and the Baroque Gypsies, Ensemble Caprice, directed by Matthias Maute, Analekta Records, 2009.
Uhrovska zbierka tancov z roku 1742 (Uhrovska Collection of Dances from 1742), Critical Edition prepared by Maria Jana Terrayova (Martin: Matica Slovenska, 1990).

Musical change in the liturgy of the Abayudaya (Jewish people) of Uganda

Oded, Arye, *Religion and Politics in Uganda: A Study of Islam and Judaism* (Nairobi, 1994).
Shiloah, Amnon and Erik Cohen, 'The Dynamics of Change in Jewish Oriental Ethnic Music in Israel', *Ethnomusicology*, 27:2 (1987), 227–52.
Sizomu, Rabbi Gershom, *Sing for Joy: Ugandan Jewish Music*, San Francisco: Be'chol Lashon (In Every Tongue), Institute for Jewish and Community Research, compact disc, 2007.
Sobol, Richard (photographs and text) and Jeffrey A. Summit (compact disc recorded and annotated), *Abayudaya: The Jews of Uganda* (New York, 2002).
Summit, Jeffrey A., compiled and annotated, *Abayudaya: Music from the Jewish People of Uganda*, CD 40504, Washington, DC: Smithsonian Folkways Recordings, compact disc, 2003.
Twaddle, Michael, *Kakungulu and the Creation of Uganda, 1868–1928* (1993).

Go down Moses and other examples of direct speech

Beckerman, Michael Brim, *New Worlds of Dvorak* (New York, 2004).
Simpson, Anne Key, *Hard Trials: The Life and Music of Harry Burleigh* (New York, 1990).

Marshall Islands

Kiste, Robert C., *The Bikinians: A Study in Forced Migration* (Menlo Park, CA, 1974).
McArthur, Philip Henry, 'The Social Life of Narrative: Marshall Islands' (Ph.D. thesis, Bloomington: Indiana University, 1995).
Malkki, Liisa H., *Purity and Exile: Violence, Memory, and National Cosmology among Hutu Refugees in Tanzania* (Chicago, 1995).

Mason, Leonard Edward, 'Relocation of the Bikini Marshallese: A Study in Group Migration' (Ph.D. thesis, Yale University, 1954).

Nadel, Alan, *Containment Culture: American Narratives, Postmodernism, and the Atomic Age* (Durham, NC, and London, 1995).

Niedenthal, Jack, *The People of Bikini: From Exodus to Resettlement* (Majuro: Bikini Atoll Local Government, 1996).

For the Good of Mankind: A History of the People of Bikini and their Islands (Micronitor/Bravo Publishers, 2001).

Weisgall, Johnathan M., *Operation Crossroads: The Atomic Tests at Bikini Atoll* (Annapolis, MD, 1994).

ROYAL HISTORICAL SOCIETY
REPORT OF COUNCIL
SESSION 2011–2012

Officers and Council

- At the Anniversary Meeting on 25 November 2011 the Officers of the Society were re-elected.
- The Vice-Presidents retiring under By-law XVII were Professor G W Bernard and Ms J Innes. Professor N A Miller, MA, MPhil, DPhil and Professor A D Pettegree, MA, DPhil were elected in their place.
- The Officer retiring under By-law XV was Professor V Harding, Honorary Secretary. Dr A I P Smith, BA, MA, PhD was elected to replace her.
- The Members of Council retiring under By-law XX were Professor C Given Wilson, Professor M Ormrod, and Dr D Thomas. Dr L Fischer, BA, PhD, Professor P A Williamson, PhD and Professor D R Wootton, MA, PhD were elected in their place.
- The Society's administrative staff consists of Sue Carr, Executive Secretary and Melanie Ransom, Administrative Secretary.
- Kingston Smith were re-appointed auditors for the year 2011–2012 under By-law XXXIX.
- Brewin Dolphin Securities were re-appointed to manage the Society's investment funds.

Activities of the Society during the year

As in previous years, the Society has played a leading role in articulating the interests of the discipline within Higher Education, to government and funding councils, and to the wider society. Through its publication programme and research support, it has also worked to support the work of professional historians, especially postgraduates and early career researchers. The Society's work is carried out largely through sub-committees. Reports from each are below. Two of the sub-committees exist to co-ordinate the Society's policy and advocacy in relation to research and education. As detailed below, these committees have been extremely active this year. Research Policy has monitored, responded and lobbied relevant bodies in relation to the details of the forthcoming

REF, changes to research funding policy, and the proposed 'Open Access' model of publishing among other things. Education Policy has dealt with the continuing fall-out for History Departments from the introduction of some of the highest HE fees in the world. The coalition government has also introduced new policies, or rumours of new policies, in relation to the National Curriculum at primary and Key Stage 3, GCSEs and A Levels. In other words, at all levels of the education system there is upheaval or the threat of it. The Society is determined to represent and advance the interests of history as a discipline and of historians as a profession in all these areas. We believe that there are opportunities as well as threats in the proposed changes, but we will continue to work closely on these issues and build as many contacts as we can with other interested parties.

The other five sub-committees deal with aspects of the Society's internal activities, including the awarding of research grants to postgraduate students and overseeing the Society's publications, which include the *Camden* series of edited texts, the *Studies in History* series of monographs by new authors, the *Bibliography of British and Irish History*, and *Transactions*.

The Society's aim of representing the interests of all parts of the historical profession has been advanced through collaboration with other bodies. Indeed, we believe that without such collaboration, the interests of the discipline cannot be properly defended. We have worked closely with the Historical Association over the issue of the government's proposed A-Level reforms, with the British Academy over 'Open Access', and with History UK across all areas. A successful joint meeting was held with History Lab Plus which represents early career researchers not yet in a permanent post and a representative from History Lab Plus has been co-opted onto Research Committee to ensure that we always hear the voice of an ECR at those meetings. The Society continues to work closely with the IHR and its Director, Professor Miles Taylor. Termly meetings of representatives of the Society, the IHR, the HA, and History UK have been held at the IHR. The Honorary Secretary participated in the interviews for Postgraduate Fellowships at the IHR in June, including the Society's Centenary and Marshall Fellowships. A joint reception was held following the Prothero Lecture on 4 July 2012. Collaboration with TNA and the Institute of Historical Research also continues in the form of the Gerald Aylmer seminar 'Locating the Past', held this year on 29 February at the Institute of Historical Research, focusing on the changing interface between history and geography and new approaches and technologies. We hope to build on these collaborations with other historical organisations in the coming years. As the political environment in which we work continues to change, it may be especially beneficial for the Society to forge links with other Learned Societies in the humanities and social sciences.

Two of the Society's meetings were held outside London, at the University of Glamorgan on 3 November 2011 and the University of Sheffield on 26 April 2012. At Glamorgan, Dr Richard Sugget, Royal Commission and Ancient and Historical Monuments in Wales, presented a sponsored plenary lecture 'Landscape and Mindscapes: Visualising the Historic Environment of late-Medieval and Early-Modern Wales'. The President chaired a plenary session at the symposium sponsored by the Society 'Visualising the Past: History, Heritage and Technology'. At Sheffield, Council members held meetings with academic and research staff and postgraduate research students in the Department of History and the Centre for Peace History, and the visit concluded with a well-received lecture by Professor Phil Withington, University of Cambridge, 'The Semantics of Peace in Early Modern England'.

Council and the Officers record their warm gratitude to the Society's excellent administrative staff: the Executive Secretary, Sue Carr and the Administrative Secretary, Melanie Ransom. We also welcome Jane Gerson to a temporary position while Melanie Ransom is on maternity leave. We thank them all for their expert and dedicated work on the Society's many activities.

RESEARCH POLICY COMMITTEE, 2011–12

Joanna Innes chaired the Committee for its September 2011 meeting, the last one of her dedicated and accomplished three years of service. Nicola Miller chaired the February 2012 meeting and the joint meeting with Teaching Policy Committee held, as in 2011, in July.

The Committee has continued its work of building contacts with the research councils and other research-related institutions, thinking about how to work effectively with the other organisations/societies that represent the historical profession. After support was expressed for co-opting an early career researcher onto the committee, we were delighted to welcome Emily Robinson of History Lab, who joined us for the July meeting and will serve henceforth as a co-opted member.

Research Councils

Relations continued to develop well, building on the work done in previous years. The new Director of Research at AHRC, Professor Mark Llewellyn, attended the joint meeting of Research Policy and Teaching Policy Committees in July. Council received a report on the meeting, which focused on the implications of BGP2, especially for MA funding; the consequences for the discipline of "strategic" research funding; and the importance of working towards establishing more effective mechanisms for meaningful consultation between AHRC and the subject community.

These concerns were also raised at a meeting with Rick Rylance convened by Robin Osborne's Arts and Humanities Users Group (AHUG), held in the Council Room, at which both the RHS and the EHA were represented. Discussions were also held with the Economic History Association to identify shared concerns about the policies of both ESRC and AHRC, notably their 'demand management' strategies; threats to postgraduate funding; the inadequacy of the AHRC Peer Review College. There was concern that the AHRC had difficulty recruiting appropriate people to the college, and over the targeting of AHRC funding toward strategic priorities.

The British Academy

The Committee welcomed the restoration of the Small Grants Scheme, following agreement from government to vire any under-spend on BA Fellowships to this scheme.

The National Archives

Concerns continued to be expressed about the effectiveness of the new catalogue search tool, which has several problems for academic researchers, particularly that it can access only a small percentage of material and offers no online training for research students: essentially it targets entry-level researchers and does little to develop the skills and sophistication of current users. To bring the tool up to professional standard it would benefit from the following additions: a 'search archival description only' key, a browse option for the descriptive catalogue and the online training tools. Ms Innes and Professor Harding expressed willingness to help TNA to develop the tool. Valerie Johnson of TNA gave a report to the February meeting on the new research strategy agreed in the light of limited staffing and reduced budgets; TNA has set out new priorities, in particular the digitisation of archival records and the 20-Year Rule project. It will also look particularly at the effect of digital resources on research and research behaviour.

The British Library

Professor Hitchcock is on the new advisory panel at the BL. Concerns about lack of provision for academic historians, similar to those in relation to TNA, were expressed about the new BL catalogue and its related iPad app. The committee will seek and monitor responses from the community.

The All-Party Parliamentary Group for Archives and History

Good contacts have been developed with this group, which includes Hywel Francis MP, Tristram Hunt MP and Lord Bew. The President and the President-elect Professor Mandler now attend meetings of the group as observers.

REF 2014

The Committee continued to make an active contribution to discussion about REF 2014, doing most of the groundwork that enables the Society to articulate the interests and concerns of members. A very helpful meeting was held in September 2011 with Councillors, Professor Chris Wickham, chair of the History Sub-Panel and invited representatives from other institutes. The RHS responded to the REF consultation document, commending good practice on Panel C as well as raising concerns expressed by Councillors and other members of the profession, especially definitions of 'publication', given the development of electronic media and increasing electronic publication of theses; preference for 'world-leading' rather than 'national' or 'international' excellence; the importance of giving credit for editing; continuing problems with the distinction between evidence of dissemination and evidence of impact. After publication of the Panel Criteria and Working Methods document, the Committee emphasised that there were three aspects of the REF criteria which needed to be communicated clearly to non-historians in university management positions: (i) the relaxed rules on overlap; (ii) the generous rules on the double weighting of books; (iii) the flexible interpretation of evidence needed to demonstrate dissemination of 'impact'.

Research Policy Forum

The Committee discussed the possibility of utilising the RHS website to raise a forum for research policy issues and improve the Committee's presence in the public arena. This idea will be taken forward in the coming year.

Open Access Publishing

In light of the publication of the Finch Report in June 2012, followed by the President's letter to the membership, the possible implications of OA publishing for the historical profession are the subject of ongoing discussions.

EDUCATION POLICY COMMITTEE, 2011–12

The Education Policy Committee considers all aspects of history in education from schools to postgraduate level, although naturally it relies very much on other organizations to take the lead in areas where they have specific expertise – for example, the Historical Association for schools and History UK (HE) for universities. To this end the Committee co-opts representatives from the HA, History UK and the Higher Education Academy, so that it might serve as a meeting-point for the various bodies that share an interest in this area. The Society is grateful to Dr Andrew Foster, Dr Jason Peacey, and Mr Peter D'Sena (HEA Subject Lead for History) and also to Dr Michael Maddison (Ofsted National Adviser for History) for acting in this capacity.

Government proposals to reform the school curriculum dominated the Committee's deliberations this year. At first attention was focused on the national curriculum (to age 14, although some proposals would have extended its purview to age 16). The Society's interest lay particularly in the knock-on effects that reform of the national curriculum might have for History at GCSE and A-Level. However, as it became clear that the national curriculum would not be extended to schools with academy status, and as more secondary schools acquired academy status, the relevance of national-curriculum reform even to government seemed to wane. Attention then shifted to A-Levels. The Secretary of State for Education proposed that universities and learned societies play a much greater role in the development and validation of A-Levels; here the Society's interests were very much at stake, and the Committee has discussed the future of A-Levels extensively with academics, the examination boards, the Historical Association, and others. A formal response was made to the Ofqual consultation on the Secretary of State's proposals over the summer of 2012.

The Committee continues to monitor closely the uptake of History GCSE and A-Level, principally through its annual meeting with representatives of the examination boards for England and Wales, which was held again this year, though now also more regularly and informally with our network of contacts in those boards. The institution of the 'English Baccalaureate' will have effects on the extent and nature of this uptake that the Committee will consider at its next meeting in autumn 2012.

As a result of the Committee's deliberations on school curriculum issues, Council agreed to cosponsor with the Raphael Samuel History Centre and the Historical Association a major national conference on 'History, the Nation and the Schools', which was held at the Bishopsgate Institute in London in July 2012. The conference was organized by Professor Barbara Taylor of the RSHC and the University of East

London, and the Society was delighted to be able to work with Professor Taylor, the RSHG and the HA to help stimulate national debates on History in the school curriculum at a time of rapidly-changing public policy.

The Committee also monitored the effects of the new tuition fee regime on applications for admission to History courses beginning in 2012. History applications dropped 7.4% vs. 2011, almost exactly the average for all subjects. The meeting that the President organized with the Universities Minister, David Willetts, provided an opportunity for representatives of the Society to raise these issues with the Minister and his Chief of Staff.

Concern was also expressed about the effects of the new fee regime on progression to postgraduate study. There was particular anxiety about the prospects of sharp increases in postgraduate fees and about the decision by the Arts and Humanities Research Council to phase out Master's funding and curtail PhD funding. The Society instigated a meeting of learned societies (through the good offices of the Arts and Humanities User Group, organized by Professor Robin Osborne) to discuss these latter cuts with Professor Rick Rylance, chief executive of the AHRC, and the annual joint meeting between the Education and Research Policy Committees in June was held to meet with Professor Mark Llewellyn, the AHRC's director of research. These efforts to convey the high value that all learned societies in the humanities place on the AHRC's investment in postgraduate education seemed to bear fruit, and it was hoped that the Society would continue to cooperate closely with other learned societies in order to provide a clear and united voice for the humanities at a time when fiscal and utilitarian considerations seem to be putting our subjects at a discount.

GENERAL PURPOSES COMMITTEE, 2011–12

The remit of this committee ranges across many activities of the Society. It receives suggestions from Fellows and Council for paper-givers and makes recommendations to Council on the card of session, taking into account the need for a balanced programme in terms of chronological and geographical spread. In addition to the regular sessions held at UCL and outside London, it is also responsible for the Prothero Lecture, the Colin Matthew Lecture and the Gerald Aylmer Seminar.

The programme of lectures and visits for 2012 was confirmed, including visits to Sheffield University in May and the University of Southampton in October. Proposals for 2013 have been discussed and speakers invited. Regional symposia and visits to Bath Spa University and the University of Leeds will take place in 2013. The Committee continues to review the purpose and success of both lectures and visits, and to consider ways of increasing their reach, for example through podcasting and repeat lectures. The Committee was pleased to receive several proposals for regional symposia, and would like to encourage more departments to make such proposals. The 2012 Gerald Aylmer Seminar was held in February on 'Locating the Past' (reported above) and discussions with TNA and the IHR for the 2013 seminar are under way.

The Committee is also responsible for the appointment of assessors for the Society's prizes, and receives their reports and proposals for award winners. It regularly reviews the terms and conditions of the awards. It is grateful to members of Council for their hard work in reading entries and selecting the prize winners. Attracting entries for the Alexander Prize and the Rees Davies Prize continues to be problematic.

This year the Committee has also considered broader administrative and developmental issues aimed at raising the Society's profile within the academic community. Several initiatives have resulted from the questionnaire circulated to the membership. Work on the website and on the database of Fellows and Members, past and present, has continued.

Meetings of the Society

Five papers were given in London this year.

At the ordinary meetings of the Society the following papers were read:

Prothero Lecture: 'History from the Top, from Below – AND from the Middle', Professor Paul Kennedy (29 June 2011)

'The challenger: Hugh Hamilton Lindsay and the rise of British Asia, 1830s-60s' Professor Robert Bickers (23 September 2011)

The Colin Matthew Memorial Lecture for the Public Understanding of History was given on Wednesday 16 November 2011 by Professor Alun Howkins 'A Lark Arising: the rural past and urban histories, 1881–2011'. These lectures continue to be given in memory of the late Professor Colin Matthew, a former Literary Director and Vice-President of the Society.

At the Anniversary Meeting on 25 November 2011, the President, Professor Colin Jones delivered his third address on 'French Crossings III: The Smile of the Tiger'.

'Entrusting Western Europe to the Church, 400–750', Professor Ian Wood (3 February 2012)

'Supernatural Politics in Stalin's Russia and Mao's China', Professor Steve Smith (4 May 2012)

Prizes

The Society's annual prizes were awarded as follows:

The Alexander Prize for 2011 attracted thirteen entries and was awarded to Levi Roach for his article, 'Public Rites and Public Wrongs: Ritual Aspects of Diplomas in Tenth- and Eleventh-Century England', *Early Medieval Europe* 19 (2011), 182–203.

The judges' citation read:

A meticulous and thought-provoking piece of comparative history, this article skilfully analyses Anglo-Saxon diplomas by drawing on insights about medieval ritual that have previously been applied to sources from continental Europe. After a succinct survey of the current historiography, it offers a fascinating account of public rituals of conveyance in ninth- and tenth-century England. Adventurous in the questions it poses, but discriminating in its assessment of what answers the methodological approach adopted can offer, this article is an exemplary addition to the literature on ritual in medieval society. It will be of interest not only to all medievalists but also to historians of any period interested in the ritual aspects of power.

The judges nominated a proxime accessit:

John Sabapathy, 'A Medieval Officer and a Modern Mentality? *Podesta* and the Quality of Accountability', *The Medieval Journal*, 1:2 (2011), 43–79.

The David Berry Prize for an article on Scottish history for 2011 attracted seven entries and was awarded to Aaron M. Allen for his article 'Conquering the Suburbs: Politics and Work in Early Modern Edinburgh', *Journal of Urban History*, 37(3) (2011), 423–443.

The judges' citation read:

The winning article by Aaron M. Allen, entitled, 'Conquering the Suburbs: Politics and Work in Early Modern Edinburgh', stood out for its deftness of expression, fluency and lucidity, in addition to the other qualities which it shared with the rest of the submissions. The article sets the phenomenon of the early modern suburb in its wider European context, and highlights the sharp contrast in meaning between the suburb of today and its counterpart of the early modern era. Far from being a leafy commuter dormitory, the early modern suburb was a scene of lawlessness beyond the reach of municipal jurisdiction; though, by the same token, it was also a place of refuge beyond the rigidities of entrenched civic establishments. Moreover, certain trades tried to evade onerous civic burdens by relocating outside the formal bounds of the city. Suburbs became important elements in the urban economy, though it was sometimes difficult to define the differences between mere suburbs and neighbouring burghs. The article traces the difficulties faced by the Edinburgh authorities in asserting control, by way of obtaining feudal superiority, over nearby burghs of barony and regality. The suburbanization of neighbouring towns was a means of absorbing potential economic rivals. The article is characterised by a patient attention to detail, a rich blend of analysis and illustration, and an outward-looking comparative approach which is the hallmark of the new generation of Scottish historians.

The Whitfield Book Prize for a first book on British history attracted forty-four entries.

The prize for 2011 was awarded to:

Jacqueline Rose for *Godly Kingship in Restoration England: The Politics of the Royal Supremacy, 1660–1688* (Cambridge University Press, 2011).

The judges' citation read:

Godly Kingship is an outstanding book. It is based on deeply impressive research, which establishes the different lines of argument in what are often difficult theological, ecclesiastical, legal and political tracts. Time and again, her readings are rich and sensitive. It has a long (and appropriate) chronological span, and it offers new interpretations of central historical problems. As well as the main argument about the large implications of the royal supremacy and its flexible and disputed qualities, it has numerous particular interpretations that will variously engage historians of the Reformation, the Elizabethan and early Stuart periods, the Interregnum, the Restoration and 1688, and historians of religion, the churches, politics, ideas and the law. It offers the most compelling account yet of the 'long Reformation'. This is a book which is already influencing historical discussions. More importantly, it has the breadth, assurance and insight to ensure that it will be a book of substantial and enduring significance.

The judges nominated a proxime accessit:

Helen Jacobsen for *Luxury and Power: The Material World of the Stuart Diplomat, 1660–1714* (Oxford University Press, 2011).

The Gladstone Book Prize for a first book on non-British history attracted sixteen entries.

The Prize for 2011 was awarded to:

Wendy Ugolini for *Experiencing War as the 'Enemy Other': Italian Scottish Experience in World War II* (Manchester University Press, 2011).

The judges' citation read:

This book explores the phenomenon of 'hybrid identity', of belonging to two cultures which are at war with each other, in this case second generation Italian migrants in Scotland in the Second World War. The Italians had brought ice-cream parlours and, so the author argues, fish and chip shops to Scotland and many of their sons fought in the British Armed Forces. But their shop windows were broken and they were vilified as fascists when war broke out. In June 1940 internment was introduced and twenty per cent of the Scottish-Italian community of 5000 was locked up. Weeks later the *Andora Star*, a liner which had been converted into a troop ship to transport the internees across the Atlantic, was sunk on its voyage to Canada. Over four hundred Italian internees from Scotland were drowned. Wendy Ugolini examines the impact of this tragedy on the Scottish Italians themselves and on their neighbours. Using interviews with 45 members of the community, she looks at the role of Italian and *fasci* clubs in the 1930s and the increased suspicion of all things Italian which developed early in the war. The book contrasts personal narratives with national and local government records, secret service reports and newspapers to paint an informative and detailed account of the lives of one small alien community. In so doing it adds another dimension to our knowledge of social interaction and identity in the Second World War.

The judges nominated a proxime accessit:

Tim Grady for *The German-Jewish Soldiers of the First World War in History and Memory* (Liverpool University Press, 2011).

The Society's Rees Davies Essay Prize for the best article based on a conference paper delivered by a recipient of a Royal Historical Society travel grant attracted seven entries.

No prize was awarded in 2011.

In order to recognise the high quality of work now being produced at undergraduate level in the form of third-year dissertations, the Society continued, in association with *History Today* magazine, to award an annual prize for the best undergraduate dissertation. Departments are asked to nominate annually their best dissertation and a joint committee of the Society and *History Today* select in the autumn the national prizewinner from among these nominations. The prize also recognizes the Society's close relations with *History Today* and the important role the magazine has played in disseminating scholarly research to a wider audience. Thirty submissions were made.

The Prize for 2011 was awarded to:

Richard Lowe-Lauri (University of Durham) for his essay *The Decline of the Stamford Bull-Running, c. 1788–1849.*

An article by the prize-winner presenting his research will appear in *History Today* in 2012.

The German History Society, in association with the Society, agrees to award a prize to the winner of an essay competition. The essay, on any aspect of German history, including the history of German-speaking people both within and beyond Europe, was open to any postgraduate registered for a degree in a university in either the United Kingdom or the Republic of Ireland. No prizewinner was announced in 2011.

The Frampton and Beazley Prizes for A-level performances in 2011 were awarded to the following nominations from the examining bodies:

Frampton Prize:

OCR: Kishan Koria (Kent College, Canterbury)
AQA: Helena Kipling (Parkstone Grammar School, Dorset)

Beazley Prize:

CEA: Andrew Henderson (Banbridge Academy, Belfast)
SQA: Alice Williamson (George Watson's College, Edinburgh)

The Director of the Institute of Historical Research announced the winners of the Pollard Prize 2011 awarded annually to the best postgraduate student paper presented in a seminar at the IHR, and the Sir

John Neale Prize for the best essay on the study of 16th century England by a postgraduate student. The Pollard Prize for 2011 was awarded jointly to Samantha Sagui for her paper on 'The Hue and Cry in English Towns', and Christopher Dillon for his paper on '"Tolerance Means Weakness": the Dachau Concentration Camp SS, Militarism, and Masculinity'. The articles will appear in *Historical Research* in 2013. The Sir John Neale Prize for 2011 was awarded to Victoria Smith for her essay 'The Elizabethan Succession Question in Roger Edwardes's "Castra Regia" (1569) and "Cista Pacis Anglie"(1576)'.

PUBLICATIONS COMMITTEE, 2011–12

The Publications Committee remains responsible for the ongoing programme. Professor Arthur Burns represents the Society's interests on the *Studies in History* Editorial Board, while Dr Ian Archer edits *Transactions*, and they share responsibility for Camden volumes. Professor Stephen Taylor is Honorary Academic Editor of the Bibliography of British and Irish History (BBIH).

In 2012 the Bibliography of British and Irish History (BBIH) celebrated its 10th anniversary as an on-line resource. The project has continued to develop smoothly, thanks largely to the work of Peter Salt, Simon Baker and the team of academic section editors – close to 15,000 records have again been added to the database over the past twelve months and minor improvements have been made to the user interface. The most significant developments have been the offer of a reduced rate subscription for Fellows and Members of the Society and the creation of a Project Board. The latter, chaired by Professor Phillip Schofield of Aberystwyth University brings together the academic project team, Brepols (our publisher) and representatives of various user groups to provide feedback and advice on the future development of the Bibliography.

Transactions, Sixth Series, Volume 21 was published during the session, and *Transactions*, Sixth Series, Volume 22 went to press.

In the Camden, Fifth Series, *The Making of the East London Mosque, 1910–1951*, ed. Humayun Ansari (vol. 38), *The Papers of the Hothams: Governors of Hull during the Civil War*, ed. Andrew Hopper (vol. 39) and *A Monastic Community in Local Society: the Beauchief Cartulary*, eds, David Luscombe, David Hey and Lisa Liddy (vol. 40) were published during the session. Ansari's volume was launched at a well attended reception at the East London Mosque, at which all the copies of the volume on the publisher's stand were sold, indicating the level of interest in the local community in this particular volume, which both in subject matter and period represents an important development for the series. The Society continues to receive excellent proposals for editions of texts for all periods, with the twentieth century now beginning to generate a significant number among them. The inclusion of the Camden series within the online resources made available by Cambridge University Press has seen the volumes reach new audiences worldwide; the Committee will seek to work with the publishers to develop the full potential of this resource in the coming years.

Documents on Conservative Foreign Policy, 1852–1878, eds, Geoff Hicks, John Charmley and Bendor Grosvenor (vol. 41), and *The Diary of Robert Woodford, 1637–1641*, ed., John Fielding (vol. 42) went to press for publication in 2012–13.

The *Studies in History* Editorial Board continued to meet throughout the year. The Second Series continues to produce exciting and widely discussed volumes (one of the 2011 titles, Samantha Williams' *Poverty, Gender and Life-Cycle under the English Poor Law, 1760–1834*, attained the distinction of featuring on the *Today* programme on BBC Radio 4). Professor Hannah Barker and Professor Alex Walsham retired from and Dr Selina Todd and Professor Alec Ryrie joined the Editorial Board. The following volumes went to press during the session for publication in 2012–13:

o *The Local Church and Generational Change: Mainstream Christianity in Birmingham, c. 1945–1998*, Ian Jones
o *Chasing Pirates: the War at Sea in Ireland, 1641–1653*, Elaine Murphy

As in previous subscription years, volumes in the *Studies in History* Series were offered to the membership at a favourably discounted price. Many Fellows, Associates and Members accepted the offer for volumes published during the year, and the advance orders for further copies of the volumes to be published in the year 2012–2013 were encouraging. Boydell and Brewer's decision to republish a number of volumes in a paperback format has proved extremely successful and it is intended to extend the selection from the backlist that will be made available in this form. Next year will see some of the series become available as e-publications for the first time.

The series has a considerable number of manuscripts under development with their authors for publication, and continues to receive a steady flow of high-quality proposals. During the course of the year it was decided that the Society should offer its authors a contract at an earlier stage in the development of their volumes in recognition of the importance of commitments to the career prospects of many early career scholars.

The Society acknowledges its gratitude for the continuing subventions from the Economic History Society and the Past and Present Society to the *Studies in History* series.

Finance

FINANCE COMMITTEE 2011–12

The Finance Committee approves the Society's accounts each financial year and its estimates for the following year. This year, as before, the accounts were professionally audited by Kingston Smith. They are presented elsewhere in *Transactions*, together with the Trustees' Annual Report. Since that report discusses the main financial developments of the year, there is little more to say here.

The Society's expenditure was broadly in line with estimates. Income was much higher than anticipated, however, largely due a greater than expected income from the joint publishing agreement with Cambridge University Press (due to on-going sales of the new digital archive). The Society is declaring a surplus of £100,107 for the year 2011–12.

The Society has run a surplus for a number of years, which has allowed it to build up a significant cash reserve. The Finance Committee recognises that the coming years will be much more challenging financially than recent years, particularly as income from the digitisation component of the publishing agreement with Cambridge University Press declines sharply. It is for this reason that the Society anticipates continuing to hold a substantial cash reserve in the expectation that it will be drawn down in future years to cover a series of planned in-year deficits.

The value of the Society's investments rose to £2.36 millions in June 2012, a decline from the previous year's figure of £2.54 million. The total return was below the APCIMS Balanced (Total Return) index against which performance is benchmarked. The issue has been extensively discussed by Finance Committee and with the fund managers (Brewin Dolphin). The Society's portfolio is invested for the long-term and members of Finance Committee are confident that the current spread of investments is appropriate. Dividend income increased in 2011–12.

The Society introduced a new system of identifying and weighting risk during the year. Each meeting of Finance Committee considers whether the current risk assessment - on matters both financial and non-financial - is appropriate (and reports accordingly to Council).

- Council records with gratitude the benefactions made to the Society by:
  - Dr G Bakker
  - Professor T B Barry
  - Professor R P Bartlett
  - Professor D R Bates
  - Mr J Berg
  - The Bibliographical Society
  - Dr G F Burgess
  - Dr J T Cliff
  - Professor C R Cole
  - Dr P Cunich
  - Professor P J Dennis
  - Economic History Society

- Professor Sir Geoffrey Elton
- Dr M H Fitzpatrick
- Professor D H Francis
- Dr I A Gregg
- Dr R P Hallion
- Miss B F Harvey
- Miss V London
- Dr P C Lowe
- Dr M Lynn
- Professor P Mandler
- Professor P J Marshall
- Dr H M R E Mayr-Harting
- Mr J D Milner
- Dr A M Moatt
- Dr M Morrissey
- Professor H Ono
- Past & Present Society
- Sir George Prothero
- Dr L Rausing
- Miss E M Robinson
- Professor D M Schurman
- Professor D P Smyth
- Dr A F Sutton
- Professor E Treharne
- Mr T V Ward
- Dr F L Wiswall

MEMBERSHIP COMMITTEE 2011–12

The Committee reviews all applications for Fellowship and Membership received by the Society, and makes recommendations to Council. The Committee is keen to encourage applications for Fellowship on the basis of scholarly achievement in history, whose definition is not limited to traditional forms of publication, but also includes, for example, the curatorship of exhibitions and publication in newer media. The Committee is glad to receive applications to join the Society in either the Fellowship or Membership category, and emphasises that it favours a broad view of what constitutes history when assessing candidates.

The Anniversary Meeting in November 2011 approved the introduction of the new category of Emeritus Fellow, to commence in the 2012–13 subscription year. Fellows over the age of seventy-five years or who have forty or more consecutive years of Fellowship of the Society may request to transfer to this category which does not incur a subscription. Emeriti will continue to enjoy the usual benefits of Fellowship with the exception of the annual copy of *Transactions* which may be purchased separately. The number of senior Fellows transferring to this category has been encouraging.

The Committee would also like to draw the attention of supervisors and postgraduate students to the recently introduced category of Postgraduate Member. The first intake of Postgraduate Members started their Membership in the July 2010- June 2011 subscription year. Postgraduate Members apply in the same way as regular Members but if they are current research postgraduates (UK or overseas) they are entitled to their first two years' subscriptions at £10 (with all the same benefits of regular Membership), after which they automatically revert to normal Member status. The discounted first two years still applies even if the students finish their degree during that time. The Society does require proof of postgraduate research student status, but only at the time of election.

The following were elected to the Fellowship:

William J Adam, BA, LLM, PhD
John R Alban, BA, PhD
Dhara Anjaria, BA, PhD
Sarah L T Apetrei, BA, DipTh, MSt, DPhil
Nir Arielli, BA, MA, PhD
Lauren Arrington, BA, MA, DPhil
Bruce E Baker, MA, PhD
Sara K Barker, BA, MA, PhD
Melodee H Beals, BA, MA, PhD
Charles Beem, BA, MA, PhD
Jonathan W Bell, MA, MPhil, PhD
John D Belshaw, BA, MA, PhD
Vivian M Bentinck
Helen Birkett, BA, MA, PhD
Nicholas Black, BA, MA, PhD
Lucy Bland, BA, MA, PhD
Timothy M Boon, BA, MSc, PhD
Karin Bowie, BA, MBA, MPhil, PhD
Charles F Briggs, BA, MLitt, PhD
Linda Bryder, MA, DPhil
Adam Budd, BA, MA, MA, PhD
Tanja Bueltmann, MA, PhD
Garry Campion, BA, PhD
Jane Caplan, BA, MA, DPhil
Augustine Casiday, PhD
Arthur J Chapman, MPhil, MA, EdD
Arianne Chernock, BA, MA, PhD
Marcus Collins, BA, MA, MPhil, PhD
Viccy Coltman, BA, MA, PhD

Andrew P Connell, MA, MSc, PhD
Marie-Louise Coolahan, BA, MPhil, PhD
Robert Crowcroft, BA, MA, PhD
John E Crowley, AB, MA, PhD
Gordon D Cumming, MA, PhD
Ian G d'Alton, BA, MA, PhD
James Davis, BA, MPhil, PhD
Denis De Lucca, BA, BArch, PhD
Joanne C Fox, BA, PhD
David H Francis, BA, PhD
Matthew Frank, BA, MSt, DPhil
Peter D Funnell, BA, DPhil
Andrea Gamberini, BA, MA, PhD
Perry Gauci, BA, MPhil, DPhil
Travis F Glasson, BA, MA, PhD
Graham D Goodlad, MA, PhD
Drew D Gray, BA, PhD
Madeleine Gray, BA, PhD
Richard S Grayson, BA, DPhil
Gerwyn L H Griffiths, LLB, MPhil, PhD
Benjamin Grob-Fitzgibbon, BA, MA, PhD
Anna Groundwater, MA, MSc, PhD
David I Grummitt, BA, MA, PhD
Christopher G Harding, BA, MSt, DPhil
Philip Harling, PhD
Rhodri L Hayward, BA, MSc, PhD
Martin R V Heale, BA, MPhil, PhD
Padhraig Higgins, BA, PhD
Douglas B Hindmarsh, BA, MA, DPhil
Eva J Holmberg, PhD
Victoria C Honeyman, BA, MA, PhD
Peter G Hore
Louise A Jackson, BA, MA, PhD
Sam Johnson, BA, PhD
John Johnson-Allen, MA
Clive A R Jones, BA, MA, PhD
Robert W Jones, BA, MA, PhD
Nicholas E Karn, MSt, MA, DPhil
Karly Kehoe, BA, PhD
Torrance Kirby, BA, MA, DPhil
Laurence S Kirkpatrick, BA, BD, PhD
Robert G Knight, BA, PhD
Peter Kruschwitz, MA, PhD
Tom O Licence, MA, MPhil, PhD
Max Lieberman, MSt, DPhil

Benno Lowe, BA, MA, PhD
Catriona Macdonald, MA, PGCE, PhD
Graham D Macklin, BA, PhD
Giacomo Macola, PCCHE, PhD
John Maiden, BA, PhD
Patrick N Major, BA, DPhil
Alexander J Marr, BA, MSt, DPhil
Annalisa Marzano, MPhil, PhD
John McAleer, BA, MA, PhD
Helen McCarthy, MA, MA, PhD
Shane McCorristine, BA, MA, PhD
Irina V Metzler, BA, MA, PhD
Alexander Mikaberidze, LLB, MA, PhD
Alexander S Morrison, MA, DPhil
Mary Morrissey, BA, MLitt, PhD
Adam Mosley, MA, MPhil, PhD
Paul M Mulvey, BA, MA, PhD
Katrina Navickas, BA, MSt, DPhil
Tillman W Nechtman, BSc, MA, MA, PhD
Elizabeth A New, BA, MA, PhD
Thomas A O'Donoghue, BA, MA, MEd, PhD
Kendrick J Oliver, BA, PhD
Tudor Parfitt, MA, DPhil
Helen J Paul, MA, MLitt, PhD
Sharrona H Pearl, PhD
Sarah M S Pearsall, BA, MA, MA, PhD
Catriona L Pennell, BA, MSc, PhD
Michael R Peplar, BA, MA, PhD
Andrew J Prescott, BA, PhD
Mark E Purcell, BA, MA
Paul Quigley, BA, MA, PhD
Sadiah Qureshi, BA, MA, MPhil, PhD
Gianluca Raccagni, MPhil, PhD
David A Redvaldsen, BA, MA, PhD
Colin W Reid, BA, MA, PhD
Antony D Rich, BSc, BA, PhD
Diane Robinson-Dunn, PhD
Jacqueline E Rose, BA, MPhil, PhD
James A Ross, BA, MSt, DPhil
Lynette Russell, BA, PhD
Judith R Ryder, MA, MPhil, DPhil
Kay Schiller, MA, PhD
Nicholas J Schofield, STB, MA
William F Sheehan, BA, MA, PhD
Stephen M Sheppard, BA, JD, LLM, MLitt, JSD

James Siemens, BA, BTh, MDiv, PhD, LicDD
Adam I P Smith, BA, MA, PhD
Sarah B Snyder, PhD
George Southcombe, BA, MSt, DPhil
Tracey A Sowerby, BA, MSt, DPhil
Jonathan W Spangler, BA, MSt, DPhil
Dionysios Stathakopoulos, MA, PhD
Philip J Stern, BA, MA, MPhil, PhD
Matthew F Stevens, BA, PhD
Gareth Stockey, MA, MA, PhD
Simon R S Szreter, MA, PhD
Brian R Talbot, BA, BD, PhD
Jeremy Taylor, BA, BA, PhD
Nicklaus Thomas-Symonds, MA, PgDipLaw, BVC
Malcolm Thurlby, BA, PhD
Hakeem I Tijani, BA, MA, MPhil, PhD
Mark Towsey, MA, MLitt, PhD
Elaine Treharne, BA, MArAd, PhD
Robert L Tyler, BA, PGCE, MA, PhD
Laura Ugolini, BA, MA, PhD
Wendy Ugolini, BA, MA, PhD
Andrew Vincent, BA, PhD
Bryan Ward-Perkins, BA, DPhil
Giles Waterfield, BA, MA
Jennifer A Weir, BA, PhD
Emily R West, BA, MA, PhD
Samantha K Williams, BA, MSc, PhD
Tim Wilson, BA, MA, DPhil
Alun R Withey, BA, MA, PhD
Matthew J Wright, BA, BA, MA
Nigel G Wright, BA, BD, MTh, PhD
Margaret Yates, BA, DPhil
Jonathan Yeager, BA, MCA, ThM, PhD
Natalie A Zacek, BA, MA, PhD
Eric Zuelow, BA, MA, PhD

The following were announced in the Queen's Honours Lists during the year:

Professor Diarmaid MacCulloch – Fellow – KBE for Services to Scholarship
Professor Richard J Evans – Fellow – KBE for Services to Scholarship

Council was advised of and recorded with regret the deaths of 1 Honorary Vice-President, 11 Fellows, 14 Retired Fellows, 2 Corresponding Fellows and 1 Associate.

Mr J S Appleby – Fellow
Professor J M Bean – Fellow
Dr P F Brandon – Fellow
Mr G R Bussey – Retired Fellow
Dr M Chibnall, FBA – Retired Fellow
Professor P Collinson – Honorary Vice-President
Professor J P Cornford – Fellow
Dr A F Cowan – Retired Fellow
Professor F M Crouzet – Corresponding Fellow
Professor C M Crowder – Retired Fellow
Dr M J C Dowling - Fellow
Mr J P W Ehrman – Retired Fellow
Mrs S J Gurney – Associate
Professor N Hampson, FBA – Retired Fellow
Dr M Heppell – Retired Fellow
Professor K Honeyman - Fellow
Professor S W Jackman – Retired Fellow
Dr R J Lee – Fellow
Dr P C Lowe – Retired Fellow
Dr P H Lyon – Fellow
Professor W H Maehl – Retired Fellow
Reverend Dr J C A Mantle – Fellow
Professor R B McDowell – Retired Fellow
Professor J M Powell – Corresponding Fellow
Professor W Rodney – Retired Fellow
Professor K M Sharpe – Fellow
Rt Reverend Dr K W Stevenson – Fellow
Professor R B Tate – Retired Fellow
Miss J A Youings – Retired Fellow

Over the year ending on 30 June 2012, 154 Fellows and 119 Members were elected, and the total membership of the Society on that date was 3,209 (including 1,980 Fellows, 691 Retired Fellows, 14 Honorary Vice-Presidents, 79 Corresponding and Honorary Fellows, 41 Associates and 404 Members).

The Society exchanged publications with 15 societies, British and foreign.

Representatives of the Society

- The representation of the Society upon other various bodies was as follows:
  - Dr Julia Crick on the Joint Committee of the Society and the British Academy established to prepare an edition of Anglo-Saxon charters;

o Professor Claire Cross on the Council of the British Association for Local History; and on the British Sub-Commission of the Commission Internationale d' Histoire Ecclesiastique Comparée;

o Professor Colin Jones on the board of the Panizzi Foundation and the Advisory Council of the Committee for the Export of Objects of Cultural Interest;

o Professor Chris Whatley on the Court of the University of Stirling

o Professor V Harding on the Board of the British Records Association

Grants

RESEARCH SUPPORT COMMITTEE, 2011–12:

The Committee met five times in the course of the year to distribute research funds to early career historians (primarily research students but also recent PhDs not yet in full-time employment) through a process of peer review. In total, the Committee made 115 awards to researchers at over forty UK institutions, of which 15 grants were to support research within the UK, 35 to support research outside the UK, 33 to support attendance at conferences to deliver papers, 31 to allow conference organisers to subsidise attendance of early career researchers at their events and one (the Martin Lynn Scholarship) to support research within Africa. The topics funded by the Committee demonstrate the Society's contribution to the full spectrum of sub-fields within the discipline of History as well as to interdisciplinary research with a substantial historical component. Successful applicants' end-of-award reports confirm that RHS funding significantly enhances early career researchers' opportunities to conduct original archival research and to hone their ensuing dissertation chapters and first publications through participation in national and international workshops and conferences. The calibre of applicants continues to be high: the supply of fundable applications consistently and significantly exceeds our available funding.

In last year's report, the committee noted that recent and impending reductions of research funding at both university and Research Council-level would place increasing pressures on its resources. To respond to this increased demand, the Society augmented the committee's annual allocation by £5,000 and sought additional external funding for its research support activities. We are delighted to report that two generous subventions have been received for this purpose. *History Workshop Journal* has awarded the Society a £5,000 subvention for each of the next two years, with priority to be given to 'self-funding' PhD students (that is, doctoral students who are not in receipt of a full fees and maintenance award for their studies). The *Past & Present* Society has awarded the RHS a three-year annual subvention of £5,000, a sum which will allow us to expand our funding of early career researchers regardless of nationality. Together these two generous and timely awards will significantly enhance the Research Support Committee's ability to foster the growth of the profession by investing in the next generation of historians.

The Royal Historical Society Centenary Fellowship was awarded in the academic year 2011–2012 to Roberta Cimino (University of St Andrews) for research on 'Italian queens in the ninth and tenth centuries'.

The Society's P J Marshall Fellowship was awarded in the academic year 2011–2012 to Anish Vanaik (Balliol College, Oxford) for research on 'Changing the plot: Property Relations in Colonial Delhi, 1857–1`920'.

Travel to Conferences (Training Bursaries)

- Jason Berg, University of Leeds
  Histories on the Margin: Contemporary Approaches to Conceptualizing the 'Other', Alberta, 1st-2nd March 2012
- Alexander Berland, University of Nottingham
  International Conference of Historical Geographers, Prague, Czech Republic, 6th-10th August 2012
- Richard Blakemore, University of Cambridge
  6th International Congress of Maritime History, Gent, Belgium, 2nd-6th July 2012
- Anna Bocking-Welch, University of York
  North American Conference on British Studies, Denver, Colorado, 18th-20th November 2011
- Charles Bow, University of Edinburgh
  Eighteenth Century Scottish Studies Society Annual Conference 2011, University of Aberdeen, 7th-10th July 2011
- Sophie Brockmann, University of Cambridge
  XVIth World Economic History Congress, Stellenbosch, South Africa, 9th-13th July 2012
- Erica Buchberger, University of Oxford
  International Congress on Medieval Studies, Kalamazoo, 10th-13th May 2012
- Lise Butler, University of Oxford
  Empire and International History: The 4th Annual Postgraduate Intensive, Sydney, Australia, 26th-27th July 2012
- William Carruthers, University of Cambridge
  8th Science and Technology in the European Periphery Meeting, Corfu, Greece, 21st-25th June 2012
- Sarah Chaney, UCL
  Body and Mind in the History of Medicine and Health, Utrecht, 1st-4th September 2011
- Nathalie Chernoff, Lancaster University

119th American Psychological Association Annual Convention, Washington, DC, 4th-7th August 2011

o Eleanor Davey, Queen Mary, University of London
International Conference on Human Rights and the Humanities, Beirut, 9th-11th May 2012

o Lucinda Dean, University of Stirling
Kings and Queens: Politics, Power, Patronage and Personalities in Medieval and Early Modern Monarchy, Corsham Court, 19th-20th April 2012

o Virginia Dillon, University of Oxford
News in Early Modern Europe, Sussex, 5th-7th June 2012

o Val Dufeu, University of Stirling
International Medieval Congress, Leeds, 9th-12th July 2012

o Joanne Edge, Royal Holloway, University of London
Science and the Occult: From Antiquity through the Early Modern Period, 2012, Purdue University, Indiana, 20th-21st April 2012

o David Feller, University of Cambridge
North American Conference on British Studies, Denver, Colorado, 18th-20th November 2011

o Gergely Gallai, University of Southampton
14th International Congress of Medieval Canon Law, Toronto, Canada, 5th-11th August 2012

o Mark Hailwood, IHR
North American Conference on British Studies, Denver, Colorado, 18th-20th November 2011

o Alexander Hall, University of Manchester
North American Conference on British Studies, Denver, Colorado, 18th-20th November 2011

o Eilidh Harris, University of St Andrews
Leeds International Medieval Congress, Leeds, 9th-12th July 2012

o David Hary, University of Bristol
Religious Men in the Middle Ages, Huddersfield, 6th-8th July 2012

o Liam Haydon, University of Manchester
Renaissance Old Worlds, London, 29th June – 1st July 2012

o Alexander Hodgkins, University of Leeds
Sixteenth Century Society Conference, Fort Worth, Texas, 27th-30th October 2011

o Samantha Hughes-Johnson, Birmingham City University
The 58th Annual Meeting of the Renaissance Society of America, Washington D.C., 22nd-24th March 2012

o Laure Humbert, University of Exeter
East-West Cultural Exchanges During the Cold War, Jyvaskyla, Finland, 14th-16th June 2012

o Simon Huxtable, Birkbeck, University of London

Association for Slavonic, East European and Eurasian Studies Annual Conference, Washington D.C., 17th-20th November 2011

o Aaron Jaffer, University of Warwick
  Community and the Sea in the Age of Sail, Aalborg, Denmark, 24th-25th May 2012

o Olesya Khromeychuk, UCL
  Association for Slavic, East European and Eurasian Studies, Washington, DC, 17th-20th November 2011

o Kimberley Knight, University of St Andrews
  Religious Men in the Middle Ages, Huddersfield, 6th-8th July 2012

o Marie-Louise Leonard, University of Glasgow
  International Congress on Medieval Studies, Kalamazoo, 10th-13th May 2012

o Eilidh Macrae, University of Glasgow
  North American Society for Sport History, California, 1st-4th June 2012

o Jessica Moody, University of York
  Slavery and Memory Sessions: American Association of Geographers Annual Conference, New York, 24th-28th February 2012

o Margery Masterson, University of Bristol
  Race, Nation and Empire on the Victorian Popular Stage, Lancaster, 11th-14th July 2012

o Stephen Miles, University of Glasgow
  International Geographical Union Pre-Conference Symposium, Trier, Germany, 22nd-25th August 2012

o Catriona Murray, University of Edinburgh
  The 58th Annual Meeting of the Renaissance Society of America, Washington D.C., 22nd-24th March 2012

o Raluca Musat, UCL
  European Social Science History Conference 2012, Glasgow, 11th-14th April 2012

o Christian O'Connell, Heidelberg Spring Academy, Heidelberg, 26th-30th March 2012

o Ben Offiler, University of Nottingham
  Continuity and Change in US Presidential Foreign Policy: Plans, Policies and Doctrines, Salzburg, 6th-10th October 2011

o Kenneth Parker, Royal Holloway, University of London
  Eighth Quadrennial Conference of the Society for the Study of the Crusades and the Latin East, Caceres, Spain, 25th-29th June 2012

o Laura Paterson, University of Dundee
  Social History Society Annual Conference, Brighton, 3rd-5th April 2012

o Emily Rootham, Glasgow Caledonian University
  European Conference on Educational Research 2011, Berlin, 13th-16th September 2011

o Melania Savino, SOAS

Cultures of Curating: Curatorial Practices and the Production of Meaning 1650–2000, Lincoln, 12th-13th July 2012

o Louise Seaward, University of Leeds
'Communities and Networks' – Annual Meeting of the American Historical Association, Chicago, 5th-8th January 2012

o Samantha Shave, University of Sussex
European Social Science History Conference 2012, Glasgow, 11th-14th April 2012

o Daniel Smith, UCL
Reading Conference in Early Modern Studies, University of Reading, 18th-20th July 2011

o Nimrod Tal, University of Oxford
The Legacy of the Civil War: An Interdisciplinary Conference, Philadelphia, 10th-12th November 2011

o Steven Taylor, University of Leicester
Social History Society Annual Conference, Brighton, 3rd-5th April 2012

o Laura Tompkins, University of St Andrews
International Medieval Congress, Leeds, 9th-12th July 2012.

o Martha Vandrei, King's College London
North American Conference on British Studies, Denver, Colorado, 18th-20th November 2011

o Caroline Watkinson, Queen Mary, University of London
North American Conference on British Studies, Denver, Colorado, 18th-20th November 2011

o Christopher Webb, University of Huddersfield
International Oral History Conference 2012, Buenos Aires, Argentina, 4th-7th September 2012

o Reza Zia-Ebrahimi, University of Oxford
9th Biennial Iranian Studies Conference, Istanbul, Turkey, 1st-5th August 2012.

Research Expenses Within the United Kingdom

o William Arthur, University of Oxford
Archives in London, August – October 2011

o Lise Butler, University of Oxford
Archives in Glasgow, Cambridge, Brighton and London, May – June 2012.

o Miriam Cady, University of Leicester
Archives in Doncaster, Carlisle, Penrith and London, September – October 2011

o Derek Elliott, University of Cambridge
Archives in London, July – September 2011

o Claire Fetherstonhaugh, University of Cambridge

Archives in London, 24th July – 21st August 2011

- Chikara Hashimoto, Aberystwyth University
  Archives in London, Cambridge, Oxford and Coventry, November 2011 – February 2012
- Mark King, University of Cambridge
  Archives in London, January – February 2012
- Shivan Mahendrarajah, University of Cambridge
  Archives in London and Oxford 2012
- Brant Moscovitch, University of Oxford
  Archives in London and Hull, October – December 2011
- Cai Parry-Jones, Bangor University
  Archives and interviews in Wrexham and Welshpool, January – February 2012
- Helen Rajabi, University of Manchester
  Archives in London and Aberystwyth, October – November 2011
- Helen Walsh, Manchester Metropolitan University
  Archives and interviews in London and Bognor Regis, August 2011
- Tracey Wedge, University of Southampton
  Archives in London, March 2012

Research Expenses Outside the United Kingdom

- George Adamson, University of Brighton
  Archives in India
- Judith Allan, University of Birmingham
  Archives in Florence, Italy, June 2012
- Lida Barner, UCL
  Archives in Russia, February 2012
- Emily Baughan, University of Bristol
  Archives in California, USA, October 2012
- Andras Becker, University of Southampton
  Archives in the USA, 1st-14th September 2011
- Eliud Biegon, University of Cambridge
  Archives and interviews in Datoga, Tanzania, December 2012.
- Kristin Bourassa, University of York
  Archives in Paris and Chantilly, France, and Vienna, Austria, July – August 2012
- Denis Clark, University of Oxford
  Archives in the USA, France and Poland, January – March 2012
- William Carruthers, University of Cambridge
  Archives in Egypt, 5th September 2011 – 30th June 2012
- Tamina Chowdhury, University of Cambridge
  Archives in New Delhi and Kolkata, India, June – September 2012
- William Coleman, UCL

Archives in Washington, D.C., March – May 2012
- Mark Condos, University of Cambridge
  Archives in New Delhi, Chandigarh and London, September 2011 –
  January 2012
- Katie Crone Barber, University of Sheffield
  Archives in the USA, 1st-30th September 2011
- Tom Cutterham, University of Oxford
  Archives in the USA, September 2011
- Stephen Dean, King's College London
  Archives in Ireland and the UK, February 2012
- Karst de Jong, Queen's University Belfast
  Archives in Jamaica, October 2012
- Stephanie Derrick, University of Stirling
  Archives in Wheaton and New York, 23rd February – 17th March 2012
- James Doherty, University of Southampton
  Archives in Dublin, Ireland and Belfast, Northern Ireland, May – June
  2012.
- Josette Duncan, University of Warwick
  Archives in Greece, October 2011
- Emma Folwell, University of Leicester
  Archives in Mississippi, May – June 2012
- Oliver Godsmark, University of Leeds
  Archives in India, January – April 2012
- Allison Goudie, University of Oxford
  Archives in Naples, Autumn 2011
- Giovanni Graglia, LSE
  Archives in Rome, 19th-31st March 2012
- Rachel Hoffman, University of Cambridge
  Archives in Berlin, November 2011
- Jack Hogan, University of Kent
  Archives and interviews in Zambia, August – November 2011
- Simon John, Swansea University
  Archives in France, December 2011
- Iain Johnston, University of Cambridge
  Archives in Canada, September 2011
- Nicola Kindersley, University of Durham
  Archives in Amsterdam, 1st-14th April 2012
- Michael Martin, King's College London
  Archives and interviews in Kabul, Afghanistan, May 2012.
- Ruth Martin, University of Cambridge
  Archives in the USA, 5th-16th September 2011
- Julia McClure, University of Sheffield
  Archives in Spain, 1st-19th August 2011

- Aaron McGaughey, University of Nottingham
  Archives in Finland and Russia, June – September 2012
- Stephen McNair, University of Edinburgh
  Archives, interviews and site visits in the USA, April – May 2012
- Christopher Minty, University of Stirling
  Archives in New York, 4th-15th June 2012
- James Perkins, Birkbeck College, University of London
  Archives in Montreal, Canada, September 2012.
- Catherine Porter, University of Cambridge
  Archives and interviews in Katanga Province, Democratic Republic of Congo, July-October 2012
- Mindaugas Sapoka, University of Aberdeen
  Archives in Poland, December 2011 – March 2012
- Teresa Segura-Garcia, University of Cambridge
  Archives in India, 9th October – 20th December 2011
- Carin Peller Semmens, University of Sussex
  Archives in the USA, 25th April – 5th June 2012
- Spike Sweeting, University of Warwick
  Archives in New Haven, Boston and Philadelphia, 28th May – 16th June 2012
- Declan Taggart, University of Aberdeen
  Manuscript Studies, Eighth International Summer School, Reykjavik, 10th-18th August 2011
- Edward Teversham, University of Oxford
  Archives and interviews in Skukuza and Bushbuckridge, South Africa, June – July 2012
- Darshi Thoradeniya, University of Warwick
  Archives in the USA, 29th August – 19th September 2011
- Jennifer Tomlinson, University of York
  Archives in France, January – July 2012
- Justine Trombley, University of St Andrews
  Archives in Italy, March 2012
- Pheroze Unwalla, SOAS
  Archives in Turkey, January – April 2012
- Danelle Van Zyl-Hermann, University of Cambridge
  Archives and interviews in Somerset West and Cape Town, South Africa, July – September 2012
- Joanna Warson, University of Portsmouth
  Archives in Aix-en-Provence, France, September 2012
- Michael Weatherburn, Imperial College, London
  Archives in New York, New Jersey, Maryland and Ottawa, 1st-27th May 2012
- Harriett Webster, University of Bristol

Archives in France, 2nd-8th September 2011
- Katherine Weikert, University of Winchester
  Site visits in Normandy, France, July 2012
- Elliott Weiss, UCL
  Archives in Pennsylvania and Illinois, USA, June 2012
- Fiona Whelan, University of Oxford
  Archives in France, January 2012
- Rachael Whitbread, University of York
  Archives in Paris, France, June 2012
- Naomi Wood, University of Warwick
  Archives in Pennsylvania, USA, September 2012
- Larysa Zariczniak, University of Exeter
  Archives and interviews in Kiev and Lviv, Ukraine, June 2012

Conference Organisation (Workshops)

- Rabah Aissaoui
  Algeria Revisited: Contested Identities in the Colonial and Postcolonial Periods, University of Leicester, 11th-13th April 2012
- Harriet Archer
  The Mirror for Magistrates, 1559–1946, Magdalen College, Oxford, 14th-15th September 2012
- Lucy Bland
  'Looking Back – Looking Forward': The Twentieth Annual Women's History Network Conference, The Women's Library, 9th-11th September 2011
- Mike Carr
  The Writing of Medieval History: Debates, Definitions and Approaches, Senate House, London, 15th June 2012
- Lucinda Dean
  Representations of Authority to 1707: Scotland and her Nearest Neighbours, University of Stirling, 20th-21st August 2012
- Sylvia Gill
  22nd Annual Conference of the European Reformation Research Group, University of Durham, 3rd-4th September 2012
- Craig Griffiths
  What is LGBT(Q) History and where do we stand? History Postgraduates and LGBT History, Queen Mary, University of London, 7th November 2012
- Kate Hill
  Cultures of Curating: Curatorial Practices and the Production of Meaning c.1650–2000, University of Lincoln, 12th-13th July 2012
- Jonathan Lawrence

Research Colloquium on the Secondary Analysis of British Social Survey Data, Emmanuel College, Cambridge, 7th-8th September 2012
o Eilidh Macrae
Fresh Perspectives on the Past, University of Glasgow, 3rd-4th May 2012
o Christopher Nicholson
Crisis: Interruptions, Reactions and Continuities in Central and Eastern Europe, UCL, 15th-17th February 2012
o Adam Marks
English Communities Abroad, c.1500–1800, University of Manchester, September 2012
o Christopher Millington
Political Violence in Interwar Europe, Cardiff University, 19th-21st September 2012
o Sunil Purushotham
Genealogies of Colonial Violence, University of Cambridge, 1st-2nd June 2012
o Daniel Roach
Orderic Vitalis: New Perspectives on the Historian and his World, University of Durham, 9th-11th April 2013
o Alec Ryrie
Reformation Studies Colloquium 2012, University of Durham, 4th-6th September 2012
o Pamela Schievenin
Association for the Study of Modern Italy Postgraduate Summer School 2012, UCL, 28th-29th June 2012
o Patricia Skinner
Care and Cure: diseases, disabilities and therapies, Swansea University, 15th-16th June 2012
o Robert Smith
Writing the Lives of People and Things, AD 500–1700, Chawton House Library, 1st-2nd March 2012
o Letty Ten Harkel
Landscape and Scale: the first in a series of one-day symposia on the study of landscapes from prehistory to the Middle Ages, Oxford, 13th June 2012
o Jan Vandeburie
Contextualising the Fifth Crusade: an interdisciplinary colloquium on the Crusading Movement in the First Half of the 13th Century, University of Kent, 13th April 2012
o Marie Ventura
The Changing Experience of Time in the Long 19th Century: Local, Regional, Transnational and Global Perspectives, University of St Andrews, 18th-19th May 2012

o Ulrike Weiss
   Emblems of Nationhood: Britishness 1707–1901, University of St
   Andrews, 10th-12th August 2012

Workshop Funding for Marshall and Centenary Fellows

Graham Barrett
Jack Lord

Martin Lynn Scholarship

Zoe Cormack, University of Durham
Archives and interviews in South Sudan, October – December 2011

Royal Historical Society Postgraduate Speakers Series

Newcastle University
University of Liverpool

FINANCIAL STATEMENTS
FOR THE YEAR ENDED
30 JUNE 2012

THE ROYAL HISTORICAL SOCIETY
REPORT OF THE COUNCIL (THE TRUSTEES)
FOR THE YEAR ENDED 30 JUNE 2012

The members of Council present their report and audited accounts for the year ended 30 June 2012. The information shown on page 1 forms a part of these financial statements.

STRUCTURE, GOVERNANCE AND MANAGEMENT

The Society was founded on 23 November 1868 and received its Royal Charter in 1889. It is governed by the document 'The By-Laws of the Royal Historical Society', which was last amended in June 2010. The elected Officers of the Society are the President, six Vice-Presidents, the Treasurer, the Secretary, the Director of Communications, not more than two Literary Directors and the Honorary Academic Editor (BBIH). These officers, together with twelve Councillors constitute the governing body of the Society, and therefore its trustees. The Society also has two executive officers: an Executive Secretary and an Administrative Secretary.

Appointment of Trustees

The identity of the trustees is indicated above. All Fellows and Members of the Society are able to nominate Councillors; they are elected by a ballot of Fellows. Other trustees are elected by Council.

The President shall be *ex-officio* a member of all Committees appointed by the Council; and the Treasurer, the Secretary, the Director of Communications, the Literary Directors and the Honorary Academic Editor shall, unless the Council otherwise determine, also be *ex-officio* members of all such Committees.

In accordance with By-law XVII, the Vice-Presidents shall hold office normally for a term of three years. Two of them shall retire by rotation, in order of seniority in office, at each Anniversary Meeting and shall not be eligible for re-election before the Anniversary Meeting of the next year. In accordance with By-law XX, the Councillors shall hold office normally for a term of four years. Three of them shall retire by rotation, in order of seniority in office, at each Anniversary Meeting and shall not be eligible for re-election before the Anniversary Meeting of the next year.

At the Anniversary Meeting on 25 November 2011, the Vice-Presidents retiring under By-law XVII were Professor G Bernard and Ms J Innes. Professor N Miller and Professor A Pettegree were elected in their place. The Members of Council retiring under By-law XX were Professor C Given Wilson, Professor M Ormrod and Dr D Thomas . In accordance with By-law XXI, Dr L Fischer, Professor P Williamson and Professor D Wootton were elected in their place.

Trustee training and induction process

New trustees are welcomed in writing before their initial meeting, and sent details of the coming year's meeting schedule and other information about the Society and their duties. They are advised of Committee structure and receive papers in advance of the appropriate Committee and Council meetings, including minutes of the previous meetings. Trustees are already Fellows of the Society and have received regular information including the annual volume of *Transactions of the Royal Historical Society* which includes the annual report and accounts. They have therefore been kept apprised of any changes in the Society's business. Details of a Review on the restructuring of the Society in 1993 are available to all Members of Council.

MEMBERSHIP COMMITTEE:	Professor C Kidd – Chair
	Professor S Barton
	Professor K Fincham (from November 2011)
	Professor C Whatley (to November 2011)
	Professor P Williamson (from November 2011)
RESEARCH SUPPORT COMMITTEE:	Professor M Finn – Chair
	Professor M Cornwall
	Professor D Feldman
	Professor K Fincham (to November 2011)
	Dr A Thacker
	Professor N Miller (from November 2011)

Risk assessment

The trustees are satisfied that they have considered the major risks to which the charity is exposed, that they have taken action to mitigate or manage those risks and that they have systems in place to monitor any change to those risks.

OBJECTS, OBJECTIVES, ACTIVITIES AND PUBLIC BENEFIT

The Society has referred to the guidance in the Charity Commission's general guidance on Public Benefit when reviewing its aims and objectives and in planning its future activities. In particular, the trustees consider how planned activities will contribute to the aims and objectives they have set.

The Society remains the foremost society in Great Britain promoting and defending the scholarly study of the past. The Society promotes discussion of history by means of a full programme of public lectures and conferences, and disseminates the results of historical research and debate through its many publications. It also speaks for the interests of history and historians for the benefit of the public.

The Society offers grants to support research training, and annual prizes for historical essays and publications. It produces (in conjunction with Brepols Publishers and the Institute of Historical Research) the Bibliography of British and Irish History, a database of over 500,000 records, by far the most complete online bibliographical resource on British and Irish history, including relations with the empire and the Commonwealth. The Bibliography is kept updated, and includes near-comprehensive coverage of works since 1901 and selected earlier works.

The Society's specific new objectives for the year are set out in 'Plans for Future Periods' below.

The Society relies on volunteers from among its Fellows to act as its elected Officers, Councillors and Vice-Presidents. In many of its activities it also relies on the goodwill of Fellows and others interested in the study of the past. It has two salaried staff, and also pays a stipend to the Series Editor of Studies in History and to certain individuals for work on the Society's Bibliography.

ACHIEVEMENTS AND PERFORMANCE

Grants

The Society awards funds to assist advanced historical research by distributing grants to individuals. A wide range of individuals are eligible for these research and conference grants, including all postgraduate students registered for a research degree at United Kingdom institutions of higher education (full-time and part-time). The Society also considers applications from individuals who have completed doctoral dissertations within the last two years and are not yet in full-time employment. The Society's Research Support Committee considers applications at meetings held regularly throughout the year. In turn the Research Support Committee reports to Council. This year the grants budget was raised to £35,000.

The Society was also able to award its Centenary and Marshall Fellowships this year. Those eligible are doctoral students who are engaged in the completion of a PhD in history (broadly defined) and who will have completed at least two years' research on their chosen topic (and not more than four years full-time or six years part-time) at the beginning of the session for which the awards are made. Full details and a list of awards made are provided in the Society's Annual Report.

Lectures and other meetings

During the year the Society held meetings in London and at universities outside London at which papers are delivered. Lectures are open to the public and are advertised on the website. In 2011–12 it sponsored sessions at the University of Glamorgan (co-organised by the University of Swansea) and the University of Sheffield. It continues to sponsor the joint lecture for a wider public with Gresham College. It meets with other bodies to consider teaching and research policy issues of national importance. Together with The National Archives, it organised the annual Gerald Aylmer seminar, between historians and archivists. Full details are provided in the Annual Report.

Publications

During 2011 the RHS has delivered an ambitious programme of publications – a volume of *Transactions*, three volumes of edited texts in the *Camden* Series and a number of further volumes in the *Studies in History* Series have appeared. It has continued its financial support for the Bibliography of British and Irish History. The Bibliography is offered to all universities at institutional rates, and made available free to members consulting it at the Institute of Historical Research. Fellows who are not attached to an academic institution will in future be able to subscribe to the Bibliography at a preferential rate payable on top of the normal subscription.

Library

The Society continues to subscribe to a range of record series publications, which, with its other holdings, are housed either in the Council Room or in the room immediately across the corridor, in the UCL History

Library. A catalogue of the Society's private library holdings and listings of record series and regional history society publications (Texts and Calendars) have been made available on the Society's website.

Membership services

In accordance with the Society's 'By-laws', the membership is entitled to receive, after payment of subscription, a copy of the Society's *Transactions*, and to buy at a preferential rate copies of volumes published in the *Camden* series, and the *Studies in History* series. Society Newsletters continue to be circulated to the membership twice annually, in an accessible format. The membership benefits from many other activities of the Society including the frequent representations to various official bodies where the interests of historical scholarship are involved.

Investment performance

The Society holds an investment portfolio with a market value of about £2.36 millions at 30 June 2012 (2011: £2.54 million). It has adopted a "total return" approach to its investment policy. This means that the funds are invested solely on the basis of seeking to secure the best total level of financial return compatible with the duty to make safe investments but regardless of the form the return takes. The Society has adopted this approach to ensure even-handedness between current and future beneficiaries, since the focus of many investments lies in maximising capital value rather than producing income. The total return strategy does not make distinctions between income and capital returns. It lumps together all forms of return on investment – dividends, interest, and capital gains etc, to produce a "total return". Some of the total return is then used to meet the needs of present beneficiaries, while the remainder is added to the existing investment portfolios to help meet the needs of future beneficiaries.

During the year Brewin Dolphin plc continued to act as investment managers. They report all transactions to the Honorary Treasurer and provide regular reports on the portfolios, which are considered by the Society's Finance Committee which meets three times a year. In turn the Finance Committee reports to Council. A manager from Brewin attends two Finance Committee meetings a year.

The Society assesses investment performance against the FTSE APCIMS Balanced (Total Return) index. Investment returns on the Society's portfolio were below the benchmark in 2011–12. This was against the background of a turbulent market (it should be noted that in 2010–11 investment performance was well ahead of the benchmark). The reasons for the underperformance have been discussed extensively both with the investment managers and by Finance Committee. The Society can afford to take a long view of its investment portfolio and is confident that the investment strategy remains prudent. Fees are 0.5% of the portfolio. The Society has a policy of not drawing down more than 4% of the market value of the portfolio (valued over a 3-year rolling period). The drawdown in 2011–12 was less than 3.3% (measured against the portfolio value at year end).

FINANCIAL REVIEW

Results

The Society generated a surplus of £100,868 (£2010–11: £42,189). This very high surplus was accounted for by income from Society's joint publishing agreement with Cambridge University Press which was once again ahead of expectations in 2011–12 due to on-going sales of the digital archive. Subscription income was slightly increased over the previous year. There was a slight increase in investment income compared with 2010–11 (although as noted earlier the capital value of the portfolio declined). Expenditure in 2011–12 was slightly higher than the previous year (in part reflecting an increase in support offered to postgraduate students). The Society continues to bear substantial costs for the production of the Bibliography of British and Irish History. The cost to the Society is estimated to average £25,000 per year over the next two years. The Society maintains a very significant cash reserve as a result of the accumulated surplus of the previous few years. The Society expects to enter a period over the next few years when it declares significant in-year deficits which will be funded by part of this accumulated surplus. This surplus will also be used to fund potential new initiatives.

Fixed assets

Information relating to changes in fixed assets is given in notes 5 and 6 to the accounts.

Reserves policy

Council has reviewed the reserves of the Society. To safeguard the core activities in excess of the members' subscription income, Council has determined to establish unrestricted, general, free reserves to cover three years operational costs (approximately £750,000). Unrestricted and general free reserves at 30 June 2012 were around £2.4 million (after adjusting for fixed assets).

The Society's restricted funds consist of a number of different funds where the donor has imposed restrictions on the use of the funds which are legally binding. The purposes of these funds are set out in Notes 10–13.

PLANS FOR FUTURE PERIODS

Council plans to develop its website in order to improve communication with both Fellows and the General Public. Council will also continue to monitor closely how policy and funding changes at the national level are likely to impact on the work of historians. It will also continue to monitor the challenges currently faced by local archives in an uncertain funding environment. Council is also paying considerable attention to current policy initiatives that affect the teaching of History in schools and colleges. It will continue to offer support for wide-ranging seminar/lecture events outside London each year, some to be held at universities, and some run by consortia of local universities and other academic institutions. Council will continue to review the role, function, and membership of its committees.

The Society intends to increase considerably the level of its current financial support to postgraduate and other young historians (primarily due to generous support offered by *History Workshop Journal* and *Past and Present*). It will continue to support the stipends for the Centenary and Marshall Fellowships (and will continue to be involved in the selection procedure for the Fellowships, organised by the Institute of Historical Research). As noted above, the Society anticipates running deficits in future years in order to fund these developments and its other activities, following a period in which it has built up a cash surplus.

STATEMENT OF COUNCIL'S RESPONSIBILITIES

The Council members are responsible for preparing the Trustees' Report and the financial statements in accordance with applicable law and United Kingdom Accounting Standards (United Kingdom Generally Accepted Accounting Practice.)

The law applicable to charities in England & Wales requires the Council to prepare financial statements for each financial year which give a true and fair view of the state of the affairs of the charity and of the incoming resources and application of resources of the charity for that period. In preparing these financial statements, the trustees are required to:

- select suitable accounting policies and then apply them consistently;
- observe the methods and principles in the Charities SORP;
- make judgements and estimates that are reasonable and prudent;
- state whether applicable accounting standards have been followed, subject to any material departures disclosed and explained in the financial statements;
- prepare the financial statements on the going concern basis unless it is inappropriate to presume that the charity will continue in business.

The Council is responsible for keeping proper accounting records that disclose with reasonable accuracy at any time the financial position of the charity and enable them to ensure that the financial statements comply with the Charities Act 1993, the Charity (Accounts and Reports) Regulations 2008 and the provisions of the Royal Charter. It is also responsible for safeguarding the assets of the charity and hence for taking reasonable steps for the prevention and detection of fraud and other irregularities.

In determining how amounts are presented within items in the statement of financial activities and balance sheet, the Council has had regard to the substance of the reported transaction or arrangement, in accordance with generally accepted accounting policies or practice.

AUDITORS

Kingston Smith LLP have indicated their willingness to continue in office and a proposal for their re-appointment will be presented at the Anniversary meeting.

By Order of the Board

Honorary Secretary

Dr A Smith

21 September 2012

THE ROYAL HISTORICAL SOCIETY
INDEPENDENT AUDITORS' REPORT TO THE TRUSTEES
OF THE ROYAL HISTORIAL SOCIETY

We have audited the financial statements of The Royal Historical Society for the year ended 30 June 2012 which comprise the Statement of Financial Activities, the Balance Sheet and the related notes. The financial reporting framework that has been applied in their preparation is applicable laws and United Kingdom Accounting Standards (United Kingston Generally Accepted Accounting Practice).

This report is made solely to the charity's trustees, as a body, in accordance with Chapter 3 of Part 8 of the Charities Act 2011. Our audit work has been undertaken so that we might state to the charity's trustees those matters which we are required to state to them in an auditors' report and for no other purpose. To the fullest extent permitted by law, we do not accept or assume responsibility to any party other than the charity and charity's trustees as a body, for our audit work, for this report, or for the opinions we have formed.

Respective responsibilities of trustees and auditor
As explained more fully in the Trustees' Responsibilities Statement, the trustees are responsible for the preparation of financial statements which give a true and fair view. We have been appointed as auditors under section 145 of the Charities Act 2011 and report in accordance with that Act. Our responsibility is to audit and express an opinion on the financial statements in accordance with applicable law and International Standards on Auditor (UK and Ireland). Those standards require us to comply with the Auditing Practices Board's Ethical Standards for Auditors.

Scope of the audit of the financial statements
An audit involves obtaining evidence about the amounts and disclosures in the financial statements sufficient to give reasonable assurance that the financial statements are free from material misstatement, whether caused by fraud or error. This includes an assessment of: whether the accounting policies are appropriate to the charity's circumstances and have been consistently applied and adequately disclosed; the reasonableness of significant accounting estimates made by the trustees; and the overall presentation of the financial statements. In addition we read all the financial and non-financial information in the Annual Report to identify material inconsistencies with the audited financial statements. If we become aware of any apparent material misstatements or inconsistencies we consider the implications for our report.

Opinion on the financial statements
In our opinion:

- give a true and fair view of the state of the charity's affairs as at 30 June 2012 and of the charity incoming/outgoing resources and application of resources for the year then ended; and
- have been properly prepared in accordance with United Kingdom Generally Accepted Accounting Practice applicable to Smaller Entities; and
- have been prepared in accordance with the requirements of the Charities Act 2011.

Matters on which we are required to report by exception
We have nothing to report in respect of the following matters where the Charities Act 2011 requires us to report to you if, in our opinion:

- the information given in the Annual Report is inconsistent in any material respects with the financial statements; or
- sufficient accounting records have not been kept; or
- the financial statements are not in agreement with the accounting records and returns; or
- we have not received all the information and explanations we require for our audit; or
- the trustees were not entitled to prepare the financial statements in accordance with the small companies regime and take advantage of the small companies exemption in preparing the Trustees' Annual Report.

Devonshire House
60 Goswell Road   **Kingston Smith LLP**
London EC1M 7AD   Statutory auditor

Date:

Kingston Smith LLP is eligible to act as auditor in terms of Section 1212 of the Companies Act 2006.

THE ROYAL HISTORICAL SOCIETY

STATEMENT OF FINANCIAL ACTIVITIES
FOR THE YEAR ENDED 30 JUNE 2012

	Note	Unrestricted Funds £	Endowment Funds £	Restricted Funds £	Total Funds 2012 £	Total Funds 2011 £
INCOMING RESOURCES						
Incoming resources from generated funds						
Donations, legacies and similar incoming resources	2	9,612	–	1,000	10,612	16,545
Investment income	6	77,309	–	2,361	79,670	74,944
Incoming resources from charitable activities						
Grants for awards		–	–	13,100	13,100	11,000
Grants for publications		5,000	–	–	5,000	5,000
Subscriptions		110,499	–	–	110,499	106,657
Royalties		127,335	–	–	127,335	64,810
Other incoming resources		1,394	–	–	1,394	124
TOTAL INCOMING RESOURCES		331,148	–	16,461	347,609	279,080
RESOURCES EXPENDED						
Cost of generating funds						
Investment manager's fees		11,270	–	349	11,619	11,530
Charitable activities						
Grants for awards	3	57,902	–	15,350	73,252	66,632
Lectures and meetings		15,806	–	–	15,806	12,336
Publications		68,573	–	–	68,573	74,038
Library		7,155	–	–	7,155	5,405
Membership services		50,793	–	–	50,793	48,271
Governance		19,543	–	–	19,543	18,679
TOTAL RESOURCES EXPENDED	4a	231,042	–	15,699	246,741	236,891
NET INCOMING/(OUTGOING) RESOURCES BEFORE TRANSFERS		100,107	–	762	100,868	42,189
Gross transfers between funds		–	–	–	–	–
NET INCOMING/(OUTGOING) RESOURCES BEFORE GAINS		100,107	–	762	100,868	42,189
Other recognised gains and losses						
Net (loss)/gain on investments	6	(161,926)	(5,008)		(166,934)	388,905
NET MOVEMENT IN FUNDS		(61,819)	(5,008)	762	(66,066)	431,094
Balance at 1 July		2,618,310	73,944	4,228	2,696,483	2,265,389
Balance at 30 June		2,556,491	68,936	4,990	2,630,418	2,696,483

The notes on pages 11 to 18 form part of these financial statements.

THE ROYAL HISTORICAL SOCIETY

BALANCE SHEET AT 30 JUNE 2012

	Note	2012 £	2012 £	2011 £	2011 £
FIXED ASSETS					
Tangible assets	5		568		681
Investments	6		2,358,108		2,535,967
COIF Investments			81,209		115,302
			2,439,885		2,651,950
CURRENT ASSETS					
Debtors	7	11,018		6,156	
Cash at bank and in hand		216,668		82,646	
		227,687		88,802	
LESS: CREDITORS					
Amounts due within one year	8	(37,154)		(44,269)	
NET CURRENT ASSETS			190,533		44,533
NET ASSETS			2,630,418		2,696,483
REPRESENTED BY:					
Endowment Funds	10				
A S Whitfield Prize Fund			46,136		49,475
The David Berry Essay Trust			22,800		24,469
Restricted Funds	11				
A S Whitfield Prize Fund			2,060		1,806
P J Marshall Fellowship			–		–
The David Berry Essay Trust			1,931		1,422
The Martin Lynn Bequest			1,000		1,000
Unrestricted Funds					
Designated – E M Robinson Bequest	12		117,904		126,798
General Fund	13		2,438,587		2,491,513
			2,630,418		2,696,483

The accounts have been prepared in accordance with the Financial Reporting Standard for Smaller Entities (effective April 2008).

The notes on pages 11 to 18 form part of these financial statements.

The financial statements were approved and authorised for issue by the Council on 21 September 2012 and were signed on its behalf by:

....

Professor C Jones – **President**   Professor M J Hughes – **Honorary Treasurer**

THE ROYAL HISTORICAL SOCIETY

NOTES TO THE FINANCIAL STATEMENTS FOR THE YEAR ENDED 30 JUNE 2012

1. ACCOUNTING POLICIES

Basis of Accounting

These financial statements have been prepared under the historical cost convention and in accordance with the revised Statement of Recommended Practice (SORP 2005) "Accounting and Reporting by Charities" and applicable accounting standards.

The following principal accounting policies, which are unchanged from the previous year, have been consistently applied in preparing the financial statements.

Incoming Resources

All incoming resources are included in the Statement of Financial Activities (SOFA) when the charity is legally entitled to receipt and the amount is quantifiable.

Grant income

Grant income is deferred only where the donor has specified that it may only be used for a future period or has imposed conditions that must be met before the charity has unconditional entitlement to the grant.

Subscription income

Subscription income is recognised in the year it became receivable with a provision against any subscription not received.

Donations and Other Voluntary Income

Donations and other voluntary income are recognised when the Society becomes legally entitled to such monies.

Royalties

Royalties are recoginised on an accruals basis in accordance with the terms of the relevant agreement.

Resources expended

All expenditure is accounted for on an accruals basis and has been classified under headings that aggregate all costs related to the category. Wherever possible costs are directly attributed to these headings. Costs common to more than one area are apportioned on the basis of staff time spent on each area.

Grants Payable

Grants payable are recognised in the year in which they are approved and notified to recipients.

Cost of generating funds

The costs of generating funds are those costs of seeking potential funders and applying for funding.

Allocation of costs

Indirect costs are those costs incurred in support of the charitable objectives. These have been allocated to the resources expended on a basis that fairly reflects the true use of those resource within the organisation.

Governance costs

Governance costs are those incurred in the governance of the charity and are primarily associated with the constitutional and statutory requirements.

Library and Archives

The cost of additions to the library and archives is written off in the year of purchase.

Pensions

Pension costs are charged to the SOFA when payments fall due. The Society contributed 12.5% of gross salary to the personal pension plan of two of the employees.

Investments

Investments are stated at market value. Any surplus/deficit arising on revaluation is included in the Statement of Financial Activities. Dividend income is accounted for when the Society becomes entitled to such monies.

Depreciation

Depreciation is calculated by reference to the cost of fixed assets using a straight line basis at rates considered appropriate having regard to the expected lives of the fixed assets. The annual rates of depreciation in use are:

Furniture and equipment   10%
Computer equipment   25%

Funds

Unrestricted:

These are funds which can be used in accordance with the charitable objects of the Royal Historical Society at the discretion of the trustees.

Designated:

These are unrestricted funds which have been set aside by the trustees for specific purposes.

Restricted:

These are funds that can only be used for particular restricted purposes defined by the benefactor and within the objects of the charity.

Endowment:

Permanent endowment funds must be held permanently by the trustees and income arising is separately included in restricted funds for specific use as defined by the donors.

The purpose and use of endowment, restricted and designated funds are disclosed in the notes to the accounts.

2.	DONATIONS AND LEGACIES	2012 £	2011 £
	Donations via membership	5,336	1,487
	Gladstone Memorial Trust	600	600
	Vera London	–	4,696
	Lisbet Rausing trust	–	5,500
	Martin Lynn scholarship	1,000	1,000
	Sundry income	–	–
	Gift Aid reclaimed	3,089	3,262
		10,612	16,545

3.	GRANTS FOR AWARDS	Unrestricted Funds £	Restricted Funds £	Total funds 2012 £	Total funds 2011 £
	RHS Centenary Fellowship	12,100	–	12,100	13,200
	Research support grants (see below)	31,838	1,000	32,838	29,632
	A-Level prizes	400	–	400	400
	AS Whitfield prize	–	1,000	1,000	1,000
	Gladstone history book prize	1,000	–	1,000	1,000
	P J Marshall Fellowship	2,863	13,100	15,963	11,740
	David Berry Prize	–	250	250	250
	Alexander Prize	250	–	250	500
	Rees Davies Prize	100	–	100	100
	Staff and support costs (Note 4a)	9,352	–	9,352	8,810
		57,902	15,350	73,252	
	30 June 2011	52,642	13,990		66,632

During the year Society awarded grants to a value of £34,281 (2011 - £29,632) to 139 (2011 - 127) individuals.

GRANTS PAYABLE	2012 £	2011 £
Commitments at 1 July	7,305	8,069
Commitments made in the year	63,901	57,822
Grants paid during the year	(65,344)	(58,586)
Commitments at 30 June	5,862	7,305

Commitments at 30 June 2012 and 2011 are included in creditors.

4a. TOTAL RESOURCES EXPENDED

	Staff costs £	Support costs £	Direct costs £	Total £
Cost of generating funds				
Investment manager's fee	–	–	11,618	11,618
Charitable activities				
Grants for awards (Note 3)	6,182	3,170	63,900	73,252
Lectures and meetings	6,182	1,585	8,039	15,806
Publications	10,991	6,339	51,243	68,573
Library	2,748	1,585	2,823	7,155
Membership services	34,347	15,849	596	50,793
Governance	8,243	3,170	8,130	19,543
Total Resources Expended	68,693	31,697	146,349	246,741
30 June 2011	67,360	27,481	142,049	236,891
	(Note 4b)	**(Note 4c)**		

4b. STAFF COSTS

	2012 £	2011 £
Wages and salaries	55,988	55,030
Social security costs	5,729	5,570
Other pension costs	6,976	6,760
	68,694	67,360

4c. SUPPORT COSTS

	2012 £	2011 £
Stationery, photocopying and postage	16,861	15,382
Computer support	1,425	392
Insurance	1,032	951
Telephone	311	287
Depreciation	113	113
Other	11,955	10,356
	31,697	27,481

The average number of employees in the year was 2 (2011 - 2). There were no employees whose emoluments exceeded £60,000 in this year or in the previous year.

During the year travel expenses were reimbursed to 22 (2011: 16) Councillors attending Council meetings at a cost of £5,566 (2011 - £3,866). No Councillor received any remuneration during the year (2011 - £Nil).

Included in governance is the following:

	2012 £	2011 £
Auditors Remuneration - current year	8,130	7,848

5. TANGIBLE FIXED ASSETS

	Computer Equipment £	Furniture and Equipment £	Total £
COST			
At 1 July 2011	33,224	1,134	34,358
At 30 June 2012	33,224	1,134	34,358
DEPRECIATION			
At 1 July 2011	33,224	453	33,677
Charge for the year	–	113	113
At 30 June 2012	33,224	566	33,790
NET BOOK VALUE			
At 30 June 2012	–	568	568
At 30 June 2011	–	681	681

All tangible fixed assets are used in the furtherance of the Society's objects.

6. INVESTMENTS

	General Fund £	Designated Robinson Bequest £	Whitfield Prize Fund £	David Berry Essay Trust £	Total £
Market value at 1 July 2011	2,333,090	126,798	50,719	25,360	2,535,967
Additions	295,070	16,036	6,414	3,208	320,728
Disposals	(305,120)	(16,583)	(6,633)	(3,317)	(331,653)
Net loss on investments	(153,579)	(8,347)	(3,339)	(1,669)	(166,934)
Market value at 30 June 2012	2,169,461	117,904	47,161	23,582	2,358,108
Cost at 30 June 2012	2,331,997	126,798	51,281	25,891	2,535,967

	2012 £	2011 £
UK Equities	1,160,664	1,831,858
UK Government Stock and Bonds	469,889	–
Overseas Equities	690,345	659,937
Uninvested Cash	37,211	44,173
	2,358,109	2,535,968
Dividends and interest on listed investments	78,693	74,294
Interest on cash deposits	977	650
	79,670	74,944

7. DEBTORS

	2012 £	2011 £
Other debtors	6,632	4,056
Royalty debtor	3,448	1,162
Prepayments	938	938
	11,018	6,156

8. CREDITORS: Amounts due within one year

	2012 £	2011 £
Sundry creditors	15,325	17,080
Taxes and social security	1,565	1,566
Subscriptions received in advance	4,814	7,416
Accruals and deferred income	15,450	18,207
	37,154	44,269

Included within Sundry creditors is an amount of £582 (2011: £577) relating to pension liabilities.

9. LEASE COMMITMENTS

The Society has the following annual commitments under non-cancellable operating leases which expire:

	2012 £	2011 £
Under the 1 year	–	3,282
Within 1 – 2 years	–	–
Within 2 – 5 years	5,900	–

10. ENDOWMENT FUNDS

	Balance at 1 July 2011 £	Investment Loss £	Balance at 30 June 2012 £
A S Whitfield Prize Fund	49,475	(3,339)	46,136
The David Berry Essay Trust	24,469	(1,669)	22,800
	73,944	(5,008)	68,936

A S Whitfield Prize Fund

The A S Whitfield Prize Fund is an endowment used to provide income for an annual prize for the best first monograph for British history published in the calendar year.

The David Berry Essay Trust

The David Berry Essay Trust is an endowment to provide income for annual prizes for essays on subjects dealing with Scottish history.

11. RESTRICTED FUNDS	Balance at 1 July 2011 £	Incoming Resources £	Outgoing Resources £	Transfers £	Balance at 30 June 2012 £
A S Whitfield Prize Fund	1,806	1,486	(1,232)	–	2,060
P J Marshall Fellowship	–	13,100	(13,100)	–	–
The David Berry Essay Trust	1,422	875	(366)	–	1,931
Martin Lynn Bequest	1,000	1,000	(1,000)	–	1,000
	4,228	16,461	(15,699)	–	4,990

A S Whitfield Prize Fund Income

Income from the A S Whitfield Prize Fund is used to provide an annual prize for the best first monograph for British history published in the calendar year.

P J Marshall Fellowship

The P J Marshall Fellowship is used to provide a sum sufficient to cover the stipend for a one-year doctoral research fellowship alongside the existing Royal Historical Society Centenary Fellowship at the Institute of Historical Research.

The David Berry Essay Trust Income

Income from the David Berry Trust is to provide annual prizes for essays on subjects dealing with Scottish history.

The Martin Lynn Bequest

This annual bequest is used by the Society to give financial assistance to postgraduates researching topics in African history.

12. DESIGNATED FUND	Balance at 1 July 2011 £	Incoming Resources £	Outgoing Resources £	Investment Loss £	Transfers £	Balance at 30 June 2012 £
E M Robinson Bequest	126,798	3,935	(4,481)	(8,347)	–	117,904

E M Robinson Bequest

Income from the E M Robinson Bequest is to further the study of history and to date has been used to provide grants to the Dulwich Picture Gallery.

13. GENERAL FUND	Balance at 1 July 2011 £	Incoming Resources £	Outgoing Resources £	Investment Loss £	Transfers £	Balance at 30 June 2012 £
	2,491,513	327,213	(226,561)	(153,578)	–	2,438,587

14. ANALYSIS OF NET ASSETS BETWEEN FUNDS

	General Fund £	Designated Fund £	Restricted Funds £	Endowment Funds £	Total £
Fixed assets	568	–	–	–	568
Investments	2,169,461	117,904	1,807	68,936	2,358,108
COIF investments	81,209	–	–	–	81,209
	2,251,238	117,904	1,807	68,936	2,439,885
Current assets	224,504	–	3,183	–	227,687
Less: Creditors	(37,154)	–	–	–	(37,154)
Net current assets/(liabilities)	187,350	–	3,183	–	190,533
Net Assets	2,438,587	117,904	4,990	68,936	2,630,418